TRANSGENDERISM

A QUESTION OF IDENTITY

FRANCIS ETHEREDGE

A Biography and Foreword by
Kiki Latimer

A Spiritual Biography and Afterword
of 'a poet of the Lord', James Sale, and his piece,
"The Father of All Lights"

En Route Books and Media, LLC
Saint Louis, MO
USA

⊕ENROUTE
Make the time

En Route Books and Media, LLC

5705 Rhodes Avenue

St. Louis, MO 63109

Contact us at

contactus@enroutebooksandmedia.com

Cover Credit: Sebastian Mahfood

Copyright 2025 Francis Etheredge

ISBN-13: 979-8-88870-389-2

Library of Congress Control Number: 2025941300

Table of Contents

So where to begin?; Gender ideology: A coincidence of causes or a
systematic Program? A real quest for an identity: Digging a foundation (cf.
Lk 6: 46-49); Scripture says, the wise man has many counsellors (cf.
Proverbs 15: 22): Growing opposition to puberty blockers and surgery; Our

culture and our questions in the context of philosophy and the Christian, Catholic Faith; Vocation, who we are and the times in which we live; An experience of the Good Shepherd

Prose and a Prayer: for the Protection of Women Globally: "Woman"

By way, then, of a summary statement of the integral reality of being a woman, consider the following account; Now consider the conception of a human being, as from conception and not from "birth"; 'biological sex and the socio-cultural role of sex (gender) can be distinguished but not separated'; and woman

The running sores in our society starting with suicides; The suffocation of suffering; The beauty of becoming a mother; The Irish Constitution's advance of abortion and defence of mothers; Running away, suicide, and deterioration of mental health; Depopulation and the un-popularity of marriage; Shrinking populations; The possibility of the transmission of faith; Blessed Dominic Barberi (1792-1849); Carmen Hernández (1930-2016); An episode from my own life (1956-); The suffering we experience

The starting point of dignity A brief account of the possibility of a vocation; Basic questions; Conflicts in society; Masculinity in crisis: toxic or not?; Freedom or career; Meaning includes and transcends what expresses it;

Spoiling the gift of being; Youth unhappiness, the media and relationships;
Where are we now; Acting together: Concordantly; Simple answers and the
need for divine help

Physicalism; Ideas about identity or ideology? A question of evidence:
What defines evidence?; Authoritatively given but unfounded advice;
Gaping evidence and suicide; The possibility of the law losing its credibility
as an expression of Justice; Life is so much more in its ongoing unfolding
than specific crises; Training people to think or to be subservient to the
thought of others; What is the right to self-expression? The mirror of the
Word

What is happening to people on-line and does it help boys and girls be
ready, if they are called and choose, to court and to marry? The effect of
social media on girls; Recovering womanhood; The effect of social media on
boys; Carlo Acutis (1991-2006); Masculinity in crisis; Masculinity: Toxic
or not?; Why the decline in real fatherhood – Is it a decline in real-time in
family life and in real friendships generally?; Meaning includes and
transcends what expresses it; What kind of being are we? Being-in-
relationship

Making a history of our own investigations; Masculinity: Healed and connected; Divorce and annulment; Population fears: Who benefits?; Disquiet, discernment and decision; Sexual ethics: Promoting the body's expression of the soul; Revisiting the foundations of human identity and relevant disciplines; Deeper than grave but external changes; Forgetting elemental truths; What does Christian marriage express distinctly?

Prose and Prayer to Protect the Environment: "Incorporation"[1]:
Reflecting on the Discoveries

A Spiritual Biography of 'a poet of the Lord', James Sale, and his piece, "The Father of All Lights" And my Response: "A-Lighting Together"

Postscript: On the heart's desire (Psalm 20: 4)

Posing the Question; Some Preliminary Points; More Specifically in the case of Gender Dysphoria

---

[1] Published, as are a number of these prayers, by Gordon Nary, the editor of "Profiles in Catholicism"; just google the website and see for yourself.

BIOGRAPHY and FOREWORD

Kiki Latimer

Kiki Latimer, host of The Catholic Bookworm podcast, has a BA in the Oral Interpretation of Literature, Psychology, & Philosophy from the University of Rhode Island and a Master's in Moral Theology from Holy Apostles College & Seminary in Cromwell, Ct, where she taught Homiletics. She is the author of Home for the Homily-The Sacred Art of Homiletics, Seeing God's Face-A Catholic American Woman in India, and her Haiti memoir There Be Hope. She is co-author with Stephen Schwarz of Philosophy Begins in Wonder and Understanding Abortion- From Mixed Feelings to Rational Thought. Kiki has also taught courses on Silence & Solitude, as well as Metaphysics, Epistemology, Virtue Ethics, and Understanding Abortion. In addition, she is a children's author with four published books: *Islands of Hope*, *The WaterFire Duck*, *BubbleButt*, and *Heal of the Hand*. (www.kikilatimer.com).

She has four grown children and is grandmother to fourteen grandchildren. She is a 1985 convert to Catholicism and lives with her husband Jim in Hope Valley, RI.

Conversion

My journey into the Catholic Church was one of grace, faith, and reason. During my teenage years I attended an Anglican Church with a pastor, Fr. Robert Creech, who believed in the Real Presence in the Eucharist and had a devotion to Mary, Mother of God. Fr. Creech, who later converted to Orthodoxy, was a strong foundational influence on my own conversion to Catholicism years later. In 1980, at a secular college my husband and I found ourselves immersed in a very Catholic philosophy department that began to form our understanding of contraception, abortion, and sexuality in a manner that was reason-based, rather than our society-based confusions. At the same time we were attending an American Episcopal ecclesial community that upheld abortion, divorce, contraception, and homosexuality as human rights. In the end, it was the issue of women in the priesthood that pressed the decision to become Catholic as the importance of the Real Presence in the Eucharist was vital to us. We began to realize that all the arguments in the Episcopal community were based on sociological demands rather than philosophical and theological reasoning. To consider many aspects of faith guided by reason, my husband and I delved into the writings of C S Lewis, G K Chesterton, Joseph Ratzinger, Thomas Aquinas, Peter Kreeft, Thomas Merton, Deitrich von Hildebrand, Christopher Derrick, and many papal encyclicals of the Church. At the same time, Pope John Paul II was illuminating the Church and the world with his saintly papal greatness. Conversion is always a matter of the whirlwind of grace and the Holy Spirit, and we soon found ourselves in a perfect storm that pulled us out of a sea of irrational chaos and into the Holy See of Peter.

"Out of the Dark into the Light"

Deep down in both the soul of the human person and the soul of a society is the question of identity. All of human happiness and/or misery depends on how this question of identity is answered. When answered, as it has been for the past one hundred years, with the erroneous tunnel vision of radical individualism, separated from one another and from the common good of family and society, we see the slow demise of a once more wholesome society and the human misery that follows. When the answer to our identity is that we must individually create ourselves from scratch, create our own meaning from nothingness, forge our way in life by guesswork, and pull ourselves up by our own bootstraps, is it any wonder that many of our young people are drowning in a morass of moral, sexual, and personal confusion?

I Awoke in a Dark Wood

If you think this an exaggeration, consider U.S. Supreme Court Justice Anthony Kennedy's 1992 statement: *"At the heart of liberty is the right to define one's own concept of existence, of meaning, of the universe, and of the mystery of human life."* Here we see the monumentally impossible task that our young people are coping with, and now in most recent years, via transgender ideology. Young people are now told that they can add their very *being* as male or female to this list of "liberty" that they are called to define. They do so with no grounding in religion, no objective philosophy of the human person, bombarded by a culture run sexually amuck, and with a blurring of even the basic concepts of natural law. Furthermore, they now attempt to "define their own concept of existence" with the pressure of their social media, their school systems, teachers, and medical professionals, all encouraging them to try on any manner of deluded existence except an objective reality. Just make it up as you go along. That's the heart of liberty? No, rather it is the dark heart, the hardness of heart, of license, the black hole of human unhappiness.

"Nel mezzo del cammin di nostra vita mi ritrovai per una selva oscura,ché la diritta via era smarrita." So begins Dante's journey through hell, *"In the middle of the road of life I awoke in a dark wood where the true way was wholly lost."* Sadly, due to our degraded misguided culture, many of our young people find themselves in a dark wood, a life crisis, far earlier than Dante did, far earlier than past generations did. In very recent times, a several century's old brewing philosophical and theological lie has finally gurgled to the surface of our Western society. This lie is now so deeply

insinuated and in situated into our society as to twist the ontological reality of the human person into an unrecognizable deformity of grotesque proportions. This is a lie that conjures our young people to hate their bodies, reject their procreative powers, and abhor the very beauty of themselves. This is a lie that tells our young people that God did not make them incarnate male and female as His children in His own beloved image and likeness, but rather tossed them precariously and thoughtlessly into a random body of meat from which they must extricate themselves through sterility hormones and medical mutilation.

We Are Made from God's Stuff

The question is whether or not young people who struggle with body/soul dysmorphia, in a society that promotes a false and evil social and sexual ideology, will find a Virgil, a guardian angel, a guide of light in the darkness, by which they might find their way out of this ideological hell. Will they make it out before the darkness leads them to extremely sorrowful repercussions and deep personal unhappiness? It is my sincere hope that this book, *Transgenderism: A Question of Identity* by author Francis Etheredge, will be such a light. Light is the only way out of darkness; hopefully young people, their parents, extended family members, teachers, social workers, therapists, doctors, pastors, and those serving the common good in government will begin to find many such sources of illumination as found here in this work.

I am reminded of an old story about God and Satan: Satan tells God that if given enough time, he too could create the universe and all that's in it from primordial dust. God takes him up on this challenge and says He will give Satan several billion years to accomplish this. Satan smirks smugly and reaches down for a handful of dust, the primordial stuff. God stops him and says "Oh, no, you have to get your own stuff!" We have been created from God's stuff, God's dust. Satan understood this and gave up the challenge. But now in our post-Judeo-Christian culture he whispers to *us* that this is not the case, whispers that we are *not* made wholly of God's stuff, but rather we must and are free to create ourselves with our own stuff. We may throw off whatever we have been given by God, abandon the body in which we were created in love, and recreate ourselves. Sadly, we fail to understand that apart from God, we have no stuff.

Distorting Mirrors or a True Reflection?

When my son Daniel was five years old we had an interesting discussion one morning when I asked him what he wanted to be when he grew up. Without missing a beat he announced "A dolphin!" I looked at him in confusion and asked "What?!" He repeated "A dolphin!" I explained "I'm sorry but you can't be a dolphin because you are a boy!" Miserable and angry he responded "But you said that I could be anything I wanted to be when I grow up!" Well, yes, I explained, in primer philosophical terms, yes, within the realm of your nature given to you by God. You have the nature of a boy. And that means you cannot be a dolphin. And that was that. He would go on to learn to swim, boogie board, surf, and snorkel, but he would never be a dolphin. He was to become a man, the only version of his nature possible.

Imagine that instead I had affirmed his delusion of dolphinhood. Imagine that I had taken him to medical professionals and asked that his legs be amputated, that he be given puberty blockers, dolphin hormones, and a prosthetic tail. Imagine that his friends, teachers, and doctors all supported his decision to define his own existence by encouraging this desired delusion. This would be like an anorexic young woman being told that her delusions of being overweight are correct and so we'll gladly give her a gastric bypass to allow her to better starve herself to death. This is the transgender ideology in a nutshell: take a confused young person who has gender body dysmorphia, affirm and encourage this dysmorphia, act on it with sterilizing chemicals and surgical medical mutilation, and then tout this ideology of the affirmation of delusion from the rooftops as a new and grand freedom of the human person.

This affirmation of delusion begins with an even deeper and more foundational deception that is rarely understood concerning the transgender ideology. This is a fundamental misunderstanding about internal perception and personal identity. Internal perceptions are those inner perceptions of the human person that are incommunicable. What does my pain feel like, what does the color red look like to me, what does a banana taste like to me, and going deeper, what it feels like to be *me*, what my own consciousness feels like, my "I" as known to my reflective self alone? These inner perceptions, which we try in various ways to vaguely communicate to others, are really and fully known only to ourselves and God. These internal perceptions cannot truly be communicated to another human person. So, when I say that "I feel like a girl" what I am really only capable of saying, from inner perception, is that "I feel like myself." I can relate this feeling to external stereotypes and cultural norms, but I have no way of relating it to or comparing it to any other person's internal perception because I have no access to those perceptions of others.

When you touch my body, me, you touch me! Constancy and Change

Our internal perception comes through our intrinsic unity with our body. The physical brain which allows our mind and soul to understand the world through our senses, sight, hearing, taste, smell, touch, gives us internal and external access to ourselves and only external access to others. We perceive one another, glimpse the soul of others, primarily through the bodily presence of one another.

If a stranger approaches and caresses my arm, it makes sense that I would say "Stop touching me!" If the stranger were to respond, "I'm not touching *you*, I'm only touching *your arm*!" we would think them crazy. My body *is* me. It would be insanity to agree with them, to think some part of my body, in this case my arm, is not *me*. Our body, male or female down to the very cellular DNA level, *is* the mysterious revelation of our self, as created male or female. If I were to mentally malfunction and suddenly think that my arm, my leg, my eyes, or, more privately speaking, my genitalia, are not me, the medical and psychiatric sciences would rationally (until recently) see this as a form of mental disorder.

Think on this! When you touch my body, you touch *me*! Our spiritual-soul-self knows its own nature, not through the inaccessible inner perception of others, but through our own accessible physical-body-self. Our body offers a revelation of our soul. When you physically touch *me* you touch *me*! As the Incarnation of God the Son reveals to us something of the nature of God, so too our body reveals something of our nature to ourselves and others, first and foremost, whether we were created male or female. When you touch my body, *me*, you touch *me*!

When a young boy/man says that he "feels like a girl/woman" or a young girl/woman says she "feels like a boy/man" this can be based only on internal perception disconnected from the given, the created-by-God objective external revelation by the body. This is a mind disorder, a mind that has gravely detached from its body. This erroneous belief, this misperception, has no means of any objective comparison to the incommunicable internal perception inside other persons, and has refused the revelation of its very own accessible body. In other words, no matter the misguided perception of what the person *believes* is perceived inside others, he or she is really only capable of perceiving that "I feel like myself" as revealed, male or female, by the gift of their body. He or she can only mentally conjure up the notion that this *feeling* does not correspond to how others feel. And he or she must ignore the reality that when he or she is physically touched, he or she *is* touched. The person must distance themselves from their own given objective reality that: When you touch my body, you touch *me*! Rather, in delusion, a transgender person thinks: What is touched, that arm, or leg, or genitalia, is *not me*! Objectively speaking, there's no basis in reality for this claim.

Furthermore, there is personal identity, that deep aspect of the soul that remains constant during our lifetime. While I certainly change over the years, these changes occur in and to a constant me. This inner constant of personal identity allows me to have memories, change for the better or for the worse over time, be held responsible for past actions, and make plans for the me in the future. I can look back on old photographs and say: "that's me!" Have I changed? Surely! But I'm still me. Personal identity is deeply wedded to internal perception. "It's me, still me, always me in here!" Others have no access to this internal perception in me and I have no access to their internal perception. Nor can we toss personal identity off, get rid of it, or exchange it for another me. (Only a severe brain dysfunction can push it into hiding; it is retained after death.) The entire transgender ideology is based on the erroneous belief that we have access to others' internal perceptions and can forsake our own personal identity.

Losing and Finding the Light of Christ

This is the sorrowful ideology that is crushing our society, our families, and especially our young people. This radically individualistic view of the human person apart from God, apart from community, apart from their family, apart from the common good is a misery of current post-Christian Western civilization, as it none too gradually becomes an uncivilization. It was for some time thought that we could continue to have and enjoy the fruits of the Judeo-Christian tree of life without the actual tree itself. It seemed that the good, the true, and the beautiful, the fruits of science, medicine, law, politics, civil discourse, art, music, that all of these aspects of a wholesome society that upheld the common goods of marriage, family, and children could and would continue without the Judeo-Christian world view that brought them into existence. But this is obviously not the case. We might do well to recall Jesus' words "Apart from me you can do nothing."

This radical individualism, by its very nature, assumes that our identity can be found within ourselves, apart from others. That deep in my soul is a lone *me*. Our young people are told to create themselves within themselves, in a vacuum so to speak, but we are truly capable of personal growth only in love and service to others. I read once of a very successful agricultural study that took place in a third world country. At the end of the several years long project the women of the village were asked via an interpreter how the project had affected their lives for the better. First they were asked about their community, and then about their families. They had lots to say about the benefits they had all experienced. But then they were asked how the project had affected them as individuals. They did not understand the question! They were sisters, daughters, wives, mothers, aunts, grandmothers, friends, community leaders; they were not *individuals*, but rather every moment of their lives was lived in communion with others, their loved ones, their community. As Joseph Ratzinger (Pope Benedict XVI) wrote in *God & the World* "It is always the case that a person first recognizes himself in others and through others. No one can arrive at knowledge of himself just by looking within himself and trying to build up his personality from what he finds there. Man as a being is so constructed for relationships that he grows in relation to others. So that his own meaning, his task in life, and his potential are unlocked in his meeting with others…meeting with Jesus, among all those other meetings we have need of, is the truly decisive one. At our meeting with him the fundamental light dawns, by which I can understand God, man, the world, mission, and meaning."

Sadly, we now have had three generations brought up, for the most part, separated from our Judeo-Christian roots. We've joked about how the nuns became nones, and we've taken lightly the possible consequences. But now the consequences of the loss of Judeo-Christianity and the highly celebrated sexual revolution that arrived in its wake have left our society in tatters, our families in ruins, our children confused and often broken. Pope John Paul II coined the term "culture of death" and we would be wise to take note of its reality. While the Chinese people hated their politically enforced one-child policy, many in the United States and Europe self-embraced their own close-to-zero child policy. The brave new Western world has moved from contraception to pornography to divorce to abortion to euthanasia to assisted suicide to homosexuality to, now, transgenderism. We have been culturally instructed to celebrate each event as a matter of relativistic liberty. With no objective understanding of the human person in place, only consent is required for morality.

If, on the other hand, the human person has an objective nature, as claimed by Judeo-Christianity, then it's time to understand that nature, and to realize that true freedom for the human person has boundaries. Without boundaries it is merely license. License cannot ever lead to human happiness. The human body is one boundary that acts as a safeguard and home for the heart and soul of the human person. Transgenderism is an ideological frontier of evil experimentation on the human person that particularly targets those with other comorbidities, usually young people struggling with many aspects of their identity, often dealing with depression, anxiety, emotional/physical abuse, substance abuse, mental issues, and other family issues. It targets the very boundary of their own body; it tells them that their own body is a source, not of safety but of betrayal. It posits that if there is a god, then this god is one of confusion, carelessness, and ignorance, a god who could not even get their body right. It directs a floundering young person, not to science and facts, but to political and sexual propaganda. It turns our most vulnerable young people's very bodies into a profitable industry for a post-Judeo-Christian medical and pharmaceutical industry that has long since abandoned its oath to "do no harm."

Time and Space, Light and Love for the Journey

One of the most simple, but perhaps hardest, things to do when faced with a child or young person questioning their identity is to just wait. Just wait. Give them time, space, love, and affirmation grounded in objective reality. Some years back we knew a little boy who at the very young age of four suddenly wanted to be dressed in pink, wanted his nails painted pink, wanted his whole image to be, in our minds, very girly. His family convened a meeting to discuss the matter. The decision was made to be gentle, affirmative of him as a person, not push the issue in <u>any</u> direction, and just wait. What the family learned over time was that this was not about a delusion to become a girl, but a recognition that girls wear more beautiful things than boys do, and this young boy had a deep appreciation for beauty. He soon transitioned, <u>not his body</u>, but his mind and heart, to conform to finding beauty in realistic ways available to his nature as a boy. He just needed time. He needed his family to just wait.

Finally, we are beginning to see Europe pull the brakes on the rush to encourage delusional transitioning and medical mutilation. A return to some basic common sense, the human decency of giving a young person a chance, time and space, to figure themselves out, is emerging. Young people who transitioned (now usually sterile) want to "de-transition", often because they find out that after transitioning, they are on the inside "still me." Internal perception and personal identity remain in a now traumatized body. Finding no recourse for help, they are beginning to make their voices heard. After the use of permanent-sterility puberty blockers, hormone therapies, mastectomies, and genital mutilations, after having caused a tsunami of human devastation, there finally appears a ray of light in the darkness of this assault on the human person.

This book, by Francis Etheredge, joins that effort of light, to shine the brilliance of faith and reason into many of the aspects of this transgender darkness. Transgenderism affects so many aspects of our society's demise: from an individual's personal bodily mutilation and sterility, to endangering the long fought for world of women's sports, to undermining men and women in marriage and family life, to weakening our trust in the medical world, to compromising the now sexualized public education system. Without a clear, true, objective metaphysical, epistemological and theological understanding of the human person as created by God, as created male and female, as created in love, there can be no flourishing of a society.

We are indeed in a dark wood, but the true way need not be wholly lost! We need only to awaken and make, with Virgil, our journey out of this darkness. We do this in relationship with others and God. By grace. We cannot do it alone. We climb out of this darkness in communion with others. And we pray that one day we might proclaim, as Dante did: *"We climbed, he first, I following his steps, Till on our view the beautiful lights of heav'n dawn'd through a circular opening in the cave: Thus issuing we again beheld the stars."*

What is this Book about?
From a Healing Heart to a Hurting Heart

We come through a society which will either foster a recognition of reality or, like distorting mirrors, will jeopardize the growing up and living in society which we do. Either we return to the original definition of do good and avoid harm, or we lose the reality of right and wrong!

This book, then, is about the various crises which have emerged in our time: that people are dying from the destruction of human relationships; that this is impacted destructively by the media; and that we are becoming a more virtual people. But, more and more, this book sets a context for focusing, as it does, on the confusion about being a boy or a girl; and, therefore, speaking from the author's own experience of thinking these thoughts, comes a wide-ranging answer to the search for identity. All these factors, then, impact the basic questions we have as we grow up. In other words, if we are without solid foundations, recognizing imperfections and wounds, whether in ourselves or others, then we are vulnerable to "identity-kit" solutions which obscure and sometimes mutilate who we are. Thus prudence and a loving expression of the truth is necessary at all times.

This concern, however, for the well-being of the young who are suffering the appalling effects of the idea that a human being is neither male nor female but what each person chooses, has turned into a recognition that these ideas, which are so incredibly well funded, are part of a strategy to disorder and dominate society, destroy human sexuality and make people infertile. For, apart from the immense profit to be made from chemicals and unnecessary surgeries, there appears to be no other explanation for the indifference of gender change advocates to the multiplying evidence of harm to an increasing number of people and peoples.

Unless, then, there is a restoration of our relationship to evidence, truth and to God, there is little hope for the restoration of our relationships to each other. Let us, therefore, be willing to re-explore the fullness of human being and life that our Savior, Jesus Christ, seeks for all of us: "I come to give you life and life to the full" (Jn. 10: 10).

A Dedication

To our Lord Jesus Christ and His Church, and to all those who seek the truth sincerely and who, like my wife and eleven children, three of whom are holding the door open for the rest of us in the hereafter, are hoping in the help of the Christian life day by day.

A special dedication to Mary: The Destroyer of all heresies

From her conception on, and in her assumption into heaven, Mary is herself a beautiful expression of the graced unity of the human person, wholly human and wholly female. In view of her vocation as the Mother of God, *The Immaculate Conception*, and the Mother of the Church, she expresses in herself all that pertains to the truth of the saving work of her Son, Jesus Christ, who is wholly man wholly God. This title, then, 'Mary as the *Destroyer of all heresies*' is both ancient and ever relevant. In our present time, she 'defends the truth about the human person. Specifically, by her Assumption, she reveals and destroys the error that plagues us now: the error about the human body'[1]: the error that the body is not integral to the human person being male or female.

As St. John Paul II says, of the human person, made in the image and likeness of God:

'Love is therefore the fundamental and innate vocation of every human being'[2].

---

[1] Fr. Paul Scalia, August 14th, 2016, "Mary, Destroyer of All Heresies": https://www.thecatholicthing.org/2016/08/14/mary-destroyer-of-all-heresies/.

[2] *Familiaris Consortio*, 11.

Our externality visibly expresses our identity as a man or a woman entailing, as it does, our uniquely present individuality[3].

Let us beg the Lord to have mercy on us! Let us beg Mary, St. Joseph, and all the angels and saints to pray for us!

---

[3] Cf. *Familiaris Consortio*, 11.

Why is the Title of this Book Appropriate?

Why "Transgenderism: A Question of Identity"? A book has a history, then, with its author and this one is no different except it has now run to a third title – if not a fourth title.

A book about marriage

To begin with, I thought I was writing a book about marriage, beginning with a survey of the problems in society through which we come, bearing in mind that they both reflect the damage being done to our humanity and the healing that is necessary. Indeed, as such, this was very much a sequel to the last book, "The Word in Your Heart: Mary, Youth, and Mental Health", which looked at how philosophy, the word of God, and pilgrimage, were more than a necessary help to bringing young people through to life and its fullness (cf. Jn. 10: 10). However, the more I read about the crises that people are going through, particularly our young people, the clearer it is that for many, young and old, the major questions of life are not being answered. So, it began to seem as if there were two books, one about the society in which we live and one about marriage – but I persevered with one long book; but then, ignoring the prompt to divide the book into two, I then lost a whole chapter, which decided me to accept that this could be a "word of God" and to accept that the long book needed dividing into two.

Thus, the original book title was "The Marriage Tomb: Exploring the Resurrection", which was an attempt to show the difficulties that people come to marriage with and from which they need healing or at least help to live with and through. Then, when dividing the long book into two, book one was called "Identity and Communion", reflecting the two major concerns with who I am and how I relate to others.

In search of an identity

But, as I have said, having been on a vocational pilgrimage for young people, which entails being open to the question of what plan of love has God for each one of us, I decided on a simpler, more direct title, of "Who Am I? A Snapshot".

So, although many people will marry, and some will be called to other vocations, there will be others who are still struggling to identify who they are and what their identity and vocation is, carrying whatever wounds and healing God has made possible. But whatever stage, step or moment in life a person is in, I hope you will find that this book is an encouragement to discover more deeply the human nature that we all have in common and the deep personal identity that God has made possible for each one of us: that each of us is an embodied person: a man or a woman with an unfolding gift and direction which, the more we align with the gift we have received, the more we understand and grasp the mystery of being given life.

In a somewhat unexpected and perhaps surprising turn up of the two parts of this title, "Who Am I? A SnapShot!", a social scientist said in two different places in one of her books, what amounts to two inadvertent endorsements of the words that then became the next title of this book.

On the one hand Mary Eberstadt said: 'The decline of the family, combined with the closely related eclipse of organized religion, has left many atomized Western individuals unable to supply an answer to the eternal questions, *Who am I?*, by resort to conventional models of family or faith'[1].

---

[1] Mary Eberstadt, *Adam and Eve after the Pill: Revisited*, Foreword by Cardinal George Pell, Ignatius Press: San Francisco, 2023, p. 19.

On the other hand, giving a few examples of how people had concretely responded to the first of these two books, reviewing the contradictions and fall out of the sexual revolution, Eberstadt spoke of giving "A few snap-shots"[2]. Together, then, these different references encouraged me to think that this present book, although written very differently to Eberstadt's books, is nevertheless ploughing a similar furrow through the culture of "today". In a word, there are many influences upon our identity as we re-view the crises in our culture; however, as we zoom out, we realize that amidst the many cross-currents that swirl around, there is a particular focus on to how to help the young "come to themselves" (cf. Lk 15).

A current risk of becoming lost in the search for an identity

Finally, however, Dr. Ronda Chervin[3] has been reading the draft text and pointed out that the title "Who Am I? A SnapShot!" set up an expectation of a series of photos in a book about the author, indeed a bi-ography of me written by someone else; and, therefore, while she acknowl-edged that there were various autobiographical elements in the book, she said: "but [the title] is really a metaphor for the biography of the sexed human person". Gradually, Ronda saw that the autobiographical elements of the book were helpful examples in terms of a concrete search for iden-tity; and, in my own mind, these were attempts to show the reality of hu-man life often entailing working through confusions without them being compounded by erroneous affirmations, the need for study and an expe-rience of life, and persevering through difficulties even when a goal is clearer – not just because of the impulse of life and talent within us but

---

[2] Eberstadt, *Adam and Eve after the Pill: Revisited*, 2023, pp. 14, 60, 92, 166; see also a song by Beth Porch: https://www.youtube.com/ watch?v=qThGfJXf81A.

[3] Email correspondence between the author and Dr. Ronda Chervin, 18th to the 22nd of October, 2024.

because of the active help of God and wise counsellors who bring good out of our often messy lives.

Thus, reflecting on all this, she suggested a more direct title, "Transgenderism: A Fresh New Perspective". Thinking over Ronda's comments, it is clear that when someone else sees what we are doing clearly, they can make us see ourselves or our work with that same clarity. Similarly, I remember my father saying the same thing when others looked at his paintings and saw, more explicitly, what he was "saying". Thus, thinking about all this, it is very much the point of this book to say to young people: *find those who will help you see yourself as you actually are and not as "they" want you to be.* In other words, false affirmations just confirm confusions and lead to dreadfully harmful outcomes.

So why is, "Transgenderism", in the title? Because "isms" are renowned for focusing on an aspect of human activity; and, indeed, this 'ism" is focusing almost exclusively on a person's self-affirmation, affirmed by others, irrespective of its wholesome truth: as if it is self-validating that a woman can become a man, or nothing, or anything in between. Thus the aspect of truth here is that the central issue is how to help a person, particularly a young person, find the right relationship between their identity and the affirmation of the fullness of their being a human person, male or female, which allows their identity to unfold as a whole and as fully and constructively as possible. But, given the relationship between these three things: transgenderism; the metaphor of needing others to help us be clear about ourselves; and the search for an identity - the final title is, I hope, the clearest and most direct of all: "Transgenderism: A Question of Identity".

However, before we proceed further, let us take a core definition of transgenderism: 'the concept of gender is seen as dependent upon the subjective mindset of each person, who can choose a gender not corresponding to his or her biological sex, and therefore with the way others see that

person (transgenderism)'[4]. 'Gender identity theory   [, then,] emerged in
the early 1990s and spread throughout the world in succeeding decades.
At the same time, there are even earlier origins to this ultimately anti-life
mentality. St. Pope Paul VI published his document on the transmission
of life, in 1968, in Latin, *Humanae Vitae.* According to 'Elizabeth Holmes
... 'the 1968 cultural revolution, [entailed] the re-launching of feminism
and the project launched – almost simultaneously – to control the growth
of population globally'[5]. However, we already know of Malthus' (1766-
1834) infamous population forecasts in 1798 and, possibly, an indirect or
even direct effect on anti-population attitudes[6]. According to Holmes,
Aldous Huxley's (1894-1963) program to control population growth inspired the 'civil society' movement. Having obtained political representa-
tion[7], 'civil society' sought to further an anti-family agenda: 'Within UN

[4] Feast of the Presentation of the Lord. Giuseppe Cardinal Versaldi Prefect
Archbishop Angelo Vincenzo ani Secretary Congregation for Catholic Education,
2019, Vatican City: "Male and Female He Created Them" Towards a Path of Dialogue on the Question of Gender Theory in Education", paragraph 11, p. 8:
https://www.vatican.va/roman_curia/congregations/ccatheduc/documents/rc_
con_ccatheduc_doc_20190202_maschio-e-femmina_en.pdf.

[5] Elizabeth Holmes, *The Contemporary Socio-Political Context of the Family*,
Birmingham, Maryvale Institute, 2012, p. 10; taken from Etheredge, A trilogy
called *Truth from truth: Volume II: Faith and Reason in Dialogue*, "CHAPTER
EIGHT: THE CHURCH AT THE HEART OF A SOCIAL DIALOGUE ABOUT
THE VALUE OF THE FAMILY: A PERSONAL, SOCIAL AND GLOBAL
GOOD", pp. 217-218, Cambridge Scholars Publications, 2016: https://www.cam-
bridgescholars.com/product/978-1-4438-8911-7.

[6] Note the prejudice towards being pregnant in the middle of the 19th century:
clothes used to hide or hinder pregnancy as well anti-pregnant women employers
cf. Emily Bach, "Victorian Image of Pregnancy through Corsetry": Victorian Image of Pregnancy through Corsetry – Maryland Center for History and Culture:
https://www.mdhistory.org/victorian-image-of-pregnancy-through-corsetry/.
But a discussion of this takes us too far from our present subject.

[7] Holmes, *The Contemporary Socio-Political Context of the Family*, pp. 84-85.

civil society, the unity of the family's voice is fragmented into the separate categories of children, men ... [and] women'[8]. It is precisely through the organs of the United Nations and the European Union[9], therefore, that 'civil society' brings about an anti-family mentality'[10]. What those who have investigated this anti-family mentality discover is that there is a mixture of recognizing that injustice and discrimination exist while using these imperfections to justify redefining the family, sex, gender, particular people and thus constantly obscuring the fundamentally constant reality of man, woman, marriage and the family. In other words, that there is a fundamentally manipulative mentality at work which seeks to undermine the good of man, woman, and the family[11].

Without going into more detail, let us return to the subject of gender-distortions which, ultimately, seem to express a mutation of the anti-population policies of the founders of 'civil society'. The thought that a person's gender is fluid expresses the idea, taken to an extreme, that there are social influences that contribute to our identity[12]. The extreme, then, to which social influence is taken, is the extreme that there is no "nature" in the dialogue between "nurture" and "nature". In other words, there is a wholesale contradiction of an outwardly expressed inwardness in the body of a man or a woman; but, paradoxically, transgenderism claims that a person can express an identity which has no outward expression: that of being in the "wrong body". Clearly, the social influence theory ends up as a

---

[8] Holmes, The Contemporary Socio-Political Context of the Family, p. 84.

[9] Holmes, The Contemporary Socio-Political Context of the Family, p. 70.

[10] Quoted and discussed in Etheredge, A trilogy called *Truth from truth: Volume II: Faith and Reason in Dialogue*, pp. 232-233.

[11] Cf. Jane Adolphe, "The Holy See and UDHR: Towards a Legal Anthropology of Human Rights and the Family", *Ave Maria Law Review (2006)*: pp. 371-376. Online at C:\Users\Francis\Downloads\HS and UDHR_stamped.pdf

[12] Vincenzo ani Secretary Congregation for Catholic Education, 2019, Vatican City: "MALE AND FEMALE HE CREATED THEM", paragraphs 8-9, p. 7.

justification for children being persuaded by others to think that they are in the "wrong body"; and, in its weaponization, it objects to anyone else helping the child to see the wholesome truth about being an embodied person, either male or female. As a consequence of this type of thinking, even differences between men and women in sport are construed as due to 'bias' and not 'biology': 'The claim in Scientific American attributing "inequity between male and female athletes" to bias rather than biology is false'[13]. This point recurs in the course of this book's research. Thus this type of thinking leads to the denial of whatever stands to contradict this over emphasis on social influence, whether it be nature, parents, clinicians, or indeed anyone who opposes it.

Transgenderism ideologically dismisses biological and scientific categories of male and female in favour of an individual constructing a "gender" of their own choosing'[14]. At the same time, turning the tide on isolationism, which often goes with this type of thinking, we can see with Pope Benedict XVI how dialogue is essential to discovering our identity: 'In reality, "the essential fact is that the human person becomes himself only with the other'[15]. However, 'Following the example of Pope Francis in this

---

[13] Robert Gagnon, December 19th, 2024, "The Left's Takeover Of 'Science' Is Obvious When It Comes To Sex Differences": https://thefederalist.com/2024/12/19/the-lefts-takeover-of-science-is-obvious-when-it-comes-to-sex-differences/.

[14] Simon Caldwell, April 25th, 2024, "Catholic Bishops of England and Wales in 'absolute harmony' with Vatican against gender ideology": https://catholicherald.co.uk/catholic-bishops-of-england-and-wales-in-absolute-harmony-with-vatican-against-gender-ideology/

[15] Congregation for Catholic Education, 2019, Vatican City: "MALE AND FEMALE HE CREATED THEM", pp. 18-19, citing: Benedict XV, Address to the General Assembly of the Italian Episcopal Conference, 27 May 2010.

sensitive area, we too distinguish between pastoral care of the person experiencing these struggles and '[trans]gender ideology"[16].

Having discussed the development of the title and acknowledged the
many influences of those who contributed to it and, indeed, to the book
itself, it is possible to see that what is emerging more and more is that those
who sounded an early warning about transgenderism are being vindicated
– even if they were once vilified[17].

> Given that dialogue is necessary to human development, particularly
> through our late adolescent and early adult years, we need to be careful
> that we are not funnelled through a one thought only process. In other
> words, are the people who are influencing me, *interested in my good for
> its own sake*, or am I being led to where they benefit from what happens
> to me?[18]

---

[16] Page 4 of "A pastoral reflection on gender by the Catholic Bishops of England and Wales", "Intricately Woven by the Lord": https://www.cbcew.org.uk/
wp-content/uploads/sites/3/2024/04/REFLECTION-Intricately-Woven-By-The-
Lord.pdf. This follows an earlier, very brief but pertinent reflection: April 20th,
2018, "A Statement on Gender from the Catholic Bishops of England and Wales":
https://www.cbcew.org.uk/a-statement-on-gender-from-the-catholic-bishops-
of-england-and-wales/.

[17] Cf. By the Editors of the "Free Press", 18th December, 2024, "Abigail Shrier
Was Vilified. Now She's Been Vindicated »: https://www.thefp.com/p/abigail-
shrier-was-vilified-youth-gender-care?utm_source=linkedin&utm_medium=or-
ganic-social; cf. also the disparaged work of psychologist, Deborah Littman, cited
by Dr. Moira McQueen and Bambi, in the January 15th, 2025, edition of "CCBI
News: Gender Affirmation – Changing Approaches": Canadian Catholic Bioethics Institute – Affiliated with the University of St. Michael's College in the University of Toronto: **https://www.ccbi-utoronto.ca/**

[18] The following article helped me see this more clearly: Rondall Reynoso, *first
published on March 14, 2014, and has been lightly edited and updated*, "Philosophy
for Theology: Aesthetics and Theology": https://www.faithonview.com/philoso-
phy-for-theology-aesthetics-and-theology/; and, what is more, this coheres with

Three kinds of published work

The following titles are now on Amazon, in production or, as with this book, in the process of being written; but I list them here in three groups: Scripture; theology and philosophy; Bioethics; and autobiographical; indeed, the third group began with a prayer in front of the Lady Chapel at our local Catholic Church, in the hope of writing a more widely accessible read.

Scripture: A Unique Word (2014); A trilogy on Faith and Reason called, From Truth and truth: Volume I-Faithful Reason (2016), Volume II-Faith and Reason in Dialogue (2016), Volume III-Faith is Married Reason (2016).

The Human Person: A Bioethical Word (2017); Conception: An Icon of the Beginning (2019); Mary and Bioethics: An Exploration (2020); Reaching for the Resurrection: A Pastoral Bioethics (2020); and Unfolding a Post-Roe World (2022); and Human Nature: Moral Norm (2023). Furthermore, the *National Catholic Bioethics Centre* of America has invited a contribution to a second edition of a book on the *Embryo Adoption Debate* (the title is to be confirmed); my contribution is called "The Annunciation and Embryo Adoption" and argues that embryo adoption is a Marian participation in the saving work of Jesus Christ (Forthcoming, 2025). While the following two books have autobiographical elements, as do most other books, they are more about the situation of our times than personal experience and, therefore, they warrant being in this section. The Word in Your

---

what the Second Vatican Council said about the love for God for us: 'Indeed, the Lord Jesus, when He prayed to the Father, "that all may be one. . . as we are one" (John 17:21-22) opened up vistas closed to human reason, for He implied a certain likeness between the union of the divine Persons, and the unity of God's sons in truth and charity. This likeness reveals that man, who is the only creature on earth which God willed for itself, cannot fully find himself except through a sincere gift of himself' (*Gaudium et Spes*, 24).

Heart: Mary, Youth, and Mental Health (2024); and now this one, Transgenderism: A Question of Identity (2025).

The Family on Pilgrimage: God Leads Through Dead Ends (2018); The Prayerful Kiss: A Collection of Poetry and Prose (2019); Honest Rust and Gold: A Second Collection of Prose and Poetry (2020); Within Reach of You: A Book of Prose and Prayers (2021); and now Lord, Do You Mean Me? A father-Catechist!" (2023), An Unlikely Gardener: A Book of Prose and Poetry (2023).

Thank you

Having said all this, I wish to thank all those who have contributed to the various books, either directly or by way of a review or an endorsement; and, here, I wish to thank those who have helped to bring this book to publication. I particularly thank Dr. Anthony Williams for his careful proofreading of this text which, in view of my later additions, does not exclude errors of my own. And, what is more, I am also deeply grateful to Dr. Sebastian Mahfood, OP, of *En Route Books and Media*, for his ongoing encouragement of a persevering author.

Prose and a Prayer
"The Blessing of Beauty"

'We are God's work of art, created in Christ Jesus for the good works which God has already designated to make up our way of life' (Ephesians, 2: 10).

So, we are not discussing those medical emergencies when an accident, a growth anomaly, or a war injury, has seriously damaged a person and there needs to be surgical and other kinds of help; but, by contrast, we are discussing the increasingly "medical-kit" solutions to what are not medical problems – but obstacles to fulfilling the injunction: 'You must love your neighbour as yourself' (Matthew, 22: 39). And, as we discuss elsewhere, it maybe that we cannot love ourselves because we do not love God (cf. Mt. 22: 37): we do not believe He loves us (cf. John 3: 16). Nor is it supposed that there are not difficult sufferings, including bleeding for years as a grossly enlarged prostate operation slipped off the waiting list. Not to mention war and its tragic and ongoing consequences, not least of which has to go beyond defence, retaliation and revenge so that reconciliation brings the possibility of a new future.

So, while it may seem trivial by comparison, nevertheless large problems can start small. If my head is not in my phone what do I see? As the book unfolds and we realize how the outdoors has diminished in young people's experience, although clearly the phone and the computer have their positive uses, nevertheless it is possible to appreciate that there are many sights and sounds that will escape being noticed. But, perhaps equally if not more important, is the time to think and wonder as we walk, more often with others than not, and either share or simply savour an account of what strikes us, whether the rippling motion of the almost black caterpillar that walked past us or the subtle movements of the leaves, slightly shivering, even watery-wavy, but coloured with the on-off lights of the evening light, now shining and shimmering now not and dull but not colourless. Indeed, what we notice of the beauty around us can lead us to the "One" who created it (cf. Romans 1: 20); and, indeed, the time we gain from not scrolling on a phone or a computer, can be time to look and wonder at the possibility of a Creator of beauty[1].

The theme of this piece arose, then, somewhat unexpectedly, from everyday walks in the countryside, through parks, down and round about the roads as, with it being Autumn, it has been impossible not to notice the extraordinarily rich and mixed colours that float about, lie in the wet, catch the light on the tree as if the whole is a kind of translucent collection of pomegranate pearls. In other words, the presence, one way or another of natural beauty, seemed such a contrast to the sufferings described and indicated in this book that, almost, this is an antidote to what we can experience if we are "on-line", immersed in a virtual world of arbitrary and unhealthy changes, whether because a person does not like his or her nose, cheeks or any other part of their body. Or, of course, there is a virtual world in which a face and a body shape can be made after the "idea" of the designer. Indeed, more pervasively, 'If we can use technology any way we like as long as the outcome results in our own happiness, then all reality is "virtual reality," open to construal in any way we like'[2].

Take, for example, the case of a young man or woman who does not like his or her nose, of another who wanted to be taller, or another who is too round, too thin, or another who is too pale – all of which is not objectionable in itself nor indicative of illness or other problems but is

---

[1] Cf. Billy Hallowell, 11/10/24, "Pastor Reveals How Smartphones, Tech Are 'Decimating' Kids' Self-Esteem, Sowing Chaos": https://cbn.com/news/world/pastor-reveals-how-smartphones-tech-are-decimating-kids-self-esteem-sowing-chaos

[2] Rod Dreher, *The Benedict Option*, New York: Sentinel, Penguin Random House, 2017, p. 220.

objectionable to the person whose body it is. Clearly, some of these outward features respond to exercise or makeup and imply some kind of "perfect" body type to which "my" body does not correspond. However, have
you ever thought of blessing God for the gift of you? Whatever the shape
of your nose, hips, shoulders, face, or any other part that somehow stands
out from the unconscious but ever-present perfect mould out of which we
never came – nevertheless we are a gift! Because, as we know from experience, falling into the trap of feeling sorry for ourselves is not just a trapdoor
but opens into a pit of sin, very often the sin of pornography. Indeed, given
the willingness of a UN resolution to retain various kinds of pornography
in their "so-called" ban on it, violating the otherwise binding treaty on the
protection of the child, there are clearly grave reasons for considering that
part of the problem resides in countries "advocating" for pornography rather than rejecting it. Thus what changed the position of the United States?
Who benefits from retaining pornography, such that governments are vot-
ing to retain it? Are there links between pornographic companies and
those advocating for it internationally? 'The United States' support for
these provisions is surprising, given that the United States government was
the main promoter of the strict standard against child pornography in the
Optional Protocol of the Convention on the Rights of the Child only
twenty-five years ago. That treaty established groundbreaking rules to help
combat child pornography, including strict liability for mere possession of
child pornography'[3]. And so why is there a retraction on what was a binding treaty for the benefit of children? Are these documents based on what

---

[3] Stefano Gennarini, J.D. (https://c-fam.org/author/stefano-gennarini-j-d/) |
August 15, 2024, "New UN Cybercrime Treaty Opens Door to Pedophilia and
Legalizes Child Sexting": https://c-fam.org/friday_fax/new-un-cybercrime-
treaty-opens-door-to-pedophilia-and-legalizes-child-sexting/.

is lasting or political pawns in a world at war with children's right to inno-
cence?

So, this is something of the background to the theme of the following
piece.

"The Blessing of Beauty"

Where does the time come from to gaze and ponder
the slightly pink and purply pearls, some twisting and
others drooping, like translucent pomegranates, dying in
and out of colour as the evening light glows amidst them,
and then a passing change and the shining, shimmering,
slightly shivering, even water-wavy leaves are suddenly
dull, dulled, but not colourless or inactive but speaking
silently, as the announcement of brilliance, balance, the
upright glory of the whole tree still stands, but shadowed,
suggesting the mixed palette of the never really black dark?

Simply waiting, it is true, in a car, to collect my daughter and
her friend as the time goes on and they overrun and I notice,
more and more, what at first seemed slight and unseeable.

Where does the time come from to lift my head from cycling
down to the station, sitting on the floor of the train, reading for
an essay for more qualifications, all the while trying to keep awake from
having been up in the night with young children who needed settling,
not to mention the journey on through the traffic,
the holiday deadlines, both for work and for time off, as well
as illness and work manipulations ending up with sitting on the
beach, slumped, so heavily slumped, weary beyond weariness,

as I bear the burden of the impossibility of extricating myself from
"purely administrative changes" that strip the gifts of work?

Simply seeing, at a certain moment, that the damp is rising and
needs cleaning, that exhaustion benefits no one, that we can
manage if I write full-time – even if life is full of uncertainties.

Where does the time come from to look, and walk, and pause
in front of the once running, now rushing and churning brown
waters as they pour through little more than gulleys, channelling the
downpour of days before down into the duck, ducking pond
at the end of the lakes, surrounded by the golden fleece of tree between
trees, some of which are alight with reds that run up and
flame up and out, while still there are greens and yellows, all
making as if to rise like blades of flourishing fire, rising without
smoke except the fuel of colour changes cascading up through
to the top, while leaves drop, a few at a time, enriching the grass?

Walking, I know, not alone, although it can be as I stoop, a little
embarrassed, collecting leaves for the garden but, more often than
not, with others, finding a stunning and stranded star-fish leaf.

Where does the time come from to stop, in front of a plant in the
garden, when the writing does not pay, but needs to be done, and some
of the vegetables are growing too well and need planting out
and time and time again taking time to manure the boxes, drop in
vegetable waste, weed around the new shoots, and watch, with care, the
rise of slugs and snails and their devouring ways, finding
the best time to pick them off before the runner beans are twigs,

scarcely a green shoot left, as the endless supply of feeders rise out of the ground and dine out, night after night, on the delicacies
served up and undefendable as the nighttime is their dining time?

Gradually the panic of having to work all the time subsides, along with the memory of previously working impossible hours of self-employ-ment, so managing because of providence impacts today.

Where does the time come from to write and run the children around to various activities, providing a natural opportunity, as "Taxi-dad", to talk about the day, what is going on in our lives, what plans and hopes and fears we have, what vocation, if any, has become clear, what my experience of life has shown me about the call to marriage and what I am learning about the vocations of others, all the while listening to the word of God and the help of other people's wisdom, learning and com-pany, unfolding an amplified breadth and wealth of experience that multiplies and rings out, like a chorus of bells, ringing to the tune of truthfulness.

It comes from a Way of walking, slowly, over many years, with a com-munity who are called together to listen to the possibility of receiving the *Christian Faith* that fruits in many unexpected ways.

A Summarising Preface

"I do not want to regret not telling you the truth. I do not want you to regret not hearing the truth from me. You will always be my child, but I love you too much to not tell you the truth"[1]. You are a 'beloved son or daughter of the Father. It is helpful to do so with kind and gentle language'[2]. Establish or re-establish wide communication 'by expanding topics of conversation rather than limiting them'[3].

'Those who suffer from distress about their bodies need to hear the same message all of us need to hear. God loves you with an age-old love (see Jer 31: 3). He had you in mind from all eternity, and he brought you into existence at his chosen moment with great joy'[4]. And, welcoming this word of life (cf. Jn. 10: 10) entails unfolding the path of life He invites us to walk.

---

[1] Schnippel, Chapter 20: "Pastoral Care for Families", pp. 338-339, of pp. 333-344 of *Gender Ideology and Pastoral Practice: A Handbook for Catholic Clergy, Counselors, and Ministerial Leaders*, edited by Theresa Farnan, Susan Selner-Wright and Robert L. Fastiggi, St. Louis, MO: En Route Books and Media, LLC, 2024.

[2] Schnippel, Chapter 20: "Pastoral Care for Families", p. 343, of pp. 333-344 of *Gender Ideology and Pastoral Practice*, 2024.

[3] Schnippel, Chapter 20: "Pastoral Care for Families", p. 338, of pp. 333-344 of *Gender Ideology and Pastoral Practice*, 2024.

[4] Ryan, Chapter 14: "Sacramental Care", pp. 252-253 of pp. 243-255 of *Gender Ideology and Pastoral Practice*, 2024.

Winston Churchill: "Some people's idea of [free speech] is that they are free to say what they like, but if anyone says anything back, that is an outrage". (1943)[5]

The lie of contraception of a giving that is not wholly given: 'Thus the innate language that expresses the total reciprocal self-giving of husband and wife is overlaid, through contraception, by an objectively contradictory language, namely, that of not giving oneself totally to the other'[6]. Why does this matter? Because relationships of the living are being dropped for virtual relationships; and, to the extent that the virtual dominates, so people are dominated by the loss of personal identity that is a fruit of relationship.

Truth does not burn[7] but builds and reduces untruth to ash – not wasted but thrown to ground to grow what's there; indeed, truth converts: because truth does not contradict truth[8] and shows that Catholic Teaching is "coherent and consistent"[9]. Thus if a society loses its grip on truth, there is an undoing of the scaffolding that shapes our thinking and our young people's identity.

---

[5] August 2nd, 1964, "*THE CHURCHILL SPIRIT—IN HIS OWN WORDS*": https://www.nytimes.com/1964/08/02/archives/the-churchill-spiritin-his-own-words.html.

[6] St. John Paul II, *Familiaris Consortio*, 32.

[7] This is an adaptation of a quote by Mikhail Bulgakov's 'masterpiece *The Master and Margarita*', which is: "Manuscripts don't burn", cited by Mary Eberstadt on p. 170 of *Adam and Eve After the Pill: Revisited*, Foreword by Cardinal George Pell, Ignatius Press: San Francisco, 2023.

[8] Dogmatic Constitution "Dei Filius": Chapter 4: Faith and Reason: https://inters.org/Vatican-Council-I-Dei-Filius.

[9] Eberstadt, *Adam and Eve After the Pill: Revisited*, p. 175.

Truth is a person, the person of Jesus Christ (Jn. 14: 6), who comes to
establish life-giving relationships with His Father through the power
of the Holy Spirit in the Church (*Lumen Gentium*, 8).

Working on a book like this is almost about discovering the synthesis
in the course of writing it and, therefore, coming at the subject from
many different points of view until arriving, as it were, at the basic questions and eventually addressing them more directly. And, therefore, as
the discussion unfolds it will become clearer why Churchill's words are
so apt for our times!

A key question, then, is this: Is a person sexed or is sex an almost "add
on" to the identity of the person? In other words, is a woman a female
person and a man a male person or are male and female a kind of ex-
trinsic, outward and even an external attribute of the person? Clearly,
as this book proceeds, clarity about the basic question contributes to
finding a helpful answer to crises of identity. Similarly, therefore, are
psychological processes involved and integral to the development of
gender distress, not just outwardly because of prejudice, but inwardly
because of trauma and an inability to identify with one's own sex? Then
there is the question, once we understand what is happening, of what
helps a young person navigate the path to the person he or she is, beginning with listening?

But to be clear from the outset, we are not discussing true intersex conditions where, in reality, there is a condition concerning the external
expression of sexuality which needs careful investigation; but, not to
pass the subject without recognizing the seriousness of it, let me say:
'The sound medical response is to identify the predominant underlying
sex and then take measures to provide health and functioning, as far as

possible, through hormones and possibly surgery. This, therefore, is not a source of evidence for gender dysphoria as intersex is a condition which manifests itself very early on and is dependent, for its manifestation, not on social or psychological factors but on chromosomal anomalies[10]. At the same time, then, the argument that sex is assigned at birth, is almost a caricature of a profound medical condition, in that a real intersex condition presents at birth and has to be investigated as to which sex founds the child's identity. However, as has been said, this is not a case of gender dysphoria nor, therefore, can the specific case of a true intersex condition be used as a general argument for justifying determining sex at birth.

So where to begin?

We begin with the heart, which both ancient philosophy and the Holy Bible describe as the centre, as it were, of who we are: '[The heart of a person] usually indicates our true intentions, what we really think, believe and desire, the "secrets" that we tell no one: in a word, the naked truth about ourselves'[11]. Any investigation of the times in which we live, especially concerning our views about reality, our young people and their agonies and concerns, is essentially a journey into the interior: that from whatever external starting point we begin, we gravitate to the "heart" of the person; and, as such, the heart is the locus of our

---

[10] But for a helpful and sensitive introduction that particular condition, cf. Ryan T. Anderson, *When Harry Became Sally: Responding to the Transgender Moment*, Encounter Books, London and New York, 2018-2019, p. 91, pp. 88-91.

[11] Pope Francis, *Dilexit Nos, He Loved Us*, paragraph 5, but others too: https://www.vatican.va/content/francesco/en/encyclicals/documents/20241024-enciclica-dilexit-nos.html#_ftnref196.

relationships[12]: the place where we encounter our hatred and our love of ourselves and others. As 'Marguerite Stern, a former radical feminist turned pro-family advocate' says, 'After years of embracing radical feminism and the LGBT agenda, Stern realized that transgender ideology in particular "does not create but destroys," and is rooted in "self-hatred"'[13]. In other words, turning to the truth of what is in the heart is, at the same time, turning for help; and, as with all real change, we need the help of God to begin, to proceed, and to continue.

The heart of the person, therefore, communicates the totality of the person in a single image which, more deeply and comprehensively than other expressions, expresses the psychosomatic whole of each one of us; and, therefore, it is to the heart and its needs that this book is addressed: the 'personal centre', 'where 'heart' means the unifying centre of the person'[14]. But, in the Tradition, Teaching and Scripture of the Catholic Church, we are directed to contemplate the heart of Christ: the One to whom we need to draw close and who, in His everlasting love of us, wants to help us to love ourselves and our neighbour with the love with which He loves us.

---

[12] Cf. Alessandro Gisotti, November 5th, 2024, "Cardinal Tagle: Placing the heart at the center of the Jubilee": https://www.vaticannews.va/en/vatican-city/news/2024-11/cardinal-tagle-interview-dilexit-nos-heart-jubilee.html.

[13] Clare Marie Merkowsky (https://www.lifesitenews.com/author/clare-marie-merkowsky/), November 6th, 2024, "Ex-feminist apologizes for 2013 anti-Catholic protest at Notre Dame Cathedral": https://www.lifesitenews.com/news/ex-feminist-apologizes-for-2013-anti-catholic-protest-at-notre-dame-cathedral/

[14] Joseph Ivel Mendanha, C.Ss.R. S.T.D, October 26th, 2024, "'He Loved Us': Pope Francis' new encyclical on the Sacred Heart of Jesus", who quotes from *Dilexit Nos*: https://www.cssr.news/2024/10/he-loved-us-pope-francis-new-encyclical-on-the-sacred-heart-of-jesus/.

On the one hand, we hope that each one of us begins life in the bosom of the family, unfolding our identity as a whole through 'Secure attachment bonds with healthy parents in a stable family coupled with good peer relations (especially with same-sex peers) serve to protect children from developing gender identities discordant from natal bodily sex'[15] (a person's sex from conception and generally visible at birth).

On the other hand, we know that there are all kind of ways that even a person brought up in a Catholic family, as I was, can sin, suffer in silence and grow up estranged from reality; and, therefore, let this book be part of that journey of healing heart to hurting heart: of *hurting heart to healing heart.*

Owing to a contradictory, materialistic conception of human being, as if there is no psychological structure to human being, or problems of psychological development, questions of identity are very often being resolved into questions of physical treatments. Thus 'Attempts are made to explain all manifestations of his life as simple consequences of material processes (physical, chemical, biological) occurring in the body'[16]. But to even think this is to transcend the particular and to express a generalization typical of the capacity of the human being for thought: for that which seeks to understand and think through the nature of what exists.

By contrast, however, there is a recent American survey which says, without giving individual reasons, that '83% of all U.S. adults believe people have a soul or spirit in addition to their physical body'[17]. Indeed,

---

[15] Dowdell and Sodergreen, Chapter 3.1: "Becoming Who We Are", p. 57 of *Gender Ideology and Pastoral Practice.*

[16] Mazurkiewicz, Chapter 8: "Christian Anthropology", p. 148 of pp. 143-161 of *Gender Ideology and Pastoral Practice*, p. 148.

[17] December 7th, 2023, "Spirituality Among Americans": https://www.pewresearch.org/religion/2023/12/07/spirituality-among-americans/.

echoing this, a South Korean was awarded the Nobel Prize for Literature, in part, because her work expressed a "unique awareness of the connections between body and soul, the living and the dead"[18].

Clearly, then, there is the question of how that recognition of the soul or spirit has come about or can be educated; but, nevertheless, and even if we cannot quantify it, there is an immense, world-wide recognition of spirituality, the awareness of more than the physical, pointing to the existence of a soul or spirit and, as some may know, there are ancient and recurring arguments for the existence of the human soul and God. In sum, the soul expresses that which determines our existence to be personal, manifesting its God-given invisible presence from the first instant of human conception[19], such that as the physiological and psychological processes come to maturity, so the "I" who exists-in-relationship, unfolds more fully through the whole of life. Hence the help of the reality of the human heart to anchor our understanding of the whole person in an intelligible simplicity; indeed, as it says in the *Catechism of the Catholic Church*:

'The spiritual tradition of the Church also emphasizes the *heart*, in the biblical sense of the depths of one's being, where the person decides for or against God' (CCC, 368)[20].

By contrast, as we shall see, there is an immense practical embodiment of physicalism in numerous kinds of medical practice. As one psychiatrist recently put the change from the search for meaning to physicalist

---

[18] Christian Edwards, October 10th, 2024, "Han Kang wins Nobel Prize in literature for 'intense poetic prose' confronting human fragility": https://edition.cnn.com/2024/10/10/style/han-kang-nobel-prize-literature-intl

[19] Cf. *The Catechism of the Catholic Church*, CCC, 362-368, and St. John Paul II, *Evangelium Vitae*.

[20] The footnote to this paragraph cites the following texts: 'Cf. Jer 31:33; Deut 6:5; 29:3; Isa 29:13; Ezek 36:26; Mt 6:21; Lk 8:15; Rom 5:5.'

treatments: "Psychology, until recent times, was seen as the study of the soul …. There was a journey to be made, into the transcendent realms, the metaphysical and the spiritual". But now "The human person is reduced to a material thing". And "psychiatry has been reduced to the study of symptoms and the prescribing of the appropriate treatment"[21].

We have the relatively recent precedent of the investigation and use of pharmacological agents that attempt to nullify being female and capable of bearing children, or of being a man and capable of fathering children and now, not only pursuing the destruction and sale of the parts of a child-from-the-womb, but it is also now possible to order the chemicals that abort a child by post and end up hating the bathroom in which a child is lost – never mind the increasing number of harmful effects on the mothers[22] and the eco-system. Similarly, what about the following: "'If Atrazine, a common pesticide, can turn male frogs into females, imagine what it's doing to our kids' hormones." However, the effect of 'Atrazine' on a frog is to feminize it while it remains a male frog; and, as regards men 'atrazine exposure is highly correlated ($P < 0.009$) with low sperm count, poor semen quality, and impaired fertility in humans'[23].

---

[21] Dr Pravin Thevasathan's May 2024, review of "The Quest for Who We Are? Modern Psychology and the Sacred": https://www.cmq.org.uk/CMQ/2024/May/book_review_psychology.html.

[22] Cf. Valerie Richardson, September 5th, 2024, Study finds 75% of women treated at ERs after taking abortion pills rated 'severe or critical': https://www.washingtontimes.com/news/2024/sep/5/three-quarters-of-women-seen-at-ers-after-taking-a/. See later in the book for further details of this discussion.

[23] Tyrone B Hayes (https://pubmed.ncbi.nlm.nih.gov/?term=%22Hayes%20TB%22%5BAuthor%5D) [a,1], Vicky Khoury (https://pubmed.ncbi.nlm.nih.gov/?term=%22Khoury%20V%22%5BAuthor%5D) [a,2], Anne Narayan (https://pubmed.ncbi.nlm.nih.gov/?term=%22Narayan%20A%22%5BAuthor%5D) [a,2], Mariam Nazir (https://pubmed.ncbi.nlm.nih.gov/?term=%22Nazir%20M%22%5BAuthor%5D) [a,2], Andrew Park (https://pubmed.ncbi.nlm.nih.gov/?term=%22

And we wonder why testosterone levels in men are at an all-time low!'[24] In other words, as we go down into more and more unnecessary and harmful actions on human beings, we have reached a point of almost complete relational, ethical and evidential blindness.

Gender ideology: A coincidence of causes or a systematic program?

As we will see, as this book progresses and focuses on the evidence emerging from all kinds of sources, that the experimental use of puberty blockers and mutilating surgeries on minors contradicts,

---

Park%20A%22%5BAuthor%5D) [a,2], Travis Brown (https://pubmed.ncbi.nlm.nih.gov/?term=%22Brown%20T%22%5BAuthor%5D)[a], Lillian Adame (https://pubmed.ncbi.nlm.nih.gov/?term=%22Adame%20L%22%5BAuthor%5D [a], Elton Chan (https://pubmed.ncbi.nlm.nih.gov/?term=%22Chan%20E%22%5BAuthor%5D) [a], Daniel Buchholz (https://pubmed.ncbi.nlm.nih.gov/?term=%22Buchholz%20D%22%5BAuthor%5D [b], Theresa Stueve (https://pubmed.ncbi.nlm.nih.gov/?term=%22Stueve%20T%22%5BAuthor%5D [a], Sherrie Gallipeau (https://pubmed.ncbi.nlm.nih.gov/?term=%22Gallipeau%20S%22%5BAuthor%5D) [a]

"Atrazine induces complete feminization and chemical castration in male African clawed frogs (*Xenopus laevis*)": https://pmc.ncbi.nlm.nih.gov/articles/PMC2842049/.

[24] John F. Kennedy, environmental lawyer, quoted by Simo at: Simo: https://x.com/yoursimmo/status/1831769933367115842: 'RFK Jr. [Robert F. Kennedy, Jr.] just dropped a bombshell: "If Atrazine, a common pesticide, can turn male frogs into females, imagine what it's doing to our kids' hormones." And we wonder why testosterone levels in men are at an all-time low!' And cf. Tyrone B. Hayes,[a,1] Vicky Khoury,[a,2] Anne Narayan,[a,2] Mariam Nazir,[a,2] Andrew Park,[a,2] Travis Brown,[a] Lillian Adame,[a] Elton Chan,[a] Daniel Buchholz,[b] Theresa Stueve,[a] and Sherrie Gallipeau[a], March 9th, 2010, "Atrazine induces complete feminization and chemical castration in male African clawed frogs (*Xenopus laevis*)": https://www.ncbi.nlm.nih.gov/pmc/articles/PMC2842049/: 'In fact, more than a half million pounds of atrazine are precipitated in rainfall each year in the United States.'

wholesale, the safeguards agreed by various protocols for the benefit of the vulnerable in research, particularly the *World Medical Association*, not to mention the disregard for full disclosure of the possible harms, the lack of record keeping, follow-up, and the question of whether or not there is a relationship between those who endorse gender ideology and those who profit from it[25].

The following excerpt acknowledges not only the relationship between money and mutilating surgeries but the "profit" from the extended, long-term effects of it, which are not reversible: 'Dr. Shayne Sebold Taylor … promoting male-to-female and female-to-male surgical procedures as hugely lucrative for hospitals.

'"These surgeries make a lot of money," she said, noting that "chest reconstruction" can mean $40,000 per patient, and vaginoplasties well over $20,000. "These surgeries are labor intensive, there are a lot of follow-ups, they require a lot of our time, and they make money"'[26].

---

[25] Cf. World Medical Association, October 19th, 2024, "World Medical Association Declaration of Helsinki: Ethical Principles for Medical Research Involving Human Participants": https://jamanetwork.com/journals/jama/fullarticle/2825290; a case is going to go before the Supreme Court of America, whereby a state has enacted a law protecting minors from unwarranted chemical and surgical changes and that law is being challenged by the Biden Administration and three families: Tylor Arnold, October 23rd, 2024, "Supreme Court will hear case on Tennessee law banning transgender surgeries for minors": https://www.catholic-newsagency.com/news/260027/supreme-court-will-hear-case-on-tennessee-law-banning-transgender-surgeries-for-minors. The specific case of a father defending the good health of his child, is plain to see: Calvin Freiburger, October 11th, 2024, "Jeffrey Younger says he has 'last shot' to stop ex-wife from 'castrating' son James in November": https://www.lifesitenews.com/news/ jeffrey-younger-says-he-has-last-shot-to-stop-ex-wife-from-castrating-son-james-in-november/.
[26] Calvin Freiburger, September 21st, 2022, "Explosive report reveals Vanderbilt promoted transgender surgeries to make 'huge money'": https://www.life-

Now, more generally, even more millions if not billions are poured into what is now called the transgender industry[27]; and, what is more, this 'market is forecast to be worth $6.2 billion dollars by 2030'[28]. But another figure is that the '"LGBTQ market" was valued at $1.4 trillion'[29]. It may even be that keeping the classification 'gender dysphoria' may be about accessing 'financial reimbursements for gender transitioning services' for which, in America, a 'diagnostic code is required'[30]. In other words, 'Gender ideology is a top-down, well-funded ideological movement that is pushing millions of dollars into LGBTQ advocacy', and attempting to use conditional aid, or 'economic coercion'[31], to replace cultures and countries that have 'strong religious traditions'[32] with an account of human sexuality that is both sexless and infertile. The European Union, it seems, uses trade agreements to coerce countries into agreeing to 'gender ideology' and other

---

sitenews.com/news/explosive-report-reveals-vanderbilt-founded-transgender-clinic-to-make-huge-money/.

[27] Cf. Michael Cook, August 30th, 2024, "Exposing the transgender money machine": https://www.mercatornet.com/exposing_the_transgender_money_machine.

[28] Hasson, Chapter 5: "The Impact of Gender Ideology", p. 93 of pp. 87-107 of *Gender Ideology and Pastoral Practice*, 2024.

[29] Hasson, Chapter 5: "The Impact of Gender Ideology", p. 102 of pp. 87-107 of *Gender Ideology and Pastoral Practice*, 2024.

[30] *Gender Ideology and Pastoral Practice*, 2024, p. 34, footnote 3, of Dowdell and Sodergreen, Chapter 3: "Becoming Who We Are".

[31] Adolphe, Chapter 6: The UN Independent Expert on Sexual Orientation", p. 109 of pp. 109-122 of *Gender Ideology and Pastoral Practice*, 2024; cf. also Giuliani, Chapter 7: "Ideological Colonization in Belize", pp. 123-140 of *Gender Ideology and Pastoral Practice*, 2024.

[32] Hasson, Chapter 5: "The Impact of Gender Ideology", p. 107 of pp. 87-107, of *Gender Ideology and Pastoral Practice*, 2024.

policies and practices harmful to the family[33]. At the same time, gender ideology has gone from a 'fringe' movement to a high-profile advocacy activism, which is where a public figure argues in the public spaces for those who are now 'fat cats who wield unprecedented cultural power pulling in massive salaries by claiming that things are worse for LGBT-identifying people than ever'[34]. Again, the question has to be asked, where does all the money come from? Again, why is the European Union taking Hungary to the European Court of Human Rights over legislation which protects children?

Hungary's 'national legislation recognizes identity based on biological sex and prohibits exposing minors to pornographic content, inappropriate sexuality, homosexuality, gender ideology, and sex changes[35]'.

What is more, these ideas are permeating the unofficial documents of the United Nations, as if they are official[36], and are often contrary to the founding documents of the United Nations; and, in addition, there is a gender ideology language which changes the relationship between words

---

[33] Austin Ruse, December 5th, 2024, "Speakers Warn Conservatives of EU Attacks to Democracy and Freedom": https://c-fam.org/friday_fax/speakers-warn-conservatives-of-eu-attacks-to-democracy-and-freedom/.

[34] Jonathon Van Maren, Wed Aug 14, 2024, "LGBT activism has gone from a fringe movement to a multi-million-dollar propaganda industry": https://lifesitenews.com/blogs/lgbt-activism-has-gone-from-a-fringe-movement-to-a-multi-million-dollar-propaganda-industry/.

[35] Rodrigo Ballester (https://europeanconservative.com/articles/author/rodrigo-ballester/)— December 11, 2024 (https://europeanconservative.com/articles/2024/12/11/), "Why the Battle Over Hungary's Child Protection Law Matters for Europe": https://europeanconservative.com/articles/commentary/why-the-battle-over-hungarys-child-protection-law-matters-for-europe/.

[36] Adolphe, Chapter 6: The UN Independent Expert on Sexual Orientation", pp. 110-112 of pp. 109-122 of *Gender Ideology and Pastoral Practice*, 2024.

and reality[37], entails an insistence on others using this new language[38] and is, therefore, dividing families, interfering with the workplace[39], schools[40] and universities, Catholic Health Care[41], and changing the meaning of laws and documents, all of which ends up being a systematically disordering domination of society.

This is because of the investment of the following agencies, which seek to manipulate the United Nations for profit, promoting and marketing anti-population policies: 'big pharma, tech, media, [and] finance'[42]. The founding documents of the United Nations, however, recognized 'the human person (endowed with reason and conscience), male and female .... the rights of the natural family based on marriage between a male and a female .... as well as the rights of parents and of children and duties of the community' including the protection of these rights by 'society and the state'[43]. Remember, too, the United Nations Declaration on the Rights of the Child: 'It is a human right for every child, as far as possible, 'to know

---

[37] Farnan and Hasson, Chapter 27.4: "General Guidance regarding Pronouns", pp. 452-458 of *Gender Ideology and Pastoral Practice*, 2024. Note, however, if a name is changed in law, and the person is an adult, discretion is necessary with regard to how to react, taking account of prudence and a loving expression of the truth at all times.

[38] Hasson, Chapter 26: Corrupting Language, Creating Confusion", p. 433 of pp. 429-437 of *Gender Ideology and Pastoral Practice*, 2024.

[39] Cf. Griffin, Chapter 27.1: "Stand Fast on the Pronouns", pp.439-444 of *Gender Ideology and Pastoral Practice*, 2024.

[40] Farnan and Hasson, Chapter 27.3: "Guidance Regarding Pronouns and "New" Names in Schools Settings", pp. 448-452 of *Gender Ideology and Pastoral Practice*, 2024.

[41] Zalot, Chapter 27.2: "Navigating Pronouns in Catholic Health Care", pp. 444-447 of *Gender Ideology and Pastoral Practice*, 2024.

[42] Adolphe, Chapter 6: The UN Independent Expert on Sexual Orientation", p. 111 of pp. 109-122 of *Gender Ideology and Pastoral Practice*, 2024.

[43] Adolphe, Chapter 6: The UN Independent Expert on Sexual Orientation", p. 113 of pp. 109-122 of *Gender Ideology and Pastoral Practice*, 2024.

and be cared for by his or her parents' (United Nations Convention on the Rights of the Child, art. 7.1)[44]. It is necessary to recall this when it comes to recognizing that while the good of the child is not always the first concern of his or her parents, there is at least the presumption of this before the state, or any other organization, presumes to act on behalf of that child. In other words, when a child is influenced to the point of seeking what is obviously a harmful procedure, just as a parent has a right to protect the child from harming themselves, so the parents have a right to protect the child from the undue and harmful influence of others. In other words, why and how has it come to pass that the rights of parents are increasingly, and unjustifiably, undermined and overruled?

On the one hand, there does seem to be a groundswell of parental objections to the harmful practices of those who want to invade female spaces with males, destroying the girls right to privacy and encouraging a delusional, if not perverse, outlook in boys[45]. In particular, as this book will show, there has to be a rebuttal of 'emotivism'[46]: the argument which plays

---

[44] "A Joint Christian Declaration on 'Diversity of Gender and Sexuality': A Norwegian Christian Ecumenical Project 2024: https://felleskristen.no/file/1joint-christian-declaration-on-diversity-of-gender-and-sexuality-2024-one-page.pdf. Clearly, this reference to the UN declaration also pertains to children conceived from "anonymous" egg and sperm donors.

[45] Johnathon Van Maren, Fri Jan 3, 2025, "The horrors of transgenderism are still plaguing our children despite growing pushback": https://www.lifesitenews.com/blogs/the-horrors-of-transgenderism-are-still-plaguing-our-children-despite-growing-pushback/.

[46] Cf. *Lived Experience and the Search for Truth: Revisiting Catholic Sexual Morality*, edited by Deborah Savage and Robert Fastiggi, St. Louis, En Route Books and Media, 2024, "Introduction", p. 1. The authors, drawing on MacIntyre, define emotivism as 'the assumption that personal preference – and not self-evident first principles – is the starting place of all moral discourse.' Clearly this applies to test-tube babies, emphasizing the plight of the mother, abortion, euthanasia etc. But in the above, I bring out the more "emotional impact of this type of

upon the emotions of people, particularly those of parents claiming, without reference to the full psychological reality of the child, that to avoid suicide a child has to be fast-forwarded through some bodily altering process.

On the other hand, there are specific "feeders" into this crisis as some bureaucratic documents of the UN are disseminating confusion by using terms that entail more than what they seem[47]. A term that has been used in bureaucratic documents for a number of years, 'life-skills', has become explicitly connected to advancing "'COMPREHENSIVE SEXUALITY EDUCATION!'" In other words, 'life skills' had become a 'synonym' for advancing 'homosexuality, trans, and abortion'[48]. Furthermore, these bureaucratic claims have spawned all kinds of intimidating legislation which has brough a rein of fear into the public discourse on protecting children from harm[49]. Thus, realistically, the United Nations needs to be recalled to the meaning of its founding documents[50]. What is more, a recent UN reporter on 'Violence Against Women' did precisely this when she said:

---

argument which, as has been said, does not recognize real human rights proceeding from human nature.

[47] Cf. Stefano Gennarini, J.D. | September 12, 2024, "UN Abortion Activists Publicly Admit Stealth Plot": https://c-fam.org/friday_fax/un-abortion-activists-publicly-admit-stealth-plot/.

[48] Austin Ruse, austin.ruse@c-fam.org, October 17th, 2024, ""Life Skills" is a Poisonous Term at the UN? YES! ».

[49] Cf. Clare Marie Merkowsky (https://www.lifesitenews.com/author/clare-marie-merkowsky/), Thu Jan 2, 2025, "Poilievre promises to keep men out of women's jails after 'sadistic' murderer claims to be female": https://www.lifesitenews.com/news/poilievre-promises-to-keep-men-out-of-womens-jails-after-sadistic-murderer-claims-to-be-female/. Moreover, in the course of this book, there are numerous, further examples, of the ways that the law has been used to intimidate, oppress, and victimize those who legitimately object to engendering gender confusion and funnelling children to mutilating procedures and operations.

[50] Cf. Adolphe, Chapter 6: The UN Independent Expert on Sexual Orientation", p. 119 of pp. 109-122 of *Gender Ideology and Pastoral Practice*, 2024.

'"Sex must be understood in its ordinary meaning to mean biological sex," Alsaleem said, quoting the landmark 1995 UN women's agreement at the Beijing conference.' How wonderful would it be if the common sense and wisdom of this woman was thought through to its logical conclusion, restoring the reality of what is legally binding instead of conflating bureaucratic documents with international, legally binding declarations:

'"Nondiscrimination based on sex is recognized in all major international human rights agreements," she said whereas, "conflating sex and gender identity through the creation of a legal sex category (gender as distinct from sex) has been confusing and problematic"[51]. This term, 'gender', was bracketed at the Beijing Conference on Women, in 1995, precisely because it was a term being used to mean multiple ideas, not just 'men and women' and, therefore, had to be properly defined. In other words there were those who were using gender as a trojan horse, bringing the idea of multiple genders into the UN document which, in the end, was rejected[52]. Similarly, now, Iowa is in the process of restating that gender applies, specifically, to being a man or a woman[53].

---

[51] By Stefano Gennarini, J.D. (https://c-fam.org/author/stefano-gennarini-j-d/)| October 10, 2024, "UN Official Defends Women's Sports Against Male Incursion": https://c-fam.org/friday_fax/un-official-defends-womens-sports-against-male-incursion/.

[52] "WCAT TV presents . . . John Klink on Bracketing Gender at the World Conference on Women in Beijing: https://www.youtube.com/watch?v=9GmapwVtteI.

[53] Associated Press, February 27th, 2025, "Vote expected on Iowa bill that would remove right of people to self-declare their gender": https://afn.net/ap/politics/vote-expected-on-iowa-bill-that-would-remove-right-of-people-to-self-declare-their-gender/.

Indeed, it is precisely for this reason that Italy refuses to recognize a legal, non-binary, sexual identity: 'Italy's constitutional court has refused to legally recognize a 'non-binary' sexual identity—on the grounds that it would disrupt Italy's entire social and legal system'[54].

America, then, under President Trump, is now moving back to a recognition of two sexes; and, in so far as it is possible, to remedy the confusion in official documents. Moreover, to be biologically clearer, the 'executive order' defines a person's sex according to his or her 'reproductive function'. A person is a female if she has a 'large reproductive cell' (the ovum or egg) or the person is a male who has 'a small reproductive cell' (the sperm)[55]. What is more, the actual "Executive Order" goes further and specifies the sex of the person from conception: '(d) "Female" means a person belonging, at conception, to the sex that produces the large reproductive cell'; '(e) "Male" means a person belonging, at conception, to the sex that produces the small reproductive cell'[56]. Indeed, is it possible that this reference to 'conception' will transform the

---

[54] Bridget Ryder, August 2nd, 2024, "Victory in Italy's Constitutional Court Over Gender Ideology": https://europeanconservative.com/articles/news/victory-in-italys-constitutional-court-over-gender-ideology/.

[55] Brooke Migdon (https://thehill.com/author/brooke-migdon/) - 01/20/25 9:40 PM ET, « Trump signs executive order recognizing only 2 sexes": https://thehill.com/homenews/administration/ 5097278-trump-executive-order-gender-transition/. Clearly, there has to be a recognition that a true "intersex" condition is resolved in terms of one sex or the other by a medical investigation. But that is outside the remit of this document.

[56] January 20th, Executive Order", "Presidential Actions: Defending Women from Gender Ideology Extremism and Restoring Biological Truth to the Federal Government": https://www.whitehouse.gov/presidential-actions/2025/01/defending-women-from-gender-ideology-extremism-and-restoring-biological-truth-to-the-federal-government/

abortion debate, because it refers to 'the sex of the *person* from conception'[57].

In other words, thinking through what is said in 1995, in Beijing, is a good basis for clarifying what is going on more widely, in society, with its confusing and unscientific accounts of sex. Thus changing the appearance of children scarcely able to understand everyday life never mind the questions of human identity that we can pass through in the course of growing up is more and more exposed as a business and a politically driven manipulation of language. What happened to ethical safeguards, the wisdom of parents to object, the legal protection of minors, the recognition of the harm done already and the accountability of those who mutilate children? And of course there are other questions, such as is there a connection between so called gender services and the transgender industry's claims[58], just as there is between contraceptive and abortion providing activities and money making, just as there was an agenda of the men who experimented on women in order to develop hormonal contraceptives, taking advantage of those who were poor or scarcely understood what the so-called

---

[57] Emphasis added. 'Ethics and Public Theology professor Andrew T. Walker on X called (https://x.com/andrewtwalk/status/1881852625307779455?s=51) the language a "brilliantly stealth" move": connecting conception and personhood. Emily Mangiaracina, January 22nd, 2025, "Trump's executive order against gender ideology recognizes personhood at conception": https://www.lifesitenews.com/news/trumps-executive-order-against-gender-ideology-recognizes-personhood-at-conception/. Also cf. Etheredge, *Unfolding a Post-Roe World*: https://enroutebooksandmedia.com/post-roe/: for a discussion on the American Constitution defining, by implication, a citizen from conception.

[58] Cf. also Calvin Freiburger, September 26th, "21 states threaten top medical group with legal action for claiming puberty blockers are 'reversible'": https://www.lifesitenews.com/news/21-states-threaten-top-medical-group-with-legal-action-for-claiming-puberty-blockers-are-reversible/?utm_source=daily-usa-2024-09-27&utm_medium=email.

scientists were doing[59]. Even now, then, there is the ongoing question of what value there is to the almost permanent use of hormonal contraceptives on women when, it seems, they have simply embodied a mentality that they must be used long term, which astronomically increases the turnover of the pharmaceutical providers[60] who continue to ignore the side effects or simply manufacture a pacifying variant of what is on the market already[61]. This raises questions about the value and purpose of a number of pharmaceutical products and those who have turned medicine into simply providing what the "customer" wants[62], whether it is changing facial or bodily structures for superficially cosmetic reason, mutilating surgeries or death. In other words, the "objectivity of diagnosis" is being obscured by other factors, whether monetary or psychological[63]. Moreover,

---

[59] By Drew C. Pendergrass (https://www.thecrimson.com/writer/1213303/Drew_C._Pendergrass/) and Michelle Y. Raji (https://www.thecrimson.com/writer/1211646/Michelle _Y._Raji/), September 28th, 2017, "The Bitter Pill: Harvard and the Dark History of Birth Control": https://www.thecrimson.com/article/2017/9/28/the-bitter-pill/.

[60] Doug Mainwaring, August 26th, 2025, "Tucker Carlson now troubled by birth control pill, says his views are 'radically changing'": https://www.lifesitenews.com/news/tucker-carlson-now-troubled-by-birth-control-pill-says-his-views-are-radically-changing/?utm_source=digest-prolife-2024-08-27&utm_medium=email

[61] Cf. the work of an investigative feminist, not in favor of the Catholic Church, who yet recognizes that her objections to contraception put her in the same field, as it were, especially as regards medical objections to contraceptives: Holly Grigg-Spall, *Sweetening The Pill: Or How We Got Hooked On Hormonal Birth Control*, Zero Books: Winchester, UK, 2013.

[62] Anderson, *When Harry Became Sally*, pp. 114-115, particularly on p. 114 where it is said that 'health care in general, and mental health care in particular, [is viewed] as primarily a matter of fulfilling a patient's desires.'

[63] Anderson, *When Harry Became Sally*, p. 115: 'The Dutch doctors who pioneered puberty blocking for children with gender dysphoria defended their approach by saying it was "proof of solidarity of the health professional with the plight of the applicant."' This does not tell us about the uncertain validity of the

there is the complicating possibility that the movement to think that sex is changeable, is actually a preliminary step in the incremental steps that are being made to change human nature as if, by adding electronics to people's brains, it is possible to "enhance" human beings – disregarding the impact on a person's humanity when he or she is "hackable", on-line constantly, or otherwise treated as an "object"[64]. Thus, will the depersonalized human being turn on the personalized, given that the depersonalized person realizes that he or she is losing the possibility of personal intimacy and so runs the risk of becoming the enemy of the person who is not undergoing what is depersonalizing?

Thus, as I will go to show from experience, I know both how demanding these questions of identity are, hence all the studying I have done, and how misleading it is to pursue every kind of problem as if human nature is monosyllabically physical – as if there is no such thing as evidence, argument and truth: as if we do not already know that puberty blockers harm children and young people as they interfere with bone density and fertility[65]. But first a grasp of the complexity of the present situation in which inexperienced people find themselves.

Scripture says, the wise man has many counsellors (cf. Proverbs 15: 22): Growing opposition to puberty blockers and surgery

---

treatment, its applicability to what there is to be treated, or the objective distance between doctor and patient.

[64] *Lived Experience and the Search for Truth: Revisiting Catholic Sexual Morality*, 2024, edited by Deborah Savage and Robert Fastiggi, En Route Books and Media, 2024, J. Budziszewski, Chapter 9: "Transsexualism as Transhumanism", p. 230-231..

[65] For a comprehensive account of what is already known, go to p. 130 and p. 131 of Anderson, *When Harry Became Sally*.

A surgeon, and indeed any health care professional, but in particular 'Surgery means "work done with the hand", "operation of the hand". And that is exactly what it is: in order to heal, surgeons must wound, cut. Therefore, when you have the body of a person in your hands, created in the image of God, act as "artisans of health", working on others with the same care with which you yourself would wish to be treated'[66].

Notably, then, there seems to be a growing agreement about forestalling, if not stopping, the use of puberty blockers on children: Chile, along with other 'countries … [has] also decided to stop this type of treatment due to the lack of solid scientific evidence about its effectiveness and side effects in adolescents.' Among these 'are the United Kingdom[67], Germany, Finland, the Netherlands, Norway, France and Sweden'. And then even in those countries that still permit it, regrettably, 'Canada, Australia or some US states such as Arkansas or Missouri, medical professionals and associations also warn of the low evidence available on the efficacy and safety of these therapies and the need for a review of these procedures'[68]. Indeed, just recently, 'Dr. Steven Williams, president of the American Society of Plastic Surgeons,' said that there is insufficient data on the 'psychiatric and long-term results' of physical treatments for adolescents

---

[66] "Audience with members of the Italian Society of Surgery, 16.10.2024": https://www.vatican.va/content/salastampa/en/bollettino/pubblico/2024/10/16/241016g.html.

[67] Cf. Andreas Wailzer, December 11th, 2024, "BREAKING: UK to ban puberty blockers for minors indefinitely": https://www.lifesitenews.com/news/breaking-uk-bans-puberty-blockers-for-minors-indefinitely/.

[68] "Bioethics Observatory", September 9th, "In Chile, hormone blockers will not be prescribed to adolescents with gender dysphoria": https://bioethicsobservatory.org/2024/09/in-chile-hormone-blockers-will-not-be-prescribed-to-adolescents-with-gender-dysphoria/47053/.

presenting with gender dysphoria[69]. More recently still, more than half of the US States have banned "'gender affirming' sex changes for minors'[70]. Thus there needs to be a grounding of the rights of the child in concrete evidence that surpasses political swings. So why has experienced and professional advice been ignored; and, as the Scripture says, the wise man has many counsellors (cf. Proverbs 15: 22) – but unless we listen to the counsellors there is no benefit from their advice.

So, in addition to all the other ethical problems, how is it possible to conduct experimental studies on children knowing, already, that that there are harmful effects[71]; in particular, what is the justification of continuing with an "experimental" use of puberty blockers if they are already banned for '18' year olds for being harmful?[72] How is that this inconsistency is not both unethical and unscientific: that there is a ban on puberty blockers for under 18s except for under 18 'clinical trials?[73] More widely, if numerous people regret the mutilation of their bodies as well as the long-term consequences of unnecessary and sometimes multiple operations which can

---

[69] Taylor Penley, September 10th, 2024, "Top US surgeon cautions against administering gender-affirming care to minors: 'Not enough evidence'": https://www.foxnews.com/media/top-us-surgeon-cautions-administering-gender-affirming-care-minors-evidence.

[70] Adam Wittenberg (https://readlion.com/authors/adam-wittenberg/), December 16th, 2024, "More than half of US states have banned 'gender-affirming' sex changes for minors, showing wide support for protecting kids": https://readlion.com/more-than-half-of-us-states-have-banned-gender-affirming-sex-changes-for-minors-showing-wide-support-for-keeping-kids-safe/.

[71] Cf. Julio Tudela and Ester Bosch, July 30th, 2024, "European policies regarding minors with gender dysphoria: A comparative analysis": https://bioethicsobservatory.org/2024/07/european-policies-regarding-minors-with-gender-dysphoria-a-comparative-analysis/47056/.

[72] Andreas Wailzer, December 11th, 2024, "BREAKING: UK to ban puberty blockers for minors indefinitely".

[73] Andreas Wailzer, December 11th, 2024, "BREAKING: UK to ban puberty blockers for minors indefinitely".

lead to life-long medications and ongoing harm and disruption to life, why is this not considered evidence against these procedures? On the one hand, 'The Finnish psychiatrist [Prof Riittakerttu Kaltiala] stresses the importance of studying why patients stop hormone treatments. This will help better predict who is suitable for this radical treatment.'

Indeed, this statement still assumes that this 'radical treatment' is helpful to anyone; but, nevertheless, even recognizing that a number of clinics did not keep records and therefore cannot trace people[74], she is still beginning to see an evidence base contrary to the claims of the benefits of this so-called treatment. And, on the other hand, 'She also wants there to be appropriate care for those who stop treatment that has caused irreversible changes in their previously healthy bodies'[75]. And, indeed, what about the testimonies of those who have or are de-transitioning[76], as it is called? Note what the psychiatrist says about 'irreversible changes in their previously healthy bodies'. Note that American lawyers are considering legal action against the American Academy of Paediatrics (AAP) who continue to claim 'that the "use of puberty blockers on children is safe and reversible'[77]

---

[74] The Cass Report lamented the lack of proper record keeping; as we will see later in the book.

[75] Cf. Tineke van der Vaal, 7th of September, 2024, "Finnish research: Number of people regretting gender change increases": https://cne.news/article/4417-finnish-research-number-of-people-regretting-gender-change-increases. *This article was translated by CNE news and published by the Dutch daily Reformatorisch Dagblad* (https://www.rd.nl/artikel/1076001-fins-onderzoek-spijt-bij-geslachtsverandering-neemt-toe) *on September 2, 2024.*

[76] Cf. Anderson, *When Harry Became Sally*, pp. 49-76.

[77] Calvin Freiburger, September 26th, "21 states threaten top medical group with legal action for claiming puberty blockers are 'reversible'": https://www.lifesitenews.com/news/21-states-threaten-top-medical-group-with-legal-action-for-claiming-puberty-blockers-are-reversible/?utm_source=daily-usa-2024-09-27&utm_medium=email. ; and cf. above for sources of evidence of the harm done.

and is clearly not based on widespread evidence to the contrary. At the same time, if there is not objectivity in the psychiatric help given to those suffering often, a variety of problems, then, 'Unfortunately, many clinicians – particularly those who work in gender clinics – disregard desistance [that is, when a person (generally an adolescent) reverts to their biological sex before major surgical changes[78]] in their headlong rush to move children to puberty-blocking and cross-sex hormones'[79].

In other words, harm has been done; as opposed to the first principle of the natural law: which is to do good and avoid harm. So why has this principle been submerged in this debate? Why, then, is it surprising that those who regret these procedures and outcomes do not want to go back to those who accelerated their progress through them?[80] Why are these advocates of puberty blockers so dependent on the law protecting their claims that they are acting in the best interests of children and yet are so isolated from the genuinely scientific, evidence-based community? What of those who witness, in their own bodies, the irreversibly harmful changes due to puberty blockers, never mind surgery?[81]

Thus questions of identity continue, very often, to be resolved into questions of medication and appearance: as if changing our appearance changes our identity. And, therefore, even if a person's appearance is changed, then it is likely that the underlying question of identity will reappear. Thus, the question of identity being deeper than questions of

---

[78] "What do the terms 'detransition' and 'desistance' mean?": https://can-sg.org/frequently-asked-questions/what-do-the-terms-detransition-and-desistance-mean/.

[79] Zalot, Chapter 25: "Guidance for Catholic Health Care", p. 425 off pp. 407-426 of *Gender Ideology and Pastoral Practice*, 2024.

[80] This is referenced later in the book.

[81] Madison Ayers, June 15th, 2024, "Is it true that puberty blockers "pause" puberty? Hint: The answer isn't what we've been told": https://naturalwomanhood.org/puberty-blockers-pause-puberty/.

appearance, very often resolving the question of identity brings about an acceptance of being male or female[82]. One immense problem with focusing on a moment of confusion is that it does not take account of the future; it is like "stopping time", as if it can be stopped, and enclosing people in a bubble of preoccupation with gender until it bursts! We are no longer discussing individual ideas but, rather, a cultural turn, whereby the law is used to express a point – as if the legal judgement is self-evident: 'Justice Robert Bromwich declared that, under Australian law, sex is "fluid and not necessarily binary"'[83]. It may be that it is self-evident that this is what Australian law states; but it is far from self-evident that this is true. Similarly, and more widely, any example of self-identification, by a man, claiming to be a woman, is an expression of redefining what a woman is[84].

However, this is not a redefinition of reality it is, rather, a redefinition of a word which substitutes an idea for an actual reality; and, indeed, this is taking hold more and more as the language expressing marriage and infertility is used, not to express either, but to express a different reality. In other words, defining infertile 'couples who are not just medically infertile, but also relationally infertile'[85] takes us into the realm of relationally infertile meaning two men or two women who live together. Again and again, UN bureaucrats are seeking to make it so familiar, that 'abortion is a right', that it will creep into more and more UN documents when, patently, this

---

[82] Cf. Anderson, *When Harry Became Sally*, p. 119.

[83] Makeda, August 27th, 2024, "Australia abolishes womanhood": https://www.christianvoice.org.uk/index.php/australia-abolishes-womanhood/. (altered speech marks to include the whole quote).

[84] Cf. Anderson, *When Harry Became Sally*, p. 190-196.

[85] Travis K. Kircher, 1st of October, 2024, "California redefines infertility to include same-sex couples": https://wng.org/sift/california-redefines-infertility-to-include-same-sex-couples-1727807152.

has neither been proved nor agreed[86]. Thus, in view of the question of the relationship between words and reality, we are opening chasms between what exists and the words which refer to it; and, therefore, where will this type of invention stop and why will it not lead to more and more moral confusion among our young and those who, already, are unable to critically assess what is going on. Thus we enter more and more into a linguistic world which is more an expression of an imagined virtuality that reveals the thought of the thinker, rather than revealing the reality of what exists.

It may be true, for example, that drugs of one kind or another can alter the body's sexual expression, introducing breasts or shrinking testes; but it does not follow that the sex of the person can be isolated from the whole person and that, therefore, the sexual identity of the person is fluid. The whole person is male or female not just the body parts; as, indeed, we recognize from the chromosomal pattern of XX for a female and XY for a male: the chromosomal pattern pervades the whole body and determines, from the beginning, a sequential development of the whole person.

In other words, for the sake of those who have manipulated the law to oppose criticism of their philosophy, their lack of accountability, their methods, their lack of records[87] and their lack of follow-up on who goes through these distressing and harmful procedures, many people are being

---

[86] Rebecca Oas, Ph.D. (https://c-fam.org/author/rebecca-oas-ph-d/) | December 12, 2024, "Amnesty International Says Abortionists are Human Rights Defenders": https://c-fam.org/friday_fax/amnesty-international-says-abortionists-are-human-rights-defenders/.

[87] Melissa Rudy, August 16th, "'Gender-affirming' breast removal surgeries may have been performed on hundreds of young girls since 2017: Number rises to thousands of girls under age 18, according to Manhattan Institute analysis": https://www.foxnews.com/health/gender-affirming-breast-removal-surgeries-may-performed-hundreds-girls-since-2017. The analysts used insurance data to discover these statistics, not clinical data from those who performed these operations and, what is more this may not be the full number. So why are there no easily accessible records of these acts?

funnelled through a "straitjacket solution" that is supposed to apply to all when, ordinarily, a diagnosis takes account of the specifics of each person's case[88]. At the same time, why is an insurance company exempt from the ethical question of funding such operations as double breast removals when there is no cancer or medical reason to do so[89]. One young woman who regrets her loss of breasts is suing the clinician who did not enquire about why she had problems with her femininity, which actually arose from early abuse, in the hope that others will be spared what she is going through[90]. In this very physicalist account of human development, which overlooks, to the tremendous detriment of many people, the psychological development of human beings and the characteristic openness of human beings to the divine, there is very often a trampling upon the relationship of evidence to outcome. What about, for example, the evidence that 'the vast majority of children with gender dysphoria -80 to 95%- grow out of it, if they aren't encouraged to transition'[91]. Indeed, in the dialogue of faith,

---

[88] Cf. Spencer Lindquist (https://www.dailywire.com/author/spencer-lindquist), Dec 27, 2024, "How One Of America's Largest School Districts Became A Pipeline For A Trans Youth Clinic": https://www.dailywire.com/news/how-one-of-americas-largest-school-districts-became-a-pipeline-for-a-trans-youth-clinic.

[89] Elizabeth Troutman Mitchell, December 20th, 2024, "UnitedHealthcare Covers Double Mastectomies for 17-Year-Olds With Gender Dysphoria": https://www.dailysignal.com/2024/12/20/united-healthcare-covers-double-mastectomies-17-year-olds-gender-dysphoria/.

[90] Elizabeth Troutman Mitchell (https://www.dailysignal.com/author/elizabeth-troutman/)| December 11, 2024, "'EGREGIOUS': Detransitioner Sues Doctor Who Prescribed Her Irreversible Sex-Change Drugs at 12": https://www.dailysignal.com/2024/12/11/ill-never-know-body-wouldve-looked-detransitioner-sues-doctor-pushed-irreversible-trans-hormones-surgery/.

[91] Cf. Anderson, *When Harry Became Sally*, p. 119; and, what is more, this is what comes out of any number de-transitioning testimonies throughout this book. There are some clear examples of how responding carefully to young children's thoughts about gender can help them to realize why there is a discordant

reason, lived experience, prayer, grace and help, it is clear that a number
of conditions are more transient than some think, namely same-sex attraction, gender dysphoria, as has been pointed out, and generally being "lost"
when it comes to growing up[92]. But let us note, again, the comment, 'if they
[children] aren't encouraged to transition.' Thus encouragement may
make more difference to either delaying a child's recognition of his or her
sex at conception or reinforcing the claim of being in the 'wrong body'
than we realize[93].

A real quest for an identity: Digging a foundation
    (cf. Lk 6: 46-49)

Clearly, then, there are questions to investigate and to answer but it will
take an investigative journalist to do so, whereas my concern is with the
underlying vulnerability of people who do not understand the life-questions that are involved in all this.

Searching for an identity can be like scrabbling in the mud, as did St.
Bernadette, scooping out the muck[94] that clots up our lives and makes us

---

note between their thinking and their sex and, it seems, this helps to resolve the
discrepancy: pp. 136-138.

[92] In the middle chapters of *Lived Experience and the Search for Truth: Revisiting Catholic Sexual Morality*, 2024, edited by Deborah Savage and Robert
Fastiggi, there is a wonderful selection of people experiencing a profound dialogue, as it were, ultimately between each person and God, which results, not necessarily easily, in the resolution of a variety of disturbances in the course of growing up. A fact confirmed by many other testimonies throughout the book.

[93] This is discussed more fully, later in the book, under the heading of the
influence of others; as, indeed, a child or indeed any person can live, uncritically,
in an "influencer's social media world".

[94] Cf. Marge Fenelon, February 18th, 2018, "The Holy Grit of St. Bernadette
Soubirous": https://margefenelon.com/5905/the-holy-grit-of-st-bernadette-
soubirous/.

ignorant of what our real talents are, or that we are following a false idea owing to a hidden attraction in what is advanced, as you will see below. But, over time, we may see that sufferings in our lives that we hated so much, such as the injustices I suffered at school being caned for failing exams, were in fact sufferings that kept alive the question of what my life was about and why I was the way I was, unable to find my way and succeed at anything.

Even as a young man, before mobile phones existed, or if they did I did not know of their existence, I was wondering if it would be easier to be a woman instead of being a man because I would not have to earn a living, or so I thought, and answer all the troubling questions about what my talents were, what was I to do with my life, and how was I going to earn a living. In other words, I was as ignorant of the real nature of being a woman as I was of being myself a man. As, clearly, women no less than men have to identify talents, training and opportunities for the development of their lives.

But there was no advocacy group or program to turn my thoughts into actions and, indeed, it was a long time before I even admitted to myself that I even thought these things. And so, believe me, these questions of identity are really demanding but wholly worthwhile to pursue[95]. There is a difference, however, to these questions arising in the course of growing up and being driven, or provoked and promoted, as it were, by groups that

---

[95] Cf. also the experience of a woman, by Tineke van der Vaal 27th of September, 2022, "Anne is happy that she did not go for gender reassignment": https://cne.news/article/1760-anne-is-happy-that-she-did-not-go-for-gender-reassignment. Anne's name has been changed but is known to the editors. *This article was translated by CNE news and published by the Reformatorisch Dagblad (https://www.rd.nl/artikel/991903-juist-in-kerk-zou-genderdysforie-bespreekbaar-moeten-zijn) on September 24.*

fly them in a questionnaire at an age in which the child has scarcely begun to think and to reason[96].

When, as a young man, exhausted from the questions of the meaning of life, studying, relationships, I ended up in a psychiatric hospital I was prescribed a tranquilizer; however, after a few weeks of regular food and sleep, I concealed the fact that I was not taking them until, pointing this out to the doctor, I was discharged into the care of my parents.

But there is also the unexpected, not just the quest we are on for the meaning and purpose of our lives, but there is also the dialogue with God who acts amidst this pursuit, calling us to Him even if it takes us years to realize what Christ is doing and that He speaks in dreams and visions and words of Scripture adapted to us at the particular time; and, patient as ever, keeps calling on us to recognize who He is and the help He offers – but He also seeks us to really know ourselves and so to seek Him for the saviour He is, even if it takes us many years to grasp the reality of sin in our lives![97]

Our culture and our questions in the context of philosophy and the Christian, Catholic Faith

But, as many may know, the question of identity is not answered without the question of belonging, of connectedness and, at depth, of communion: of being able to speak a common language about being a person, growing up and connecting with others and what is good in existence.

---

[96] Evert van Vlastuin, 1st of July, 2021, "The end of male & female: what is the belief behind gender mainstreaming?": https://cne.news/article/100-the-end-of-male-female-what-is-the-belief-behind-gender-mainstreaming. *This article was published previously in the Dutch Reformatorisch Dagblad* (https://www.rd.nl/artikel/664197-het-einde-van-man-vrouw) *on June 1st 2016.*

[97] There are various autobiographical books which go into the question of my own development more closely; go to: https://enroutebooksandmedia.com/francisetheredge/.

Even if, then, a person temporarily identifies with a particular group, like those who claim, mistakenly, to be in the "wrong body", their human development will in due course open them to the wider questions of human identity unless, of course, the group acts in an insular way and keeps people from examining the wider questions of their identity. Ultimately, life experience, the impulse of the sources of our identity that are deeper than changing appearance, good dialogue, philosophy and being able to find that questions of who we are and what our relationships are about are immeasurably rooted, clarified and enriched in *Jesus Christ and His Church.* But even this is not automatic as I know and have written elsewhere about a search that led to being found by God at forty!

Thus, the subject of personal identity must pass by way of the subject, singular, of "identity and communion", as these twin principles express an irreplaceable relationship between the individual and the society in which we live. Thus, in the course of this investigation we have to look at why people take their own lives and not just regard it as one more statistic of the times in which we live but look at the meaning of suffering, isolation, being apart from others or losing hope. At the same time, we cannot overlook the help of the forgiveness of sins, of those who have hurt us, mediated as it is by the mission of the Catholic Church, which is always in need of renewal.

But, given the relationship between what changes in a society and what remains constant, both in the origin of human identity and in human relationships, it follows that there is a sense in which taking the pulse at any given time, in any given moment of writing, there will be a certain amount of noting what is not only of "moment" but of the "moment" too. Therefore this book is both searching for what is constant as well as what changes and so is, ultimately a combination of answers to the question of "Who Am I?" and the glimpse afforded of a "Snapshot" of the times in which this question, ever old and ever new, is being asked.

Not forgetting, however, that identity runs deeper than even psychological accounts of human development and even philosophical ideas of what the human person is, we will take account of what God has revealed about who and "what" we are. Thus we enter the scenario of our times from a different perspective to that of social studies, which glimpses ideas about the human person, to the more deeply rooted accounts of human being. And so, unpopular or unintelligible to many as it may be, we need to engage with what is "sin" and "grace": with what detracts from our humanity and what help God gives to restore and perfect it, bearing in mind that just as we come into existence through relationships so we live and die in the course of living out the love of God and our neighbour, whether that neighbour is our family or beyond. Thus:

"All attempts to find a way out of the plight of today's world are fruitless," warned Solzhenitsyn, "unless we redirect our consciousness, in repentance, to the Creator of all: without this, no exit will be illumined, and we shall seek it in vain"[98].

'We ... need theology because the challenges posed by progress in science and technology ... are presently forcing us to work towards a common understanding of *what it means to be human*, what is worthy of our nature as human beings, what aspect of our humanity is irreducible because it is divine, that is, made in the image and likeness of God in Christ.'

---

[98] Quoted by Jordan J. Ballor, June 6th, 2024, in "Mere Humanity: An Ecumenical Anthropology for Human Flourishing": https://www.thepublicdiscourse.com/2024/06/95092/

And 'For theologians … are like *the scouting party* sent by Joshua to explore the land of Canaan: they are charged with finding the right paths towards the inculturation of the faith.'

Theology has to be 'a discipline critical for the life of every human being and the entire People of God, uniting science and virtue, critical reasoning and love. Catholic faith is a faith that works through charity: otherwise it is a dead faith (cf. *Jas* 2:26). A sapiential theology is thus a theology of love, because "whoever does not love does not know God, for God is love" (*1 Jn* 4:8)'[99].

These statements excised, for the most part, from an address by Pope Francis to theologians, help me to see that while an investigation of what is happening now is going to impact human identity, so it is necessary that we go more deeply, at the same time, into what it is to be human and the help of God to become more fully human, 'unto the full stature of Christ' (Eph. 4: 13). Clearly, going deeper means going beyond "polemics" about the opposition of science and the Catholic religion; and, without overlooking well known points of conflict or disagreement, there is a growing recognition of the contribution that members of the Church have made to the development of science[100]. Thus, as always, we are searching for that coherence of truth which accords with both reason and faith.

---

[99] *Greeting of His Holiness Pope Francis to the Members of the International Network of Societies for Catholic Theology. (INSeCT), Friday, 10 May 2024*: https://www.vatican.va/content/francesco/en/speeches/2024/may/documents/20240510-insect.html.

[100] Even if the relationship between science and the Catholic Faith has not been without its difficulties, besides well-known Christians, like the Abbe Mendel, there are many who have contributed to science through the basic coherence discernible in the universe and human affairs, that contribute, to the evidence for the existence of God; cf. Olivier Bonnassies, "Christianity gave rise to modern

Vocation, who we are and the times in which we live

But I am no longer the youth I was and God has acted powerfully to bring me, as you will see, at forty, to marriage; but even that is so many years ago as I am now, almost 28 years married with eleven children, three of whom are in heaven and, at the present time, a writer. So there is a point to passing through the culture in which we live, the experiences we have had, good and bad, that both built us up and destroyed us, so that the person I am now has a history of salvation: a journey; and, I hope, you will too: a journey through what we are going through in our time with a view to who you are and where you are going and what God's love wants to bring about in your life.

And, indeed, whatever vocation we discover, whether the single life, marriage, the priesthood or the religious life, we will no doubt need to address what obscures if not obstructs our recognition of the path to the meaning and purpose of that vocation. While there are no doubt many ways to discovering the help and healing of many vocations, I will often draw on the many experiences and helps of the *Neocatechumenal Way*[101].

At the same time, however, healing is ongoing as indeed are the crises of life; and, therefore, vocation is not so much an answer in the past as a path to further answers. Thus my own waywardness calls me to renewal, constantly, such that at times my marriage is like a ragged cross, ragged and full of splinter like protrusions that really get into my flesh; and, therefore, at the start of a recent pilgrimage I was given a definite invitation to seek afresh the unique gift of my wife. My wife, for her part, instead of devoting her energies to worrying, is being called to seek the will of God

---

science": https://1000raisonsdecroire.com/en/christianity-gave-rise-to-modern-science.

[101] Chapter One will give more on the charism of the *Neocatechumenal Way*.

in what goes awry. Thus vocation, as you will see, is not just a static answer
to a question but the beginning of a new quest.

An experience of the Good Shepherd

I am 68. Around 45 or more years ago, the Good Shepherd came to visit
me, to call me back to the Catholic Church; indeed, at the time, I did not
know what the visit was about or even, as I say, that I needed calling back
to the Church. My initial thoughts were about a possible vocation to the
priesthood; but I really did not know what the visit was about. I was relatively young, working and studying to become a psychiatric nurse and on
holiday in another country. Indeed, having accepted an invitation to go
and visit an elderly woman, I unexpectedly found myself in a small nudist
camp, in a remote place among mountains and streams.

On my return to England, I went to see my local Bishop and his assistant took offence at either what I said or how I was dressed, or both, and
would not even allow me to talk to the Bishop. It took nearly 20 years for
me to finally return to the Catholic Church, having travelled up and down
the country, in and out of universities and courses, different denominations and places of work. In other words, returning to the Catholic Church
was like going through a maze, and I would very often end up leaving, being disorientated or just confused and troubled by the people I saw, who
did not seem to know what the Church teaches or how to help a questioning, generally ignorant, sinful, wandering, returning member of the
Church. This is not to say there were not people who tried to help or even
did help; but, it is to say, that the light of Christ and the call to conversion
were dim to the point of going out.

By contrast, returning to the Church through the *Neocatechumenal
Way* was a much more direct route even if, being the sinner I am, I left it
and went back to my sin like a dog to its vomit (cf. Proverbs, 26: 11); but,

after reading in the *Catechism of the Catholic Church*, that if God can create everything from nothing He can make a new beginning for the sinner[102], I was suddenly changed. As a part of a public park moment of evangelization, while others were singing psalms, I spoke to an Anglican man from Zimbabwe, who kept repeating the summary phrase of what I said, that God makes a "New beginning for the sinner". And, in the context of ecumenism, that exchange between denominations was an instance of the 'Evangelization [that] proceeds by dialogue'[103]; and, in the course of our conversation, we exchanged both names and the blessings that God had given us.

After this experience of discovering that God acted in me, at 40, I returned to the Way and went on a pilgrimage. As time has gone on, the contrast has been amazing. This is Eastertide, celebrating Eucharists with abundantly beautiful flowers, which fill my heart with the imagery of marriage, of the marriage between Christ and His Church, it seemed like Easter in the *Neocatechumenal Way* is like entering a blazing gate, full of the light of Christ, speaking of Christ's love for the sinner and bringing me to rejoice in a community with whom I and my wife walk.

Within a year of returning to the Church at 40, God had resolved a decades long agony about whether to marry, to become a priest or a religious; and I married within a few months of courting and have been married, now, for almost 28 years, and we have eight children. If this seems like a scandalously short courtship, Louis and Zelie Martin, the parents of St. Therese of Lisieux, married after three months![104] And while my history

---

[102] CCC, paragraph, 298.

[103] Pope Benedict XVI, 2013, "Doctrinal Note on Some Aspects of Evangelization": https://www.papalencyclicals.net/ben16/cdfdoctrineevang1207.htm.

[104] Rev. Paulinus Redmond, *Louis and Zelie Marrtin : The Seed and The Root of the Little Flower*, 1995, p. 32.

and theirs is very different, nevertheless God can and did work miracles in the life of a sinner, like me, just as He can and does so in the lives of others.

Having experienced all this, I now see how essential it is to be well informed as to what the Catholic, Christian Faith is, as to what Christ has done in my life, and to what practical acts of evangelization I am called, both in the family and beyond. But, in addition, as I hope this book will show, there is a great need for a philosophical grounding of the person[105] to help to navigate so many crises of our times which thrive on trying to straitjacket the human person into a physicalist account: as if the human person is an indecipherable body-bag of a being and that we are doomed to guess what is in the bag without any real help leading up to our opening it.

---

[105] Cf. Etheredge, Part I of the Trilogy, *Truth from truth, Volume I: Faithful Reason*, "Chapter I: What is Philosophy? Philosophy is Thinking "through" Reality. Beginning with General Questions about Philosophy and Reason, this Essay Articulates Seven Aspects of Philosophy: Anthropology; Epistemology; Cosmology; Philosophy of Science; Metaphysics; Ethics; and, finally, Politics": https://www.cambridgescholars.com/product/978-1-4438-8680-2.

Prose and a Prayer

for the Protection of Women Globally: "Woman"

In this two-part essay, the second part of which comes later in the book under the title "Women in Sport", there is both the gathering of different views and a discussion of evidence and, at the same time, an exploration of the claims that revolve around our identity, as men and women, and as boys and girls. In other words, while it is commonplace to see prominent members of science, sport or indeed many other kinds of expert, declaring that there is no scientific definition of being male or female, they have clearly overlooked both the classification of ages and, simultaneously, the incredible architecture of the human person, in particular the woman. The emphasis, then, in view of the often-repeated remark, that there is no scientific definition of woman, is on an exposition of the "identity" of being a woman.

In an essay on the harmful impact of various kinds of contraceptives on the woman's body, it is clear that there is an immense difference between a few outward changes, advocated by some, and the immensely intricate and complex timing, psychological characteristics, and capacity for childbearing of the woman-in-reality[1]. None of which is possible in the man. In other words, to advance outward bodily changes in the vain attempt to physically right a psychological problem, is to draw such a caricature of the woman and, as it happens, of the man, that a person has to be educationally uninformed to believe it; and, if uninformed, then

---

[1] *Lived Experience* and the *Search for Truth*: Revisiting Catholic Sexual Morality, edited by Deborah Savage and Robert Fastiggi, Saint Louis, MO: En Route Books and Media, 2024, Chapter 21: Angela Lanfranchi, MD, FACS, "Hormonal Contraception and the Physiology of Human Sexuality", as I said, mainly on the subject of the harmful impact on the woman.

vulnerable to fear, manipulation and, unfortunately, the possibility of the mutilation of a healthy body. Again, if we take the argument that what makes a woman or a man is their 'performative' behaviour, what they actually do, then so long as this remains superficial and pertains to make-up, how a person walks and talks, then clearly, according to the argument, a man is behaving like a woman and therefore is a woman[2]. But, again, the argument is by definition superficial, as it supposes that external changes can change, not just an internal reality but a whole person's reality. Therefore there is no change of sex. Furthermore, if these thought are taken further, then there is the idea of "designer, intersex babies", whereby some have 'discussed their desire to have intersex or hermaphrodite babies so that their children can "choose later" their gender or sex'[3]. In other words, the child has become an "object" in the perception of transgender ideology; and, therefore, the victim of it. For any unwarranted interference with the normal development of the child is, as the whole transgenderism ideology proposes, a harm to healthy children[4]. And, as regards the child having choice, that is already false as it is the parents who have chosen this "interstate" condition for their children. Thus, once humanity has departed from the child as a gift, an original gift, people will give way to any and every kind of biological abuse of the child[5].

---

[2] Sandra Pertot, February 25th, 2025, « No Room for Sex": https://www.genderclinicnews.com/p/no-room-for-sex.

[3] Thomas Stevenson, February 25th, 2025, "CIA, NSA officials use government chat to say they want 'intersex' babies so children can 'choose' gender later: report": https://thepostmillennial.com/cia-nsa-officials-use-government-chat-to-say-they-want-intersex-babies-so-children-can-choose-gender-later-report.

[4] As discussed elsewhere in this book, a true "intersex" condition entails a careful and thorough investigation for the good of the child; it is not a parental or otherwise deliberate experiment.

[5] As we have already seen with IVF's discarding of human, embryonic children, freezing them, and experimenting upon them.

This, moreover, raises the concern that if our young people, and people generally, are living in a "virtual world", maybe this is more of a reason for our discovery, as it were, of people's inability to "access" reality. In an unexpected confirmation of this, note the effect of watching Charlie Chaplin use an umbrella as a parachute on Pope Francis' younger brother, when they were relatively street wise children: Alberto 'opened the umbrella and launched himself off with no hesitation'. Fortunately, Alberto was not injured; but the 'landing from the first floor was by no means as soft as the one onscreen'[6]. So what does this tell us about the gullibility of young children; and, therefore, their susceptibility to being led into serious health problems by misguided adults?

Before, then, discussing the two forms of addressing our present concerns, there is a preamble about the integral reality of the woman's human conception, and the legitimate, if variable, relationship between sex and gender.

By way, then, of a summary statement of the integral reality of being a woman, consider the following account

Are you a biological realist? Given the identification of a creature by its characteristics, what do we find on considering the practical expression of a woman's motherhood? To begin with, the outward structures of the woman are not merely external - but external expressions of what is internal to the woman and indicative of a mothering relationship to a child. In other words, the relationship of mother to child is of person to person but "mediated", as it were, bodily. Granted, however, that not all women become actual mothers nevertheless, in reality, the potentially is biologically structured in the woman, beginning with the existence of the ovaries, the

---

[6] Pope Francis, Hope, The Autobiography, with Carlo Musso, translated from the Italian by Richard Dixon, UK: Penguin: Viking, 2025, p. 58.

production of eggs, which generally ripen and pass into a Fallopian tube. This gives rise to a subtle but real change in the woman's temperature, along with other changes, and contributes to the possibility of deliberately conceiving or avoiding, for good reason[7], the conception of a child. Moreover, conceiving and bearing the received child, can entail an inward awareness of the presence of a person, hence the grief in response to a miscarriage, even an early miscarriage. In addition, however, there is an expression, as it were, of an epigenetic relationship between the child's gene expression and the mother. Thus there is an interaction between the embryonic child's unfolding of genetic instructions, in other words the sequence of the baby's gene expressions and the mother, so that the mother has a maternal influence on the expression of her child's embryonic genes. In other words, the possibility of "transferring" what is embodied in a woman's existence, expressed in a mother's response to her child, is so subtle and, as a whole, as to be inconceivable.

Similarly, the intimately personal consciousness of the life within, being given as he or she grows, the subtle nutrients, the stellar processes under hormonal control, not to mention the possible connection between cravings and the growth of the child, raises not just a biological function but a relationship between mother and child. Moreover, the particular loosening or adaptation of the pelvis in the course of the growing child, not to mention the whole manifestation of the timing and the activity of giving birth, shows abundantly clearly that what is outward manifests the external expression of what is wholly internal.

In a word, changing the externality of a woman's body, does not make a body that was feminine masculine; rather, it robs what was feminine from what remains a woman.

---

[7] Cf. Pope St. Paul VI, *Humanae Vitae*: https://www.vatican.va/content/paul-vi/en/encyclicals/documents/hf_p-vi_enc_25071968_humanae-vitae.html

Now consider the conception of a human being, as from conception and not from "birth"

But, note, it is not possible to be born in the wrong body, as if there is some kind of personal separation from bodily existence, prior to birth, that allows you to be born in the wrong body. There is no body, as it were, prior to personalization. In other words, from the very first instant of fertilization a process of active change, growth, and maturation, has begun and continues uninterrupted not only until birth - but until death! Not only is there an outward sign of conception, among other things, in the enclosure of what is now the human embryonic child in an embryonic wall, but there is the continuous process of "who" has come to exist being made manifest throughout the process[8]. Once contact has been made between the docking of the sperm and the open pore of the egg, there is a calcium ion-wave-triggering of the formation of the embryonic wall, enclosing and establishing the human embryo as a whole entity. Through from the initial contact of sperm and egg, the fusion of the two nuclei, yielding an X from the man's sperm and an X from the woman's egg for a girl, there is the founding, from the process of fertilization, of the child's identity, in this case, as female, and as wholly orientated to the unfolding of the person-woman.

Thus the natural autonomy of the child in the mother's womb is an outward sign of the reality of the child's personal, independent, but inter-relational existence, as will be demonstrated abundantly by the child's birth, at which point the "the feeding and breathing gear" of the placenta is discarded.

Clearly, however, there can be many factors that influence the healthy, holistic growth of the girl or the boy into the woman and the man which

---

[8] Cf. Etheredge, *Conception: An Icon of the Beginning*, En Route Books and Media, including expert testimony from two Spanish physicians in Chapter 5: Part II: https://enroutebooksandmedia.com/conception/.

is inner goal of the whole process, from start to finish. And, similarly, there are many harmful factors which introduce all kinds of impediments into what is otherwise a goal-determined process from conception. Thus we need to distinguish between what is medicine, what is the activity of aiding the natural process of human growth, and mutilation, which is the harm that is inflicted on an otherwise healthy process of growth and development. And, in the course of distinguishing health from harm, there needs to be a process of recognizing the psychological processes which, while variable, are yet intrinsic to the complete development of the girl or boy's identity.

'biological sex and the socio-cultural role of sex (gender) can be distinguished but not separated'[9]

In brief, this is not an argument denying the cultural impact on the vocations and activities of women as, clearly, in some societies there are more public opportunities for education, employment, and advancement than in others. However, this is an argument for recognizing that being a female person permeates the action and activities of a woman and, therefore, has a bearing on how she lives out her feminine genius[10].

Moreover, although this is often denied, sidelined or disregarded, there is an immense heritage of the diverse activities of women in the life of the Catholic Church, whether as Doctors of the Church, founders of Religious Orders, and indeed as influencers on the life of the Church in their day and afterwards.

---

[9] Declaration of the Dicastery for the Doctrine of the Faith "Dignitas Infinita" on Human Dignity, 08.04.2024: https://press.vatican.va/content/salastampa/en/bollettino/pubblico/2024/04/08/240408c.html.

[10] Cf. Pope St. John Paul II, *Letter to Women.*

Woman

In contrast to the uncertainty to be discussed, the vision of Pope St. John Paul II, seeing what was going on in the world of culture and thought wrote extensively on the human person, establishing before all else the centrality of the person-as-gift[11]. This illuminating discernment of the person, drawing as it does on the mystery of the Blessed Trinity, each of whom makes a "gift" of themselves to the "Other" and thus reveals that, made as we are in the image of the divine "We", we are made to be, to each other, a person-gift. Whether we are a person-gift in marriage, the religious life or in friendship, this is the language of being-in-relationship.

On the one hand, John Paul II wrote about the reciprocal gift of marital love, taking account of the reality-difference in the sexuality of the woman and the man; and, on the other hand, he searched out the orientation of the man-person to truth and the woman-person to the "other". And, therefore, our whole being informs our understanding of who we are and how to relate to each other as, even what arises within us, arises out of our whole identity as man and woman and not just from a "part" of it. Thus it becomes clear that in losing the language of human reality, we lose the "reference" in our humanity to the God who created us (cf. *Gaudium et Spes*, 14). As we survey the problem of defining "woman" let us remember, then, that the wisdom of God prepared us to think through our relationship to reality: a reality not reduced to "use" but opening upon the mystery of the love that is God.

---

[11] Pope St. John Paul II, wrote: *The Way to Christ: Spiritual Exercises,* published in English in 1994 but from his time as Bishop, *Love and Responsibility,* published in Polish in 1960 and in English in 1981, *Person and Act,* 1969 in Polish and 2020 in English, *Male and Female He Created Them,* 1979-1984, *The Dignity of Woman* 1988, *Letter to Families,* 1994, *Letter to Women,* 1995, etc. etc.

These foundational documents of the Catholic Church reflect, as I say, an early perception of the development of thought that disassociated person and nature, making the body an instrument of manipulation and a "raw material" of the will. Thus advancing the view that freedom is unrestricted and unrelated to the compass of truth; and, therefore, in and of themselves, these ideas contradict any claim to being scientific and indeed express a denial of a relationship to reality as other than subjectively asserted[12]: what exists is what "I" want to exist.

'Townhall has covered time and time again how so-called "transgender" women [who are men] have taken away awards and opportunities for females. This has occurred in sports (https://townhall.com/tipsheet/madelineleesman/2024/06/14/lia-thomas-was-banned-from-competing-in-womens-sports-heres-how-his-former-teammate-reacted-n2640471), beauty pageants (https://townhall.com/tipsheet/madelineleesman/2024/06/07/transgender-beauty-pageant-n2640112), and brand partnerships (https://townhall.com/tipsheet/madelineleesman/2022/10/17/ulta-trans-backlash-n2614606)'[13].

In an age where "woman" has become an uncertain term and even a document designed to signal the health gap between men and women, reporting on the detrimental effect of this gap on women, leads to the authors saying: that 'not all people who identify as women are born

---

[12] This ongoing evaluation of transgenderism persists through from St. John Paul II, Benedict XVI, to the pontificate of Pope Francis. Specific documents are referred to throughout this book and, following the articles or declarations, are a host of specific interventions on the subject and, indeed, a few by the Bishops of England and Wales.

[13] Madeline Leesman (https://townhall.com/tipsheet/madelineleesman) | September 18, 2024, « A 'Trans' Actor Was Nominated for 'Best Supporting Actress'": https://townhall.com/tipsheet/madelineleesman/2024/09/18/transgender-actor-nominated-for-womens-award-n2644900.

biologically female'[14]. In other words, while it is perfectly legitimate to recognize the health needs of those men who have self-identified as women, it is clearly confusing to call self-identifying men, women. These are actually men in healthcare and, as such, they could, potentially, obscure the facts of the report, as is happening in sport. In the end, if there is no clarity about who is a "woman" even if, then women do not benefit from a report on women. In this case, however, it looks as if this report does in fact focus on women who are women from conception. In another survey, this time of UK women, it is again clear that there is no real reflection on the harm of abortion, both to the child and the woman, abortion pills, and contraceptives; and, by contrast, there is no mention of the benefit to the woman of learning and understanding her own body through natural family planning methods[15].

The evidence for considering that the report specifies women from conception is the type of conditions referred to, many of which pertain to the menstrual and giving birth related conditions[16]; and, more generally, the claim that 'Questions about sex-based differences were rarely investigated or recorded, with the assumption – now known to be false – that there are few important differences in the functioning of organs and

---

[14] Lucy Pérez and Shyam Bishen, January 2024, "Closing the Women's Health Gap: A $1 Trillion Opportunity to Improve Lives and Economies": Introduction and Chapter 2, pp. 5, 8 and 14 of this report: https://www3.weforum.org/docs/WEF_Closing_the_Women%E2%80%99s_Health_Gap_2024.pdf.

[15] Public Health England, June 2018, "What do women say? Reproductive health is a public health issue": (https://assets.publishing.service.gov.uk/media/5b64731940f0b668806ca8e1/What_do_women_say_reproductive_health_is_a_public_health_issue.pdf). Cf. Etheredge, *Human Nature: Moral Norm*: https://enroutebooksandmedia.com/humannature/. This book contains a lot of references and summaries to research from the point of view of Natural Family Planning and its benefit to the woman's general healthcare.

[16] Pérez, Bishen, January 2024, "Closing the Women's Health Gap", p. 11.

systems in men and women beyond reproduction'[17]. In other words, there is an understandable call for research that is questioning the 'traditional understanding of disease [which] is focused primarily on the male body'[18]; and, likewise, there is a move to differentiate seat-belts for women from those designed for men[19]. Indeed, if proposing 'sex as a biological variable'[20] means collecting sex specific data, for either men or women, then it is obviously going to be helpful; however, unless it is more carefully worded we are back to a confusion of information because it is not clear "who" it is collected from. But if, as the report goes on to say, it is clearer that sex-specific research is intended: 'healthcare professionals of all specialties must be equipped with accurate and updated knowledge of biological differences, including sex-specific manifestations of symptoms'[21].

Let us continue to note, however, that the new "Executive Order" promulgated by the American Government recognizes that the female person exists from conception, it being biologically determined that she is the 'sex that produces the large reproductive cell'[22] (otherwise known as ovum or egg).

However, this same report "masks" problems that arise from inappropriate care for women where health care problems arise precisely from contraceptives, abortions, whether surgical or by pill and, at the same time, neglecting to point out the many benefits of the comparatively "cost-free"

---

[17] Pérez, Bishen, January 2024, "Closing the Women's Health Gap", p. 10.

[18] Pérez, Bishen, January 2024, "Closing the Women's Health Gap", p. 31.

[19] This is referred to later in the book, when discussing male and female differences in sport.

[20] Pérez, Bishen, January 2024, "Closing the Women's Health Gap", p. 31.

[21] Pérez, Bishen, January 2024, "Closing the Women's Health Gap", p. 32.

[22] "Executive Order", January 20th, 2025: https://www.whitehouse.gov/presidential-actions/2025/01/defending-women-from-gender-ideology-extremism-and-restoring-biological-truth-to-the-federal-government/: (d).

natural family planning health care[23]. On the one hand, there is the death of a child or, in rare cases, the child's surviving an abortion. On the other hand, perhaps because of an insistent presence of the facts, the evidence of harm to women when it comes to both surgical and pill abortions, not to mention the overwhelming number of pregnant women who are presenting with psychiatric problems, may be part of the background where even the "idol" of abortion is beginning to fall from its pedestal as a call to monitor and report on complications is going through the UK House of Lords[24].

In the United Kingdom alone the unrestricted access to social media's content of violent pornography and derogatory portrayals of women, making billions out of accessible vice, is fuelling actual assaults on real people. 'Between 2019 and 2022, it suggested a 40% increase in reports of sexual assaults and rapes where both the alleged victim and perpetrator were under 18. There was a 33% increase in rape reports and a 26% increase in reports where the allegation was against a child aged under 10'[25].

At the same time, there is an '81% rise in reported incidents that took place on school property. One leading expert said the problem had reached "alarming levels"'[26]. What has happened to limiting the power of making

---

[23] Pérez, Bishen, January 2024, "Closing the Women's Health Gap", p. 19; cf. also, Etheredge, *Human Nature: Moral Norm*, "Part V: The Word of Truth-in-Love and Conscience", discussing the advantages of intensive, well understood care of women from Natural Family Practitioners.

[24] December 13th, 2024, "British House of Lords Approves Bill to Compile Report on How Abortion Pills Hurt Women": https://www.lifenews.com/2024/12/13/british-house-of-lords-approves-bill-to-compile-report-on-how-abortion-pills-hurt-women/.

[25] Michael Savage, 17th February, 2024, "'Toxic' online culture fuelling rise in sexual assaults on children by other children, police warn": https://www.theguardian.com/society/2024/feb/17/toxic-online-culture-fuelling-rise-in-sexual-assaults-on-children-by-other-children-police-warn.

[26] Michael Savage, "'Toxic' online culture fuelling rise in sexual assaults'.

money out of what is destroying human relationships? And, therefore, if the availability of these images is going to exponentially increase, owing to 'sextortion' and artificial intelligence – God help this generation because it is already beyond the help of self-help and statutory willingness to stop money-making out of human carnage.

By contrast, Pope Francis says: 'All these women [I would like to mention them by name: Josephine Bakhita, Magdeleine de Jesus, Elizabeth Ann Seton, Mary MacKillop, Laura Montoya, Kateri Tekakwitha, Teresa of Calcutta, Rafqa Pietra Choboq Ar-Rayès, Maria Beltrame Quattrocchi and Daphrose Mukasanga], at different times and in different cultures, each in her own distinct way, gave proof through initiatives of charity, education and prayer, of how the "feminine genius" can uniquely reflect God's holiness in the midst of our world. Indeed, precisely at times in history when women were largely excluded from social and ecclesial life, the "Holy Spirit raised up saints whose attractiveness produced new spiritual vigour and important reforms in the Church". Here too, "I think of all those unknown or forgotten women who, each in her own way, sustained and transformed families and communities by the power of their witness" (*Gaudete et Exsultate*, 12). The Church needs to keep this in mind, because the Church is herself a woman: a daughter, a bride and a mother. And who better than women can reveal her face? Let us help one another, putting aside any aggressive and divisive attitudes, and exercising careful discernment, to discover, in docility to the voice of the Spirit and in faithful communion, fitting ways for the grandeur and the place of women to be increasingly valued in the People of God.'

'That is why it is important to make the saints better known, especially women saints, in all the depth and reality of their humanity. In this way, education will be increasingly capable of touching each person in his or her wholeness and uniqueness'[27].

Where, then, there is a certain cultural ignorance, denial or rejection of the value and contribution of women to society, whether in the society of the Church or the world, it is important to emphasize the reality of the women who have contributed and, by implication, all those who remain unnamed or cannot be named for the time being.

But whether we are talking about the violent outbreaks of the rejection of women's rights and education, as if she is less than human, or the number of men who are in prison because of offences to women, we are talking about a society of men who have lost their way, thinking that the suppression of women is an answer to their own sinful tendencies. At the same time, prudence in dress is a good thing and, equally, let us not suppose that women are without sin any more than men – but this introduction is not about citing the sins of women; rather, it is about recognizing that there needs to be a re-education of men in the light of reason, evidence and faith, about the reality of being a woman and that 'The Church needs to keep this in mind, because the Church is herself a woman: a daughter, a bride and a mother. And who better than women can reveal her face?'[28] (and[29]).

Thus, again, Christianity is neither about blaming woman for sin, as if man has not sinned from the beginning, nor about exalting women, unless God reveals the exceptional nature of a woman, in particular, Mary, the

---

[27] Audience with participants in the International Interuniversity Conference "Women in the Church: Builders of humanity", 07.03.2024: https://press.vatican.va/content/salastampa/en/bollettino/pubblico/2024/03/07/240307d.html.

[28] Pope Francis (as above).

[29] Not in any chronological order but think of all the work of St. John Paul II on the identity of woman: *Redemptoris Mater, Letter to Women, Mulieris Dignitatem,* and many exhortations at one time or another, beginning very early in his life with *Spiritual Talks to Men and Women,* including criticism of men's relationship to women.

Mother of God – who made full and generous use of the gift of being *the Immaculate Conception*: the one conceived without sin and, in that, like her Son, but unlike her Son, not God. So, Christianity, whatever its historical and actual imperfections, is about trumpeting the equality in dignity of men and women, made in the image and likeness of God.

"Woman"

We know, Lord, the common image of a showingly-shaped woman draped over a car, but there is also the less well known and trained woman who is lying on the ground, using tools needed to mend it.

We also know, Joseph, about the exploitation of various kinds of enslaved women, hidden from sight but no less human, trapped in a variety of ways, but helped by helpers and those who have escaped.

We know too, Mary, the need to clothe the shapely-unclothed, to help the woman standing close to the kerb and the girls led, lonely, to indescribable brutality all of which should make men ashamed.

Lord, you paused after the first burstingly-beautiful flowering of the intimately pulsing universe, alive with life and multiplying, and you reflected on the mysteriousness of being *Three*, creating a dignified, dual-unity, called man and woman, open to the gift of a child-third?

How amazing, Joseph, guardian of the redeemer, that your love of Mary was enriched by a grace of being prepared to risk scandal and to accept a woman translucent to the mystery of God, revealing in her modesty the immense dignity that God's gift endowed her with.

How, Mary, were you able to dwell in the almost totally hidden life, letting the Church discover through the centuries the foundational humility that can only be called God-like, in view of how hidden a wealth of holiness, scarcely believable, was to be mirrored in you?

And so, Lord, you took the word "woman" and made this word re-sound from the beginning, as you spoke to us through speaking to your mother: "O woman, what have you to do with me? My hour has not yet come" (Jn. 2: 4); and then again, towards the end of your poured out love, suffering and crucifixion, you gave us to your inex-tricably suffering mother, saying: "Woman, here is your son" (Jn. 19: 26).

Oh Lord, you addressed the woman at the well, revealing the open-wide arms of the love you promised to give in the form of living wa-ter, with these words: "Woman, believe me, the hour is coming ...., and now is, when the true worshipers will worship the Father in spirit and truth, for such the Father seeks to worship him. God is spirit, and those who worship him must worship in spirit and truth" (Jn. 4: 21-24).

How wonderfully you have drawn back to the beginning, the gift of woman, drawing afresh on the magnificent nature in which you have chosen to express the inexpressibly hidden face of your mys-tery, even saying you long to gather your children like a 'hen gathers her chicks', disclosing a mothering love in the mystery of God (Mt. 23: 37).

Oh Lord my God, your words transformed a woman you healed from a flow of blood; indeed, from a woman who reached out with a flow of blood, and you recognized her as your "Daughter, [saying that] your faith has healed you. Go in peace" (Luke 8 : 47), express-ing the same wisdom as when you said that whoever does the will of God is my mother, and brother and sister (cf. Mk. 3: 35).

What is more, Oh Lord, you entrusted the discovery of your resurrection to a woman, whom you had recovered, renewed and filled with love, sending her as the apostle to the apostles to announce the new news, not just to them but to all who are to follow and to experience, as she did, the mystery of being taken out of sin's disfigurements into the beaconing light-life of the resurrection!

So, Lord, what will help us to rediscover the cherishing of women, whether in the newly bright spring, the autumn's array of light-lit colours, not forgetting the wintered suffering and the summer's fullness, all of which comes in every shade of blemished beauty, colour, and shape, all of which express the wondrous reality of sharing the expression of the mystery of God, perhaps more fully for expressing the mystery of being-in-relationship more clearly?

In answer, Oh Blessed Trinity, you have said how you have expressed your own, blazing love for the mystery of woman in the act both through and beyond words of a reality scarcely imaginable: that you chose a woman, Mary, from the first instant of her being, to be the mother of the only begotten Son of the Father, Jesus Christ, conceived through the Holy Spirit (cf. Lk 1) and constantly rediscovered under ever new and old titles as the Mother of the living and of the Church.

Chapter One

Crises in Society and Crises in the Christian Life

Before we get into the particularities of gender crises, this chapter gives context to some of the numerous intersecting crises in society, within which the challenges to our youth and their identity are taking place; and, thereafter, there is a gradual movement to the pervasive influence of social media, accessible on the phone, and its general impact on impressionable identities. Perhaps, at root, this impulse to be "out there" is an expression of our nature that seeks to go from "being alone" to "being in communion"; and, therefore, if recognized for what it is, a person will seek real and not virtual relationships that take us into the real, relational world, in which we forge our identity, reciprocally, in the process of coming to discover ourselves as a gift to give and a gift to be received[1].

And so, even before we enter this arena of conflicting ideas, single-idea ideologies, crosscurrents of one kind or another, we need help. In a certain sense, it is possible to argue that if adults and children are not well prepared, philosophically, for the challenges of life, that that vacuum will be filled with prevailing, often single-sided ideas, swamping the intelligence of the person, especially in view of these views being authoritatively expressed or reinforced by the application of insufficiently discriminating legislation. Where, then, do we begin?

We need hope and hope is not optimism, says Pope Francis, 'Hope is fed by each person's commitment to the good; it grows when we feel we

---

[1] Mazurkiewicz, Chapter 8: "Christian Anthropology", pp. 143-148 of pp. 143-161 of *Gender Ideology and Pastoral Practice*.

are participating and involved in giving meaning to our own lives and the lives of others. Nurturing hope is therefore social, intellectual, artistic, political action in the highest sense of the word; it is putting one's skills and resources at the service of the common good, it is *sowing the future*. Hope generates change and improves the future. It is the smallest of virtues, said Peguy, it is the smallest, but it is the one that takes you the furthest! And hope does not disappoint. There are so many *Turandots* in life today who say: "Hope is always dashed". The Bible tells us: "Hope does not disappoint" (cf. *Rom* 5:5)'[2].

'And in this context of uncertainty and fragility, the younger generations experience more than anyone else a *feeling of precariousness*, so that tomorrow seems like a mountain impossible to climb.' Thus we are in a crisis. 'But let us remember two things about crises: we do not emerge from a crisis alone, either we all come out or we do not; and we do not emerge from a crisis the same: we come out better or worse. Let us remember this'[3].

There are a growing number of "nones": of people of no religion. According to a website advertising *Youth Work* through forming 'small group ministries', '80% of Catholics who leave the Church to join the ranks of the "nones" are younger than age 23'[4]. Indeed, according to another American source, although 'historic Protestant denominations' are dropping by as much as 70% and the Catholic Church benefits from

---

[2] "Address of the Holy Father Francis to the participants in the third edition of the States General on Natality, 12.05.2023": https://press.vatican.va/content/sal.astampa/en/bollettino/pubblico/2023/05/12/230512a.html

[3] Address of the Holy Father Francis to the participants in the third edition of the States General on Natality, 12.05.2023".

[4] "Andrew Ministries : We build world-changing, high- impact, small group ministries": https://andrew-ministries.com/.

immigration, non-denominational, often biblically based churches[5], are drawing converts, while among the "nones", 'young adults who grow up in non-religious families are more likely to stay non-religious than religious young people are to continue to identify with the faith in which they were raised'[6]. According to one survey, it seems as if the decline of religious observance is more about the use of time to do good things, like laundry or go for a walk, than questions of salvation. In other words, there does not seem to be a sense of either salvation or life after death[7]. But then a different piece says: 'Consider once more that the most unchurched generation in America, the "nones", is also the most mentally afflicted'[8]. So maybe there is not a clear connection between mental health and the help of God or the help of God and salvation. Or even that the help of God is possible.

So one of the questions that arises is to do with what kind of faith is being transmitted, if young people are unlikely to 'identify with the faith in which they were raised'? What if the problem is to do with whether or not people are living that faith? In other words, what if the fall-out, as it were, from the Church, is also a sign that the Christian Faith has withered in the pews, either because of a lack of reality watering or because the urgency to leave the Church is greater than the desire to meet the God who created and loves us? But, the question remains, why the increase of the 'mentally afflicted' among the 'nones'?

---

[5] "Non-Denominal Churches Explained": https://graceplano.church/about/non-denominational-churches-explained/.

[6] Brendan Hodge, April 3rd, 2024, "The Faith of the Next Generation": https://www.pillarcatholic.com/p/the-faith-of-the-next-generation.

[7] Jana Reiss, November 18th, 2024, "7 ways Americans who leave religion are basically pretty boring": https://religionnews.com/2024/11/18/7-ways-americans-who-leave-religion-are-basically-pretty-boring/.

[8] Eberstadt, *Adam and Eve after the Pill: Revisited*, 2023, p. 178.

'Many congregants arrive late, are dressed inappropriately, do not sing the hymns, become lifeless during the homily, receive Holy Communion indifferently, and then scramble to the exits at the first opportunity'[9].

Indeed, according to one social researcher, just as 'Mainline' Protestant Churches accommodate the social mores of our time, in terms of contraception and abortion, and other imitations of secular culture, so attendance, donations, Christian identity and mission proportionately drop[10]. Thus it seems that as the family declines so does religious affiliation[11]; and, indeed, does this explain the mentality that seeks to destroy the family through whatever measure it can? What about the unimaginable millions dedicated to 'limiting … fertility' through the promotion of contraceptives?[12] Could not that money be put to a better way to help overpopulated cities or struggling families? So pharmaceutical companies get richer, polluting the human and ecological environment, with all its deleterious effects, and the poor person who uses it – what happens to them and their societies?

If, then, there is no gratitude to God, then will there be gratitude for what God gives us in our lives, namely talents, the possibility of marriage, a family, a providential help in all the uncertainties of life? Will, then, we call on a God whom we flee from meeting? Are we ending up like the man

[9] Fr. Robert McTeigue, May 23rd, 2024, "Why Do (Mass-going) Catholics Resent God?": https://crisismagazine.com/opinion/why-do-mass-going-catholics-resent-god.

[10] Eberstadt, *Adam and Eve after the Pill: Revisited*, p. 138, but also the whole chapter, "The Doomed Experiment of Christianity Lite".

[11] Eberstadt, *Adam and Eve after the Pill: Revisited*, p. 151 and the whole chapter, "What Causes Secularisation?"

[12] Eberstadt, *Adam and Eve after the Pill: Revisited*, p. 64.

who buried his talent because he was afraid of the taskmaster who yet wanted an account of what he had been given but, afraid as he was, he did not deposit the gift with the bank so that he earnt interest on it but buried what he had been given? (cf. Mt. 25: 24-30). So what is the talent of the Christian Faith? Conversion! What God has shown that I am like, as a sinner, and that He loves me!

Incidentally, although non-denominational churches have problems of fracturing over the very doctrinal principles they resist; however, they have a certain appeal to the 'often technocentric mindsets of the millennial generation, which has little patience for ritual and tradition'. There is also the view that these churches are more 'relational and less institutional'[13]. Nevertheless, it is impossible to escape the irony that there is a vestige of the very structure, in the non-denominational church, which resolves doctrinal disputes, and which remotely resembles the *Teaching Authority, the Magisterium*, of the Catholic Church, namely, 'the elders' to whom differences between pastors, of practice or belief, can be referred[14].

Nevertheless, whatever beginnings a person makes, it is better to make that beginning than to remain adrift; for Christ is forever walking the waters to see who will call out to Him for help! (cf. Mt 14: 29-33). Moreover, in the course of my wandering years I went to many fellowship or small church services and both discovered a genuine ignorance about the Catholic Faith, in others as well as in myself, as well as many welcomes. What is more, however, witness is common ground. When I once spoke to an almost anti-Catholic Protestant group of students, I shared my experience of how Christ had acted in my life; and, afterwards, the Principal of the College said, as he was passing, he heard the applause and wondered, as the students did not applaud him, why they were applauding me? Because they recognized my testimony to the saving work of Jesus Christ!

---

[13] "Non-Denominal Churches Explained": see above.
[14] "Non-Denominal Churches Explained": see above.

In the *Book of Tobit* we have, in the prayers of Tobit and Sarah (Tobit, 3: 1-6, 11-15), the young and the old who are so distressed that they want to die: that they want God to take their life from them or help them – but God helps both of them and His Providence embraces us all. In other words, there is this dialogue with God that allows each of them, young and old, to put before Him how they are and the real circumstances and impossible sufferings in their lives. But, if this dialogue is no longer there, what is left? Ultimately, our faith is about God acting in our relationships. We are called, after all, to love God and our neighbour. If, therefore, people withdraw from the Christian Faith, not only is there the question of how vulnerable we are to the destruction of our relationships – but also and, in a way more importantly, what will enable us to see why it is worth returning to Christ and His Church? In other words, while we need healing from what afflicts us, we also need hope in the possibilities of life, whether that be a vocation to marriage, the priesthood, or the religious life and so it is not just a matter of our ailments, as it were, but what will take us out of their orbit and into life.

Let us consider, then, a brief review of a number of sufferings in our society, many if not all of which centre on our relationships; indeed, the more on-line use of social media the more it seems to leave 'heavy users starving for social connection'[15]. Thus, along with that 'starvation', is the whole possibility of the vulnerability of young people, generally, to being taken advantage of. Moreover, as we discover the extent to which the media has been patrolled by people unwilling to discuss the reality of mutilating operations, if for no other reason than that the "platform" on which they speak will censor them, then it becomes increasingly clear why so

---

[15] Jonathan Haidt, *The Anxious Generation: How the Great Rewiring of Childhood Is Causing an Epidemic of Mental Illness*, Allen Lane, an imprint of Penguin Books, 2024, p. 65, and then see pages 67-68 developing this on-line vulnerability, even under the nose of a 'helicopter parent' (p. 68).

many people, especially young people, were prey to these uncritically dis-
seminated ideas and practices[16]. And, therefore, while respecting the cour-
tesy of speech, it is vital that these tenacles of the movement that advances
these ideas are brought to light and addressed from the point of view of
the right to open discussion of what is obviously harmful.

'To cite just one example: When trans activists claimed last year that
Scotland's new Hate Crime Act applied to "misgendering," Rowling
promptly "broke" the law on X and challenged authorities to arrest her
(https://thebridgehead.ca/2024/05/07/elites-against-the-elites-how-j-
k-rowling-and-elon-musk-smashed-the-transgender-consensus/).
Shortly thereafter, the police sheepishly affirmed that she had not broken the law — although there is doubt that absent any platform, they
would have been willing to continue quietly suppressing dissenting
voices'[17].

In other words, as the book progresses, we will see many examples of
how discussion has been strangled, using the law, restrictions, employment terms, bureaucratic pronouncements and, in the end, the ignorance and vulnerability of the many people who do not know how to
investigate and repudiate the often emotional claims that being 'born
in the wrong body' is a valid declaration, warranting life-harming
changes to the boy or girl who, often, somewhat innocently declares
these thoughts. The question arises, too, how was it possible that 'The
transgender movement captured the institutions of Big Tech almost

---

[16]

[17] Johnathon Van Maren, January 9th, 2024, "Big Tech's about-face on free
speech takes away transgender activists' advantage": https://www.lifesi-
tenews.com/blogs/big-techs-about-face-on-free-speech-takes-away-transgender-
activists-advantage/.

overnight, and the cultural power this granted them was extra-ordi-nary'[18], including 'the absurd practice of providing feminine menstrual hygiene products to men'[19], in that discussion and disagreement were so trenchantly suppressed, as it continues to be in most parts of Can-ada[20].

On the other hand, a company that was founded to provide women only products, 'as it is only women who get periods', affirming 'biolog-ical reality', has thrived. 'While some took offense at Maxson's firm po-sition on biology, many more celebrated the way Garnuu [meaning '"rescue" in Nepali'] was upholding the dignity of women, leading to the small company's growth'[21].

Already, then, owing to the relaxation of censorship on the social media platforms, 'Dr. McHugh, the former psychiatrist-in-chief for Johns Hopkins Hospital and its current Distinguished Service Professor of Psychiatry (https://profiles.hopkinsmedicine.org/provider/paul-r-mc-hugh/2777430), has said that:

---

[18] Van Maren, January 9th, 2024, "Big Tech's about-face on free speech takes away transgender activists' advantage".

[19] Libby Emmons, January 10th, 2025, "Mark Zuckerberg removes tampons from men's bathrooms at Meta offices: report": https://thepostmillennial.com/mark-zuckerberg-removes-tampons-from-mens-bathrooms-at-meta-offices.

[20] Johnathon Van Maren, January 9th, 2025, Canadian media continues to suppress the horror of child mutilation in the name of 'gender'": https://www.lifesitenews.com/blogs/canadian-media-continues-to-suppress-the-horror-of-child-mutilation-in-the-name-of-gender/.

[21] Virginia Allen and Kristen Eichamer, February 26th, 2025, "Tampon Com-pany CEO Stood Against Gender Ideology Movement. Her Business Is Thriving": https://www.dailysignal.com/2025/02/26/tampon-company-ceo-stood-against-gender-ideology-movement-her-business-is-thriving/.

- Transgenderism is a "mental disorder" that merits treatment,
- Sex change is "biologically impossible," and
- People who promote sexual reassignment surgery are collaborating with and promoting a mental disorder'[22].

Increasingly, then, as this book develops we will see how many tentacles the transgender movement has, from the bureaucracies of the United Nations to the control of the social media, the misuse and weaponization of the law. In other words, amidst the social disorder which seems to be so very widespread, there has been a long-term plan to introduce, ratify and disseminate ideas about being in "the wrong body" for some time. It is not at all a "novel" or "suddenly" appearing ideology or a single, dominant idea; it is, rather, the outcome of a long-term and strategic plan. But where does the money come from? Who is the paymaster of this particular group of anti-life strategies? How can a coordinated outbreak of an idea not be funded?

However, the context of this particular manifestation of disordered thinking are the many and varied other sufferings, all of which, together, manifest a real crisis of our times and a kind of smokescreen which obscures our perception of the reality of the present. Together with Pope Francis, we acknowledge the need for '"media literacy education" in promoting critical thinking and individual growth'[23]. Perhaps, in the light of this call, one of the main ways to progress 'media literacy' is to engage in

---

[22] Craig Bannister (https://www.mrctv.org/author/craig-bannister)| January 8, 2025, « Facebook Now Allows John Hopkins Psychiatrist to Call Transgender a 'Mental Disorder'": https://www.mrctv.org/blog/craig-bannister/facebook-now-allows-john-hopkins-psychiatrist-call-transgender-mental-disorder.

[23] Elise Ann Allen (https://cruxnow.com/author/elise-ann-allen), January 9th, 2024, "Pope says 'fake news' foments hate, leads to acts such as Trump assassination attempt": https://cruxnow.com/vatican/2025/01/pope-says-fake-news-foments-hate-leads-to-acts-such-as-trump-assassination-attempt.

the traditional, intellectual practice, of finding for or against, a particular position – thus derailing the juggernaut of the advocacy of "single ideas".

The running sores in our society starting with suicide

Now we have rocketing rates of suicide, where people kill themselves. In a shocking comparison, the death of American soldiers due to suicide is the following, in that it is already tragic to lose a life in war; but, over the last twenty years: '30,177 active duty personnel and veterans who served in the military after 9/11 have died by suicide - compared to the 7,057 service members killed in combat in those same 20 years.' And what is helping is that sense of being 'connected' to people at home is lost[24]; and, by implication, those who are at the greatest risk of suicide are those of us who feel the most disconnected to others, beginning with our own families. Again, by way of confirmation of this situation, there is a rising number of construction workers in America who are committing suicide as they are experiencing this lack of contact with their own families and the pride of being unable to confide their weakness to others because of the risk of losing their jobs: they are too often under pressure to work away from home, long hours and are only just beginning to share the circumstances that lead them to come out of this culture of silence and admit that they are almost ready to kill themselves[25].

We will revisit this theme of "connection" in the course of this book as it underlies so many problems, whether as a child in the family, an estranged father or husband, divorce, dying without anyone knowing and

---

[24] "Concerns Rise Over Military Suicide Rates; Here's How the USO is Trying to Help": https://www.uso.org/stories/2664-military-suicide-rates-are-at-an-all-time-high-heres-how-were-trying-to-help.

[25] Shannon Pettypiece, June 24th, 2024, "Construction workers are dying by suicide at an alarming rate": https://www.yahoo.com/news/construction-workers-dying-suicide-alarming-140042793.html.

suicide. At the same time there is increasing empirical evidence of the impact of contraception on the rise of abortion, illegitimacy, 'decrease in marriage and married fatherhood for men' and the rise of single men being prone to 'substance abuse, incarceration, and arrests, to name just three'[26]. In tandem with contraception, pornography emasculates men and makes them impotent[27], not just in its obvious sense but in terms of the real connection necessary to another, equal human being: pornography results in the 'dystopic creation of chronically stupefied young men for whom love and romance have become unachievable, thanks to pornography'[28]. In other words, there are multiple factors at work in the breakdown of family relationships. But, clearly, being connected to others is central to human identity. And, conversely, whatever takes us away from actual relationships, whether it is pornography, contraception, abortion, immersion in social media, remaining in our rooms, takes us away from the life-giving suffering of real relationships.

The suffocation of suffering

This was certainly my experience as a child when it came to my own attempted suicide at 14. I felt almost no connection to my own parents and brothers and sisters and, more generally, I had no friends except those with whom I gambled, and we certainly did not share what was going on in our lives. Indeed, my thoughts and feelings were all about being afraid of my parents finding out, being discovered when I stole money from home, and how long it would take me to walk home after losing my bus money in the

---

[26] Mary Eberstadt, *Adam and Eve after the Pill: Paradoxes of the Sexual Revolution*, San Francisco: Ignatius Press, 2012, p. 138.

[27] Rod Dreher, *The Benedict Option*, New York: Sentinel, Penguin Random House, 2017, pp. 215-216; and, as it happens, a number of priest say it is the by far the most common sin confessed to them.

[28] Eberstadt, *Adam and Eve after the Pill: Revisited*, 2023, p. 22.

card games. And, although I took no drugs, I completely repressed the experience of suffering at the root of this unhappiness and suffered memory loss as a result until, a few years later, I went in search of who I was. Pride was the reason I said to myself: "I will not cry and show my suffering". At a certain point, I experienced a dam breaking and a flood of memories being restored to consciousness. Now consider the current crisis among boys and men in the UK:

'Suicide is the biggest killer of people under the age of 35 and the biggest killer of men under the age of 50. It is the leading cause of death in the UK for 10-19 year olds'[29]. In other words, while there is some merit in popular remedies for suicide[30], they are no more than a starting point and just as the problems lie deeper they need deeper answers: answers about who we are and the help we need. Also in the UK, following the introduction of smart phones, 'One in five young people (https://www.england.nhs.uk/2023/11/one-in-five-children-and-young-people-had-a-probable-mental-disorder-in-2023/) is reckoned to suffer a mental disorder, with a 53% rise in emergency referrals (https://www.theguardian.com/society/2024/feb/07/childrens-emergency-mental-health-referrals-in-england-soar-by-53) in three years. Half a million children are awaiting psychiatric help'[31].

---

[29] "Suicide Prevention": https://www.stuartroadsurgery.co.uk/health-information/suicide-prevention/.

[30] Caitlin Moran, 1st July, 2023, "Caitlin Moran: what's gone wrong for men – and the thing that can fix them": https://www.theguardian.com/society/2023/jul/01/caitlin-moran-whats-gone-wrong-for-men-and-the-thing-that-can-fix-them.

[31] Simon Jenkins, 17th December, 2024, "If you've got children, you need to watch Swiped – and see how sick their phones are making them": https://www.theguardian.com/commentisfree/2024/dec/17/children-swiped-channel-4-smartphones-mental-health-addiction?CMP=oth_b-aplnews_d-5.

Then there is euthanasia, the active killing of a person. There is even a suggestion of bringing in a category of euthanasia for those who are called, "terminally anorexic", except that one young person was very grateful that death was not available to her when her anorexia was threatening her life[32]. Indeed, there are numerous ways to suffocate suffering: drugs; endless videos; drink; and abortion. However, where there is trading in what are euphemistically called "recreational drugs", remember it is like starting on the outside rim of a coin drop which, the longer it runs, the more irresistible is the descent of the money to the bottom of the container; and, therefore, in reality, if the vulnerable person is escaping his reality, he or she is escaping into the arms of a lobster pot: it is easy to get in and almost impossible to get out – but there are communities of hope to go to. Pope Francis calls for the conversion of drug dealers and help for their victims:

'The Lord Jesus paused, drew near, healed wounds. In the style of His closeness, we too are called to act, to pause before situations of fragility and pain, to know how to listen to the cry of loneliness and anguish, to stoop to lift up and bring back to life those who fall into the slavery of drugs."[6] And we pray, too, for these criminals who spend and give drugs to the young: they are criminals, they are murderers. Let us pray for their conversion'[33].

---

[32] Cf. Chelsea Rolf, February 23rd, 2024, "I Was Anorexic—I Would Have Chosen Assisted Dying": https://www.newsweek.com/i-was-anorexic-would-have-chosen-assisted-dying-1870648; cf. also a woman suffering from cancer, who wanted assisted suicide but who was persuaded to accept the treatment for cancer and lived: March 3rd, 2024, "24 Years ago, Jeanette Hall had terminal cancer and she wanted assisted suicide. She is happy to be alive today": https://alexschadenberg.blogspot.com/2024/03/24-years-ago-jeanette-hall.html.

[33] Pope Francis' address, "Catechesis. On the occasion of the International Day. Against Drug Abuse and Illicit Trafficking » : https://www.vatican.va/content/francesco/en/audiences/2024/documents/20240626-udienza-generale.html.

In addition, the widespread availability of drugs via internet platforms changes the situation radically in that around 1,500 minors are accessing contaminated drugs and dying, per year, in America[34]; but, presumably, the problem is more widespread and points towards how the availability of the social media has radically changed the lives of children. This will come up again and again throughout this book. Indeed, the questions arise as to how and why these children are able to get these drugs, as well as what can be done to prevent access to them.

While abortion is advocated as a "solution" to the problem of pregnancy, the reality of abortion is that there is the death of a child. As Pope Francis says so clearly: "Doing [an abortion] is killing a human being. You like the word or you don't like… but it is killing"[35]. At the same time, as science says, there is a beginning that when the sperm interacts with the egg, or ovum, and there is a new being formed, which is expressed by the sperm head's incorporation into the now body-mass of the newly formed and encapsulated embryo: encapsulated because as the sperm comes into contact with the egg it "triggers" the new entity to form its own outer-covering and, as the embryo develops, so this outward sign of the new human being changes[36]. Thus the embryo and the life-saving diving gear, known

---

[34] Barbara Ortutay, September 13th, 2024, "How social media became a storefront for deadly fake pills": https://www.ap.org/news-highlights/spotlights/2024/how-social-media-became-a-storefront-for-deadly-fake-pills/.

[35] Catholic Vote, September 13th, 2024, "Pope Francis: US Catholic voters 'have to choose the lesser evil,' according to conscience": https://catholicvote.org/pope-francis-us-catholic-voters-choose-lesser-evil-conscience.

[36] Cf. Etheredge, *Conception: An Icon of the Beginning*, particularly Chapter 5: Part II, co-written by two Spanish professor specialists in embryology: En Route Books and Media: https://enroutebooksandmedia.com/conception/; and there is substantial agreement between this account and that in *Gender Ideology and Pastoral Practice: A Handbook for Catholic Clergy, Counselors, and Ministerial Leaders*, 2024, Chapter 1: Susan Selner-Wright, Ph.D, "Biology and Metaphysics of

as the umbilical cord and placenta, develop together, with the discarding of the placenta and cord at birth. However, just as a diver would die if his or her air-pipe was cut when he or she is at depth, so the placenta and umbilical are necessary for the well-being of the child in the womb.

What is more, with the growing number of available abortion pills, there is a massive increase in the number of women either admitted to the Accident and Emergency Departments or into hospital: 'In the last five years across England and Wales, at least 39,000 women have been treated at NHS hospitals for complications arising from failed or incomplete DIY medical abortions at home'[37].

An American journalist has said that abortion pills are being sold to anyone and everyone and that can include sex-traffickers; but, in terms of the health problems: 'Aside from the death of the baby, whom the mother must expel while at home, often alone, the "most common" side effects of the abortion pill, according to the Mayo Clinic (https://www.mayoclinic.org/drugs-supplements/mifepristone-oral-route/description/drg-20067123), include anxiety, blurred vision, chills, coma, confusion, depression, dizziness, fast heartbeat, headache, nausea, nervousness, nightmares, seizures, slurred speech, and swelling. But those aren't all. Women have **died** (https://aaplog.org/amber-

---

Human Embryonic and Sexual Development", pp. 5-6, 9 and indeed, the whole chapter. I disagree with the claim, however, that 'sex is ordered to generation', as only to 'generation' p. 11, as it is also and simultaneously ordered to spousal communion; and, therefore, the famous phrase of Paul VI'ths *Humanae Vitae*, of the inseparable connection between union and procreation.

[37] Kevin Duffy, May 7th, 2024, "39,000 British Women Have Been Injured by Abortion Pills in Just Five Years": https://www.lifenews.com/2024/05/07/39000-british-women-have-been-injured-by-abortion-pills-in-just-five-years/.

thurmans-tragic-death-was-caused-by-legal-abortion-drugs/) from the abortion pill or lack of care after'[38].

Note, too, the politicization of research which seeks to demonstrate the harmful effects of the abortion pill[39]: a pill that is designed, anyway, to cause harm and confirms what is said above about the massive increase of admissions to hospitals for 'complications arising from failed or incomplete DIY medical abortions at home'. If the research is valid, it will be valid independently of the controversy around it. Indeed, even now, a request to have an annual review in the UK of abortion-pill complications is being resisted by the abortion industry, which has clearly understated the pain of abortion pill abortions[40].

Clearly, there is not only the loss of the child, harm to the mother but also the trauma of the reminder that the bathroom has become a home abortion facility: 'Many of these women are now telling … about how they feel 'triggered' when in their own bathrooms'[41]. Not to mention the pollution of the chemicals and the body parts in the sewage system[42]. One

---

[38] Susan Ciancio, October 17th, 2024, "Alarming abortion pill report warns of online dangers": https://www.catholicworldreport.com/2024/10/17/alarming-abortion-pill-report-warns-of-online-dangers/.

[39] Jordan Boyd (https://thefederalist.com/author/jordandavidson/), October 04, 2024, "Scientists Sue Over 'Discriminatory' Retraction Of Studies Exposing Abortion Pill Dangers": https://thefederalist.com/2024/10/04/scientists-sue-over-discriminatory-retraction-of-studies-exposing-abortion-pill-dangers/.

[40] December 20th, 2024, "DIY abortion pain far more severe than women are told by medics, poll finds": https://spuc.org.uk/diy-abortion-pain-far-more-severe-than-women-are-told-by-medics-poll-finds/.

[41] Duffy, May 7th, 2024, "39,000 British Women Have Been Injured by Abortion Pills in Just Five Years".

[42] Cf. Steven Ertelt, May 30th, 2024, "Abortion Pills are Releasing Dangerous Chemicals, Remains of Aborted Babies in Our Water":

woman, in a recent and tragic case, had killed her twins with an abortion pill and who then died from complications[43]. May God reconcile mother and children *enroute* to heaven. There are, however, those who have reversed an abortion pill and the child has survived[44]; and, in addition, there are people who are coming forward and saying that their mother's attempted to abort them and that they survived, discovering sometimes that their mother had been coerced into submitting to it[45] and then there is also data from the clinics themselves, when they keep it – but what happens to the child is very often tragic[46]. Why, then, if the reality of the abortion pill is so problematic, are people who advocate reversing the abortion pill, both for the sake of the child and the mother – why are they targeted by state prosecutors as if the public does not have a right to know the whole truth of how a woman and child can be helped? So concerned are 7,000 pro-life gynaecologists and obstetricians that they have signed a statement stating, clearly, that these drugs have dangers and that, if help is needed, they will

---

https://www.lifenews.com/2024/05/30/abortion-pills-are-releasing-dangerous-chemicals-remains-of-aborted-babies-in-our-water/.

[43] Kelsey Hazzard, September 17th, 2024, "Abortion Pill Kills Woman, Left Remains of Her Unborn Babies Inside Her: https://www.lifenews.com/2024/09/17/abortion-pill-kills-woman-left-remains-of-her-unborn-babies-inside-her/.

[44] Grace Porto, September 17th, 2024, ""Almost Aborted" Campaign Shares Amazing Stories of Babies Saved From Abortion": https://www.lifenews.com/2024/09/17/amost-aborted-campaign-shares-amazing-stories-of-babies-saved-from-abortion/.

[45] By Adam Eley and Jo Adnitt, 5th June, 2018, "The failed abortion survivor whose mum thought she was dead": https://www.bbc.co.uk/news/health-44357373.

[46] Charlotte Lozier Institute, January 27, 2023, "Questions and Answers on Born-Alive Abortion Survivors": https://lozierinstitute.org/questions-and-answers-on-born-alive-abortion-survivors/.

help – not to abort but to help women who are misled into taking them[47]. Indeed, the complete and utter irony is that the pill to prevent an abortion is claimed to be 'experimental'[48], which is unsubstantiated – as if abortion itself, whether by pill or otherwise is harm free.

Moreover, as a longitudinal study shows, there are women suffering health problems that were not there before. 'The many women represented in this study [over 4,800 women, followed up over 17 years] were so traumatized by their abortions they sought out treatment for their deteriorating mental health'[49]. More recently, a survey of the 'reproduction history' of women aged '41-45' showed that 'women who aborted were 7 times more likely to report their pregnancy outcome was a major contributor to their suicide attempts.' Furthermore, those whose abortion was coerced, had the highest attempted suicide rate of '46.2%'[50].

Meanwhile, in the abortion industry itself, it seems that many people need help to come out of it or to recover from it: Abbey 'Johnson, who

---

[47] October 14th, 2024, "7,000 OBGYNs Confirm Abortion Pills Killed Two Women": https://www.lifenews.com/2024/10/14/7000-obgyns-confirm-abortion-pills-killed-two-women/.

[48] Liz Lykins, September 30, 2024, "A win for pro-life speech rights in New York: A court rules organizations can speak about abortion reversal treatments while lawsuit pends": https://wng.org/roundups/a-win-for-pro-life-speech-rights-in-new-york-1727725316.

[49] "Abortion's Impact on Women's Mental Health",
July 13, 2023 by Bradley Mattes (https://lifeissues.org/author/bradley-mattes/): https://lifeissues.org/2023/07/abortions-impact-on-womens-mental-health/.

[50] Laura Pham, February 27th, 2025, "Study Finds Women Having Abortions are Twice as Likely to Attempt Suicide": https://www.lifenews.com/2025/02/27/study-finds-women-having-abortions-are-twice-as-likely-to-attempt-suicide/?inf_contact_key=ff15f67df3db542f1673da7f8e523c11d18a532c4142cb79caf2b269de1401fa.

left the organization in 2009, claimed many of the workers have post-traumatic symptoms from witnessing abortions at Planned Parenthood'[51].

As if there could be any doubt about what happens in an abortion, a child who survived it was left to die by a doctor who performed it; and, in this tragic moment, there is a visible manifestation of the effect of abortion on the aborter – a heart rending heartlessness[52].

So, even the testimony of people who have survived an abortion seem incapable of convincing a pro-abortionist that a person has come to exist from conception and, while undergoing many changes, comes to manifest the person conceived – as the testimonies of those who have survived an abortion demonstrate with their very existence. What, then, has happened to our society that evidence, the evidence of a person existing from conception, is rejected? And, similarly, with frozen human embryos: that an embryonic person who is transferred to the womb and lives, demonstrates the reality of the personhood of frozen embryos![53] Justice to the unborn, then, requires that the truth be told that human conception is from the first instant[54] of the contact between sperm and egg that leads to the

---

[51] Steven Ertelt, July 8th, 2024, "Planned Parenthood Exploits More Children With Trans Hormones Than Anyone":
https://www.lifenews.com/2024/07/08/planned-parenthood-exploits-more-children-with-trans-hormones-than-anyone/.

[52] Raimondo Rojas, 3rd October, 2024, "Doctor Left This Baby to Die After He Survived a Late-Term Abortion": https://www.lifenews.com/2024/10/03/doctor-left-this-baby-to-die-after-he-survived-a-late-term-abortion/

[53] Cf. John Strege, *A Snowflake named Hannah: Ethics, Faith, and the First Adoption of a Frozen Embryo*, Kregel Publications, 2020.

[54] Etheredge, Conception: An Icon of the Beginning, Chapter 5: Part II: "The Biological Status of the early Human Embryo: When does Human Life Begin? A

embryonic wall's enclosure of the now human being's beginning. Freezing, discarding or destroying a human life is a foundational injustice to the human beings who are frozen or die[55]. If the reality of human conception is recognized, then justice can be done for the frozen human embryos[56].

In what can only be described as a miracle of grace, as many have prayed outside of Dr. Smith's clinic for a long time, a long time abortionist has come out in favour of life: 'Dr. Smith, who once performed thousands of abortions, now calls for an end to the practice, especially for viable children, saying, "There is no need to kill viable babies"[57]. Is this the real reason why pro-abortionists want protected zones around abortion clinics – not only to deny last minute help to women and babies but also because of the action of witness calling a person to repent, save and serve life?!

The beauty of becoming a mother

In America, 'Between 76 and 93 percent of OB-GYNs do not perform induced abortions. Yet they are perfectly capable of offering

---

Paper by Professors Justo Aznar and Julio Tudela » : https://enroutebooksandmedia.com/conception/.

[55] Etheredge, "Frozen and Untouchable: A Double Injustice to the Human Embryo": https://www.pdcnet.org/ncbq/content/ncbq_2016_0016_0001_0049_0054

[56] Calvin Freiburger, October 8th, 2024, "Supreme Court rejects IVF facility's appeal of wrongful death suit for killing frozen embryos": https://www.lifesitenews.com/news/supreme-court-rejects-ivf-facilitys-appeal-of-wrongful-death-suit-for-killing-frozen-embryos/.

[57] Steven Ertelt, October 22nd, 2024, "Longtime Abortionist Stops Killing Babies, Calls for End to Abortion": https://www.lifenews.com/2024/10/22/longtime-abortionist-stops-killing-babies-calls-for-end-to-abortion/.

comprehensive, high-quality reproductive health care to their patients'[58]. Indeed, is the level of coercive manipulation that attempts to
stop pro-life doctors helping their patients an indication of the extent
to which ant-life advocates are losing the argument? Similarly, in various countries, money is invested to "coerce" governments to change
their pro-life laws; and, as such, it signifies that there is a losing argument which seeks recourse to money[59]. Abortion is almost a "cash
crop".

An Italian gynaecologist, saving the lives of over a thousand babies as
he helped women seeking an abortion to accept their children, died suddenly, and 'a short time after' all his colleagues went from being pro-abortion to becoming 'conscientious objectors' to abortion. In a wonderful
summary of how Dr. Giancarlo Bertolotti worked, we read that

'he was able to make women gradually discover the beauty of becoming
mothers. This was because he also had the charisma to understand the
profound beauty of femininity. In a mystical and beautiful sense he "fell
in love" with all women. For this reason he, single and chaste as he was,
could understand the great beauty of sexuality much more than many
other 'experienced' men. He actually carried out some high level scientific studies on this matter'[60].

---

[58] Susan Bane, October 11th, "Biden Administration Bullying of Pro-Life Physicians Gets SCOTUS Smackdown": https://www.nationalreview.com/2024/10/
biden-administration-bullying-of-pro-life-physicians-gets-scotus-smackdown/.

[59] Lisa Correnti (https://c-fam.org/author/lisa-correnti/) | December 19,
2024, « Congress to investigate Biden's abortion blackmail of African country":
https://c-fam.org/friday_fax/congress-to-investigate-bidens-abortion-blackmail-
of-african-country/.

[60] "Faith in Medicine: Giancarlo Bertolotti, Servant of God - A whole life spent
in   favour   of   the   Unborn":   https://cmq.org.uk/CMQ/2024/May/faith_in_

Not to mention the amazing grace of seeing a hostile man and a pregnant woman come out of a pregnancy centre with 'baby supplies' and the reassurance, probably, that there is help to help them keep the baby: "'They went from threatening [us] to keeping their baby in less than eight days," Dan commented. "Crazy!'"[61].

What has become of us? Neither the death, injury nor pollution seems to matter to the advocates of anti-life pills and practices. Environmentalists have many blind eyes, including those that cannot see that contraceptives and abortion pills are part of what pollutes our environment! Is it any surprise, then, that if the medical profession, although actually only parts of it, are unable to accept the evidence concerning the beginning of a person's life, that they will not accept evidence in other fields? What has happened, then, to accepting the evidence of the harm that puberty blockers and mutilating operations are doing to younger and younger people?

But if justice can be done on the basis of empirical evidence, then it bodes well for justice to be established in other areas of life on the basis of empirical evidence. In terms of a guiding preoccupation of this book, it bodes well for the medical profession if the evidence of the beginning of life, or the harm of puberty blockers and mutilating surgeries, is increasingly recognized.

But, in addition to the widespread need of empirical evidence, is the willingness to accept it; and, according to Cardinal Sarah, we are a generation which is less and less willing to accept that the truth is a gift; and, therefore, we are confronted with the need for divine help!

---

medicine.html. Kindly note that this website comes up as unsafe, but I have never had a problem arising from the use of it.

[61] Shawn Carney, September 27th, 2024, "Baby Saved From Abortion When Couple Heading to Planned Parenthood Changes Their Mind": https://www.life-news.com/2024/09/27/baby-saved-from-abortion-when-couple-heading-to-planned-parenthood-changes-their-mind/.

The Irish Constitution's advance of abortion and defence of mothers

How vulnerable are the vulnerable to changes in legislation that are not based on truth: 'In 1983 the 8th amendment [of the Irish Constitution], guaranteeing the right to life of the unborn, was approved by 67% of voters in a nationwide referendum. Thirty-five years later, in 2018, the 8th amendment was rejected in another referendum by precisely the same percentage of voters: 67%'.

Why this change to the Irish Constitution? Has the truth about the beginning of each one of us changed? Or is the truth about the beginning of human life being lost in the various political cross currents that inevitably exist in any society[62]. What happened to the fact that for every mother there is a father and fathers suffer too![63] What will follow?

Is there a connection between the growing number of fatherless children, 1 in 4 children in America are without a father[64], and the destruction of the rights of the father: of recognizing that a child has a father as well as a mother? In American prisons, we see that there are 1,142, 359 men and 784 women in prison. In the UK Dad deprivation is directly related to ... [the doubling of incarceration in prison], and to suicide, which is the number one killer of British men aged under 45'[65]. However, it is clear that in England and Wales there are more men in prison than women: 'In 2023,

---

[62] Cf. *Conception: An Icon of the Beginning*: https://enroutebooksandmedia.com/conception/; and Chapter 5 of *Mary and Bioethics: An Exploration*; both of which can be found through the following webpage: https://enroutebooksandmedia.com/francisetheredge/.

[63] Cf. my experience, in prose and poetry, in *The Prayerful Kiss: A Book of Prose and Poetry*: https://enroutebooksandmedia.com/theprayerfulkiss/.

[64] "Statistics Tell the Story: Fathers Matter": https://www.fatherhood.org/father-absence-statistic.

[65] "The Story So Far": https://www.chapter2.org.uk/background.

there were 83,128 men and 3,259 women in prisons in England and Wales in 2023'. What is more, around half of the men in prison were aged between 15 and 30[66].

Does this mean that the father-son relationship is a priority in restoring a good outcome for our young men? Consider the view that fatherlessness does not just affect the child but, in turning the fatherless 'kids to gangs' it multiplies the effect on society in all kinds of ways, not least is the sense of anger that erupts in all kinds of situations[67].

At the same time, however, it does happen that fatherless boys can develop into fathering men[68], which is always a reason to give hope to others.

If another amendment is passed it could mean that Irish mothers, who are currently protected by the Constitution if they wish to stay at home with their children, will then be obligated to find work, even if they are mothers of young children[69]. In the event, the country voted to retain the explicit wording of the Irish Constitution which said "mothers shall not be obliged by economic necessity to engage in labor to the neglect of their duties in the home"[70]. In other words, although 65% of the country voted

---

[66] D. Clark, November 15th, 2023, "Number of prisoners in custody in England and Wales from 1900 to 2023, by gender": https://www.statista.com/statistics/283475/england-and-wales-prison-population-by-gender/.

[67] Eberstadt, *Adam and Eve after the Pill: Revisited*, 2023, p. 111, but also the whole chapter: "The Fury of the Fatherless", pp. 105-122.

[68] Cf. Adam B. Coleman, March 12th, 2024, "Downfall of America's children starts with the selfishness of parents": https://nypostcom.cdn.ampproject.org/c/s/nypost.com/2024/03/12/opinion/downfall-of-americas-children-starts-with-the-selfishness-of-parents/amp/.

[69] Paul Kingsnorth, February 29th, 2024, "What is a Mother?": https://paulkingsnorth.substack.com/p/what-is-a-mother.

[70] Charles Collins, March 9th, 2024, "Ireland's government suffers crushing defeat in effort to change constitution": https://cruxnow.com/church-in-uk-and-ireland/2024/03/irelands-government-suffers-crushing-defeat-in-effort-to-change-constitution.

to retain the wording, "mothers shall not be obliged … to engage in labor", the question arises as to why did 67% of the population vote to drop the Constitution's defence of unborn children when an unborn child has a mother? A woman is not a mother without a child. Why, then, is there a disconnect between being a mother, having a child, and the defence of human life?

We live in a society in which divorce is the outcome of almost half of all marriage in the UK[71] and in over a third of all marriages in America[72]. 44% of all children under 21 have not grown up with both parents[73]. One of the sufferings is simply the misunderstanding that the child goes through in which, unless he or she is helped to understand otherwise, that the divorce of the parents is the fault of the child: 'She said when she was a child and her parents divorced, in her little mind, she thought it was her fault. She'd never heard anyone, before me, say otherwise'[74]. Moreover, couples can take out a legal, 'pre-nuptial agreement' that is signed before a marriage and which specifies who gets what if there is a divorce[75]. If contraceptives, surgery which takes away fertility and abortion are all

---

[71] "Office for National Statistics sets out '13 facts about divorce'; UK Divorce Rate": https://www.astlepaterson.co.uk/13-facts-about-divorce-uk-divorce-rate/.

[72] Marija Lazic, May 20th, 2023, "13 Saddening Children of Divorce Statistics for 2022": https://legaljobs.io/blog/children-of-divorce-statistics.

[73] Fiona Apthorpe, September 1st, 2022, "New report reveals true scale of family breakdown in the UK": Commenting on a Report by Rachel de Souza, Child Commissioner: https://www.geldards.com/insights/new-report-reveals-true-scale-of-family-breakdown-in-the-uk/.

[74] Dr. Jennifer Roback Morse, "Dr. Jennifer Roback Morse, "Divorce is bad for kids", drmorse@ruthinstitute.org; or go to: https://www.youtube.com/watch?v=e1pfoK5a7Qk.

[75] FM Family Law: "Relationship Agreements": https://www.fmfamilylaw.co.uk/what-we-do/relationship-agreements/: A pre-nuptial agreement is a contract signed before a marriage. It sets out what each party can expect during the marriage and if the marriage comes to an end through divorce or death.'

unnecessary interventions, is it any surprise that there are other forms of unnecessary surgery? What, then, is the culture out of which a person comes into society? Is it a culture that is afraid of reconciliation: of being unable to forgive? Is it a culture that cannot give without, as it were, taking back what is given? Is it a culture in which appearance is paramount?

Running away, suicide, and deterioration of mental health

Running away at 14, over 50 years ago, I returned home, frightened by what was "out there"; and now, 50 years on, there are 100,000 children who run away each year[76]. Around the same time, roughly 14 years old, I tried to commit suicide. Now, in the UK, suicides in the 15-19 age group 'rose to 198 in 2021. This is the highest number in over 30 years'[77]. In America, Dr Toolin-Wilson tried to commit suicide 60 years ago[78], she has since written a book, married, obtained a doctorate and still works in higher education; now, in New York alone, suicide is the second highest cause of death after accidents 'in teens and young adults'[79]. More generally, the 'pandemic left millions of American teens suffering, mentally, and led

---

[76] The Children's Society, "I don't have to be afraid anymore": https://www.childrenssociety.org.uk/what-we-do/our-work/children-missing-home.

[77] Thursday, October 6th, 2022, "Suicide rates record high amongst 15-19 year olds": https://www.disabilityrightsuk.org/news/suicide-rates-record-high-amongst-15-19-year-olds.

[78] As she said towards the end of interviewing Francis Etheredge on his new book, "The Word in Your Heart: Mary, Youth, and Mental Health": The interview can be found here: https://www.spreaker.com/episode/episode-299-francis-etheredge-on-his-book-the-word-in-your-heart-mary-youth-and-mental-health-february-21-2024--58774423.

[79] Maria McFadden Maffucci's "Foreword", p. 6, "Enriched by Experience" to Francis Etheredge's book, "The Word in Your Heart: Mary, Youth, and Mental Health".

more than 800,000 to seriously consider suicide'[80]. For one researcher, suicide was the second highest cause of death for men in America[81]. In addition, in 2023, nearly a third of American youth went to mental health services: '8.3 million youth ages 12 to 17 received mental health care'[82].

In general, 'Covid-19 … seriously exacerbated problems such as anxiety, depression and self-harm among school-age children'[83]. With respect
to understanding 'anxiety and depression', they are understood to be 'in-
ternalizing disorders', experiencing the 'symptoms [of 'anxiety, fear, sad-
ness, and hopelessness'] inwardly'. The young people 'ruminate' and 'often
withdraw from social engagement'[84]. Anxiety can be defined as a reaction
'in anticipation of future threat'[85] suggesting an almost generalised fear of
the future; and, therefore, the possibility that depression is a reaction in
the present to the fear of the future. However, in terms of a clinical diagnosis in the context of social media, depression arises when people feel
'more socially disconnected, and depression then makes people less interested and able to seek out social connection'[86].

---

[80] Tom Hoopes, 4/12/2022, "*Over 800,000 American teens seriously considered suicide during the COVID-19 pandemic, the CDC reports…Pope Francis prophesied exactly this kind of crisis*": https://aleteia.org/2022/04/12/covid-19s-mental-health-toll-and-the-popes-advice/.

[81] Cf. Dr. Yella Hewings-Martin, June 19th, 2020, "Do all men die equally?": https://www.medicalnewstoday.com/articles/leading-causes-of-death-in-men.

[82] Sarah Holliday, August 12, 2024, "8.3 Million Minors Received Mental Care in 2023, Highlighting a 'Decaying Culture'": https://washingtonstand.com/commentary/83-million-minors-received-mental-care-in-2023-highlighting-a-decaying-culture.

[83] Francis Etheredge's book, *The Word in Your Heart: Mary, Youth, and Mental Health*: Chapter Three, "Youth, Mental Health and the Word of God", p. 116 of the pre-publication text; now published:

[84] Haidt, *The Anxious Generation*, 2024, p. 25.

[85] Haidt, The Anxious Generation, 2024, p. 27-28.

[86] Haidt, The Anxious Generation, 2024, p. 29, p. 38.

To give a glimpse of the problem of mental health, in one month, in post Covid-19 UK, there were 420,000 children 'treated for mental health problems'[87]. At the same time, these phenomena are not restricted to the UK and the USA, as there are extremes of family breakdown in Japan. 700,000 young people are not ever going out, to the point where they are called "stay-ins".

There is an amazing saying, that *it is better to light one candle than to grumble against the darkness,* and this one lady has lit this candle. But, clearly, many more need to be lit and put in the limelight.

'Finland is given as an example of a sustained drive to end homeless-ness, with the claim that there are now only about 150 homeless fami-lies. In contrast in the UK, there are more than 100,000 households cat-egorised as homeless.'

After a 20-year silence, Sabrina now advocates for the homeless, as she says: "'I sit in front of you now with a job, a home, a family and a PhD," said Sabrina, who works as a fire service chief.'

As 'a 15- and 16-year-old … Sabrina was sleeping rough, after the death of a parent and problems at home.'

'Her way out was selling the Big Issue - "I credit them with saving my life" - and once she had secure accommodation she was able to get a job in the fire service, which became her career'[88].

---

[87] "Record 420,000 children a month in England treated for mental health problems": https://www.theguardian.com/society/2022/may/22/record-420000-children-in-england-treated-for-mental-health-problems.

[88] Sean Coughlan, July 11th, 2024, "From rough sleeping to advising Prince William": https://www.bbc.co.uk/news/articles/c1weg5en21wo.

And, therefore, even without reference to God or the meaning of Sabrina's experience, we can see that she has realised that there is a time to share what has happened so that her history gives hope to others.

Depopulation and the un-popularity of marriage

The UK has now gone on the list of those countries in which the 'fertility rate' is falling very fast owing, it seems, to the cost of having more children and, therefore, to policies which do not support the family[89]. As regards a source concerning young people and marriage in South Korea[90], a country once evangelized by young people themselves who found more in Christianity than in their own philosophies[91], young people have suffered such long and stressful years of studying as children and as working as adults that now they do not want to marry and the country's birthrate is the lowest in the world[92]. The expectation that the man will be able to provide a house, in the present circumstances, is proving financially

---

[89] Adele Robinson, 12th October, 2024, "UK's fertility rate falling faster than any other G7 nation - with austerity thought to be 'principal factor'": https://news.sky.com/story/britains-fertility-rate-falling-faster-than-any-other-g7-country-with-austerity-thought-to-be-a-principal-factor-13232314.

[90] Pope Francis has chosen South Korea for the next "World Youth Day".

[91] Jacques de Guillebon is an essayist and journalist. He is a contributor to the Catholic magazine La Nef, "How Korea evangelized itself": https://1000raisonsdecroire.com/en/how-korea-evangelized-itself-18th-century; *Meg Hunter-Kilmer* (https://aleteia.org/author/meg-hunter-kilmer)- *published on 03/02/17*, "How Korea evangelized itself": https://aleteia.org/2017/03/02/how-korea-evangelized-itself: 'Korea, in fact, is the only country that evangelized itself.' And '[Now the Servant of God], Yi Byeok, a young man who began in 1770 to study a Catholic book by Servant of God Matteo Ricci, written in Chinese. At only 16, he devoted himself to the study of the faith, gathering other young (and older) men around him at Chon Jin Am, known as the birthplace of Catholicism in Korea.'

[92] Jean MacKenzie, 28th February, 2024, "Why South Korean women aren't having babies": https://www.bbc.co.uk/news/world-asia-68402139.

impossible. Indeed, the President has declared the situation an emergency
and has created a new ministry to inspire and incentivize a rise in the birth
rate; it is called "'Ministry of Low Birth Rate Counter Planning." According to a report, in addition to local reasons for this birthrate nose-dive,
there are also the following, common problems.

'Like most other countries in the world, South Korea is suffering from
the fallout of the sexual revolution that has led to collapsing birth rates
due to the normalization of abortion, contraception, divorce, and the
general breakdown of the family'[93]. More recently, owing to a positive
government campaign, the birth of children has risen. Thus 'They are
celebrating – and rightly so! – that 8,300 more babies were born in 2024
than in 2023. But by the best estimates, well over double that number
were also killed [by abortion] before they were born'[94].

At the same time, however, an American military chaplain who died in
a North Korean prisoner of war camp, has increasingly come to promi-
nence ever since Pope Francis said that the next *World Youth Day* would
be in South Korea[95].

---

[93] Andreas Wailzer, 15th May, 2024, "South Korean president declares low
birth rate a 'national emergency,' plans new ministry to address it":
https://www.lifesitenews.com/news/south-korean-president-declares-low-birth-
rate-a-national-emergency-plans-new-ministry-to-address-it/?utm_source=di-
gest-prolife-2024-05-17.

[94] Jonathon Van Maren, "South Korea's birthrate rose for the first time in a
decade, with 8,000+ more babies born last year": https://www.lifesi-
tenews.com/blogs/south-koreas-birthrate-rose-for-the-first-time-in-a-decade-
with-8000-more-babies-born-last-year/.

[95] Etheredge, The Word in Your Heart: Mary, Youth, and Mental Health, pp.
236-237: https://www.amazon.com/dp/B0D1NTBBPJ.

'One pilgrimage celebrates the life of Father Emil Kapaun, the Korean War chaplain who gave his life for his Church and country. Fr. Kapaun's body was finally discovered and returned to Kansas in 2021. The holy priest now has a process of canonization.

The pilgrimage is known as the Kansas Camino. It started about 15 years ago with only five people. The 60-mile route starts in Wichita and ends at the priestly war veteran's home parish in Pilsen, Kansas. This year, the pilgrimage had 300-plus participants'[96].

Fr. Emil Kapaun said of Christian families that wanted to be happy, like the Holy Family, that they 'must practice the virtue of self-sacrifice'[97].

However, in more recent times there has emerged a widespread monetarization of adoption that began during the mixed-race births of Korean women and Western soldiers. Around the time of Fr. Emil Kapaun's [1916-1951] death, the mixed-race children were found homes in America; however, so lucrative did this practice turn out to be that a collusion developed between private adoption agencies, the Korean Government officials and an Oregon based branch of the adoption agencies which turned what may have been a help into a baby-trade and the exporting of any

---

[96] Byron Whitcraft, June 28th, 2024, "Are Pilgrimages in America Becoming Mainstream?": https://www.tfp.org/are-pilgrimages-in-america-becoming-mainstream/?PKG=TFPE3360.

[97] Allysa Murphy, "Father Emil Kapaun: 18 Things Every Catholic Should Know About This Heroic Priest": https://www.ncregister.com/blog/father-emil-kapaun-18-things-every-catholic-should-know-about-this-heroic-priest;   and, moreover, there are two miracles under investigation as a part of the process of canonization: going from Servant of God to Saint: Roy Wenzl, "Vatican finds enough evidence to continue probe into miracle": https://www.kapaun.org/documents/fr-kapaun-canonization/29-vatican-finds-enough-evidence-to-continue/file.

number of Korean children. With the rise of contraception and abortion in the West, so rose the export of babies from Korea; but, also, so increased the suffering of Korean families whose parents were told that their child had died or was seriously ill and had to be adopted if the fees for medicine were to be paid[98]. But now, it seems, not only has this scandal come to light but, as has been said, Korean society's birthrate has spiralled down.

Shrinking populations

The Lord says 'he did not create [the earth] to be chaos,
he formed it to be lived in' (Isaiah, 45: 18).

Saying earlier: 'Woe to anyone who argues with his Maker,
one earthenware pot among many!
Does the clay say to the potter, 'What are you doing?
Your work has no hands!'
Woe to anyone who asks a father, 'Why are you begetting?'
and a woman, 'Why are you giving birth?' (Isaiah, 45; 9-10).

As regards low birthrates, in Italy, there is a crisis concerning the low birthrate: 'the country reached an all-time low with just 390,000 live births in 2023'[99]. But, interestingly enough, coincidence or providence?, a

---

[98] By Kim Tong-Hyung and Claire Galofaro, with contributions from Lori Hinnant and researcher Rhonda Shafner and Frontline's Lora Moftah and Emily Sternlicht, 19th September, 2024, "Widespread adoption fraud separated generations of Korean children from their families, AP finds": https://www.ap.org/news-highlights/spotlights/2024/widespread-adoption-fraud-separated-generations-of-korean-children-from-their-families-ap-finds/.

[99] May 11th, "Protests erupt around papal event, but Francis wasn't the target": https://cruxnow.com/vatican/2024/05/protests-erupt-around-papal-event-but-francis-wasnt-the-target.

young mother Chiara Corbella (1984-2012) had three children, the first two of whom were born with seriously compromised health, whom the parents refused to abort, and the children both died shortly after birth. Chiara, who refused aggressive cancer treatment while pregnant with her third child, and so gave birth to a third, healthy child, has now been designated *Servant of God*, like Dorothy Day, and is being put forward to become a saint. "In the edict opening Corbella's sainthood cause, the Diocese of Rome said her sacrificial choice for her child "remains as a beacon of the light of hope, a testimony of faith in God, the author of life, and an example of love greater than fear and death"[100].

The same destruction of the population, as exists in a number of other countries, exists in Canada[101], along with the deliberate killing of an increasing number of people, young and old, mentally ill or in some way suffering the question of life's meaningless and needing help with it, but not the help of being killed[102]. 'Almost by contrast in 'Asia-Pacific', where 60% of the world's youth population is, including countries like China, Russia, India, the Philippines and many others, 51 in all, there is a growing problem of teenage pregnancies; however, instead of counselling abstinence and the spiritual resources to make it possible, the *World Economic Forum* advocates contraceptives and abortion among other measures[103].

---

[100] June 21st, 2024, *The Catholic Herald* on-line edition: "Sainthood cause progress for mum who refused cancer treatment to save unborn child": https://catholicherald.co.uk/sainthood-cause-progress-for-mum-who-refused-cancer-treatment-to-save-unborn-child/.

[101] Anthony Murdoch, May 13th, 2024, "Canada's fertility, marriage rates plummet to record lows: report": https://www.lifesitenews.com/news/canadas-fertility-marriage-rates-plummet-to-record-lows-report/.

[102] Francis Etheredge, *Reaching for the Resurrection: A Pastoral Bioethics*: https://enroutebooksandmedia.com/reachingfortheresurrection/.

[103] Tomoko Fukuda (https://www.weforum.org/agenda/authors/tomoko-fukuda/) and Andreas Daugaard Jørgensen (https://www.weforum.org/agenda/authors/andreas-daugaard-jorgensen/), March 4th, 2024, "How countries can save

Meanwhile, contrary to seeing China as full of youth and vitality, which in one sense it may be, there is an unwillingness of young people to accept the transition from a terribly brutal one child policy to the government now allowing up to three children or more because of the low birth-rate. On the other hand, while there is an ageing population, there is clearly a willingness of some people's part to care for their elderly, although there is a growing number of kindergartens being turned into old people's care homes[104]. A decades long policy of persecuting women and children has obviously had a profound effect on the population as a whole; indeed, currently, there is a risk of men being unable to find wives turning to violence, because *In China, son preference and sex-selective abortion … [has] led to 32 million excess males under the age of 20 years[105].*

---

millions by prioritising young people's sexual and reproductive health": https://www.weforum.org/agenda/2024/03/how-countries-can-save-millions-by-prioritising-adolescent-sexual-and-reproductive-health/; and cf. "Asia-Pacific": https://en.wikipedia.org/wiki/Asia%E2%80%93Pacific. Cf. also *Human Nature: Moral Norm* for an in-depth investigation of how moral action expresses the gift of human nature given by the Creator: https://enroutebooksandmedia.com/humannature/.

[104] Frances Martell, 9th September, 2024, "Birth Rate Collapse: China Turning Kindergartens into Nursing Homes": https://www.breitbart.com/asia/2024/09/09/birth-rate-collapse-china-turning-kindergartens-into-nursing-homes/.

[105] Therese Hesketh (https://pubmed.ncbi.nlm.nih.gov/?term=Hesketh%20T%5BAuthor%5D), MD PhD, Li Lu (https://pubmed.ncbi.nlm.nih.gov/?term=Lu%20L%5BAuthor%5D), MD PhD, and Zhu Wei Xing (https://pubmed.ncbi.nlm.nih.gov/?term=Xing%20ZW%5BAuthor%5D), MD MPH, September 6th, 2011, "The consequences of son preference and sex-selective abortion in China and other Asian countries": https://www.ncbi.nlm.nih.gov/pmc/articles/PMC3168620/.

Additionally in China, but also in China and Russia 'the … bill is coming due in the form of the long-predicted demographic crisis' owing to the prevalence of abortion[106].

Having met a young man from China, owing to the degree of studying he had to do in his life, at times, from 5am to 11 pm, with his parents doing the work which was not examined, he has resolved to improve the lot of those whom he now teaches. Although, however, he was a child of the one-child policy years, he seemed remarkably open to having a bigger family himself and to being willing to evaluate the good he found in other cultures, particularly as regards whether or not it could help him or his students. In general, if there are others who have been saved by their work schedules from absorbing too much negativity from Chinese culture, maybe there is hope in expected places!

By contrast to these inherently harmful practices, promoted in all kinds of ways, whether in China, Africa, or by the United Nations anti-populationists' policies, there is the 'now paradoxical statement by the United Nations highlighting the value of people with disabilities and rejecting discrimination against them [which] is in open contradiction with the policies that this organization has promoted in all areas since the 1970s'[107] – but as good as a change is, is it principled and does it recognize the wholesale injustice to women because of the 'son

---

[106] Jonathon Van Maren, December 13th, 2024, "Russia faces serious demographic crisis due to its abortion culture": https://www.lifesitenews.com/blogs/russia-faces-serious-demographic-crisis-due-to-its-abortion-culture/?utm_source=digest-profamily-2024-12-17.

[107] Julio Tudela, October 2nd, 2024, "A surprising UN report now denounces discriminatory abortion practices in people with disabilities": https://bioethicsobservatory.org/2024/10/a-surprising-un-report-now-denounces-discriminatory-abortion-practices-in-people-with-disabilities/47124/.

preference and sex-selective abortion'? In other words does it go to the root of the problem of "relativism", which says that any means justifies the end, and so it rediscovering the natural law principle that taking any innocent human life is a true injustice?!

The possibility of the transmission of faith

Do, then, the young and the old have anything to offer to each other; and, if so, what is it? [108] (cf. Ps 148: 7, 12). Does anyone seek the wisdom of God (cf. Ps. 14: 2) that is to be found? (cf. Mt 7: 7-8). If, indeed, as the social evidence shows, the structure of everyday family life is breaking down, as Christianity seems to be sinking into the sand, what response can be made that will benefit young people? Indeed, if the central mystery of the suffering, death and resurrection of Christ is being drained out of our culture, what can be done to show that God loves to help us!

Testimony was the answer to how young people could increase their faith and testimony was the answer to how to transmit the parent's faith to their children; and, in both cases, to speak from the concrete reality of the family, remembering to forgive and not let the sun go down on our anger and the cold war begin in the morning. "A parish where children are not heard and the elderly are ignored," he insisted, "is not a true Christian community. Don't forget, the elderly are the memory and the children the promise." Therefore, listening to the children and the elderly is essential to family life and the witness of it'[109].

---

[108] 25th – 26th May, 2024, "Message of His Holiness Pope Francis for the First World Children's Day/: https://www.vatican.va/content/francesco/en/messages/bambini/documents/20240302_messaggio-bambini.html.

[109] "Wow Pope Francis' Surprise Community Visit saying "Let's defend the family" - "We all fall in life, but the important thing is not to stay down if you

At the same time as we have seen notable examples of men and women going forward with a view to canonization, the statistics for pilgrimages are telling us, too, that many people are on the move and are discovering their value: 'In 2012, 715,000 [went to Lourdes] and … 570,000 pilgrims attended pilgrimage events'[110]. In a recent article, there seems to be a rise of almost local pilgrimages in parts of America, both indicating the seriousness of the times in which we live but, also, signifying the outreach, as it were, in seeking the help of those already in heaven[111]. Similarly, in America there is an increase in praying in front of the Blessed Sacrament, the presence of Christ in the Catholic Eucharist[112]. Some, perhaps an increasing number of young American men are making a pilgrimage through a variety of Churches and, increasingly, being drawn into the Catholic Church – even more so than young women[113]. Globally, however, there seems to be an increase in the number of Catholics but an ongoing decrease in the number of priests and religious, albeit the number of deacons are increasing; at the same time, though, these statistics do vary

---

slip."" *June 06, 2024*: https://www.catholicnewsworld.com/2024/06/wow-pope-francis-surprise-community.html.

[110] An adapted quotation as the original was not clear, as it simply said: "In 2012, 715,000 and in 2012, 570,000 pilgrims attended pilgrimage events", « Bernadette Soubirous": https://en.wikipedia.org/wiki/Bernadette_Soubirous.

[111] Byron Whitcraft, June 28th, 2024, "Are Pilgrimages in America Becoming Mainstream?": https://www.tfp.org/are-pilgrimages-in-america-becoming-mainstream/?PKG=TFPE3360.

[112] Cf. Fr. Philip Nolan, OP, June 28th, 2024, "Adoration and the Struggle of Prayer": https://www.hprweb.com/2024/06/adoration-and-the-struggle-of-prayer/.

[113] Father Dwight Longenecker (https://www.ncregister.com/author/father-dwight-longenecker) Commentaries November 26, 2024, « The Rise of Religious Young Men": https://www.ncregister.com/commentaries/the-rise-of-religious-young-men.

according to the country or region analysed[114]. Indeed, in France, there has been a record number of 7,134 baptisms this year, 2024, with one person saying:

> 'What was at the origin, for me, of the "catechumenal path" that I have undertaken, it is clearly the encounters: attentive priests, a joyful and dynamic parish community. Through them, I discovered an open and welcoming Church, and extremely diverse! Faced with a society that appears more and more materialist and seems to promote a form of consumerist individualism, being Christian and "Catholic" (ie. universal, etymologically), is to experience that THE good is to say care, attention, and more broadly Love, is better than goods, that is to say possession, wealth, power or glory'[115].

The infancy narratives, including Zechariah and the parents of the infant Jesus' visits to the temple, the pilgrimages they make, are all saturated with references to what was, up to that point, the whole bible. In other words, the whole impression, without going into a detailed analysis of the biblical text, is of devout parents, who are immersed in the history and prayer of Israel, immersing their child in it too.

For, if pilgrimage was a regular event, and parents were called to tell their children what and why they are doing it (cf. Dt 6: 6-7, 20-25), then their family would be very preoccupied with preparations for pilgrimage,

---

[114] Cf. L'Osservatore Romano, "New Church statistics reveal more Catholics, fewer vocations": https://www.vaticannews.va/en/vatican-city/news/2024-04/vatican-central-statistical-office-church-pontifical-yearbook.html.

[115] March 27th, 2024, "Record results in 2024 for the number of catechumens in France": https://eglise.catholique.fr/espace-presse/communiques-de-presse/550845-resultats-record-en-2024-du-nombre-de-catechumenes-en-france/.

as we were[116], both in leading up to the event and going through with it. What is more, this word of God, with which they are all familiar, is a prophetic word (cf. Lk 1: 45, 55), which is constantly addressing life as it is lived and providing Mary, Joseph, and others too, with words to ponder (cf. Lk 2: 19, 51; and Lk 1: 66). Just, then, as there is this relationship between the history of Israel and the Holy Family, both immediate, extended, and those connected with them through the various events written about, so with ourselves, our Christian faith is a faith which in and of itself and how it is lived, is always a faith to be both received and transmitted.

On the one hand, Pope Francis addresses the youth of the world with his invitation to get up, like Mary, and to go in haste[117], which was taken up by people preparing to go on pilgrimage to Lisbon; and, in addition, he invited young people to meditate on various figures in the Old Testament, such as Samuel, David, the Jewish servant girl who told Naaman the leper to go and meet the prophet in Israel (cf. 2 Kg 5:2-6)[118] and, by implication, these were a witness to others in their lives too, like David witnessed to

---

[116] Cf. Francis Etheredge, *The Family on Pilgrimage: God Leads Through Dead Ends*: https://enroutebooksandmedia.com/familyonpilgrimage/; and cf. Francis Etheredge, *Mary and Bioethics: An Investigation*, "Chapter One: The Holy Family: Celibacy and Marriage: A Reflection on the "Passage" from the Jewish Rite of Marriage to the Christian Sacrament of Marriage", pp. 47-77: https://enroutebooksandmedia.com/maryandbioethics/.

[117] Pope Francis, 5th August, 2023, Apostolic Journey of His Holiness Pope Francis to Portugal on the Occasion of the XXXVII World Youth Day: (2 - 6 August 2023) (https://www.vatican.va/content/francesco/en/travels/2023/outside/documents/portogallo-gmg-2023.html): Recitation of the Holy Rosary with Sick Young People (https://www.vatican.va/news_services/liturgy/libretti/2023/20230802-06-messale-portogallo.pdf : https://www.vatican.va/content/francesco/en/speeches/2023/august/documents/20230805-portogallo-rosario.html.

[118] Pope Francis' Post-Synodal Apostolic Exhortation *Christus Vivit*, of the Holy Father Francis "To Young People and to the Entire People of God", 2019: https://www.vatican.va/content/francesco/en/apost_exhortations/documents/papa-francesco_esortazione-ap_20190325_christus-vivit.html.

Saul. Thus there is the early call of Samuel, with Eli the priest teaching him to recognize the voice of the Lord (cf. 1 Sam; indeed, helping to open his ear. David, the King, who rests from a battle that is going on and falls into sin (cf. 2 Sam 11: 1-27); and, therefore, the Lord is admonishing us to stay in the fight against sin. The Jewish servant girl giving Naaman the leper advice (2 Kings 5: 1, 14) indicating that we can point others to Christ and His word if we are clear how it has helped us. Ruth, too, was attracted to follow her mother-in-law's God after the death of her husband '(cf. *Ru* 1:1-18), yet she also showed boldness in getting ahead in life (cf. *Ru* 4:1-17)'[119]. But also, on the other hand, there are the saints[120] and those, closer to our own time, who are almost saints.

So let us consider, however briefly, their contribution to preparing or helping us to live through sufferings. For, if the withdrawal of Christianity is opening a wound in our culture, it is that we no longer know the significance of suffering or the hope of the resurrection, either now or at the end of time, such that wherever suffering breaks out, as it were, we want to suppress it, either with medicalizing numbness or with death.

Blessed Dominic Barberi (1792-1849)

In 1720, an Italian, St. Paul of the Cross (1694-1775) founded the Passionists because he saw that the passion of Christ was poorly understood and wanted to make it central to his religious order. Thus, in terms of our modern "withdrawal" from Christianity, it could be argued that it was already happening in the 18th century; and, while only remotely, this

---

[119] *Christus Vivit*, 11.

[120] In *The Word in Your Heart: Mary, Youth, and Mental Health*, there are numerous cameos of a variety of saints or religious, from one who founded a football club to help the poor in Glasgow to one who died a martyr's death in a concentration camp: https://enroutebooksandmedia.com/wordinyourheart/.

prepared for both the *Second Vatican Council's* reclaiming the relationship between the Jewish *Passover Lamb*[121], the celebration that marked Israel's departure from slavery in Egypt and founds, as it were, the Passover of Christ. Returning to St. Paul of the Cross:

he 'saw the Passion as the greatest, most overwhelming, work of God's love. For Paul the Passion was a revelation of the love of God: it was not about placating an angry God, or about guilt, or even in a sense about suffering, except in as much as the suffering of one who is loved will lead … the one who loves to compassion for the sufferer, that is, suffering-with'[122].

So Blessed Dominic Barberi, also a Passionist, practised both penance and prayed for England to return to Christ[123], such that after 28 years he arrived in England in 1841[124]. However, the point to be made here is that even when a person is trained in religion, as it were, to both accept difficulties and self-imposed penance, there can still come upon them a moment when life seems impossible : 'Last Sunday, I broke down and wept bitterly. I can do no more. The cross is too heavy. My God, if You intend to increase it, You must increase my strength too'[125]. In other words, even

---

[121] Cf. *Sacrosanctum Concilium*, of the *Second Vatican Council*, 6: https://www.vatican.va/archive/hist_councils/ii_vatican_council/documents/vat-ii_const_19631204_sacrosanctum-concilium_en.html.

[122] Martin Newell, February 14th, 2019, "A Brief History of the Passionists, from St Paul of the Cross to Today": https://passionist.life/stories/2019/02/brief-history-of-the-passionists/

[123] Gerard Skinner, *Dominic Barberi*, Leominster: Herefordshire, UK, 2021, p. 99.

[124] Blessed Dominic Barberi: https://passionist.org/blessed-dominic-barberi/.

[125] Gerard Skinner, *Dominic Barberi*, 2021, p. 113, quoted from U, 213: Young, U., *The Life and Letters of the Venerable Dominic (Barberi) C. P., Founder of the Passionists in Belgium and England*, London, 1926.

the person who is prepared to see the significance of his suffering can still cry out for help, as did the Lord (cf. Mt 26: 36-46); but what hope is there, otherwise, for people who are not prepared to suffer and who do not know the secret help that God gives.

Carmen Hernández (1930-2016)

'The Neocatechumenal Way began in 1964 in the slums of Palomeras Altas, Madrid, through the work of Mr Francisco (Kiko) Argüello and Ms Carmen Hernández who, at the request of the poor with whom they were living, began to proclaim to them the Gospel of Jesus Christ. As time passed, this kerygma [or saving announcement of the love of God for the sinner and the faraway] was embodied in a catechetical synthesis, founded on the tripod: "Word of God-Liturgy-Community", that seeks to lead people to fraternal communion and mature faith'[126].

As a child, Carmen used to go through the Cathedral on her way to school and, at some point, she heard the Gospel of the miraculous catch of fish and, in some way, it spoke to her of a possible vocation (cf. Lk 5: 1-11). As she got older and expressed her desire to become a Christian missionary, her father objected and wanted her to study chemistry, which she did. Later, when she was old enough, she left home to join the *Missionaries of Jesus Christ*, but they did not allow her to continue with them[127]. Her rejection led to a freedom to 'go anywhere' and she met Kiko 'in the shanty

[126] James Francis Card. Stafford, 29th June, 2002, "Decree of the Pontifical Council for the Laity: Approval of the Statutes of Neocatechumenal Way 'Ad Experimentum'".

[127] Maria José Atienza (https://omnesmag.com/en/author/mjose/)-December 4, 2022, "The life of Carmen Hernández represents the history of the Church in the 20th century": https://omnesmag.com/en/focus/biographer-carmen-hernandez/.

towns of Palomeras Altas, near Madrid (Spain)' and, together, they co-founded a Way of adult formation in the Christian faith[128].

Around fifteen years after beginning this missionary work with Kiko, Carmen started a diary, the first entry of which is in January 1979[129]. Thus, although this is a diary entry, it is in the context of now accompanying and being accompanied by her fellow catechist, Kiko Argüello, and sharing the work of giving catecheses with Fr. Mario Pezzi and others. The late Fr. Ian Ker, the great Newman scholar, spoke of the Holy Spirit raising up Charismatic movements which are complementary to the hierarchical Church[130].

My concern here, however, is with her suffering: that even if she is in the forefront of a post or pre-baptismal way of formation, drawing on the *Second Vatican Council's* work, including reflection on and recovery of the early catechumenate of the Church, she is full of angst about what is happening. And so, referring to her earlier life, she says of it: 'Then I was happy, today I'm sad.' But the entry continues and ends by addressing Christ: 'Come, visit me, visit your land. I love you'[131]. In other words, it is her relationship to Christ which sustains her 52-year collaboration with Kiko which, as she says in her diary, was at times helpful, inspirational and unbearable. Along with her smoking, inability to speak, at times, and the constant call to listen to others, she is always calling on Christ to help her.

Owing to the generosity of God, my wife and I were able to visit the tomb of Carmen, in Madrid, and to ask for her intercession; indeed, for so

---

[128] "WHAT IS THE NEOCATECHUMENAL WAY?" Website: https://neo-catechumenaleiter.org/en/history/.

[129] *Carmen Hernández: Diaries, 1979-1981*, translated by Pablo and Debora Martinez et al, Gondolin Press: 1915 Aster Rd, 60178 Sycamore IL, USA, 2022, p. 21,

[130] Cf. Fr. Ian Ker, "The New Ecclesial Movements": http://www.ccr.org.uk/old/archive/gn1109/g07.htm.

[131] Carmen, *Diaries*, 1979 -1981, p. 45.

many intentions it is probably impossible to know the outcome except that, in general, a prayer is never wasted! Perhaps the easiest prayer to remember is simply gratitude, in thanksgiving for so much good that has come to me, my wife and family, through the *Neocatechumenal Way*.

An episode from my own life (1956-)

As the first two examples are from the lives of religious, my third example is from my own life as a married man, given that most people want to marry, do marry, and probably hope to remain married.

To begin with, I could not marry and went through several relationships, discovering as I went, that although I periodically went to the Catholic Church, I had no faith: Marriage was, to me, an inescapable suffering and it was an impossibility for me to enter. I imagined marriage like a lobster pot: it is easy to get in but impossible to get out. At forty, then, after yet another failed relationship, I was on my own with three possibilities: going mad; going further into sin; committing suicide. As it happened, by now I had started reading the *Catechism of the Catholic Church* (CCC) as, after many failed courses, I was completing a degree in theology; and, suddenly, I read that if God can create all that exists out of nothing, He can make a new beginning for the sinner – me! (CCC, 298).

So what changed? Everything! I married and we began a family which has, thank God, continued for 26 years with 8 children with us and 2 in heaven. But, when we married, I was working as a laundry labourer, earning 3. 50 pence an hour, my wife was a library assistant, and we lived in the basement flat of my parent's house.

I recall, then, a time of crisis beyond that of having pneumonia, clots on my legs and lungs, unemployment, temporary work and little money above our daily needs. At the time of this particular crisis there were now four children already, with a fifth on the way. I was exhausted as a result of underlying illnesses and deficiencies, trying to complete yet another post-graduate course, find work, and overwhelmed with the impossibility of ever being able to have a home of our own. Thus I lay on the floor, unable to cry, but cried out to God. What happened? My mother decided to sell her house in a year's time, but it was sold one month later. Unable to come to terms with it, I reluctantly packed, along with the help of our Church Community and we moved, three times, the last time of which we ended up in our current, Council House, and have lived in it since the birth of our fifth child, some twenty years ago!

The relationship between generations, as we have seen, traverses time and draws, notably, on Mary, the Mother of God and Mother of all Christians[132], who both listens to Christ and to us.

What, then, can inform our lives when it comes to the transmission of faith both in the family and beyond?

Pope Francis speaks of a '*rupture*' in the transmission of faith; and, therefore, a need of the family, but not the family alone, to bridge that rupture between the generations[133].

Mary 'opened her heart to God's plan. She reminds us of the first and greatest of the commandments: "Hear, O Israel" (*Deut* 6:4), because more important than any precept is our need to enter into a relation-

---

[132] Cf. Documents of the *Second Vatican Council*, such as *Dei Verbum*, on the Word of God, *Lumen Gentium* on the Church, *Gaudium et Spes* on the times in which we live, all of which draws on the Church's ecumenical journey, tradition, the mystery of Christ and the Scriptures.

[133] "Audience with participants in the Plenary of the Dicastery for Evangelization - Section for Fundamental Questions regarding Evangelization in the World, 15.03.2024": https://press.vatican.va/content/salastampa/en/bollettino/pubblico/2024/03/15/240315a.html.

ship with God by accepting the gift of the love that he comes to bring us[134].

In the book of Deuteronomy, having brought them out of Egypt and a life of suffering-slavery and misery to the point of death, God says to His people, three times: 'Listen Israel' (Dt 5: 1; 6: 3; and 6: 4-5). In other words, listening to the word of God is a priority – *if not the priority!* For the word of God both illuminates who Christ is[135] and who we are. Indeed, it is God who opens our 'ear' (cf. Is 50: 5). As, then, I have read the first volume of the diaries of Carmen Hernández, I realize that so much of the work which she and others did is to listen with discernment as to whether the lives of brothers and sisters in the communities are being illuminated by the word of God: 'Listening to everyone consoles me'[136]. So maybe this Way can be understood as a fulfilment of a word from Isaiah: the 'Lord God has opened my ear' (Is 50: 5); and, therefore, on this path, we are called to listen to God and to each other.

And, therefore, a fruit of our own formation in the Catholic Christian Faith is to persevere in the passing of it to our children, and to others; however, in terms of passing it to our children, a father of six says: 'a call to love over "the long haul"; to guard, reveal, and communicate love in the hurly-burly of family life and in the midst of a profoundly confused

---

[134] *Address of His Holiness Pope Francis to the Roman Curia for the Exchange of Christmas Greetings,* 21st December, 2023: https://www.vatican.va/content/francesco/en/speeches/2023/december/documents/20231221-curia-romana.html.

[135] *Dei Verbum,* 25: St. Jerome, "Ignorance of Scripture is ignorance of Christ"; and, therefore, ignorance of Christ is ignorance of ourselves.

[136] Carmen, *Diaries,* 1979-1981, p. 28, entry 22, etc. etc.

society. This task demands of all parents heroic effort and confidence in Divine Providence'[137].

The suffering we experience

Statistics, while helpful, can only take us so far – but what, even so, can they indicate? One tentative conclusion that tends to arise is that just as women in Japan seem less likely to die alone, because they are more socially integrated, so there are dramatically fewer women in English and American prisons. As regards men who are in prison for offences against women, would it help if there was a long-term, systematic review of family relationships, beginning with parents, siblings and then those nearer to home, as it were, in terms of wives or girlfriends?[138] Conversely, how does it help these men and women if men are allowed to call themselves women and be allocated cells in the same block or prison? Does that mean that they would avoid addressing the reasons that they are in prison? What is more, given that this is already happening in schools[139], is it not more likely that this will be exploited? At the same time, as noted below, there is a billowing need of help to pregnant women and, as we have seen, transgenderism is clearly robbing resources from those who need it most.

On the one hand, does the socialization of women favour a more open and expressive culture than that of men; and, therefore, while not freeing them from all difficulty, yet have they a contribution to make to the problems that men face in relating to each other and to women themselves? On the other hand, why are there so many women seeking help while pregnant

---

[137] Michael D. O'Brien, *The Family and the New Totalitarianism*, Wiseblood Books-Divine Providence Press, 2019, p. 26.

[138] This thought arose out a conversation with one of my daughters, as regards the incidence of certain types of male crime (23rd September, 2024).

[139] Anderson, *When Harry Became Sally: Responding to the Transgender Moment*, pp. 178-190

which, in one sense, is good in that pregnant women are admitting the need for help; but then, there is also the question of why: Is there less "connect" between first time mothers and their own mothers and others? Does motherhood raise serious questions about wellbeing and the meaning of suffering in a person's life? Are there other reasons?

'A record 57,000 new and expectant mothers received specialist support for mental health problems in 2023, according to NHS England.' One wonders if there is a need for *love* and *community* that the young, expectant mother, is in the process of discovering, especially if broken families, marriages and other social problems make the new situation overwhelming[140].

"There needs to be more joint working between clinicians so that issues are spotted earlier, better training – and the time to undertake such training – and specialist midwives to meet the increasingly complex needs of these women and families. Mental ill-health ranks with physical factors as one of the leading causes of maternal deaths in the UK, and yet this is not reflected in the resources allocated to it"[141].

Why is there poor care health care for women?[142] Is it a symptom of a heath service that advances contraceptives and aborts lots of children

---

[140] Abigail Boeser (https://www.hprweb.com/author/abigail-boeser/), December 30th, 204, "Meeting at the Well: Relational Pro-Life Ministry in the Post-Roe Era": https://www.hprweb.com/2024/12/meeting-at-the-well/#comments.

[141] There is no intended disregarded for the emphasis of the article on the neglected care of black women; but, in view of the general statistics, there is clearly a crisis about the needs of pregnant women. Why? Tobi Thomas, 6th of May, 2024, "Black mothers twice as likely as white mothers to be hospitalised with perinatal mental illness": https://www.theguardian.com/world/article/2024/may/06/black-mothers-twice-likely-white-hospitalised-perinatal-mental-illness.

[142] Tobi Thomas, 11th December, 2024, "'Medical misogyny' condemns women to years of gynaecological pain, MPs told":

and even challenges a doctor who wants to reverse the abortion pill and help women and children?

Coming back, then, to the theme of the intelligibility of suffering, on the one hand there is the possibility that we will not understand all we want to, possibility because God calls us to humility and the mystery of entering the depths of suffering, like Christ, in which, almost, all we can do is cry out: *My God, my God, why have you forsaken me?* (cf. Mt 27: 47). And, in the depths of Christ's suffering and resurrection, we encounter the deepest mystery of all: the suffering of the innocents: of those aborted; of those who have lost their lives while children, on the edge of war and not a part of it, of those doing good and who are killed and, ultimately, of those martyred for the truth and for their Christian faith.

On the other hand, there are insights, as it were, that we can gain from the word of God which both help us to see that we share many sins with our generation and that, therefore, we are called to share, also, the hope of help we have received in this life and the possibility of eternal life to come. In the context, then, of Morning Prayer, parents can share how God has helped them with their sufferings, even before marriage, but certainly in marriage, so that the children experience both an opportunity to share their own trials but also to give substance to the hope that Christ comes to help marriage and family life (cf. Jn 2: 1-12). Thus re-founding the vocation to Christian marriage on the Christian life.

In a word, if diverse people in different states of the Christian life experience sufferings which cause them to cry out, like Christ. How much more do young people need to be drawn into this Christian heritage and to rediscover what helps a person to persevere, to be able to offer a word of hope for our children, and to awaken us all to the horizon of eternal life.

---

https://www.theguardian.com/society/2024/dec/11/medical-misogyny-condemns-women-to-years-of-gynaecological-pain-mps-told.

So, taking account of the ancient wisdom of the Church, maybe the adage, to Christ through Mary is more relevant than we realise![143]

---

[143] Cf. Fr. Donald Calloway's autobiography, *No Turning Back: A Witness to Mercy*, Stockbridge, MA: Marian Press, 2020.

A Prayer for Palliative Care and Hospice Staff: "A Soft Singing"

We live in a time of unprincipled death, death being caused by being aborted, determining by tests the death of the disabled, the death of girls, the death of those with mental health issues, the death of young people indeed, almost, the death of anyone who is unfortunate enough to experience a suffering, in a country, where the answer is the deliberate cause of that person's death.

But how we die can be a sign of how we have lived the life of our relationships.

The dying of my diabetic father, then, owing to an unforeseen bleeding through his bones was, by contrast, not a deliberate bringing about of his death; and, similarly, my eighty plus year old mother dying, step by step, as her mobility and health was sliced away by her cancer – but again was not a deliberate death even if the medicine for helping her breath had a foreseeable but unintended consequence of shortening her life. In the case of my father, we were warned that, unexpectedly, he was bleeding to death in the course of a back operation; and, therefore, those of my parent's adult seven children who could make it, were there along with my mother, praying an "Our Father" together, and any number of other, silent prayers.

Thus these deaths, and others too, were profoundly lived, in a certain sense sudden in that there does come a point when all the measures are zero, in contrast to what is claimed as "brain death" which, as controversial as it is, is far less clearly a death of the whole person[1]. While the possibilities

---

[1] Etheredge, *Reaching for the Resurrection: A Pastoral Bioethics.*

were there that death would take one of my parents, unexpectedly, as one of my grandfathers died going to buy a paper dropped dead on the street, the event of death can still come slowly, even stealthily, depending on the underlying health problems that exist – but even then there is still the shock of death: of the event of a person, suddenly, no longer living!

So whether the death is expected, owing to illness, or sudden, owing to unexpected events, there is still the shock of loss and the gnawing grief of "if only"; but, in fact, the event of death is beyond, the event of actually passing from this life is "out of our reach" and takes us beyond our human capabilities, calling us to pray as the only way to accompany a person's passing through death.

In what follows, there could be more acknowledgement of all those un-named helpers who sweep the floor, do the medicine rounds, check the equipment, monitor how we are, pass by on their rounds, bring the tea and juice, the meals, check on us and keep abreast of who is visiting who and who needs help – but, nevertheless, there are many kinds of everyday good being done as I know from the numerous times I have been in hospital myself!

"A Soft Singing"

As I sat beside my mother, Lord, the late hours went to midnight
And her breathing was more and more laboured, slow, and a kind
Of rattling that made me think, more and more, she does not have
Long to live and, as the ward was quiet and there were few awake,
I remembered that the last of the senses to go was hearing and so
I sang the psalms from the prayer book, softly, hoping her heart
Was still open to the meaning and melody of the comfort in words.

As my thoughts turned to my wife and children I left and drove

Home, hoping to return in the morning and praying for the final
Hours to pass peacefully, even if her breathing was a new labour
Unto eternal life, leading like birth pangs, not without my heart
Touched, keenly, by the help she needed to be comfortable but
Not hastened to the door and so the doctor prescribed what was
Needed and, as I drove and prayed, Lord, it was dark and silent.

As day dawned, my Lord, and the family got organized and then
I left for the ward, so dark and quiet the night before, I panicked
Over parking and had to pay and delay before I could visit again.

Meanwhile, in those few minutes, my mother died to the sound of
Two of my sisters reading psalms aloud to her, making me think of
Mary, the Mother of the Word, being present as I arrived and cried.

How many were the hours, Mary, from her decline from a busy, Eighty-
year-old mum and bicycle, as my father went ahead and the
House my wife and I had founded our family in, went from big to
Smaller, from hosting teas for us on a Friday evening to bearing
With our noisy visits and the comings and goings of all our eight
Children, drifting in and out of the garden, playing, not noticing
The faltering step, the long-time sitting, the falls and final leaving.

Oh Mary, can one life speak to all as each of us dies in unforeseen Ways,
with or without our family around and the help we need?
But then what is the death of your Son if not the humble entrance
To the mystery of suffering and suffering with, patient and painful
As it is, yet great and majestic in the eyes of God who suffers with
Us by being with all who pass, silently or struggling, into the open,

Eternal heart, that throbbed a last beat, and the last drop of blood And
water that fell and blessed the earth from which we depart.

Oh Joseph, how many pass, alone, unnoticed, and need but another
To be there, whether speaking or singing, whether silent or holding
A hand, whether family or from the family of man, standing in as You
did as the father of the Son of God, whether as brother, uncle,
Neighbour, or those whose care it is to take us through the last days
Of our life, nurturing not just the passing of time and enabling the Peace,
but preparing us for the abrupt departure to everlasting love.

Oh Holy Family, call together all those who will, when others leave,
Or cannot stay and are called away, who will stay and bear the loss, And
share the grief of parting and, through praying, begin the rejoicing as yet
another, we hope, has entered the Holy of Holies where the great and unimaginable beauty, of the being of God, dwells as an everlasting fountain
of health to share with all who come to be in the presence of the Blessed
Trinity, now and forever.

Chapter Two
The Cultural Context of Being Single

As we saw in the first chapter, there are already many factors which constitute a kaleidoscopic impression of both what is going on in our society and the challenges of the transmission of faith and indeed of the obstacles to persevering in the Catholic Faith. But these are not just obstacles to persevering in the Catholic Faith, these are obstacles to developing through life's challenges; and, if a person is not grounded in an intelligent understanding of human nature and life, then how much more are they susceptible to being misled and going down a dangerously brutal dead end.

So what are the first principles, as it were, of a rational and Christian understanding of the human person? Into what setting, while still imperfect and challenged by sin, does the person come to exist and, hopefully, flourish? We have already touched upon a number of challenges to young people generally, but what does all this tell us about how deep we need to go to find help? And what about that help that comes from above?

The starting point of dignity

(*Dignitas infinita*) Every human person possesses an infinite dignity, inalienably grounded in his or her very being, which prevails in and beyond every circumstance, state, or situation the person may ever encounter. This principle, which is fully recognizable even by reason alone, underlies the primacy of the human person and the protection of human rights. In the light of Revelation, the Church resolutely reiterates and confirms the ontological dignity of the human person, created in the image and likeness of God and redeemed in Jesus Christ. From this truth, the Church draws the reasons for her commitment to the weak and those less endowed with power, always insisting on "the

primacy of the human person and the defense of his or her dignity beyond every circumstance"[1].

Similarly, there is a dignity to truth, whether biblical or natural, in that
we do not invent either and both are a benefit to us, whether helping us to
"see" reality as a whole or "ourselves" as we are; and, therefore, just as imperfections in the Church and society call for renewal rather than 'rede-
signing"[2], retaining what is God-given, so we are called and persuaded to
return to the search for truth, which is indeed natural to the use of our very
reason[3]. Thus, as gifts are not given in isolation with one another, just as
soil and plants, seeds and growth make a whole, so seeking truth is not
separable from the love, the good we are called to do, from the human nature that is enlightened and developed through our human activity[4].

In terms of the possibility of vocations, whether to the priesthood, the
religious life or to marriage, it seems likely that if the well-founded religious life of a Catholic family orientates young men to the possibility of
the priesthood then it does so to other vocations too. In America it was
found that 'The data shows that families continue to be the seedbed of religious vocations: of the 392 respondents, 95% were raised by their biological parents, and 88% were raised by a married couple who lived together'[5].

---

[1] Declaration *"Dignitas Infinita"*, on "Human Dignity", Presentation: paragraph 1: https://press.vatican.va/content/salastampa/it/bollettino/pubblico/2024/
04/08/0284/00588.html#en.

[2] Ryan Patrick Budd, April 14th, 2024, "Truth in Crisis": https://theimagina-
tiveconservative.org/2024/04/truth-crisis-ryan-patrick-budd.html.

[3] *Dignitatis Humanae*, 1-3: https://www.vatican.va/archive/hist_coun-
cils/ii_vatican_council/documents/vat-ii_decl_19651207_dignitatis-huma-
nae_en.html.

[4] Cf. St. John Paul II, *Veritatis Splendor*.

[5] April 15th, 2024, "New Survey of Men Being Ordained to the Priesthood Un-
derscores the Significant Influence of Parents on Children's Vocational

Nevertheless, the power of God being what it is, vocations can come from the unlikeliest ground and almost literally, overnight; and, therefore, one young man entered the priesthood after dedicating his life to stealing, drugs, and girls, although it was a slow process as he had to make up for the education that he missed[6].

If, then, families are the 'seedbed' of religious vocations then it is likely, also, that the same family orientates the male and female children to the variety of vocations which exist. At the same time, while individual Catholic families may seem to exist and dispose their children to the vocations of the Church, including marriage, in general families themselves need to be part of a Christian milieu, whether it is the 50,000 pro-life people on the streets in Warsaw, Poland[7], or all the different ways that cultures encourage what is good in the family and the Church while, however, not being blind to what needs to change, to be reformed or to be rejected. Having said that, however, my own married life did not begin until 40 owing to a wandering life-style, serial girl-friends and a general disorientation about what my life was about; but, even in view of that, what made marriage possible was the word of God which said: if God can make everything out of nothing (CCC, 298[8]), He can make a new beginning for the sinner. He did. And that sinner was me.

There is, too, a dignity to love. On the one hand love is used indiscriminately to mean anything from I love the wonders of nature, these shoes,

---

Discernment":   https://www.usccb.org/news/2024/new-survey-men-being-ordained-priesthood-underscores-significant-influence-parents.

[6] Cf. Donald Calloway, *No Turning Back: A Witness to Mercy*.

[7] April 15th, 2024, "Wow 50,000 Join Poland's March for Life Defending the Unborn as the Government Debates Abortion Legalization - VIDEO - #ProLiife": https://www.catholicnewsworld.com/2024/04/wow-50000-join-polands-march-for-life.html.

[8] *Catechism of the Catholic Church*, and the numerals refer to the paragraph number.

this song, my home, and my wife; but, on the other hand, it has the more specific meaning, according to St. Thoams Aquinas, of doing what is good for the 'other'. In other words, there is an intimation, in all this, that love is an action, entailing that whatever is done is actually for the good of the other, where good is understood objectively and is not just an excuse to what we like and to call it good. But, as we have seen from our list, while love is a positive action according to the good nature of what is being loved, there is a sense in which love is also an attitude: that *love is both uncondi-tional* and *wholesome*. So, while it may seem extravagant to say so, love may well express the providential love of God for all of us: a love that ex-tends to all that God has created and which is either good or very good; and, therefore, human love, perfected through being suffused with divine love, has this characteristic of involving everything we do and everyone we are with. Thus, again, the dignity of love derives from the Creator from whom it proceeds, whether as a divine or a human gift or as a divine gift that permeates the human gift.

A brief account of the possibility of a vocation

Being single, however, brings with it the exciting, if sometimes daunt-ing prospect of what talents we possess, what vocation is given to us and with whom to share our lives, whether in friendship, religious community, or marriage. What emerges, then, besides what we have discussed so far, are those moments when our lives seem to open upon a new perception that both shows our current reality is in a way emptying of meaning and another possibility is simultaneously showing through.

Consider, then, the following testimony from a woman called Molly who was working in the business world but had begun to attend a bible study group and, increasingly, discovered a discrepancy between growing in her Christian Faith and her daily work, to the point where she decided to leave her work and pursue further studies in her faith.

"'I didn't really see a future with the company I was working for," she admitted. "So I was just at a place of real openness with the Lord, and I asked. What do I do here? What do I want to do next?"

In that moment of contemplation, God compelled Molly to reflect deeply on her encounters with the Dominican Friars in her parish and the knowledge she was acquiring regularly in Bible study'[9].

Now, it does not follow that this discrepancy between what we are doing and the call of God is so easily resolved, and indeed the reality may be more complicated even for Molly. But in my case, after much stopping and starting of different courses, the remembrance of enjoying the discussion of religious questions began to shine through, like a diamond in the mud, and so I began to study theology in my mid-thirties. However, even as I enjoyed the course and started making progress with it, so I failed the moral theology module, the module about what is good and right and wrong and disordered, so it again became clear to me that understanding the Catholic Faith is not identical to living it: living more clearly would come into its own when I returned to the *Neocatechumenal Way.*

So, having begun in a rather general way, it is each person who is being addressed by God and the prevailing challenges, as it were, that assail each one of us in the course of growing up, whether we have quite grasped that many others are going through or being "touched" by what has impacted on us, or not.

---

[9] Very Rev. Thomas Petri, O.P., April 29th, 2024, "A Journey in Theology and Illumination": https://dhs.edu/a-journey-in-theology-and-illumination/.

So what are some of the basic question with which we have to contend?

There is not one answer, as it were, to what comprises the culture out
of which many people come, emerge, are engaged with or otherwise are
simply immersed in; but, nevertheless, it is good to visit a range of what
ideas colour this generation's perception.

'In this generation "Z" 'many are turning to astrology and neo-pagan-
ism, and/or binding themselves to increasingly tribal social causes that
effectively become their very identities. Christianity seems a thing of
the past; indeed, many of their older siblings and parents are decon-
structing from their Christian upbringings, an emerging trend on Tik-
Tok and Instagram[10].

'In the classroom, de Lubac's thesis [that there is a natural desire for the
'God of Jesus Christ'] inspires me to trust that, in spite of what they
may think, students *want* to hear the Gospel; they desire to know and
love God. I … mean [that] this principle extends to all: the video-gam-
ers, the theater kids [drugged on drama[11]], the athletes, those in a gender identity crisis, the rich, the poor, the devotees of other religious traditions, the burned-out Catholic school kids who want anything but
another "religion" class, and so on. Each of these unique and unrepeatable students wants a relationship with God, whether they are con-
sciously aware of it or not. Indeed, in de Lubac's view, they are already

[10] Dr. Sarah Hulse Kirby, April 26th, 2024, "Teaching Theology to Gen Z:
Three Lessons from Henry de Lubac": https://www.hprweb.com/2024/04/teach-
ing-theology-to-gen-z/.
[11] Cf. "theatre kid": https://www.urbandictionary.com/define.php?term= the-
atre%20kid. The summary 'drugged on drama' is my own.

constitutively related to the God of Jesus Christ, in whom each of them was created, regardless of their conscious likes and dislikes'[12].

To those, very often, who felt religion was 'imposed' there is the answer of the 'proposal' of the mystery of the Blessed Trinity: of the realization that the mystery of God being the 'unity-in-diversity' answers more abundantly the intimations of reality being more than all is 'material' or that there is no 'other' only that all that exists is God[13].

At the same time, there is a kind of apocalyptic activism: 'that When it comes to environmental, economic, or social issues, today's youth are far more likely to identify with a cause and to seek to act on it—perhaps in drastic ways that can look like alarmism or overreaction'[14].

On the one hand, it is good for young people to seize their opportunities to take the need for action forward, to draw attention to what needs to be done to protect the environment; but then, by contrast, there seems to be a simplistic absence of the priority of the person: that all that matters is the obvious protest rather than understanding that each person who "appears" to be connected with an issue is not necessarily as directly responsible as we think or indeed understands the reality of what is happening. An abortion, for example, is notoriously "politicized" when, in reality, it is the tragic death, in often regrettable circumstances, of an innocent child;

---

[12] Dr. Sarah Hulse Kirby, April 26th, 2024, "Teaching Theology to Gen Z: Three Lessons from Henry de Lubac".

[13] Dr. Sarah Hulse Kirby, April 26th, 2024, "Teaching Theology to Gen Z: Three Lessons from Henry de Lubac".

[14] Benjamin Vincent, May 6th, 2024, "Goodbye Postmodernism, Hello Metamodernism: Our apologetics must evolve to engage with the new cultural mood of the next generations": https://www.christianitytoday.com/ct/2024/april-web-only/what-is-metamodernism-postmodernism-dead-next-gen-z-alpha.html.

and, just as this child was innocent, so are many more who are subject to the atrocities of war, trafficking or abuse.

In other words, there is also a call to recognize reality, as one author once said, as the first step in the process of conversion to the truth.

Conflicts in society

We live in a society which is increasingly struggling to debate what is going on without it becoming vitriolic, violent, weaponizing the law, discouraging informed debate and reasonable assessment of policies, principles, facts, ideas or even procedures. As we see from the escalation of many conflicts throughout the world, there is both a rise in armed conflicts and in the use of violence and intimidation when it comes to people advancing their point of view. In general, then, our times have become increasingly incapable of addressing contentious conflicts equitably, whether in the actual conflict itself or in the public debate and protests with respect to these conflicts. However, these conflicts spread very quickly to those not directly involved owing to a person's race or religion. Similarly, the suppression of political dissent, women's rights and, indeed, territorial rights, has increasingly taken on a violence that risks an escalation of escalating violence.

What impact, then, does all this have on the internal dynamics of marriage, family life and the prospects of our young people? Does it follow that if quasi-claimed rights, rights without a philosophical expression, can turn into laws, that this is going to escalate conflicts within families, between families and schools, between institutions in society and the members of that society? Then let the social evidence of these increasingly varied conflicts speak for itself! In other words, as Professor Cass has experienced, she has come to be personally vilified for pursuing, as best she can, the investigation of what will help young people who present as disorientated about their gender[15].

Whereas the social media has come under increasing scrutiny owing to the rise of young people's mental health problems, with a lack of face-to-face time or outdoor activities, poor sleep owing to more on-line time, day and night, being unable to follow a line of thought without being derailed by social media messages, all of which ultimately leads to dopamine type addictions: of needing that constant click on what is next[16]. What is more, what about the ability to think critically in response to what these young people are viewing or listening to or doing? Clearly, then, there is a lot of accumulating evidence that these young people seem unable to critically evaluate or access the debate constructively; indeed, if clinicians cannot do so in a relatively objective manner, what hope is there for those who are subject to debateable medical judgements?[17]. Is this a part of the problems of our times? Clinicians have been concerned that their ability to debate contentious or controversial treatments has been suppressed by the fear of this legitimate questioning of what has been passed off as self-evidently helpful use of puberty blockers, drugs that interfere with the natural

---

[15] Sammy Gecsoyler, 20th April, 2024, "Hilary Cass warned of threats to safety after 'vile' abuse over NHS gender services review": https://www.theguardian.com/society/2024/apr/20/doctor-hilary-cass-warned-of-threats-to-safety-after-vile-abuse-over-nhs-gender-services-review; and, again, Sarah Cain, 9th of May, 2024, " The Hidden Life of Hilary Cass": https://crusadergal.substack.com/p/the-hidden-life-of-hilary-cass.

[16] Cf. Heidt, *The Anxious Generation*, 2024, pp. 139-141 and the pages previously etc.

[17] Cf. Frederick Attenborough, May 25th, 2024, "The British Medical Journal (BMJ) has been accused of 'abandoning science' after it rejected research from top academics over their views on the trans debate": https://freespeechunion.org/top-academic-accuses-the-british-medical-journal-of-abandoning-science-after-rejecting-research-because-of-their-views-on-the-trans-debate/.

process of a young person's age-related maturation, being used against them in their professional lives[18].

In some countries, for example, Switzerland, 'Canada, USA, Australia' parents seeking help for their disorientated children can find that the state overreaches and puts them in care owing to the parents' reasonable objection to health altering treatments like puberty blockers and surgery. In Switzerland, a girl who is now 16, following on-line use during Covid-19, at 13, developed this gender confusion which her parents had sought help with[19].

As we will see in the course of this book, this is a specific example of what tends to happen more and more: "In 2021, following other mental health concerns, the then 13-year-old told her parents that she felt her "gender identity" was male. This happened following the COVID pandemic, when she had spent a significant amount of time alone in her room and online. But then the school and the Swiss authorities stepped in and the child is now in a government run home, regulating the visit of her parents, and all because they thought, rightly, that their daughter's best interest is not proceeding with dangerous puberty blockers and the mutilating operations that often follow[20].

---

[18] 21st April, 2024, "We are ashamed of the role psychology played in gender care": https://www.theguardian.com/theobserver/commentisfree/2024/apr/21/we-are-ashamed-of-role-psychology-played-gender-care-observer-letters.

[19] July 10th, 2024, "Swiss authorities take teen girl from family after parents refuse to endorse gender 'transition'": https://www.lifesitenews.com/news/swiss-authorities-take-teen-girl-from-family-after-parents-refuse-to-endorse-gender-transition/

[20] July 10th, 2024, "Swiss authorities take teen girl from family after parents refuse to endorse gender 'transition'".

The parents are continuing their legal battle to recover their daughter and, according to a subsequent report, 'This Swiss family is not the only one. In every jurisdiction that implements gender ideology, the state eventually comes to take children away from their parents – in Canada, the United States, and elsewhere'[21]. In America, a court upheld a school withholding from a parent a child's change of name to one of the opposite sex, claiming it did not impair the parent's ability to care for the child; however, the dissenting judge said, very clearly, '"Because accurate information in response to parents' inquiries about a child's expressed gender identity is imperative to the parents' ability to assist and guide their child, I conclude that a school's withholding of such information implicates the parents' fundamental right to raise and care for the child," she wrote'. And, what is more, in view of the gravity of what can happen to the health of a child, this is indeed information which is 'imperative to the parents' ability to assist and guide their child'[22].

By contrast, 'Cass suggested a different approach to treatment which would consider young people holistically – rather than solely focusing on distress related to gender'[23].

---

[21] Jonathon Van Maron, 1st October, 2024, "Swiss parents fight to reclaim teen daughter from state after refusing to enable 'sex change'": https://www.lifesitenews.com/blogs/swiss-parents-fight-to-reclaim-teen-daughter-from-state-after-refusing-to-enable-sex-change/.

[22] Stephen Kokx, Sat Aug 31, 2024, "New Hampshire Supreme Court sides with school district that hid student's gender confusion from mom": https://www.lifesitenews.com/news/new-hampshire-supreme-court-sides-with-school-district-that-hid-students-gender-confusion-from-mom/.

[23] Ella Rhodes, 19th, April, 2024, "'…young people caught in the middle of a stormy social discourse…'": https://www.bps.org.uk/psychologist/young-people-caught-middle-stormy-social-discourse.

Why it took the Cass Report to come to a common-sense conclusion about the need to carefully evaluate what brings a young person to question their gender, indicates how people are crippled by fear, the weaponizing of social media and the law. At the same time, although Cass says 'that there were few other areas of healthcare where professionals were so afraid to openly discuss their views'[24], she might or might not be referring to what happens to the debate about the rights of unborn children. As we see, both in America and the UK, there is an increasing public polarisation over the right to life of the unborn child, as if there is something intrinsically wrong with articulating and defending, not just the truth concerning human conception, the conception of each one of us, but the actual life of human beings. Similarly, what about the human right to be conceived within the human relationship of husband and wife, father and mother? Similarly with the advance of sex education programs which invade the lives of young children and, no doubt, contribute to their confusion and distress around these questions. Not to mention the debate about what marriage is and who can and who cannot enter into a valid marriage, where validity is not just about advancing an undefended or supposed right but is actually about explaining or investigating what constitutes marriage.

In general, then, the pursuit of truth, which includes but is more comprehensive than the claim for an evidence-based medicine, especially as it concerns the very premises on which research is founded or the influence of unexamined philosophical premises, such as it is possible to change a given sex, given that a human being is an indivisible whole and not "biological, psychological, and spiritual parts". Thus, while it is true that we need an evidence-based medicine, let us not forget that there is more to the investigation than the data collected, in that the investigator may well proceed on the basis of unexamined claims. In other words, what is the

---

[24] Ella Rhodes, 19th, April, (as above).

justification for thinking that a person is a divisible entity? Why is it claimed that psychological development is not an inward expression of biologically determined developmental processes? In other words, why is it unjustified to argue that human development is an integrated process of biological thresholds making possible the manifestation of interior, psychological developments?

Indeed, one of the constant refrains of those involved in helping people who are in the midst of these crises is the need to take account of the child or young person's psychological development; and, particularly, to be aware that 'teens fail to consider the long-term consequences of current decisions and are impulsive in decision making. Furthermore, most adolescents do not prioritize reproductive function at this stage of life'[25]. In other words, it is common sense to argue that this developmental instability, characteristic of this time, recommends itself as a reason for refraining from life-altering interventions.

Rather, it is better to advocate that each person is an unmitigated gift and, therefore, if this gift is not received with gratitude, then maybe that itself is an indicator of problematic elements in a person's psychological development[26]. In view, then, of the psychological considerations, it could be argued that there is a gross negligence concerning the educational needs of young people if there is no recognition of their developing psychological maturity.

---

[25] Paul Hruz, M.D. Ph.D., Chapter 2: "Care of People Who Have Been Exposed to "Gender Affirming" Medical Interventions', p. 25, and pp. 19-30 of *Gender Ideology and Pastoral Practice*, 2024.

[26] Cf. Etheredge, *The Human Person: A Bioethical Word*: https://enroutebooksandmedia.com/bioethicalword/; but, also, cf. Etheredge, *Mary and Bioethics: An Exploration*: https://enroutebooksandmedia.com/maryandbioethics/; and cf. Etheredge, *The Word in Your Heart: Mary, Youth, and Mental Health*: https://enroutebooksandmedia.com/wordinyourheart/.

We know, already, that there has been an erosion of the rights of fathers to witness to the life of their children and, where necessary, to rightly defend the life of their unborn child; and, therefore, there is already a trampling of the integrity of the family, rupturing the relationship between parents, even when the life of their child would, ordinarily, be what brings them together. So, similarly, with conflicts over genderism, there seems to be a tendency to selectively attribute "rights" to clinics over parents in order to advance a harmful agenda on the child when the child scarcely understands what is happening: 'The tactics of gender ideologues who aim to distance confused children from their parents are akin to those used in nasty custody disputes'[27]. All this raises the question of both the restoration of the rights of the family to its integrity and the rights of men to be fathers responsible for the welfare of their children. At the same time, it raises the question of why this haste to funnel children into a one-outcome program of life-changing drugs and operations?

And so, while there is a discordant note about masculinity, partly justified by actual behaviour but also entailing a kind of smear of what it is to be a man[28], there is nevertheless the real task of identifying what masculinity is about. According to Pope St. John Paul II, men are called in a particular way to the pursuit of truth, in love,

In 'an address to male students by Bishop Karol Wojtyla, later to become Pope John Paul II; he said that when Christ instructed the apostles to "make disciples of all nations" (Mt 28: 19): 'This means, "Go and teach," which in turn means that we must take responsibility for the

---

[27] Cf. ANDREA PICCIOTTI-BAYER: "Gender Ideology Is The New 'Parental Alienation'": https://dailycaller.com/2024/09/21/opinion-gender-ideology-the-new-parental-alienation-andrea-picciotti-bayer/.

[28] Cf. Chase Repogle, August 23rd, 2024, "The Gospel Coalition: "You Won't Find Manhood in the Shadows"": https://www.linkedin.com/pulse/you-wont-find-manhood-shadows-the-gospel-coalition-be1gf/

Gospel as Truth! In contemporary terms it means that, in accordance with our specific characteristics as men, we must take responsibility for the Gospel as *Weltanschauung* and idea' [29]. In other words, Karol Wojtyla was telling me to teach; and that, more specifically as a father, I am called to teach my children about God [30][31].

What does the Church contribute to all this if not the search for truth, the turn to God and prayer: daily prayer; world-wide prayer; prayer in the marriage and in family life and in every social situation imaginable – listen to the pope's appeal for prayer! To seek the help of God to overcome what is overcoming us! [32]

Freedom or career

Is a person a singular human being, to the point where there is almost no connection with others or is a person a being-in-relationship where, in actual fact, if there is no explicit relationship to others there is some kind of hidden, probably psychological defect that needs addressing? Or there is, as it were, simply running from the question of meaning. At the same time, there are two typical views on what being single actually means

[29] *The Way to Christ: Spiritual Exercises*, English Translation, Harper SanFrancisco, 1994, p.53.

[30] *The Way to Christ: Spiritual Exercises*, pp. 53-56.

[31] An excerpt from Etheredge, *Scripture: A Unique Word*, from Chapter Two, p. 108 of a prepublication version, but which is now published: https://www.cambridgescholars.com/product/978-1-4438-6044-4.

[32] There are so many calls for prayer by Pope Francis, almost at every opportunity, e.g. April 25th, 2024, "Pope Francis says "Pray for...the desire to build peace, to give the young generations a future of hope, not of war; a future of full cradles, not tombs; a world of fraternity..." to Pilgrims from Hungary": https://www.catholicnewsworld.com/2024/04/pope-francis-says-pray-forthe-desire-to.html.

which are, in themselves, half-truths that are taken as the whole truth of what a person is:

> the 'two types [are]: a male suspicious of marriage as nothing more than a ball and chain, and a female who prefers a career to marriage'. Moreover, it seems as if the following myths are crumbling: myths about being happy with a career, 'that family structure doesn't really matter' and that people prefer a 'soul-mate' to a stable marriage[33].

On the one hand, there is a false view of freedom which is to be free of every restraint, even the choice that expresses the equal value of a man and a woman: the choice of marriage. Perhaps, in the concrete, there is no greater evidence of equality than a marriage of one man and one woman. On the other hand, there is no objection to a woman's career; however, a woman is more than her career, just as a man is more than his work. Perhaps, then, men and women are unrealistic about how deeply fatherhood and motherhood exist in the human psyche. Thus the question: What is the more? As one woman athlete put it: 'My search for answers led me to reconsider not just my attitude to my body and to running, but to life itself. To finding meaning and purpose, to achievement and ageing and to that ultimate finish line, mortality'[34]. In other words, approaching the end, the 'finish line, mortality' perhaps can help us focus on life itself and what it is about. What is it about? For whom are we living? Whom have we loved? What have we done with our lives? While we know not everyone can have

---

[33] Chuck Chalberg, 9th of April, 2024, "Get Married! How American Families Can Save Civilization": https://theimaginativeconservative.org/2024/04/get-married-american-families-civilization-brad-wilcox-chuck-chalberg.htmll

[34] Sam Pyrah, 8th of May, 2024, "A moment that changed me: I thought fitness was my superpower. Then I realised it was a ball and chain": https://www.theguardian.com/lifeandstyle/article/2024/may/08/a-moment-that-changed-me-fitness-was-my-superpower-then-a-ball-and-chain.

children, there seems to be a growing choice not to have them. Anecdotally, couples often seem to be totally trim and running together, although some running together is done after children and is not successful for everyone[35], and one wonders if fitness training and living together has taken over from the possibility of family life and the loss of "free time, personal space, and the joint-single life-style" – with or without cats and dogs. Has the moral outrage at the cost of children, both in terms of money and to the environment, if there is one, taken people beyond the desire to be parents?[36] What about the cost of the joint-single lifestyle on the environment as against the breaking down of the limited availability of me to the point of being of service to others?

From the evidence of our time, we would think that there is more and more denial of our relationship to others, beginning with a denial of our relationship to the child in the womb, the person proposing to be euthanized, the person proposing suicide, the person who is either zipping themselves up in a body-bag and not communicating the reality of their life to others or others are zipping them up in a body-bag before they are either born or dead. In other words, while we live in a world community more than ever connected through immense, immersible media, almost to the point of witnessing the terrible tragedies that either emerge or are ongoing throughout the world, and yet more and more people are dying without discovering the meaning of their suffering: either suffocating themselves or being suffocated. We seem incapable of reasoning from

---

[35] Lily Canter, 4th January, 2018, "Why couples should never go running together": https://www.theguardian.com/lifeandstyle/the-running-blog/2018/jan/04/why-couples-should-never-go-running-together.

[36] Kathryn Bromwich, 30th March, 2024, "What is it about us dinks (dual income, no kids) that so many people dislike?": https://www.theguardian.com/commentisfree/2024/mar/30/what-is-it-about-us-dinks-dual-income-no-kids-so-many-people-dislike.

evidence and first principles, beginning with the reality that each one of us is given the gift of life[37].

Spoiling the gift of being

One of the pervading themes of our times, seems to be a dissatisfaction with our own reality, whether it be whether or not we are a man or a woman or talented or tall, or short, successful, rich, handsome or pretty; indeed, it seems that the possibilities of rejecting an aspect of our nature are many and multiple, as if there is a kind of viral rejection of what is given, where what is given is about accepting ourselves as a gift[38]. Where possible, then, some people alter their appearance with makeup, by photoshop on social media, some people pay for operations to alter what is, in so many ways, irrelevant in that it is not to correct a blemish or a defect so much as to enhance an appearance according to some abstract criteria of what we think a person needs to look like.

So, if an enemy wanted to spoil the gift of life, what would they do if not poison the very gift that has been given:

'so we pick out this natural pleasantness of change and twist it into a demand for absolute novelty'[39].

In other words, we cannot take away from the fact that a gift has been given, but someone can pull the petals off it, disfigure it, destroy it – but none of these actions, terrible as they are, can change the fact that a gift has

---

[37] Cf. Francis Etheredge, *Conception: An Icon of the Beginning*: https://enroutebooksandmedia.com/conception/; or Chapter 5 of *Mary and Bioethics: An Exploration*: https://enroutebooksandmedia.com/maryandbioethics/; or, finally, *Unfolding a Post-Roe World*: https://enroutebooksandmedia.com/post-roe/.

[38] Cf. C. S. Lewis, *The Screwtape Letters*, London: Fount Paperbacks, 1998.

[39] C. S. Lewis, *The Screwtape Letters*, London, p. 98.

been given. Maybe, then, we need to examine our dissatisfaction and see where it comes from because, if we are given existence as a gift, then why would the giver build in a dissatisfaction with the gift? It would be as if the giver has enclosed a note to the effect that this gift is not evidence of being loved by the giver. In other words, dissatisfaction has to have an origin other than the giver of the gift[40]. What attacks gratitude? Indeed what prevents gratitude taking root if not resentment?

> 'Whatever men expect they soon come to think they have a right to: the sense of disappointment can, with very little skill on our part, be turned into a sense of injury'[41].

Certainly, I can remember being grieved by my father paying me and my brother one pound after a summer's helping with alterations in the house; and, having dreamed of all the money we were going to get, and getting one pound, it was an impossible disappointment. Similarly, one present has stood out for me as almost unintelligibly irrelevant to who I was: a multiple penknife. A definition of a disappointing present that has stayed with me ever since and, almost between the two events, a kind of recoil against looking forward to anything, whether as a reward or a present. But does this explain the resentment that I experienced, even before this, towards helping my father with the building work; indeed, in retrospect, I would hardly call it helping as I was always climbing out of the garden to go and play football. In other words, already, there was planted in me a resentment that did not seem to have a justified origin, but which showed itself so powerfully that in my late teens I was asked to leave home.

---

[40] Cf. C. S. Lewis, *The Screwtape Letters*, London: the whole mentality of this book is so clear about how the slightest good or imperfection can be exaggerated and turned against the good of the person.

[41] C. S. Lewis, *The Screwtape Letters*, London, p. 118.

And, therefore, there is the question of what originated this inability to be helpful; indeed, to appreciate that the house improvements would benefit the whole family. What is more, why was it not possible to find the work enjoyable, interesting, even good from the point of view of working together with my father? In other words, resentment does not just arise; it has roots. What were its roots? What inspires resentment if not injustice? And what foments a sense of injustice if not a sense of being "wronged"?

At school, the punishment for failing end of year exams was the cane on the hand and, sometimes, on the backside; and, as I failed almost everything, repeatedly, I came in for a regular caning – either in front of the class or in the headmaster's office. To add insult to injury, as the saying goes, my father approved of the canings, presuming it was all my fault. In later years, and this took a long time to recognize, it struck me that there was a hidden justice in this situation in that I had already begun stealing, gambling and lying, none of which was discovered. In other words, while these injustices were the foundations of my resentments, the foundation of being reconciled to these injustices was beginning to see the sinful reality that I was already living as a child – but which, at the time, I did not recognize.

More widely, a sense of injustice can inspire justice; however, to dwell on the past injustice to the point of ignoring the present, is a contradiction. Therefore, even if it is true that there have been vast injustices to peoples and to specific behaviours, this does not justify everything in the present; and so, even if women have suffered terrible treatment in back street abortions, the women and children are entitled to help, not more abortions and their attendant risks. Similarly, with those who have been persecuted for being effeminate are entitled to acceptance, but that acceptance of a person does not justify everything that that person does. So discernment is necessary in our response to each other; but discernment does not mean endorsing everything done in the name of a past injustice. Injustice, I would say, is one of those "hooks" which catch people unwarily and somewhat disarms critical thinking. In other words, when 'gender ideology [is presented] as fact'[42] there is a clear indication of "group think" rather than being educated to think critically; and, as I say, if there is a "hook" it is to present emotional arguments which are intended to disarm those who object. Indeed, part of this uncritical thinking is to draw on a 'victim ideology'[43]: that a certain group is beyond criticism because they are the victims of society's prejudices. Thus foreclosing a critical evaluation of those who claim to be unjustly discriminated against; and, therefore, making it difficult to distinguish real-time prejudice from the ideological thinking expressed in a person's behaviour and thought.

Youth unhappiness, the media and relationships

As a young man, I was so frustrated with writing and rewriting, that I would end up pasting on corrections, literally cutting up the pages and resticking them, so that when I eventually sent off an article for publication, it was almost like cardboard[44]. My first degree was completed with largely handwritten essays. Having learnt to type before I dropped out of university, I had a typewriter and then a very small-screened computer. Eventually I was given a computer that "locked up" with all my written

---

[42] Hasson, Chapter 5: "The Impact of Gender Ideology", p. 93 of pp. 87-107 of *Gender Ideology and Pastoral Practice: A Handbook for Catholic Clergy, Counselors, and Ministerial Leaders*, 2024.

[43] Michael Bedar, January 15th, 2024, "How will we recover from the victimhood culture destroying our youth?": https://www.lifesitenews.com/opinion/how-will-we-recover-from-the-victimhood-culture-destroying-our-youth/.

[44] One of my first and only pieces to be accepted for this hard copy journal, "Communio: International Catholic Review", was accepted in this kind of format; it was called "A Reflection on the Language of the Body", Summer 1997, Volume 24: 2: https://www.communio-icr.com/articles/view/a-reflection-on-the-language-of-the-body.

coursework on it from further education; but, fortunately, one of my brothers is an IT expert and saved it all onto a more useable computer! The internet, both when employed and now self-employed, has enable a wonderful degree of correspondence across the world with many people whom it would have impossible to collaborate with, without the speed and dialogue that emails have made possible; and, therefore, there is no doubt about the ongoing use of this media being very positive, from a research and writing point of view.

Meanwhile, however, as I had no I-phone, or even any kind of phone, my meeting with people was almost always face to face and involved walks and coffee breaks! However, my moral life was in disarray and, therefore, lacking social media was not an obstacle to sin and, indeed, I first began to recognize what was morally wrong and it was only many years later that I saw it for what it was, namely, sin. And there were many unhappy years, throughout which the temptation to suicide was often very vivid.

Where are we now?

'The relationship of children, media, and education can be considered from two perspectives: the formation of children by the media; and the formation of children to respond appropriately to the media. A kind of reciprocity emerges which points to the responsibilities of the media as an industry and to the need for active and critical participation of readers, viewers and listeners. Within this framework, training in the proper use of the media is essential for the cultural, moral and spiritual development of children'[45].

---

[45] Pope Benedict XVI, 20th May, 2007, *Message of the Holy Father Benedict XVI for the 41st World Communications Day.* "Children and the Media: A Challenge for Education": https://www.vatican.va/content/benedict-xvi/en/messages/communications/documents/hf_ben-xvi_mes_20070124_41st-world-

In America, now, there is a national state of emergency around children's health: there are 50,000 suicides a year and 100,000 overdoses. In a 2022 national survey on drug use and health, 1 in 5 children, aged 12-17, had a major depressive episode in the last year, and nearly half of 18–25-year-olds had either a substance abuse disorder or a mental illness. All of which has risen immensely in the last 20 years[46]. But, also, to put this into a broader context, it is estimated that 21% of adult Americans 'experience mental illness'[47].

While it seems that unhappiness, the media and relationships are unconnected, the more I study what is being learnt about them the clearer it becomes that there is an unfolding set of influences where one impacts or exacerbates the other. By way of an overview, and I presume these statistics are from America as it was an American doctor and religious who reported them: 95% of teens are on social media; a third say that they are on it continuously; and one in three use it beyond midnight. Teens, it seems, who use it more than 3 hrs a day double the risk of depression and anxiety. Babies are interacting with electronic media at 2-3 months of age, by the age of 1 they are using these devices and playing games. Apparently, according to neural studies, the more there is a use of screens the less developed is the white matter is and the more it is disorganized.

---

communications-
day.html#:~:text=The%20theme%20of%20the%20Forty,the%20for-
mation%20of%20the%20media.

[46] "ITEST Webinar How Does Social Media Affect Children (April 13, 2024)" with Sr. Marysia Weber, RSM, and Dr. Kevin Powell: https://faithscience.org/children-and-social-media/. These American statistics are from Dr. Kevin Powell's presentation (who is a Lutheran), "How Social Media Affects Children".

[47] Tara Hunt McMullen, "What would you fight for? Fighting to combat America's Mental Health Crisis": https://fightingfor.nd.edu/2024/fighting-to-combat-americas-mental-health-crisis/.

In terms of behaviour, then, the more screens are used, the later a child talks, with limited and poor face to face conversation, poor writing skills, plus the feeling of being bored and isolated with books, poor tolerance of frustration and the navigation of conflict, plus phones end up competing with attending to the teacher, sleep deprivation and the rise of sex-related topics, bringing down the average contact with pornography from 14 years to 5, with 10% of all porn viewers being under 10 years of age. In a word, the hyper-stimulation of the limited senses of sight and sound, coupled with systems which "appear" interactive and ever changing, results in the over-production of dopamine in the brain and the beginning of on-line addictions[48].

By contrast, even a woman who was brought up a Lutheran, dropped out of college owing to heavy drinking, reckless living, promiscuity, and was recruited and worked pornographically for ten years, in response to a tragedy in her life started to pray. She ended up going into Catholic Church upon Catholic Church, seeking out Mary and discovering, in a sense, that Mary and St. Clare of Assisi were seeking her out, so she left what she was doing and began a *Rosary Bead* business, reflecting constantly on her gratitude to God and that her natural talent for jewellery design allows her to celebrate that beauty so beautiful that she found calling her into Catholicism.

As she says: 'I really felt like Mary was calling me. Each time I entered a church, I felt compelled to seek her out. I wanted to greet her and ask her to help me with the effects of the tragedy that had previously occurred in my life'[49].

---

[48] These two paragraphs are from Sr. Marysia Weber's contribution (who is a Catholic), called "Screen Addiction: Why You Can't Put Your Phone Down".

[49] Madalaine Elhabbal (https://catholicvote.org/author/madalaine-elhabbal/) on April 26, 2024, "How the Virgin Mary, St Clare of Assisi, and Italian

Through her experience with social media she says: 'If you're struggling, rely on your church community. Get involved in women's groups or a Bible study. Don't focus your life so much or on your online presence. Especially young women, realize that maybe 10 percent of what you see on Instagram or TikTok is real. Every image you see is an exaggeration or a filter or a green screen. Live your life comparing yourself to who you were yesterday, not to other females.
Go to Mass often and stay away from your screens. Face-to-face interactions have so much more value and are more fulfilling'[50].

As regards the deliberate design of the social media, read the following: a screenshot 'of an internal Facebook presentation, brought out by Frances Haugen' [a Facebook whistleblower], the 'caption says, "Teens' decisions and behavior are mainly driven by emotion, the intrigue of novelty and reward. While these all seem positive, they make teens very vulnerable at the elevated levels they operate on. Especially in the absence of a mature frontal cortex to help impose limits on the indulgence in these"'[51]. In other words, there is a deliberate design of these social media sites to keep teens '"engaged for longer with rewards, novelty, and emotions'[52].

A growing unhappiness has been identified in young people, with these consequences: 'When happiness wanes, so does motivation, productivity, health and life expectancy.' Among the many factors are student

architecture brought about the conversion of 'Mistress B'": (https://catholicvote.org/mistress-b-conversion-story-virgin-mary-italy-clare-assisi/).
[50] Elhabbal (https://catholicvote.org/author/madalaine-elhabbal/) on April 26, 2024, "How the Virgin Mary, St Clare of Assisi, and Italian architecture brought about the conversion of 'Mistress B'".
[51] Haidt, *The Anxious Generation*, 2024, p. 134, text from 'Figure 5.4.'
[52] Haidt, *The Anxious Generation*, 2024, p. 133.

debt, joblessness, climate change and environmental problems, the
contrast between 'increased social media' use and loneliness, and the
polarization of political conflicts. In other words, what one might call
the natural propensity of youth to be 'beacons of optimism'[53] are in real
need of the help of a hope beyond our own natural tendencies and capabilities.

With respect to social media, George Farmer, the husband of Candace
Owens, put it very succinctly when he said: 'If you sign up to Big Tech,
you sign up to being connected, and if you have Christ at the centre of
everything you do, you can use it as a force for good. But if you sign up
and you have nothing inside of you, then you inherently take in what is
out there, which is often evil, so you become a consumer and you cultivate your own internal life and become formed by what is out there.

The most important thing is that we centre ourselves on Christ'[54].

And let us realize, then, more and more deeply, that we need the help
of God not to be swept into the drains around us but to use well the devices
engineered by modern technology; and, at the same time, we need discernment to see that the forces of evil, that turn everything into money, particularly pornography, are driven by a destructive spirit that does not want
to be discovered or thrives on being denied. Thus, as Pope Francis says,

---

[53] "A generation adrift: Why young people are less happy and what we can do
about it", April 5th, 2024: https://www.weforum.org/agenda/2024/04/youth-
young-people-happiness/.

[54] Thomas Edwards, April 18th, 2024, "INTERVIEW: George Farmer on his
Catholic Faith and being married to a US media star": https://catholicher-
ald.co.uk/interview-george-farmer-on-his-catholic-faith-and-being-married-to-
a-us-media-star/.

remembering that the victory of Christ is ours to call upon and, through the Holy Spirit, 'to make His victory our own':

'Modern technology, for example, besides the many positive resources that are to be appreciated, offers also countless means to "give an opportunity to the devil", and many fall in the trap. Think of online pornography, behind which there is a flourishing market: we all know this. It is the devil at work, there. And this is a very widespread phenomenon, which Christians should beware of and strongly reject. Because any smartphone has access to this brutality, to this language of the devil: online pornography'[55].

In other words, without demonizing technology, as it has 'many positive resources that are to be appreciated', it is clear that there is a harmful use of it which goes beyond either what is natural or human and drags the human spirit into untold slaveries from which it needs to be delivered by a power greater than itself.

While it seems new in the turn it is taking, there seems to be more and more about the vulnerability of young people to electronic media; and, even if the phenomena began decades earlier, with infatuation with popular singers, magazines tending to depict "thin" as fashionable, there now seems to be a very intrusive impact of electronic media. So, for example, a social psychologist, Jonathan Haidt, argues 'that kids should have little to no access to either until they turn 16'. Why? Because there are 'climbing mental health struggles among American tweens and teens'; and what is more, this is echoed by the American Psychological Association, who say

---

[55] Pope Francis: "General Audience, 25.09.2024": https://press.vatican.va/content/salastampa/en/bollettino/pubblico/2024/09/25/240925b.html.

that many platforms should be regulated by the providers and not by children or their parents, as they are "inherently unsafe for children".

Parental fears around outdoor play led to an over enthusiastic endorsement of technological play; however, that has led to several hours a day screen time and more. Boys tend to go for games and girls for social media; however, although accidents for boys have dropped dramatically, owing to indoor play, '10-14-year-old girls' self-harming has nearly tripled since the 2010s. There has been a 'wreckage' of adolescent health with rising suicides and self-harm generally and lower test scores. More generally, 30% of teens are thinking about suicide and 30%-40% are suffering from rising anxiety levels and depression.

In general, then, if the plague of i-phone use and pornography is undermining children's health, and not just children's if it is a world-wide money maker, then it is also a spiritual battle that has to be waged if, in all, we are not to be swamped by the corrupting mentality that is in danger of being more and more prevalent. In other words, pray and act.

Acting together: Concordantly!

Haidt wants parents, governments and platform developers to act now, beginning with restricting the use of i-phones, while using ordinary phones, or not allowing the i-phone media until 16. In terms of our subject, of the context of being single with a view to the possibility of marriage, Haidt says:

'Because kids are somewhat sex-segregated online (they interact less with kids of the opposite sex), the situation is unconducive to heterosexual dating and marriage. I think the separation between boys and girls and their rising rates of anxiety are going to drive rates of marriage and heterosexual childbearing down much faster than they've been going — and they've been dropping for decades'[56].

Some 'teens' smartphones were their "constant companion that encourages regular pickups," amounting to checking their phones more than 100 times daily on average and feeling they couldn't put them down'[57].

A study in Norway has shown that banning smart phones in the school has reduced bullying and improved the grades of girls particularly. Reducing the use of phones in high school had the following result: 'The effects are most visible among girls. One explanation for this effect may be that girls use their mobile phones significantly more than boys at this age'[58]. Conversely, if there is no action to limit the use of phones in the classroom, is it surprising if a teacher resigns?[59] Why do the teachers have to compete with the unwarranted use of technological devices?

More personally, how many of us have witnessed the encroaching use of phones, even secretly, at the meal table, during Church services and, by

---

[56] Matt Vilano, April 16th, 2024, "How cell phones are killing our kids, and what we can do about it": https://edition.cnn.com/2024/04/16/health/cell-phones-jonathan-haidt-wellness/index.html.

[57] Kristen Rogers, September 26th, 2023, "Teens are exhausted by phone notifications but don't know how to quit, report finds": https://edition.cnn.com/2023/09/26/health/teen-hundreds-of-phone-notifications-report-wellness.

[58] Sigrid Folkestad, 12th February, 2024, "Mobiles Should be Out of the Classrooms": https://www.nhh.no/en/nhh-bulletin/article-archive/2024/february/mobiles-should-be-out-of-the-classrooms/.

[59] Nicholas McEntyre, 2nd June, 2024, "Arizona high school teacher Mitchell Rutherford quits job over students' cellphone 'addiction': 'They can't put it away'": https://nypost-com.cdn.ampproject.org/c/s/nypost.com/2024/06/02/us-news/arizona-high-school-teacher-mitchell-rutherford-quits-over-students-cell-phone-addiction/amp/.

implication, in some cases from dawn until dusk. Others, however, have traded the i-phone for block phones; while others have left their i-phones behind on pilgrimages so that they can be present to the whole event. More generally, young people report the problems that arise from phone or computer access to pornography, counting "likes", bullying, and being generally transfixed with screens. What is more, with the rise of social and military violence, there is a tendency for the worries of the world to overwhelm (cf. Mk 4: 19) us if we listen, as it were, unprepared for the effect on us of the crises of our times that, because of these media, that are almost "in our face" on a daily basis. Never mind the absolutely tragic situation for those for whom this is not a media but an actual, ongoing, life changing tragedy.

So, while not everyone is aware of the statistics, many people may well be aware on a day-to-day basis of the intrusiveness of social media, its tendency to increase our use of it by many kinds of "Apps". There is a clearly charted influence of social media "Content", teaching us all kinds of things, including a kind of addictive interest to all that goes on, instant contact with all that goes on, wherever it goes on. Thus we are increasingly drawn in as our attention is grabbed and, unreflectingly, it may well be forming our preoccupations, not all of which is unhealthy, but instant thinking and poorly formed inputs, as well as other dangers, abound for the unwary or the untutored and immersed user.

Simple answers and the need of divine help

Some primary schools now have signs which say: "Greet your child with a smile not a phone!" Indeed, parents admit that phones are impacting their relationship to their children: '17% of American parents report they are *often* distracted by their phone' with '52% saying they are *sometimes* distracted' from attending to their children[60]. But finding the right kind of answer, as against the 'me time' or the 'whatever makes you happy' answer, whether it is marrying someone who was already married or any number of other possible answers, they have to go beyond the transmission of values which, like laws, show us our need of salvation but do enable us to live them[61]. In this day and age, drawing on the *Christian, Catholic Faith,* has to go beyond the roundabout of going in and out of Church and be about begging God to give us faith in His Son Jesus Christ and His bride the Church. The power of media and other compulsions is so great we need a greater power: to believe that if God can create all that exists He can help all He has brought to exist (cf. Wis 11: 24).

However, as it has been indicated, it is not possible to establish limits, agreements, reasonable use of media, without individual and family prayer! God gives us many modern gifts; but it is the same God who gives us the grace to use them well. More widely, if the on-line experience of communication is not only fraught with so many dangers and difficulties, confusing "likes" for friendship and really being unable to identify easily, all who make contact, the young person seems particularly vulnerable to that primary desire for human contact and, perhaps, being inexperienced, is really susceptible not only to being deceived by "on-line impersonators" but also, because of that same inexperience in everyday relationships, being particularly unprepared for the whole ebb and flow of the dialogue of courtship and marriage. Indeed some countries are considering social-media bans until 15 or 16 even if some people can evade it[62]; however,

---

[60] Haidt, *The Anxious Generation*, 2024, p. 56.

[61] Cerith Gardiner, 12/13/23, "Is this the real danger facing our teens today?": https://aleteia.org/2023/12/13/is-this-the-real-danger-facing-our-teens-today/.

[62] Hannah Ritchie, with additional reporting by *Tiffanie Turnbull in Sydney,* November 2024, "Australian Senate approves social media ban on under-16s": https://www.bbc.co.uk/news/articles/c89vjj0lxx9o.

puzzingly, it is not entirely clear if pornography is included in what cannot be accessed[63].

One of the simplest and recurring themes of the answer to these on-line addictions, is a return to what could be called "everyday life": face-to-face meetings, outdoor activities; reading a book in the hand; getting in the dirt, whether gardening or walking in the countryside; and, essentially, unplugging and opening up the times of silence in our lives. With respect to reading, a recent report has studied and recommended the benefits of reading for recreation from an early age; but, clearly, not reading on-line but with a book in the hand. Some of the benefits are better health and well-being, less stress, good sleeping, as well as less time on-line, assuming hard copies rather than e-books:

> 'These children also had better mental wellbeing, as assessed using a number of clinical scores and reports from parents and teachers, show-ing fewer signs of stress and depression, as well as improved attention and fewer behavioural problems such as aggression and rule-break-ing'[64].

Just as reading develops good brain structure[65] so silence builds the brain, facilitates reflection, helps us let go of stress and, in the words of

---

[63] Cf. LinkedIn page: https://www.linkedin.com/feed/.

[64] "Reading for pleasure early in childhood linked to better cognitive perfor-mance and mental wellbeing in adolescence": https://www.cam.ac.uk/research/news/reading-for-pleasure-early-in-childhood-linked-to-better-cognitive-per-formance-and-mental-wellbeing; and the citation at the end of the article was to the original research document: *Yun-Jun Sun & Barbara J. Sahakian et al.* https://doi.org/10.1017/S0033291723001381. *Psychological Medicine; 28 June 2023; DOI: 10.1017/S0033291723001381.*

[65] "Reading for pleasure early in childhood" etc.

Cardinal Sarah: "Without silence, God disappears in the noise ..."[66]. Clearly, then, there are a lot of practical measures which go with this, changing phones, switching off notifications, using a home computer, no electronics in the bedrooms, while driving, while in Church, at meal-times; and, I have to say, having a family of eight growing up through these times of electronification of communication, I know how persevering parents need to be with helping each other and their children with all this.

What is entailed in living a family life? Note what a novelist says in the introduction to his book on the family.

> A family outing led to a father sitting on the hillside with his children, enjoying the beauty of the view and praying for everyone: 'We sat on the edge of the cliff for a long time, and after a while we prayed together for the people of the valley, for the many good enterprises bustling there, for our own needs, for the Church, and for families throughout the world'[67] .... [then the children] 'scattered across the mountain top in search of discoveries'[68].

The price, then, of family life is putting aside the studying, the over-time, the multitude of "my" projects and agreeing to go out, even to go out when it is difficult to leave what I am doing and to go and ramble, to talk, taking whoever is at home, our elderly mother-in-law, a widow friend, even our neighbours who come from a foreign land and have not visited outside the town, and so to be sociable and to enjoy the vast views that come from being on the hills, not least of which is the amazing wealth of the sky's colours and shapes. The

---

[66] From Sr. Marysia Weber's contribution (who is a Catholic), called "Screen Addiction: Why You Can't Put Your Phone Down".

[67] O'Brien, *The Family and the New Totalitarianism*, 2019, p. 14.

[68] O'Brien, *The Family and the New Totalitarianism*, 2019, p. 23.

price is time and the payment is in terms of "relationship".

As it says in the *Book of Wisdom* (11: 21-26):

> Yet you are merciful to all, because you are almighty,
> you overlook people's sins, so that they can repent.
> Yes, you love everything that exists,
> and nothing that you have made disgusts you,
> since, if you had hated something, you would not have made it.
> And how could a thing subsist, had you not willed it?
> Or how be preserved, if not called forth by you?
> No, you spare all, since all is yours, Lord, lover of life!'

Thus, if we can but see, to be male or female is equally a gift in that none of us choose our sex at conception; it is given, freely given, not as a punishment but out of the goodness of God and entails an implicit plan of love for each of us, both individually and in our relationships to one another and to society. Moreover, as people become aware of the deliberate design of i-phones as time-consumption devices, never mind the harm of sociogenic, contagious illnesses, bullying, manipulation and other problems, so there is a rise of the "dumbphone".

As one person, who switches the sim card between phones, says: 'With the Nokia, I've cut myself off from such meaningless digital stimuli but preserved my ability to answer texts or phone calls if necessary. (I'm too much of a millennial to actually leave the house without any phone.) I find myself looking more at my surroundings, which are particularly enjoyable in springtime, and I am more relaxed when I return from the excursions'[69].

Smartphone Free Childhood has, in a few weeks, accumulated a 60,000 membership and has inspired many similar movements world-wide. And now, interestingly enough, the pressure from parents is mounting on the i-phone companies, as parents are starting to limit their children and young people's access, so that the companies are now introducing what are nothing more than reasonable controls.

'Under mounting pressure, the tech giant [Meta, CEO Mark Zuckerberg] announced in January 2024 that it will limit the type of content that teenage users of Instagram and Facebook can see including self-harm, eating disorders, and nudity.

Some tech companies are trying to build child-friendly smartphone and social media experiences. Google launched YouTube Kids in 2015, a separate YouTube-like app with child-friendly content and parental controls.

iPhone maker Apple launched a new website recently promoting the Apple Watch for kids who are too young for smartphones. The device that would be managed by parents' iPhones so they can keep in touch with their children'[70].

---

[69] Kayle Chayka, April 10th, 2024, "The Dumbphone Boom Is Real"; https://www.newyorker.com/culture/infinite-scroll/the-dumbphone-boom-is-real.

[70] Sawdah Bhaimiya, July 17th, "A growing number of parents are refusing to give their children smartphones — and the movement is going global": https://www-cnbc-com.cdn.amppro-ject.org/c/s/www.cnbc.com/amp/2024/07/17/a-smartphone-free-childhood-a-global-movement-is-growing.html.

Prose and a Prayer for Phone Users Called: Snap-a-Shotting"

My wife and I travelled for four hours on a coach, from Valencia to Barcelona, in the course of travelling we saw an amazing array of Spanish scenery, ranging from farmland to massive mountains, some of which were excavated, presumably for building materials.

At the same time, we were on a kind of pilgrimage, in view of taking a general exhortation from a Catholic priest's homily for married couples to take a break together. While our eight children were away, one a seminarian visiting Columbia, six others visiting a second son in a seminary in Poland, this was a possible moment for our taking advantage of a time together. So, Providence, having inspired the priest's homily, arranged for us to travel to Spain, paying little more than a parking fee at the airport and buying a few pieces of fruit and vegetables the whole time we were away; and, therefore, we were given the use of a flat by a family we know, most of whom had vacated to a sea-side flat for the summer, leaving a fridge full of food and a wealth of help, including our two trips to Barcelona and Madrid.

But, getting back to the point of this piece, while we travelled, going on planes, on coaches, we continued our enjoyment of the countryside, the views, the changes in landscape, from agriculture to mining, to industrial to urban landscapes, to visiting and praying in Churches, continuing our conversation, intermittently, along the lines of our marriage and various questions we were asking ourselves from a book about marriage, it was inescapable that the phone and scrolling were everywhere. Even if we dozed, especially on the coach, it was clear that the same person who was scrolling clothes was still scrolling clothes when I woke up. At one celebration of the sacrament of reconciliation, where we go to ask the help of

God's forgiveness through the ministering priest, we were seated at the back of the Church and it was impossible not to notice the number of phones, text messages and flicking that was going on.

Clearly, those who have designed the phones to be used so almost con-stantly that there is scarcely a break between activities when the phone does not come out or does not even get put away, then it is possible to see why the data miners, the data companies that collect your movements, whether you have picked up your phone, turned it over, put it down, scrolled or texted or videoed and all the other minor, scarcely significant acts of use, have collected so much data that it can be stored in remote warehouses using unimaginable amounts of energy to cool it and, at the same time, are making a trillion pounds in the process! Whether your tril-lion is a million billions or thousand billion, it is a lot of money[1]; and, if you are counting pounds or dollars, putting one down per second, it will take you 32 years at least, non-stop, without a break or a sleep – somewhat like the phone is designed to be used!

All in all, then, this started me thinking about a possible prayer or poem, or both, on the subject of snapshotting.

Snap-a-Shotting

Keep in touch! Watch me? Send and receive! Now! Every-all-time-now! And be safe – but keep it out of reach of a smart snatch!

I search where I am going, what I find there, any questions I may have that arise, including how to say "where" in so many languages, or "please" and "thank you" and, of course, it can all be spoken too.

---

[1]   Cf.   https://www.quora.com/How-do-you-illustrate-the-difference-be-tween-a-billion-and-a-trillion.

Buy it! Book it! Pay for it! ID! Store it! Sell it! Check it on-line!

When I wear my head-phone during the day, when I am visiting, going out or coming in, travelling, going to bed, what I see is a touch screen, ticks, messages, videos, images, text, flowing through my fingers, reflecting a stream of consciousness like the debris fall-out from an advertising campaign, raising up what was repeatedly searched or searched once, replying with an almost countless number of similar plays, sliding one after another in a mime of concentration, pressing here, pushing past there, stopping, pausing, somewhere, while I see and am seen by who cannot be with me in person, all the while sending back the data, dating it all, piling it into a finite box of cooling coils and coding, using one percent plus of the world's available energy rising to about eight percent of the world's energy at what kind of cost? Earning a trillion in currency!

But what kind of cost? Costs are comparative. How many seeds could it buy? How much clean water would it provide? Free meals? Books! Training! Debt relief? Bringing down the cost of living? Paying for operations. Distributing benefits more widely?

What I look for when I am walking is a place to snap-a-shot, either on my own or with whom I am together, with a cathedral, tree, water, plate of food, when crossing the road to show that I am doing it now or down the road, at the view, masking the full account of what there is to be seen as, in the end, I am seeing myself and my friend, sitting or standing or posing anywhere and everywhere, passing time passively in that I am doing what any good user needs to do and, indeed, the device has trained us to do, namely flitting from topic to topic, picture, sound, none of which is more than passing or, at length, I stop and wonder where the day-light has gone and what I am doing on this drainage system?

But I can phone up and put the phone down. I can switch it on and off. I can take a picture and send it and stop. I could but I cannot.

I remember standing and staring like the woman on the path, waiting for us to cross a one-person wide bridge, caught in a moment's waiting, looking, as we looked, at the bird's pointed beak, grey, almost camouflaged against the rock, but moving, suddenly, flying off and over the ponds, frustrated in fishing, flying to another place, guided by a limited, but lively intelligence, somewhat languid in flight, slightly tatty winged and tall, elegantly still at times and, so I am told, stunningly swift to dive, jealous of its fishing patch, but fishing free, no licence and giving us moments of wondering about the intricately, intimate ways of nature's coming together to feed, to live, to thrive and die, probably almost oblivious of how much we have loved its passing.

What gracious ungluing of being glued is going to enable me to switch to using and not being used, to swipe without being swiped away, to be grateful without a grudge, giving my attention to the person next to me, whether my wife, my mother, my father, my children, my friend, a passer-by, a workman, a cleaner and God?

Chapter Three

Gender Confusion: Physicalism and the Danger of One-Dimensional Medicine

To begin more widely, faith and reason work together to investigate reality[1] or, in a different way, to enable the researcher to pursue his or her study, even when confronted with confusion or disappointment, knowing that for the person that strives for the truth, there will be a trail of evidence that leads to it. Pope Francis, although discussing astronomical investigations, says what is of relevance to all investigations.

Physicalism

As social researchers have commented, there is a dissatisfaction with the theory of 'pure materialism' which seems to lead many towards 'psychics, crystals, tarot, and astrological charts, or simply swap stories of the eery and the unexplained'[2].

But first, let us consider "physicalism", that there is a unitary, physical substance which is the human being. In other words, if there is the view that there is nothing more to the human being than the materialism of his or her being, then it is incomprehensible to speak of a psychological reality that arises out of it.

---

[1] Cf. "What is Reason?", Nov 6th 2024, Edited by Todd Aglialoro, Andrew Belsky: https://shop.catholic.com/blog/what-is-reason-/.

[2] Eberstadt, *Adam and Eve after the Pill: Revisited*, p. 143, citing an article by Casey Cep, "Why Did So Many Victorians Try to Speak with the Dead?"

'My view of empirical science did not include absolute truth: everything was subject to change. Progress — given priority — and new scientific discoveries would always change the models, paradigms, and scientific laws.

I didn't ask, what is real? Empirical science told me. Sometimes I wondered where I came from, and who was thinking my thoughts? A human soul was immaterial, and obviously not real'[3].

But in the course of this man's life someone explained to him that what distinguished Jesus Christ is that 'Jesus came to suffer and gave meaning to suffering'; and, in time, he sought baptism[4].

And so the question, 'who was thinking my thoughts' indicated that there had begun, as it were, a kind of openness to the possibility that there was more to reality than the bare minimum of physical science. Thus, a "slight", a way of degrading a person, is not merely the impact of a word-sound but how that word impacts on the heart of another, arousing anger or upset which, in reality, is expressed in terms of physiological changes too. Thus a word is not just an impersonal object, as if it is like a brick; rather, if the word is thrown at a person, like a brick can be thrown at a windscreen, it does damage. In other words, a word bears more than the meaning of it in that through the tone of voice and body language of the speaker, a word can be a missile into the heart. An emotional response, then, is not an abstraction from our nature but an expression of it: of the

---

[3] Mark Drogin, April 13th, 2022, "Cardinal Ratzinger described the philosophical world of my childhood": https://www.cal-catholic.com/cardinal-ratzinger-described-the-philosophical-world-of-my-childhood/.

[4] Drogin, April 13th, 2022, "Cardinal Ratzinger described the philosophical world of my childhood":

"meanness" or the "mercy" of a word-in-relationship to the person who speaks it to another. However, to reach this conclusion requires a reflection on human being that is not already imposing a uniformity on it. Thus we need to go deeper than appearances to what constitutes the origin of continuity as well as change in a human being. Asserting, then, that we are mechanisms in movement does not account for our integrity[5], our wholeness, nor does it explain how we can think and write about being what we are not, namely, intelligent, individual, capable of human relationships and of thinking beyond the specifics that merely biological beings, like birds, are capable of. So going deeper entails both philosophy and theology, evidence and reason.

'Faith and science can be united in charity, provided that science is put at the service of the men and women of our time and not misused to harm or even destroy them. I encourage you, then, to press forward to the outer limits of human knowledge. For there, we can come to experience the God of love, who fulfils the deepest yearnings of the human heart'[6].

Pope Francis said, on another occasion, something more specific to our subject: 'Gender ideology is something other than homosexual or transsexual people. Gender ideology makes everyone equal without

---

[5] Cf. William Carroll, December 10th, 2010, "Arsenic and the Meaning of Life": https://www.thepublicdiscourse.com/2010/12/2166/.

[6] Thursday, 20th June, 2024, "*Address of His Holiness Pope Francis to Participants in the 2024 LEMAÎTRE CONFERENCE of the Vatican Observatory*": https://www.vatican.va/content/francesco/en/speeches/2024/june/documents/20240620-specola-vaticana.html.

respect for personal history. .... gender ideology, ... nullifies differences. Transgender people must be accepted and integrated into society'[7].

If gender ideology 'nullifies differences', does it not have roots in the view that 'woman must be liberated above all from what characterizes her and very simply makes for her specificity: this must disappear before 'Gender, fairness and equality,' before an indistinct and uniform human being, in whose life sexuality had no other meaning than as a voluptuous drug that can be used in any manner conceivable …'[8].
Again, if gender ideology 'nullifies differences' is it related, more than superficially, to a very different kind of ideology: the Global, a-historical human being who is disconnected from his or her own history and who is the consumer of universally available marketed goods?

An 'individual, one who needs neither family nor neighbor nor even God Almighty…. [pointing] toward a hedonistic ethics of consumption'[9].

---

[7] BY JEANNINE GRAMICK, May 1st, 2024, "After Vatican text, pope tells Jeannine Gramick: Trans people 'must be accepted'": https://www.ncronline.org/vatican/vatican-news/after-vatican-text-pope-tells-jeannine-gramick-trans-people-must-be-accepted; and, therefore, the Pope's letter is in the context of an article that confuses labels with the identity of real people.
[8] O'Brien, *The Family and the New Totalitarianism*, 2019, p. 204; cf. also Etheredge, *The Word in Your Heart: Mary, Youth, and Mental Health*, pp. 135-136: from the path of feminism to gender ideology as women are stripped of their identity: https://enroutebooksandmedia.com/wordinyourheart/.
[9] Jerry Salyer, December 28th, 2019, "The Paleoconservative Eminence? Cardinal Sarah On Identity, Nationality, & Roots": https://theimaginativeconservative.org/2019/12/robert-cardinal-sarah-the-day-is-now-far-spent-jerry-salyer.html.

What, then, do we find at the origin of these mutilating operations –
but the view that 'that gender identity was nothing but a malleable social construct'. "In 1967 a Canadian couple, Ron and Janet Reimer, ap-
proached psychologist John Money, … The Reimers needed help to fix
the failed circumcision of 2-year-old David, their son, who also had a
twin brother Brian. Money, who had long argued that gender identity
was nothing but a malleable social construct, counseled the parents to
have David's genitals surgically modified to female. David became
"Brenda," Money became famous and the floodgates of sex-reassign-
ment surgery were opened.' The tragedy continues as the boy, Brenda,
grows up and rejects what was decided for him and the operation is
reversed and he reverted to the name David. But, between what happened to him and the abuse he and his brother suffered at the hands of
John Money, 'In 2003, Brian died of a drug overdose, and David committed suicide'[10].

Clearly, then, it is naïve to think that a gender identity simply springs
from within, such that we do not take account of parental preoccupations, peers, social media, and all that counts is the metaphysical self-
assertion that, contrary to my reality at conception, I can assert whatever identity I want and that is what I am[11]. However, if I assert I am a
fish, a rodent or a bacteria, presumably I would not be taken to mean
that I am a fish, a rodent, or a bacteria; however, the same evidence that
convicts me of being a human being and not a fish, a rodent or a bacteria, is the same evidence that convicts me of being a boy or a girl, a

---

[10] Joseph Freymann, June 18th, 2022, "Transgenderism Is a Dangerous Illu-
sion": https://www.ncregister.com/blog/gender-change-is-a-dangerous-illusion.

[11] Cf. Ryan T. Anderson, *When Harry Became Sally: Responding to the
Transgender Moment*, Encounter Books, London and New York, 2018-2019, pp.
29-33, pp. 45-48, p. 100.

man or a woman. In other words, if a child's sex is assigned at birth, it is not because the act of birth determines it, nor that people invent the sex of the child arbitrarily, rather it is the same evidence that we ordinarily use to identify our sex once the chromosomal development, begun at conception[12], has unfolded more fully demonstrates that we are a boy or a girl. So what has changed?

The tendency, then, to minimise differences, may contribute to cultureless individuals not only being without the critical tools of culture but also, because of that, vulnerable to whatever fashion of thought goes through the social-media stream. But, in terms of true, humane and culturally enriched individuality, so much more must be recognized in that there is an individuation to human identity, namely, that each one of us takes on an understanding of who we are which needs to be enriched by philosophy and dialogue. At the same time, a stripped-down humanity that is barely distinguishable as individuals, is itself a kind of thinking which makes a person "wear" all kinds of socially driven "illnesses" or "conditions" because each person does not know themselves well enough to know that an identity does not depend on "fashionable" identity-fashions.

Knowing, then, that Pope Francis distinguishes between ideas and the reality of the person[13], his view that 'Gender ideology is something other than homosexual or transexual people' is a similar expression in a different context. In other words, and rightly so, a person is a fuller, more complex reality than reductive expressions can communicate. And, indeed, the

---

[12] Anderson, *When Harry Became Sally,* pp. 81-85.

[13] Cf. Cf. Cardinal Francesco Coccopalmerio, translated by Andrew Guernsey, Chapter Eight of the Post-Synodal Apostolic Exhortation, Amoris Laetitia: 'Pope Francis evaluates reality through the person or, again, he puts the person first, and thereby he evaluates reality. What counts is the person, the rest comes as a logical consequence' at http://www.hprweb.com/2017/05/chapter-eight-of-thepost-synodal-apostolic-exhortation-amoris-laetitia/.

greatest help, in terms of human identity, is recognizing that man and woman are made in the image and likeness of God, are children of God, – precisely because the nature of the human person, as male or female, opens upon the mystery of God which is not, of itself, *encapsulable* except in expressions that point beyond themselves to the reality of the Blessed Trinity: Three persons in one God.

Thus, while there are many areas of profound concern with the generation rising and facing the possibility of marriage, one of them, clearly, is how to help young people navigate any distress or confusion arising out of being a boy or a girl. In other words, the first fact is the reality of an identity that informs a person's perception; however, owing to all kinds of psychological and social factors, it is possible that the given identity, of being a boy or a girl, can entail a certain amount of subjective turmoil. In other words, there is no objective basis to this turmoil except in so far as there may be psychological reasons for a boy's aversion to being a boy and a girl's aversion to being a girl. However, over time, the impact of what brings on this turmoil may diminish and, as one long term study has found, 'A majority of children who are confused about their sex grow out of that feeling by the time they become adults, according to a 15-year-old study'[14].

As regards those who do not grow out of being gender 'confused' it is possible that the problem is deeper and more difficult to resolve especially as, in our own time, there are ideological reasons for a person perpetuating their idea of who he or she is beyond the evidence. In other words, there are reasons which derive from ideas, not from the reality of a person's human identity, which perpetuate a gender-identity project. Thus, for example, the ideological idea that there is no limit to human freedom and that

---

[14] Alana Mastrangelo, 4th April, 2024, "Study: Most Children Confused About Their Sex Grow Out of It as Adults": https://www.breitbart.com/politics/2024/04/04/transgender-most-children-confused-about-their-sex-grow-out-adults/.

whatever is proposed is, therefore, in principle obtainable; and, therefore, even if it is clear to others that I am a boy or a girl, I may sustain a different claim on the basis of a misunderstanding of a "freedom to choose" my identity without reference to any kind of objective reality. Thus, while it is ideologically claimed that we can manipulate the biological sex of a given person, who is not presenting with a truly objective inter-sex condition, is to regard the bodily expression of the person as if it is like clothes: a kind of superficial "dressing" of the human person.

This leads, inexorably, to the equally unfounded view that there are no natural sexual differences; and, what is more, it entails the denial of the reality that the body expresses the person: that the objective reality of being a man or a woman expresses a subjectivity characteristic of being male or female. The objective reality, then, of a bodily expression of the person, whether male or female, is not a "temporary", "evolutionary" or otherwise surgically *surpassable* limit. In other words, there is an objectivity to the body which is an implicit guide to a person's identity and which it behoves us to respect. The impact of ideas, therefore, on human identity, has to be studied further and cannot be assumed to be irrelevant.

A wider social complication of this question is the involvement of so called "authorities" who, for whatever reason, are themselves driven by some kind of passing fascination that scarcely attends to reason and evidence; and, in the end, the "victim" is the child, not the parents, not the school-teachers or activists, or the politicians – but the child whose identity is compromised by unwarranted interventions at an age when it is widely understood that a child's identity is psychologically unstable. The "vibration" of identity, however, is not a "vibration" beyond what might be called an "oscillation" in front of the given identity of being a boy or a girl: 'This foundational difference [sexual difference] is not only the greatest imaginable difference but is also the most beautiful and most powerful of them'[15]. Thus, as some argue, caution is clearly relevant to understanding the difficulties that teenagers can experience in the climate in which we live[16].

Ideas about identity or ideology?

On the one hand, there are widespread problems in the world of research if researchers cannot distinguish and relate sex and gender in a useful way, claiming the following, vaguely defined terms: 'sex (a biological variable)' and gender (a socio-cultural variable' and yet insisting that this uncertainty be perpetuated across research programs even if 'the concept of "gender" cannot be defined but should be incorporated into all aspects of scientific research nonetheless'[17]. In other words, we see the same kind of "generating confusion" being proposed in research protocols as in some of the United Nations bureaucratic statements. Who does this confusion benefit? What is more, the *World Health Organization* has formed a relationship with a pro-abortion organization which is contrary to the charter which 'forbids the body from forming a relationship with any group that would "compromise WHO's integrity, independence, credibility, and reputation" (WHA69.10, paragraph 5)'[18]. In other words, money and

---

[15] Declaration *"Dignitas Infinita"*, on "Human Dignity", Presentation: paragraph 58.

[16] Cf. "Involve parents before pupils 'socially transition' at school, says NHS England":   https://www.theguardian.com/education/2023/sep/21/parents-should-know-if-school-pupils-socially-transition-says-nhs-england.

[17] Colleen Dean - Franciscan University of Steubenville •August 27, 2024, https://www.thecollegefix.com/author/colleen-dean-franciscan-university-of-steubenvil/ International 'equity' scholars can't define 'gender' after 5 years of research | The College Fix. https://www.thecollegefix.com/international-equity-scholars-cant-define-gender-after-5-years-of-research/

[18] Ben Johnson, June 6, 2024, "WHO OKs Partnership with Radical Abortion/Transgender Activist Lobbyists": https://washingtonstand.com/ writers/ben-

ideological influence are inseparably involved in turning an organization away from their founding principles.

On the other hand, we are beginning to see, however, a beginning of common sense breaking out of what was otherwise an immersion in ideological genderism, an uncritical claim that the body-given is "wrong" for the person whose body it is; and, therefore, attention is being drawn to the fact that the law can be used as a weapon to impose this mentality on all. Thus, it does seem as if there is a growing recognition that there are psychological factors involved in this question of identity. In a recent report by 'Dr. Hilary Cass, a former president of the Royal College of Paediatrics', says:

> [This report] recommends a shift away from medical intervention for trans-identifying children, "an area of remarkably weak evidence", to a model that prioritises therapy and considers the possibility that other mental-health issues are involved. Dr Cass concludes that "for most young people, a medical pathway will not be the best way to manage their gender-related distress"[19].

The report highlights that when the *Gender Identity Service* (known as GIDS) was set up, in 1989, the 'service saw fewer than 10 children a year', by 2009, 20 years later, 'the service saw fewer than 50 children per year', whereas referrals rose exponentially from 2014[20], particularly from 'birth

---

johnson; https://washingtonstand.com/news/-who-oks-partnership-with-radical-abortiontransgender-activist-lobbyists.

[19] April 10th, 2024, "The Cass Review damns England's youth-gender services": https://www.economist.com/britain/2024/04/10/the-cass-review-damns-englands-youth-gender-services

[20] "The Cass Review", April 2024, "Foreword from the Chair", p. 24: https://cass.independent-review.uk/wp-content/uploads/2024/04/CassReview_Final.pdf.

registered females presenting in adolescence'[21]. While, however, birth registered males continue to present in adolescence, the greatest rise by far was in birth registered females who presented over this five-year period[22]. Along with the rise of social media, there is a "causal" rise in '"sociogenic" illnesses, … illnesses caused by social influence rather than from a biological cause'[23], notably girls presenting with gender distress[24]. At the same time it is clear that there has also been an increase in 'anxiety and depression' in teenage girls, as well as 'eating disorders, tics and body dysmorphic disorder'[25]. With respect to 'anxiety and depression', one of my daughters points out that they often come together; and, as I argued earlier, if anxiety as a problem is an excessive fear of the possibility of future harm, particularly, then depression may well exert its negative impact on the mood of the person in the present. At the same time, if depression is also compounded by feeling 'socially disconnected'[26] then it raises the question of whether or not there is a real, face-to-face deficit of friendships? Thus, one wonders, is there a connection between poor relationships and, in some sense, a desire to transition from girl to boy being seen as a kind of "way out" of this experience?

Furthermore, data on referrals to the NHS adult gender clinics discovered that 'the majority of referrals were birth-registered females under the age of 25'[27]. Again, the questions arise, why do girls seem to be going through the gender-related stress? What is the reported reasons for this if, indeed, there is any summary of what these girls are going through?

---

[21] Cass Review, p. 25.

[22] Cass Review, p. 24.

[23] Haidt, *The Anxious Generation*, 2024, p. 172.

[24] Haidt, *The Anxious Generation*, 2024, p. 165.

[25] Cass Review, p. 27.

[26] Haidt, *The Anxious Generation*, 2024, p. 29.

[27] Cass Review, p. 42.

In a summary account of these findings, 'the exponential increase in adolescents in the West identifying as transgender is not a reflection of the fact that the same proportion of the population has always "been trans," and that more young people are now able to come out because of greater societal acceptance. Rather, it is in large part due to the influence of social media, which has simultaneously harmed the mental health of Gen Z—especially girls—and encouraged adolescents to attribute their loneliness, depression, and anxiety to a mismatch between their true identity and their sexed bodies'[28].

According to Haidt, the period between 2010-2015 was when 'social media companies … [started to inflict] their greatest damage on girls, and video game companies and pornography sites, which sank their hooks deepest into boys'[29]. By '2015, more than 70% of American teens carried a touch screen around with them' which, by now, was designed to attract the teen's attention[30].

Protecting children from a rush to services which may well be inapplicable and even harmful, comes from a woman legislator, Rep. Julianne Young. She has founded the development of her protection of children from transgenderism, by enacting a foundational law that defines sex biologically; and, therefore, Rep. Julianne Young says that they enacted 'legislation that gave a definition of biological sex, as opposed to gender

---

[28] Rebecca McLaughlin, April 22nd, 2024, "Transgender Meds for Kids? 4 Findings from New Report": https://www.linkedin.com/pulse/transgender-meds-kids-4-findings-from-new-report-clhcc

[29] Haidt, *The Anxious Generation,* 2024, p. 4, p. 3; but see also p. 23-24, and several pages up to p. 45 etc.

[30] Haidt, *The Anxious Generation,* 2024, p. 116 etc.

identity' and 'that she hopes that children and families will now enjoy real protection from an ideology that harms the body and destroys the family'[31].

A question of evidence: What defines evidence?

Coincidentally to the conclusions arising from my own reading of the sub-theme that many people are refusing to read the evidence of harm arising out of physical treatments for what are principally psychological and developmental questions is the longer running denial and rejection of the evidence that the use of the hormonal pill harms the woman in multiple ways[32] to the point that even an anti-Catholic feminist rails against it[33].

On the one hand, as we have seen, there is the evidence of a dramatic rise of young people, particularly girls, presenting at a *Gender Identity Service* over the last 35 years or so. What was already coming through were the reservations of those who had been pioneering what turns out to be treatments that were running into major problems[34]. On the other hand, because there has been this surge of gender crises, in an era of growing psychological ills, are there more factors to be investigated? In other words, what about the wider evidence of people managing, however imperfectly, with what they are going through, such that this recent

[31] Louis Knuffke, 23rd April, 2024, "EXCLUSIVE: Idaho lawmaker explains how Definition of Sex law protects children from gender ideology": https://www.lifesitenews.com/news/exclusive-idaho-lawmaker-explains-how-definition-of-sex-law-protects-children-from-gender-ideology/

[32] Cf. Mary Eberstadt, *Adam and Eve after the Pill: Paradoxes of the Sexual Revolution*, San Francisco: Ignatius Press, 2012.

[33] Holly Grigg-Spall, *Sweetening The Pill: Or How We Got Hooked On Hormonal Birth Control*, Zero Books: Winchester, UK, 2013.

[34] Riittakerttu Kaltiala, October 30th, 2023, 'Gender-Affirming Care Is Dangerous. I Know Because I Helped Pioneer It': https://www.thefp.com/ p/gender-affirming-care-dangerous-finland-doctor.

phenomenon really has to be examined in its own right? In other words, why has it somehow become normative to be gender confused when, very often, it is what, ordinarily, a person passes through in the course of growing up?

As the Cass Review says: 'a diagnosis of gender dysphoria ... is not reliably predictive of whether that young person will have longstanding gender incongruence in the future'[35].

At the same time, if an uncertain and possibly harmful treatment can be taken forward under a 'research protocol', what does that mean for the child, teenager or adolescent concerned?

'The Review's letter to NHS England (July 2023) advised that because puberty blockers only have clearly defined benefits in quite narrow circumstances, and because of the potential risks to neurocognitive development, psychosexual development and longer-term bone health, they should only be offered under a research protocol'[36].

But the problem with being able to advise clients about possible outcomes depends upon what is known and that is precisely the problem: a lot more is unknown, including whether or not a gender identity issue will resolve over time and, therefore, what qualifies as informed consent to a research procedure if there are so many unknowns[37]?

If, as Cass says, 'The reality is that we have no good evidence on the long-term outcomes of interventions to manage gender related distress'[38], then clearly it is for the good of all for debate and investigation to go on and, meanwhile, to protect people from irreversible decisions.

---

[35] Cass Review, p. 29.

[36] Cass Review, p. 32.

[37] Cass Review, p. 34.

[38] Cass Review, "Foreword from the Chair", p. 13 and pp. 47, 59, and p. 76-77.

In so far, however, as it is clear that the 'current evidence base suggests that children who present with gender incongruence at a young age are most likely to desist before puberty, although for a small number the incongruence will persist'[39]. In other words, if there is some presenting gender distress or 'incongruence', there is a tendency for a person's sense of identity to stabilize in the course of ongoing development. In other words, what is at work by way of psychological development that makes this possible and, therefore, what can be done to facilitate the person's further, integral development?

'The Review was unable to obtain clear criteria from the GIDS team on their criteria for referral for endocrine intervention'[40]. Moreover, when NHS gender clinics were asked to cooperate in long-term evaluation of some 9,000 people who had passed through GIDS treatment programs, cooperation was not 'forthcoming'[41].

In England, there still seems to be a lack of clarity about who is being treated by so-called gender clinics; and, as this involves the wellbeing of children, why is there so little accountability to those seeking to know what is going on: 'Nottingham also declined to hand over data on former Gids patients under their care to the Cass Review'; and now, equally, seems unable to express or confirm data on what is happening to the children for which they are responsible[42]. Where is the public accountability in all this?

Is there a connection between the NHS' inability to cooperate with legitimate investigations and a desire to hide the presence of men in women's changing rooms? According to a reported case in NHS Fife, a woman has objected to a man in a woman's changing area: 'My case is

---

[39] Cass Review, p. 41.

[40] Cass Review, p. 193.

[41] Cass Review p. 33.

[42] Hannah Barnes, 21st October, 2024, "Questions remain over NHS youth gender care, despite Cass Review": https://www.newstatesman.com/politics/health/2024/10/are-nhs-gender-services-disregarding-the-cass-review

about whether the hospital and Dr Upton subjected me to sexual harassment and discrimination by forcing me and other female colleagues to
share a changing room with a man identifying as a woman," she said'[43].
What is more, it transpires that a doctor can be double registered with the
General Medical Council, GMC, such that a doctor can be registered under
his own name but then also under a chosen name that reflects his decision
to be known as a woman. And, in view of this, 'a doctor who had been
warned or suspended could claim to have a new gender and under his new
GMC number all that would be forgotten'[44]. In other words, how is it that
this is an ethical practice? What is more, if this Council has oversight over
doctors, clearly it is not impartial and is registering itself as complicit in
the false claim that a person can change their biological sex. What are the
implications, then, for the NHS service in this country? Is the fact that a
nurse has to go to court to protect women's spaces for women a consequence of this GMC complicity in transgenderism? What other implications are there? According to a nationwide examination of public institutions in the UK, there is wide-spread confusion about record keeping because of people being allowed to change the registration and records of
men who are now claiming to be women: the data is therefore corrupted
as a result of the last ten years of 'conflating gender with sex.[45]

---

[43] Daniel Sanderson, 8/01/2025, "NHS attempt to hold trans whistleblower
tribunal in secret dismissed": NHS attempt to hold trans whistleblower tribunal
in secret dismissed. https://www.msn.com/en-gb/entertainment/music/nhs-at-
tempt-to-hold-trans-whistleblower-tribunal-in-secret-dismissed/ar-AA1xbxsL

[44] Stephen, 26th February, "GMC misleading the public over 'trans' doctors":
https://www.christianvoice.org.uk/index.php/gmc-misleading-public-trans-doc-
tors/

[45] Cf. Jill Foster, 21st, March, "From the NHS to the police, how the obsession
with gender captured the public sector": https://www.telegraph.co.uk/gift/
9c9e39f7fb92908e

Again, an American midwife student in Scotland was cleared of any 'wrongdoing' by declaring her prolife views on a midwife chat. However, the two public bodies that were taking her to task was, again, NHS Fife. Furthermore her professors at Edinburgh Napier University have continued to issue warnings to her about her social media use', when she has already been cleared of wrongdoing. What is more, the Scottish Government is reviewing abortion provision and the task is headed 'by many of whom have had a career within or around the abortion industry'. In other words, as the article says, where is the protection of free speech in the UK and where is the possibility of peacefully expressing a prolife defence of the unborn?[46]

While in a recent employment case in the government offices at Whitehall, of England, has shown that there has been a creeping policing of those legitimately critical of trans policies, suggesting that this is more widespread than just isolated departments. Ms Frances 'argued that the policy's use of politicised language and concepts – such as defining "transphobia" as including the "denial/refusal to accept" someone's gender identity – effectively compelled civil servants to recognise male people as women. Ms Frances also warned that the broader adoption of "self-identification" policies gave men access to female-only facilities in government buildings'[47]. Note, too, the teacher who has to go to an employment tribunal over raising a legitimate and serious concern, especially given the public controversies and actual harm to those who go through puberty

---

[46] Alliance Defending Freedom, "Scottish health system suspends American midwifery student over pro-life social media posts": https://www.lifesitenews.com/news/scottish-health-system-suspends-american-midwifery-student-over-pro-life-social-media-posts/?utm_source=digest-prolife-2025-03-04.

[47] Frederick Attenborough, January 13th, 2025, "Civil service to revise transgender policies following whistleblower settlement": https://freespeechunion.org/civil-service-to-revise-transgender-policies-following-whistleblower-settlement/.

blocking hormones and, possibly, their irreversible effects and that of surgery: 'A young child due to join her class wanted to be treated as a member
of the opposite sex. Because Hannah pursued safeguarding concerns over
the school's policy, she lost her job.' And, what is more, how was it that a
member of the Tribunal Panel was 'LGBT activist with an obvious bias
against Christians' and had to be changed?[48]

Note the problem of making this information available too, in America, which appears to be proceeding with puberty blockers and surgeries[49].
What of the recommendation by the World Medical Association's Helsinki document that there is an independent ethical review of what is proposed for vulnerable people?[50] Note, too, Pope Francis' call to recall the
'spirit' of Helsinki agreement: 'It is more urgent than ever to recover the
"spirit of Helsinki", with which opposing states, considered "enemies"',
succeeded in creating a space of encounter and did not abandon dialogue
as a means of resolving conflicts'[51].

Meanwhile, also in America, one wonders at the objectivity of a document that, instead of being compiled by people who can refer to evidence,

[48] Christian Concern, "Pray for teacher sacked for safeguarding concerns over
child transition": https://mailchi.mp/christianconcern/prayer-alert-hannah-re-
trial?e=e955a35045.

[49] Cf. Gabrielle M. Etzel, November 4th, 2024, « House Republicans press
NIH on suppression of federally funded puberty blocker research":
https://www.washingtonexaminer.com/policy/healthcare/3215032/house-repu-
blicans-press-nih-suppression-puberty-blocker-research/.

[50] Cf. World Medical Association, October 19th, 2024, "World Medical Association Declaration of Helsinki: Ethical Principles for Medical Research Involving
Human Participants": https://jamanetwork.com/journals/jama/fullarticle/
2825290

[51] Pope Francis, 9th January, 2025, *Address of His Holiness Pope Francis to
Members of the Diplomatic Corps Accredited to the Holy See*: https://www.vati-
can.va/content/francesco/en/speeches/2025/january/documents/20250109-
corpo-diplomatico.html.

which has not been suppressed, is edited according to a person's position rather than according to the facts: 'The documents assert, referencing original emails, that the US assistant secretary for health, Dr Rachel Levine, who is a trans woman herself, intervened in the drafting of *SOC-8* and lobbied to have age limits removed'[52]. Why would you not want to protect young people, who more often than not accept their sex from conception, from being manipulated into life-crippling decisions owing to their immaturity?

Similarly, in America, 'Louisiana Republican Sen. Bill Cassidy, who was a medical doctor before joining politics, has strongly criticized Planned Parenthood for being "opaque" in its reporting practices on transgender procedures – raising questions about whether spikes in an undisclosed category in its annual reports are from its gender program.

"Despite the rapid increase in the number of Planned Parenthood affiliates offering these types of services, the exact number of gender transition services performed is unknown because this information is captured in the organization's annual reports under the broad label of 'Other Procedures,'" Cassidy said in a press release'[53].

Clearly the inability of these organizations to make their statistics available raises serious questions about their accountability, actual practices, and follow-up on outcomes of those who are subject to these actions, not to mention what motivates their work if it is not "scientific interventions". Indeed, is "inability" to provide information to be equated with "unwillingness" to make records available, indicative of being afraid of what the records would have shown?

---

[52] Barnes, 21st October, 2024, "Questions remain over NHS youth gender care, despite Cass Review".

[53] Steven Ertelt, July 8th, 2024, "Planned Parenthood Exploits More Children With Trans Hormones Than Anyone".

Authoritatively given but unfounded advice

Why, then, is it not possible to evaluate what has already been done by gender clinics? Moreover, the attempt to set up regional centres that would contribute to a holistic care programme has discovered that there are 'considerable challenges ... within a highly emotive and politicised arena. This is well illustrated in another context where 'one of the major challenges for the Review has been the difficulty in having open, honest debate as people with differing views can find it uncomfortable to sit together in the same room or on the same stage'[54]. Or, in another context, it was found to be difficult to come to a consensus where views were so 'polarised'[55]. However, where some treatments are so radical, involving irreversible surgery, it is not necessarily the case that objecting to this surgery is expressing anything other than care for the person it could impact upon – especially in view of the tendency of many young people to grow beyond what is called 'gender distress'. Furthermore, the very nature of irreversible change, whether because of the use of hormones or surgery, is sufficient reason to avoid it except in those very cases of true intersex states and even then, only after extensive evaluation of what is necessary.

Does the use of 'puberty blockers' and surgery on a widespread basis indicate that a 'fixed idea' of one solution fits all is equivalent to advancing an ideological opinion irrespective of what is good for the child or the young person who presents with gender distress? Indeed, this also raises the question of whether or not people are holding "fixed ideas" of an ideological kind rather than basing their point of view on various findings, of whatever quality. In general, the number of times the Cass Review reported that there was an uncertain or inconclusive finding suggests that those who were looking for evidence on which to base treatment were

---

[54] Cass Review, p. 60, p. 75 and 83.
[55] Cass Review, p. 64.

finding it difficult to do so. If this concern about the weakness of the evidence base for medical interventions and the lack of professional guidance for clinicians, has impacted on the ability of the new services to recruit the appropriate multi-disciplinary workforce'[56], then it follows that there could be an issue about professional objectivity in the service to young people. A woman with fifty years clinical experience of helping people with sexual difficulties has noted a number of changes in response to young people who present with gender dysphoria to the point that she now says:

> '"Queer theory seeks to disrupt dominant and normalizing binaries that structure our understandings of gender and sexuality."

Translated, this suggests that gender-affirming care is as much a political statement as it is a health policy, which seems likely to explain the lack of a rigorous assessment and management protocol for gender-questioning young people'.[57] In another article, she points out rather more stridently, 'If health professionals who work with gender-questioning children hold … [bizarre claims that sex is also a social construct, that a person can change sex, and there are more than two sexes], what hope do their patients have for receiving safe, appropriate, evidenced-based care?[58]

Although the Cass Review has proposed an overarching service, even what exists in the current situation is far from working properly, given that 'Throughout the course of the Review, it has been evident that there has

---

[56] Cass Review, p. 36 and cf. also p. 37.

[57] Sandra Pertot, 25th March, 2025, "Puberty panic merchants": https://www.genderclinicnews.com/p/puberty-panic-merchants.

[58] Sandra Pertot, January 18th, 2025, "Who am I? Exploration, not affirmation, is the correct response to a child who believes they are the opposite sex": https://www.genderclinicnews.com/p/who-am-i. I have conflated two parts of what she says, for brevity; but, in general, both this and the previous article are excellent pieces.

been a failure to reliably collect even the most basic data and information in a consistent and comprehensive manner; data … [has] often not been shared or … [has] been unavailable'[59]. Similarly, in America, as the Supreme Court begins to examine the evidence concerning the validity of treatments, the side effects and the costs, as well as whether or not research has been shared or people have been intimidated into silence, then what emerges is an appalling lack of objectivity to the point where the ideological advance of mutilating procedures overrides all contrary evidence and argument[60]. This is beginning to be a familiar pattern. In terms of those who 'regret' what has happened and wish to 'detransition', they are reluctant to 'engage with the gender services that supported them through their initial transition'[61]. Thus, there is the following question: Why is this? What was it about their former contact with gender services that now makes the same people reluctant to access it? In relation to this, if new NHS numbers are issued for people who have made some kind of transition, there arise numerous problems involving 'safeguarding', in that this new number may mask a person's real birth identity, as well as making it difficult to gather information from long-term follow-ups[62]: a need for which has been voiced many times throughout the Cass Review.

More widely, is it significant that the countries that the Cass Review has drawn upon for its research, are the following: North America, Europe and

---

[59] Cass Review, p. 39, p. 40 and p. 74.

[60] Lisa Selin Davis, Updated December 3, 2024, "Legal challenges to red-state bans on youth gender care have illuminated a cover-up": https://archive.md/2024.12.03-170600/https://www.bostonglobe.com/2024/12/04/opinion/youth-gender-medicine-wpath-soc-8/#selection-1741.0-1741.83.

[61] Cass Review, p. 43.

[62] Cass Review, p. 44.

Australia; UK, Netherlands; Canada; Holland, Finland[63]. Moreover, it seems that 'Of this group, 63% were transitioning from female to male'[64]. Thus, one way or another, the research that emerges seems to have geographical implications, raising the possibility of cultural contexts which also need to be considered. In particular, are the countries in which people are engaging in "transitioning" those with unregulated social media platforms?

On the other hand, given the rigorous, methodological criteria for determining which reports could be accessed, with some degree of academic justification, the Cass Review may have given a skewed impression of where these problems were arising, given that there are other places where gender issues have surfaced, like Mexico, South Asia, the Philippines, Cambodia, Laos, Scythia, and Thailand[65]. Indeed, in a recent report, Professor Dianna Kenny reports these problem across a number of these countries; for example, 'US, UK, Asia, Europe, Scandinavia, and Australia'[66]. Australia and, hopefully, other countries, appear to be taking note of the evidence that physical treatments for psychological type conditions, concerning gender identity, are indeed harmful and are beginning to consider their own reviews: 'Tasmania's Liberal government has become the first Australian administration to recommend a national review of public gender services for minors'[67].

---

[63] Cass Review; the countries are grouped according to the page of the Review on which they are referred to, thus the following page references are: 84; 88; 89; 91.

[64] Cass Review, p. 89.

[65] In conversation with one of my daughters, 30/04/2024.

[66] Professor Dianna Kenny, "The Social Contagion of Gender Dysphoria": https://diannakenny.com.au/the-social-contagion-of-gender-dysphoria/.

[67] Bernard Lane, June 14th, 2024, "Inquiring mind: An Australian health minister puts the case for a nationwide review of gender clinics": https://www.gender-clinicnews.com/p/inquiring-mind.

But, in general, where there is social media there is the potential for a whole variety appearing in which enclosed peer groups form and propagate their ideas. Thus the gender crisis seems to be escalating to the point of constituting a veritable crisis in the identity of young people. What is more, the language of 'gender-affirming' care is morphing along the lines of being offered to anyone, even minors, irrespective of any evaluation of need or whether or not it is a good treatment, but 'just because' it is wanted. In other words, this is almost a statement of what has been happening already; and, therefore, is not so much a change of policy as a blunter exposition of it. But, as before, should minors, or anyone, 'be able to consent to take drugs that sterilize and surgical procedures that remove healthy body parts, just because they want them'?[68]. Thus this seems more about the provider providing what the provider wants irrespective of it possessing any merit for the person for whom it is proposed! But the question is: Why would anyone want to inflict this kind of damage on another person – especially those vulnerable through immaturity, ignorance or the influence of another? What about the basic question of what is medicine? What is it to do good? What is it to help another know who he or she is?

Gaping evidence and suicide

The 'primary piece of emotional blackmail that transgender activists have used is telling parents that by not affirming their child's gender-dysphoric thoughts, such as their son thinking he's a girl, they are putting their

---

[68] Brandon Showalter (https://www.christianpost.com/by/brandon-showalter), Friday, January 03, 2025, "No, gender doctors, kids don't have 'autonomy' to self-sterilize": https://www.christianpost.com/voices/gender-doctors-kids-self-sterilize-trans-puberty-blockers.html.

children's lives at risk because they may take their own lives as a result of not getting their way'[69].

What also emerges, among other things, from surveys of parents is that even when they want to know if their child is being "transitioned", they do not seem to be sufficiently clear about what is a boy and what is a girl to critically reject "transgenderism" wholeheartedly[70]. Are we discovering, then, a weak, intellectually undeveloped, and impoverished philosophical mentality among parents?

As we will see from the evidence, suicide rates rise dramatically if a child goes through a body mutilating process; but, in reality, is a threat of suicide a reason to abandon reason and not seek to diagnose, sensitively, what the real problems are? On the contrary, the threat of suicide does not appear to come from the child, so much as the gender activist.

According to a more recent study 'The results section stated that "from 107 583 patients, matched cohorts demonstrated that those undergoing surgery were at significantly higher risk for depression, anxiety, suicidal ideation, and substance use disorders than those without surgery." But, in addition, the study claimed, in a contradictory note, that 'the surgeries were "beneficial in affirming gender identity"'[71]. Furthermore, the "Abstract" concludes that "Gender-affirming surgery, while beneficial in affirming gender identity, is associated with increased risk of mental health

---

[69] LifeSiteNews staff, 17th October, 2024, "The transgender movement will never give up: here's why": https://www.lifesitenews.com/news/the-transgender-movement-will-never-give-up-heres-why/.

[70] **Leif Le Mahieu** (https://www.dailywire.com/author/llemahieu), Jan 6, 2025, "EXCLUSIVE: Majority Of American Parents Oppose Teaching Kids Transgender Ideology": https://www.dailywire.com/news/exclusive-majority-of-american-parents-oppose-teaching-kids-transgender-ideology.

[71] Thomas Stevenson, "Transgender surgeries associated with increased risk of suicidal ideation, depression: Oxford Academic study": https://thepostmillennial.com/sex-change-surgery-associated-with-increased-risk-of-suicidal-ideation-depression-oxford-academic-study.

issues, underscoring the need for ongoing, gender-sensitive mental health support for transgender individuals' post-surgery." Moreover, the study claims, that the mental health problems are 'partly due to stigma and lack of gender affirmation' for being transgender[72]. But another study says that there is evidence that there are psychiatric problems prior to gender dysphoria[73]. Going back to the Oxford study there is no reference, it seems, to the multiple psychiatric factors that the English Cass Report signalled in those presenting with gender dysphoria. Nor is there reference to the multiple problems of the surgery itself and the fact that there are an increasing number of people who regret it and regard it as a medical abuse.

In other words: Why the contradiction? What benefit to 'affirming gender identity' is there if the overall effect is a deterioration of mental health?[74] It looks as if there is some kind of disconnect between claiming the benefit of surgery and mental health deterioration. Moreover, it looks as if the claim that mental health problems are 'due to stigma and lack of gender affirmation', coupled with the claim of surgery being helpful and the need for more psychological care afterwards, is simply an unwarranted justification of surgery. This report needs to be looked at more closely.

---

[72] Admittedly this information is from the Abstract – but it is too clearly confirming the so-called value of gender affirming surgery as statistics lack detail: "Examining gender-specific mental health risks after gender-affirming surgery: a national database study": Joshua E Lewis, BS, Amani R Patterson, MBS, Maame A Effirim, BS, Manav M Patel, BSA, Shawn E Lim, BS, Victoria A Cuello, BS, Marc H Phan, BS, Wei-Chen Lee, PhD, 25th February, 2025: https://academic. oup.com/jsm/advance-article-abstract/doi/10.1093/jsxmed/qdaf026/8042063.

[73] Monique Robles, "The Bioethical Dilemma of Gender-Affirming Therapy in Children and Adolescents": https://www.thelinkbhutan.org/seminars/symposium_gender_dysphoria/program/presenters/robles_monique/bioethical_dilemma_monique_robles_M.D.pdf, p. 265.

[74] Thomas Stevenson, "Transgender Surgeries associated with increased risk of suicidal ideation, depression: Oxford Academic Study".

By contrast, a more exacting study, both medically and psychologically, states: 'There is no evidence that hormones or surgery benefit individuals with gender incongruence (Bra¨nstro¨m and Pachankis 2020)'[75].

In general, there is accumulating evidence of psychological "fluctuations" being resolved, adequately, in terms of the child's birth-registration. Not to mention the general caution about puberty blockers' impact on bone density and fertility, never mind irreversible operations and the problems that arise for those who want to detransition. Thus there are those who been "funnelled" through harmful treatments and who have decided to address, in the courts, the injustice of what was done to them and to raise awareness for the sake of protecting others[76]. Indeed, when it comes to a child or young person, are they really able to understand the impact on their health of an inconclusively tried type of treatment which has real body altering effects?[77] So one of the major considerations to arise out of this discussion is how ideologically driven it seems to be; and, therefore, as in numerous other areas of public debate, the difficulty of establishing what is true, normative and good concerning early to adolescent human development. In a tragic, ironic turn of events, fears that young people may be suicidal if they *do not* receive hormonal or surgical interventions, it is beginning to emerge in an American study that the suicide rate among 'those who underwent gender surgery had a suicide risk 12

---

[75] Monique Robles, "The Bioethical Dilemma of Gender-Affirming Therapy in Children and Adolescents", on p. 267. In addition, on

P. 264: if GD is "merely a natural variation, it becomes difficult to identify the purpose of or justification for medical intervention" (Griffin et al. 2020, 2).

[76] Grant Atkinson, updated November 27, 2024, "Preventable Tragedies: Why De-transitioners Are Suing Doctors": https://adflegal.org/article/preventable-tragedies-why-de-transitioners-are-suing-doctors/.

[77] Cf. Cass Review, p. 79.

times higher than those who did not, adding more data showing the dangers of the life-altering procedures'[78].

Moreover, a study in Denmark found that 'trans-identifying people had a suicide death rate 3.5 times higher and a suicide attempt rate 7.7 times higher than people who did not identify as transgender'[79].

This raises the question of assessing the possibility of suicide, independently of it being used as a "lever" to actuate actions which are harmful in their own right and profoundly complicate an already problematic condition. Thus it is unethical that 'Gender clinicians and transgender activists ... continue to misrepresent the data on suicide'[80].

In other words, as yet more studies conclude, not only was there insufficient grounds for widespread use of hormonal blocking and surgical procedures, they clearly aggravate complex psychological problems with, often, irreversible side effects. Thus, 'the administration of hormonal, blocking or transition treatments, as well as surgical ones, presents numerous side effects and complications, in many cases irreversible, and contributes to worsening the quality of life of these patients. Therefore, insisting on this type of intervention, ignoring psychological diagnosis and

---

[78] Zach Jewell, May 18th, 2024, "'The Butchers And Liars Were Murderously Wrong': New Study Finds 12-Fold Higher Suicide Risk For People Who Had Gender Surgery": https://www.dailywire.com/news/the-butchers-and-liars-were-murderously-wrong-suicide-risk-skyrockets-following-gender-affirmation-surgery-new-study-shows?inf_contact_key=2dcb9ec60a3be93f403b2f455a5c3a267e470d92b8b75168d98a0b8cac0e9c09.

[79] Jewell, May 18th, 2024, "'The Butchers And Liars Were Murderously Wrong'.

[80] Hasson and Selner-Wright, Chapter 4: "Suicidality and "Gender Affirming Care", p. 84 of pp. 69-84 of *Gender Ideology and Pastoral Practice: A Handbook for Catholic Clergy, Counselors, and Ministerial Leaders*, 2024.

assistance, implies proceeding in the opposite direction to that shown by the most recent scientific-clinical evidence'[81].

'The American College of Paediatricians (ACPeds) affirms the medical fact that the sex of an individual is based upon biology and not upon thoughts or feelings. The individual's sex is encrypted in every diploid cell of the body. Since an individual's biological sex is immutable from the moment of fertilization, it cannot be changed, regardless of hormonal or surgical interventions. Nothing in this paper should be construed to mean the College agrees with or accepts that individuals can change their given biological sex. The so-called "transition" is not a change of sex or even a change of sexual/gender identity, but rather only a change in sexual appearance or presentation'[82].

The American College of Paediatricians goes on to say that if a social transition takes place, it is likely to lead to hormonal or surgical measures because 'Social transition can then confirm to a child a new identity. Importantly, the child will have difficulty later questioning the new identity since parents and teachers have confirmed it'[83].

---

[81] Julio Tudela, Bioethics Conservatory, May 21st, 2024, "Do gender reassignment treatments reduce the risk of suicide?": https://bioethicsobservatory.org/2024/05/do-gender-reassignment-treatments-reduce-the-risk-of-suicide/46324/.

[82] Jane E. Anderson, MD, Scott Field, MD, and Patricia Lee June, February 2024, "Mental Health in Adolescents with Incongruence of Gender Identity and Biological Sex": https://acpeds.org/position-statements/mental-health-in-adolescents-with-incongruence-of-gender-identity-and-biological-sex; cf. also the excellent summary of this longer document: "American College of Paediatricians: Best for Children": https://acpeds.org/assets/positionpapers/mental-health-of-gender-incongruent-youth-fact-sheet-final.pdf.

[83] Jane E. Anderson, MD, Scott Field, MD, and Patricia Lee June, February 2024, "Mental Health in Adolescents with Incongruence of Gender Identity and Biological Sex".

As regards surgery that changed the person's sexual appearance, a Swedish study found that 'At 30 years of follow up, the suicide rate was 19 times that of age-matched controls'[84].

This report justifiably calls surgery on the sex-appearance of a child or adolescent, 'surgical mutilation' and it is coming to light that 'Studies confirm that adolescents, when faced with real life decisions, are much more likely to depend upon their emotions and peer pressure, with less use of their cognitive reasoning skills and with less concern for future consequences'[85].

A study from Germany has shown that 'A massive, [nine] years-long study shows [that] the overwhelming majority of young people who identify as transgender will grow out of the diagnosis within five years'[86].

Possibly the same study, again from Germany, overcame the limited availability of data from clinics and people generally by analysing the information collected through 'the socialized health care system' which gave results on those who withdrew from appearance altering medications or surgeries.

The following, slightly more detailed information, follows:

'"Researchers found overall that 63.6% of trans-identifying children and adolescents desisted from their clinically confirmed gender diagnosis, and 'only 36.4% had a confirmed [gender identity disorder] diagnosis after five years.'"

---

[84] Jane E. Anderson, MD, Scott Field, MD, and Patricia Lee June, February 2024, "Mental Health in Adolescents etc.

[85] Jane E. Anderson, MD, Scott Field, MD, and Patricia Lee June, February 2024, "Mental Health in Adolescents etc.

[86] Ben Johnson, June 14th, 2024, "Grow Out of Transgenderism within 5 Years": https://washingtonstand.com/news/german-study-vast-majority-of-people-will-grow-out-of-transgenderism-within-5-years.

So, nearly two out of three patients abandoned treatments. Looking more deeply revealed interesting patterns behind the overall figures.

"The most likely group to change its mind is 15-to-19-year-old females, with 72.7% desisting. But a majority (50.3%) of young men who came to their transgender identity in adulthood (males aged 20-24) also desisted in five years"[87].

Bearing in mind, however, that the time frame was five years and that in both cases the age groups were relatively young, it is possible that after a longer period more will reject what they have gone through and reverse whatever it is possible to reverse.

We will discuss the negative influence of authorities later whether that authority is medical or parental, effectively encouraging transitioning. For now, however, let it be noted that questions of identity were so often linked with all kinds of negative experience that the whole understanding of a developing adolescent has to be revisited and not just assumed to be

---

[87] Edwin Benson, July 8th, 2024, "New Evidence Shows that Two-Thirds of Sex Change Patients Regret Their Decisions": https://www.tfp.org/new-evidence-shows-that-two-thirds-of-sex-change-patients-regret-their-deci-sions/?PKG=TFPE3372; and the German study referred to could well be this one: Bachmann, C J (https://www.aerzteblatt.de/suche?archivAutor=Bachmann%2C+C+J); Golub, Y (https://www.aerzteblatt.de/suche?archivAutor=Golub%2C+Y); Holstiege, J (https://www.aerzteblatt.de/suche?archivAutor=Holstiege%2C+J); Hoffmann, F https://www.aerzteblatt.de/suche?archivAutor=Hoffmann%2C+F), 2024, "Gender identity disorders among young people in Germany: prevalence and trends, 2013–2022. An analysis of nationwide routine insurance data": https://www.aerzteblatt.de/int/archive/article/239563. For an English version of the evidence the most accessible was the following: Ben Johnson, June 15th, 2024, "German Study: Vast Majority of People Will Grow Out of Transgenderism Within 5 Years": https://www.dailysignal.com/2024/06/15/german-study-vast-majority-of-people-will-grow-out-of-transgenderism-within-5-years/.

indicative of some kind of physically rooted discordance between sex from conception and preferred gender. Thus integration, a foundational requirement for a stable identity, takes holistic medicine beyond the parameters of a reductive materialism that looks upon the body as if it is a purely material entity and not a profound expression of a person's whole identity[88]. To return to the American report, the authors cite an authority in Finland, saying:

> 'The Council for Choices in Healthcare in Finland / COHERE Finland reviewed research on gender dysphoria treatment and issued their report in 2020. For hormonal suppression, the report stated, "In cases of children and adolescents, ethical issues are concerned with the natural process of adolescent identity development, and the possibility that medical interventions may interfere with this process'[89].

In view, then, of the gaping holes in the collection of evidence, traceable outcomes of those treated, what is already known about the harmful effects of puberty blockers on bone density and fertility, obviously mutilating surgery, isolation of young people and their rejection of the service that turned them towards these procedures when they revert, the weaponizing of the law and the fear of those opposing these procedures losing their jobs or being vilified, there is no credible reason to conduct "trials" of these procedures.

---

[88] Cf. Dr. Eric Manuel Torres, *Curing and Healing*, 2024: https://enroute-booksandmedia.com/curingandhealing/.

[89] Jane E. Anderson, MD, Scott Field, MD, and Patricia Lee June, February 2024, "Mental Health in Adolescents with Incongruence of Gender Identity and Biological Sex".

The possibility of the law losing its credibility as an expression of justice

Clearly there is a necessity to examine individual cases where the law has been applied and what kind of interpretation has been given to it; but, while certain cases have been referred to already, what follows is about how the case can be skewed by what the prosecution is looking for. In other words, is it the case that minors are being operated on needlessly or is it about finding fault with a whistle-blower because what has been shown to be going on does not accord with an agenda. Let us take the case below.

An American court brought a case against a doctor who blew the whistle on staff who were continuing the mutilating surgery after they were required to stop. Instead, then, of questioning the staff, the prosecution took issue with the right of the doctor to access the files that revealed the continuing business of the hospital staff. In the end it turned out that the government had to admit that the doctor was within his rights to access the files because he was still working at the hospital. But, in hindsight, it is clear that the prosecution was more concerned about an "alleged" infringement of document confidentiality than what was really happening to the children in the hospital[90].

To put this in context, it seems that in American society there is a broad unwillingness to admit, in public, what a person thinks about 'hot button issues'; and, by implication, especially when a person's thinking is contrary to the powerful public policing of thought[91].

_____

[90] Mary Margaret Olohan (https://www.dailywire.com/author/mary-margaret-olohan), Sep 16, 2024, EXCLUSIVE: New Info Destroys DOJ Case Against Trans Surgery Whistleblower, Lawyers Say": https://www.dailywire.com/news/exclusive-new-info-destroys-doj-case-against-trans-surgery-whistleblower-lawyers-say.

[91] Naturally, I grant that there are some specifics in this article, such as 'abortion, school choice and legal immigration' but these are put too briefly to be all that clear. Rebeka Zeljko, September 25th, 2024, "Majority of Americans

More broadly, then, this case was not about the actual harm being done to the children after the hospital claimed it had ceased these mutilating acts[92]; but, rather, prosecuting someone who had acted in accord with the best interests of the children. What criteria of justice are at work, or have the courts simply become an instrument, imposing not justice but the ideology of the day? On the other hand, according to the country and its laws, there may be provision for redress if what is involved is an infringement of the reasonable right to free speech; and, therefore, in America, 'there are many protections … in federal and state law for workers who will not engage in speech or conduct that violates their deeply held religious beliefs (including beliefs about sex, gender, and human sexuality)'[93].

Life is so much more in its ongoing unfolding than specific crises

In the context of the question of the relationship between what is going on in society and the possibility of a vocation to marriage or, indeed, to any other permanent state, such as the priesthood or the religious life, there is an immense sense of the need for healing. While, in my own experience of going from a "loser life" to preparing for marriage, there was an extraordinary sense of being haunted by ghosts, as it were, as I cycled to work in a laundry on the lead up to marriage. In other words, while there may be exceptions where people walk away from a destructive way of living without consequences generally, it would appear, there is an ongoing destructive impact which has to be addressed. There is a change from an

---

[surveyed] admit to 'self-silencing' on hot button issues, survey reveals": https://readlion.com/majority-of-americans-admit-to-self-silencing-on-hot-button-issues-survey-reveals/.

[92] Mary Margaret Olohan, Sep 16, 2024, EXCLUSIVE: New Info Destroys DOJ Case Against Trans Surgery Whistleblower, Lawyers Say".

[93] Bursch, Chapter 24: "Counseling Parishioners", pp. 405-406 of pp. 393-406 of *Gender Ideology and Pastoral Practice*, 2024.

"occasional" to a permanent relationship called marriage, from promiscuity to chastity, to an engagement in what is good in itself and for the other[94], a recognition that multiple relationships may make one-man one-woman marriage a trial and a cross that can yet flower. At the same time, given the dramatic increase in the transmission of sexually transmitted diseases, which abstinence before marriage can help prevent, means that there can be physical consequences, too, of a permissive life-style[95].

In the Catholic tradition there is both the *Sacrament of Confession*, known as the *Sacrament of Reconciliation*, drawing on the practices of penance, giving alms, and spiritual direction – all of which helps, not forgetting openness of each spouse to the other. At the same time there is a difference between sin, an occasional sin, and the grip of sin which is known as a vice: 'The repetition of sins - even venial ones - engenders vices, among which are the capital sins'[96]. If the grip of sin is like a vice, a metal clamp which holds onto wood while it is worked, then we can expect to have to fight with the help of Christ to be delivered from this condition. But, as has been said, we are not our sin but we are a child of God and therefore ask for help from God Himself and His Church[97].

---

[94] Cf. Dr. Sam Serio, "Casual Sex Lifestyle": https://www.healingsexualhurt.com/casual_sex.

[95] Jonathon Van Maren, 18th December, 2024, "As STD rates skyrocket, people should 'follow the science' and realize fornication has consequences": https://www.lifesitenews.com/blogs/as-std-rates-skyrocket-people-should-follow-the-science-and-realize-fornication-has-consequences/?utm_source=digest-prolife-2024-12-19.

[96] *Catechism of the Catholic Church*, 1876; Capital sins, which engender other sins, 'are pride, avarice, envy, wrath, lust, gluttony, and sloth or acedia', cited by "Catholic Culture": https://www.catholicculture.org/culture/library/catechism/cat_view.cfm?recnum=5102.

[97] Cf. Lara Katherine Miller's experience in the "Endnote" of the book by Etheredge, *The Word in Your Heart: Mary, Youth, and Mental Health*.

Thus, there is no doubt in my mind, that the possibility of conversion, while real, does not end there, but goes on into the conversion of daily life to the new life in Christ.

Training people to think or to be subservient to the thought of Others

"Notice that [if we reject and decry a good goal because we cannot reach it that this] is the opposite of becoming large by first becoming small, as the apprentice does in the act of submission to a teacher. *Ressentiment* instead turns the objective order of value upside down"[98]. In reality, then, it is not about whether or not we will be influenced by others, whether a teacher, an argument or a modern-day activist or influencer; it is, rather, a question of which one will we submit to, like the apprentice to the tradesman. Thus, the wisdom of being an apprentice to the thinking of others, is not just any kind of choice, it is a foundational choice and needs discernment: an appreciation that the authority of the person we choose is, in reality, helping us to choose the good, the true and the beautiful and is capable of explanations, dialogue and illustrations of an argument and how to answer objections. And, therefore, let us make that choice openly, critically and with wisdom and prayer.

The problem as reported, however, is that if a group mentality develops uncritically, then there develops an "in-group" conformity and a rejection or at the very least a distancing from an "out-group". Therefore we end up with the following development across many countries and across many socially contagious problems, such as eating disorders, 'non-suicidal self-

---

[98] Matthew B. Crawford, October 10th, 2024, "Why Individualism Fails to Create Individuals: Independence of mind requires sustained submission to authority": https://hedgehogreview.com/web-features/thr/posts/why-individualism-fails-to-create-individuals.

injury', suicide, copycat suicides of prominent public figures significant in the lives of adolescents. In particular, with regard to gender distress:

'the transactivist lobby ... [o]pinion leaders operating at the centre of these networks are very influential. The level of density in a network has two effects – firstly, it enhances the circulation of information between members and secondly, it blocks the introduction of dissenting ideas and evidence ..., both observable phenomena in the transgender epidemic'[99].

Moreover, 'Parents also reported a decline in their child's mental health (47%) and relationship with parents (57%) after declaring themselves transgender. Thereafter, they preferred transgender friends, websites, and information coming from the transgender lobby'[100].

In the tragic case of a relatively isolated young man of 26, going more and more on-line, but still in contact with his loving mother, he ends up coming out as transgender, changing his name, and going on feminizing hormones after one visit to a clinic. In his case, the increasing high doses of hormones, the lack of understanding about the family history of clotting, resulted in his untimely death[101].

Thus there seems to be a tendency to isolate children and young people from those naturally around them; and, therefore, play into the "in-group-think"; but, more widely, this suggests that this breaking of family

[99] Professor Dianna Kenny, "The Social Contagion of Gender Dysphoria": https://diannakenny.com.au/the-social-contagion-of-gender-dysphoria/.

[100] Kenny, "The Social Contagion of Gender Dysphoria".

[101] Megan Brock, "EXCLUSIVE: 'They Failed Him' — Cross Sex Hormones Killed Her Gender-Confused Son": https://dailycaller.com/2025/03/03/exclusive-they-failed-him-cross-sex-hormones-killed-her-gender-confused-son/.

relationships is a part of what happens in these ideologically driven settings. Thus, the question arises, why this negativity towards family relationships; indeed, is there some kind of reason for this impervious, almost black hole mentality - unless it is simply demonstrating an inability to discuss a point of view, respond to a mental challenge or generally being unable to examine the foundations of this kind of thinking.

> Witness what a woman said, when she thought about becoming a "man": "'If I had been banned from social media as a child, I would not have transitioned," Strongin says. "I was struggling with depression and bad self-esteem. I was also just impressionable and 14... There were so many reputable people, like doctors and mental health professionals saying, 'Yep, this is the standard treatment for this'"[102].

Therefore one element, not explicit in the Cass Review, but which was remarked upon by a report from young people's involvement in programs at the United Nations, is the following:

> 'While it is normal for young people not to have all their values and beliefs clarified, what is abnormal is for adults to push them to become advocates for causes whose implications they have yet not fully grasped'[103].

Having listened, then, to a dialogue with which I am sympathetic in so far as it is stepping back from the medicalization of young people and, therefore, advocating a more psychological approach to young people's

---

[102] "From girl to 'boy' to woman: a detransitioner's story", May 29th, 2024: An email excerpt from drmorse@ruthinstitute.org.

[103] Iulia Cazan, April, "ECOSOC Youth Forum": https://www.internationalyouthcoalition.com/unmonitor/ecosoc-youth-forumnbsp.

problems, I can see a kind of mismatch between the young person presenting, really, with an identity problem and swallowing a wholly unpalatable
answer to it as he or she does not have the critical capacity to discuss "the
solution". Therefore, if the gender crisis is symptomatic, actually, of good
and true questions about identity, then answering a child with the line that
you are "in the wrong body" is like jamming the wrong key in a lock and
finding that it cannot be easily removed – because it touches on a very deep
desire in young people: a desire to understand themselves, what they are
going through and who they are[104]. On the foundation, then, of a reasonable self-understanding, it seems more likely that even older people will
drawback from chemical or surgical changes to their body[105]; and, therefore, I hope that young people gravitate to the wider questions of "Who
am I?" and not just the presenting queries about his or her body?

In other words, are our young people being taught to be reasonably
critical or are they being led, through a combination of a lack of critical
thought and people who argue polemically, to lose their self-understanding to an immersive ideological position: a position that turns all opposition into a weaponised claim of hate speech? Given, then, the various factors that seem to come into play, particularly a rather generalised but pervasive youth culture of "influencing and being influenced" there is, simply,
the emphatic need to help the 'young person' as an individual[106].

What is evident, then, is that the "umbrella" claim that a particular
group is being denied their 'right' to exist, has a kind of automatic claim
on an uncritical response of "endorsing the right that is denied"; and,
therefore, even a well-qualified professional can find that they end up

---

[104] Cf. also Francis Etheredge, "Jammed Locks or Real Keys":
https://www.catholicprofiles.org/post/jammed-locks-or-real-keys.

[105] See the discussion called "Gender-Affirming Trans Therapy Is NOT
Healthy": https://www.youtube.com/watch?v=P5QArOidi3U.

[106] Cass Review, p. 27.

advocating against the evidence and truth of these early claims until, in the end, the person rejects the starting point of injustice. But, up until that point, the claim of a supposed injustice seems to disarm critical thinking[107].

How does all this impact on our subject of unfolding an identity? One, very obvious impact, is that a lot of young people are very confused about their own identity and so tend to think that there is going to be uncertainty about so many other aspects of their lives, whether work, training, or vocation. At the same time, from the point of view of what help is available, there is an immense challenge in the provision of suitable help.

For many, it may be too simple, but for all of us there needs to be a starting point that takes the person as a whole and not just in terms of presenting problems; and, therefore, there is the simplicity of announcing the love of God: that God loves you: the whole you! And that discovering or accepting this lays a foundation to an identity based on being a child of God, which is an enduring identity, and not on what otherwise is open to change and unstable (cf. Mt 7: 24-27). For human nature, clearly understood, is a combination of what changes and develops and what remains constant. Thus the "I" of human individuality, embodied in the distinct reality of being male or female, is the enduring reality; and, at the same time, the unfolding of the "I", from conception onwards, involves the changes that manifest the presence of the person from the beginning.

What is the right to self-expression?

Where are we if a man cannot think and pray in his heart, for a 'deceased son', even if he is near those taking the lives of children? 'The prosecution acknowledged that no public complaints were made

---

[107] Alicia Hendley, April 10th, 2019, "I supported trans ideology until I couldn't anymore": https://www.feministcurrent.com/2019/04/10/i-supported-trans-ideology-until-i-couldnt-anymore/.

against Adam.' At the same time, while a council is nearing bankruptcy it can spend around 100,000 pounds on prosecuting Adam and threatening him with a 2-year prison sentence[108]. What is happening that thought crimes, never mind free speech, can be the basis of a prosecution – as we are not talking about intending to commit violence or any offence remotely akin to it. But, rather, praying for good to be done and evil avoided. What happened, even, to his right to self-expression?

Indeed, 'Abortion is considered more sacrosanct than free speech. Anyone who disagrees with this comes up against the Cancel Culture'[109].

Even before examining the phrase 'expressive individualism', what is it to be an individualist in the first place? C. S. Lewis, in *Mere Christianity*, says the following: 'If you forget that … [another person] belongs to the same organism as yourself you will become an Individualist'[110]. On the basis, then, of *Individualism* there is already a separation from a common identity based on human personhood. In other words, we are not beings-in-relationship because relationship is between creatures of the same kind; rather, already, there a sense of estrangement, so that what is 'expressive' is, as it were, already out of the human context of bearing a common humanity.

'Playing a key role behind the scenes is expressive individualism, a radical autonomy that replaces the embodied relational person, connected to

---

[108] Jeremiah Igunnubole, Legal Counsel, ADF UK: https://us12.campaign-archive.com/?e=15b1cdc82b&u=2501acea9c85acb0f71c8fc94&id=43af812e8e.

[109] Dr Stuart Blackie FRCPath, "Has Modern Medicine Moved Away from Me?": https://www.cmq.org.uk/CMQ/2024/May/has_modern_medicine_moved_away_f.html.

[110] O'Brien, *The Family and the New Totalitarianism*, 2019, p. 165.

family and human nature, with the isolated psychological self who con-
structs his or her own morality[111].

Indeed, according to the document on the infinite dignity of the human being, there is another definition of this mentality:

'It is as if the ability to express and realize every individual preference or subjective desire should be guaranteed. This perspective identifies dignity with an isolated and individualistic freedom that claims to impose particular subjective desires and propensities as "rights" to be guaranteed and funded by the community'[112].

'The ascendance of expressive individualism, which can be traced to the Sexual Revolution, is partially responsible for the breakdown of marriage and has gained a foothold in religious institutions. Among others, it combines the thinking of Simone de Beauvoir, who divorced sex from gender; psychologist Sigmund Freud, who elevated human sexuality as central to identity; and philosopher Jean-Jacques Rousseau, who argued that man is innocent and corrupted by society'[113].

Whereas a true 'self-realization', as Pope Francis says, is that 'There is therefore in the heart of every man and woman the capacity to seek the good. The Holy Spirit is given so that those who receive it can clearly

---

[111] Brenda Hafera, March 19th, 2024, "Men Without Meaning: The Harmful Effects of Expressive Individualism": https://www.heritage.org/progressivism/report/men-without-meaning-the-harmful-effects-expressive-individualism.

[112] Declaration *"Dignitas Infinita"*, on Human Dignity, Presentation: paragraph: 25.

[113] Brenda Hafera, March 19th, 2024, "Men Without Meaning: The Harmful Effects of Expressive Individualism": https://www.heritage.org/progressivism/report/men-without-meaning-the-harmful-effects-expressive-individualism.

distinguish good from evil, have the strength to adhere to good by shunning evil, and, in so doing, achieve full self-realization'[114].

Indeed, Pope Francis seeks that place in a person's life where God is: 'Even if the life of a person has been a disaster, even if it is destroyed by vices, drugs or anything else — God is in this person's life'[115].

More specifically, then, there has emerged questions about the validity of the evidence on which decisions are made concerning a young person's health; and, therefore, the question arises as to what kind of philosophical ideas may be at work that tend, as it were, to override the need for evidence and demonstrated good outcomes. One such type of idea is what, at first, seems a reasonable principle: the right to self-expression.

Ordinarily, then, there is not only a right to self-expression but a necessity to do so, given that psychological development does seem to require that a person articulates his or her actual experience; indeed, it can almost be called a psychological law of making explicit what is implicit. Indeed, I can remember very clearly how suppressing my reaction to being humiliated at school, certainly suppressed the whole development of my interior conversation, as it were, about who I was and what I wanted to do. On examination, and many years later, I saw more clearly that my unwillingness to recognize my own suffering was a form of pride: that I would not show that I was hurt; and therefore, the psychological passes, as it were,

---

[114] POPE FRANCIS, *General Audience: Saint Peter's Square, Wednesday, 24 April 2024*: https://www.vatican.va/content/francesco/en/audiences/ 2024/documents/20240424-udienza-generale.html.

[115] From the first interview of Pope Francis in 'September 2013, [by] his Jesuit confrere Fr Antonio Spadaro', in an article by Dom Pius Mary Noonan, January 9th, 2025, "Benedictine monk: Francis has given us two keys for understanding his pontificate": https://www.lifesitenews.com/opinion/benedictine-monk-francis-has-given-us-two-keys-for-understanding-his-pontificate/.

into the spiritual and opens up a further horizon of what constitutes the person. But this passage, although present at the time of being humiliated and hating to cry or otherwise show any kind of suffering to others, did not begin to be clear until many years later and a long time after, as it were, the freeing up and flooding of childhood memories. The latter event being like scrabbling around in the mud for why I was like I was and suddenly a dam breaking and a whole history of suppressed memories just flooding consciousness. So, clearly, there is a right and necessary kind of self-expression.

The Cass Review, however, says: 'Many young people do not see themselves as having a medical condition and some may feel it undermines their autonomy and right to self-determination'[116] to say that they have.

Identity and dialogue

In general, whether in professional life, in one society or another, there is a growing difficulty of discussion. 'If the smartest kids at the most elite university arguably in the world aren't able to break ground — or even exchange words — on contentious topics, what hope do we have that future generations will make progress on the issues that divide us today?

The whole situation is made even worse by the fact that their professors are too scared to lead the way.

"The only way that these institutions can be trusted to separate truth from falsity is if they are comfortable challenging sacred cows through thought experimentation, devil's advocacy, and the rigors of the

---

[116] Cass Review, p. 29.

marketplace of ideas," Lukianoff said. "Unfortunately, we are nowhere near there"[117].

Ordinarily dialogue is about exploring questions of identity which range over many subjects, aspects of a person's life or an idea that is current, floated by various people or even thought up by the growing adult. If, however, this discussion is truncated, forbidden, riddled with restrictions or fears of legal intervention, where is the opportunity for exploratory discussions which are so much a part of growing up?

The question that arises, then, is how immersed a person is in an identity, rather than that identity, as a person develops, is open to question and development. Are there limits? Is the right to speak only for those campaigning for bodily mutilations? What about those who think this is ideologically driven and unsound? In other words what about those who argue that body changes are superficial changes that do not address the person's problems as presented and, what is more, leave the subject profoundly disfigured?

The Cass 'Review is not about defining what it means to be trans, nor is it about undermining the validity of trans identities, challenging the right of people to express themselves, or rolling back on people's rights to healthcare.'

Indeed, what is this 'right of people to express themselves'[118] if it involves mutilating their own bodies, drawing in others to help them

---

[117] Rikki Schlott, October 22nd, 2024, "Over half of Harvard professors are too afraid to discuss controversial subjects with students – what's become of this bastion of free speech?": https://nypost.com/2024/10/22/opinion/over-half-of-harvard-profs-fear-controversial-topics/.

[118] "The Cass Review", April 2024, "Foreword from the Chair", p. 12.

to do it? Is it that the medical professionals are drawn into making medic-inal or surgical interventions on the basis of an overly "biological" account of the human person: as if centuries of self-insight, psychological research, philosophical and theological thought are of no value whatsoever? Con-sider, too, that if there is an overly medical model of the human person in the fields of clinical medicine, what possibility is there of a presenting child, teenager or young adult, thinking beyond the physical possibilities of how to address gender distress? Similarly, the parents, school governors, and educational institutions: How many of them will be open, detached, or simply well-formed enough, philosophically, to consider the limitations of addressing the totality of the human person with a kind of physicalist account that the body is plastic and can be manipulated in any shape or form?

What about the claim that any and every other person has to agree with what they are doing or calling themselves? What about the freedom of a clinician to make a diagnosis: to offer an informed opinion on the difficul-ties that the presenting person is experiencing? What about the freedom of a parent, sibling, friend or teacher to offer a different interpretation of what the person is going through? In other words, is the so-called right of people 'to express themselves" without limits and not equally valid for those, whether peers, parents, teachers, medical staff, lawyers, employees who disagree with what is being done?

In general, then, there are many factors that mitigate against the mar-riageability of this generation, keeping in view the experience of real, face-to-face friendships, not to mention those attempts we all make to find a husband or wife, whether painful or not, and the groundwork of com-municating ourselves to another instead of a kind of internal monologue that does not necessarily help either the person concerned or the possibil-ity of being able to be open and to share life-experience with another or others.

More widely, 'Whenever man is regarded as a one-dimensional being, he becomes fragmented, riddled with doubts, negations, and inarticulate rage. He does not know who he is and for what he was created. As his exterior and interior world becomes a shambles he must be rescued by more and more remedies. Thus, the consumer society inevitably becomes the therapeutic society'[119].

As we have already discovered, with 420,000 young people and their families presenting themselves to the mental health services in one month, in 2022, it is clear that that we are becoming that 'therapeutic society'.

The mirror of the Word

As Scripture says:

"My son, eat honey, for it is good,
 and the drippings of the honeycomb are sweet to your taste.
[14] Know that wisdom is such to your soul;
 if you find it, there will be a future,
 and your hope will not be cut off" (Proverbs, 24: 13-14).
Is the advice good? Is the method good? Is the outcome good?

By contrast, God invites us to be simple: to accept our identity as a gift: that of being the children of God: a multi-faceted identity that does not deny our full reality but unfolds it wholly and in terms of its many complementary parts – all of which is a gift which unites us with others and divides us from isolationism. In other words, our doubts and difficulties

---

[119] O'Brien, *The Family and the New Totalitarianism*, 2019, p. 126.

are in the context of a relationship to God and His word which can reveal us to ourselves more clearly, to use an expression, in the *mirror of the word*. So that we look at ourselves steadily and discover, more and more clearly, who we are and what it is right to do:

> 'Anyone who listens to the Word and takes no action is like someone who looks at his own features in a mirror and, once he has seen what he looks like, goes off and immediately forgets it. But anyone who looks steadily at the perfect law of freedom and keeps to it – not listening and forgetting, but putting it into practice – will be blessed in every undertaking' (James 1: 22-25).

Thus there is, in the word of God, a pool of wisdom which shows us how to become the person we are! At the same time the word of God, which unites us to the whole of humanity, tends to integrate us into the human family; and, therefore, the tendency to see ourselves as so unique that we cannot be members of the same human family is subjected to a healthy challenge. Thus, without a common understanding of who each of us is, whether we be male or female, there is the danger that marriage no longer makes sense of our identity as male or female, such that there is no longer a common substrate, as it were, about what it is to be a human being. Thus, for whatever end it serves, marriage itself, for one reason or another, is seen as a "disease" instead of a symptom of "health"; although, as we know, it is constantly in need of renewal.

Prose and a Prayer for Women Athletes:

"Women in Sport"

'The replacement of the female sports category with a mixed-sex category has resulted in an increasing number of female athletes losing opportunities, including medals, when competing against males. According to information received, by 30 March 2024, over 600 female athletes in more than 400 competitions have lost more than 890 medals in 29 different sports'[1].

What kind of evidence is offered to justify this: that "men who self-identify as women are women"?

'The [Irish] Government's new Science Advisor believes that biological males "are women" if they identify as transgender women.'

"I am a biologist, and I'm pretty sure that whatever you can think of, there exists both an example and a counter-example somewhere in nature," McLysaght said in a 2020 social media post'[2]. Similarly, according to current Olympic guidelines, athletes only need to have a "female" sex marker on their legal documents in order to be permitted to compete in the women's category'. The now retiring President of the Olympic Committee, 'Thomas Bach ... [he said] that there was no scientific method to determine who is a man and who is a woman'[3]. According to a law firm, testing a man's

---

[1] Reem Alsalem, in accordance with Assembly resolution 77/193, 27th August, 2024, "Violence against women and girls, its causes and consequences", p. 5: https://documents.un.org/doc/undoc/gen/n24/249/94/pdf/n2424994.pdf.

[2] Ben Scallan, October 10th, 2024, "New Government science advisor: Trans males are women": https://gript.ie/new-government-science-advisor-trans-males-are-women/.

[3] Marielena Meder, October 23rd, 2024, "GERMANY: Transgender Martial Artist Who Kicked Female Opponent So Hard She Forfeited Match Aims To

DNA is a 'scientific test that can provide conclusive' evidence of paternity[4]; how, then, can an Olympic official claim that there is no 'scientific method to determine who is a man and who is a woman'? How is it that an Olympic official can make such a contradictory claim – as it is precisely scientists who have demonstrated that an XY and an XX set of chromosomes express the sex of the person as male or female? So how do we know that the XX chromosomes come from both father and mother, whereas the X chromosome comes from the mother and the Y chromosome from the father – if not from those whose science it is to share this knowledge with us?

Where, however, is there a self-identification in nature equivalent to a man saying he is a woman and others believing him? Therefore, let us take the following, unusual example: a male sea horse has a pouch into which the female deposits her eggs and then the male fertilizes them and, after a couple of weeks, the baby sea horses leave the pouch and swim off. This, however, is not a creature in nature self-identifying as a female[5]; it is, rather, a very unique type of reproduction, whereby the male is still a male producing sperm and the female is still an egg producing female – but instead of the male depositing the seed in the female, the female deposits the unfertilized egg in the male's own sac. Therefore, the principle of reproduction remains, that the female produced the egg and the male fertilizes it. Moreover, according to an atheist biologist, even in the case of a male sea horse there are two types of 'reproductive cells' that define biological

Compete As A Woman At The 2028 Olympics": https://reduxx.info/germany-transgender-martial-artist-who-kicked-female-opponent-so-hard-she-forfeited-match-aims-to-compete-as-a-woman-at-the-2028-olympics/.

[4] "Establishing Paternity: A Comprehensive Guide": https://www.nicolsono-briensolicitors.co.uk/establishing-paternity-comprehensive-guide/.

[5] "The Only Male Animals in the World That Get Pregnant and Give Birth": https://blog.padi.com/the-only-male-animals-in-the-world-that-get-pregnant-and-give-birth/.

sex as male and female[6]. While, therefore, I may disagree with what an author says on other subjects, it is good to see biologists objecting to the falsehood that denying two sexes is scientific[7]. In other words, if evidence and reason can lead to this truth maybe it can open up other fields for investigation too.

We can note, here, too, that the 'Executive Order' of January 20th, 2025, of the Trump Administration, uses precisely this language of the 'large reproductive cell' and, what is more, goes further, saying that the female person, 'from conception', 'will produce the 'large reproductive cell'[8] (known as the egg or ovum'. At the same time, however, Trump's Administration has to recognize the inconsistency, therefore, of promoting in-vitro technology, which selects, freezes, kills and experiments upon the very human embryos who are elsewhere called, in the above Executive Order, male persons and female persons from conception. However, the Executive Order promoting IVF availability, also promotes the natural birth of children and adoption: 'He also signed into law a provision that enables new parents to withdraw up to $5,000 from their retirement accounts without penalty when they give birth to or adopt a child'[9].

---

[6] Conflating my own conclusion with of Professor 'Coyne, an emeritus professor of Ecology and Evolution at the University of Chicago': see his piece "Biology is Not Bigotry": https://www.realityslaststand.com/p/biology-is-not-bigotry.

[7] Thus I disagree with Jonathon Von Maren on this one, January 9th, 2025, "'Anti-woke' atheists who oppose gender ideology are not our allies: here's why": https://www.lifesitenews.com/news/anti-woke-atheists-who-oppose-gender-ideology-are-not-our-allies-heres-why/?utm_source=digest-profamily-2025-01-09.

[8] "Executive Order", January 20th, 2025: https://www.whitehouse.gov/presidential-actions/2025/01/defending-women-from-gender-ideology-extremism-and-restoring-biological-truth-to-the-federal-government/: (d).

[9] "Fact Sheet: President Donald J. Trump Expands Access to In Vitro Fertilization (IVF)", February 18th, 2025: https://www.whitehouse.gov/fact-

Furthermore, it has already been evidenced that where a chemical fertilizer interferes with natural development of a male frog, the frog remains male even if it is "feminized". The effect, then, of 'Atrazine' on a frog is to feminize it while it remains a male frog; and, as regards men 'atrazine exposure is highly correlated ($P < 0.009$) with low sperm count, poor semen quality, and impaired fertility in humans'[10]. In other words, even in terms of the effects of a chemical on the male species of a frog and a human being, the chemical fertilizer modifies a male and does not "create a female". Therefore the basic identity, even when influenced by chemicals, remains male. Thus there is no case for arguing that a human being can be made to change sex, even in a biological sense, by chemical means; for, the reality of the organism remains male, whether a frog or a man. And, what is more, a human being is a psychosomatic whole, which is a different kind of entity to that of a frog; and, as such, it is even more the case that altering the body does not alter the whole, which is either a male person or a female person[11].

In the case of a man who tried to become a woman at 42, he discovered that there were traumas that drove that desire to change; and, eventually, he realized that surgery was no answer to the psychological problems that he needed help with. Although, then, he could not undo the harm of the surgery he underwent, amazingly, he went on to be reconciled to being a

---

sheets/2025/02/fact-sheet-president-donald-j-trump-expands-access-to-in-vitro-fertilization-ivf/.

[10] Tyrone B Hayes [a,1], Vicky Khoury [a,2], Anne Narayan [a,2], Mariam Nazir [a,2], Andrew Park [a,2], Travis Brown [a], Lillian Adame [a], Elton Chan [a], Daniel Buchholz [b], Theresa Stueve [a], Sherrie Gallipeau [a]

"Atrazine induces complete feminization and chemical castration in male African clawed frogs (*Xenopus laevis*)": https://pmc.ncbi.nlm.nih.gov/articles/PMC2842049/.

[11] Cf. Etheredge, examples of arguments in *The Human Person: A Bioethical Word*: https://enroutebooksandmedia.com/bioethicalword/; and examples of case histories in *Mary and Bioethics: An Exploration*: https://enroutebooksandmedia.com/maryandbioethics/.

man: 'Instead of encouraging them to undergo unnecessary and destructive surgery, let's affirm and love our young people just the way they are'[12].

What evidence is offered to identify and classify the multifaceted injustice to women in sport?

In what follows there is a stunning statement for its clarity and objectivity, not only stating the obvious science but drawing attention to what is binding in international law. 'Alsaleem [the UN Special Rapporteur on Violence Against Women, in her latest report to the General Assembly,] insisted that it is factually correct to refer to these individuals as "men who self-identify as women." She said, "Human rights language and principles must continue to be consistent with science and facts, including biological ones."

Thus, recently, it has been evidenced that a male martial artist, claiming to be a woman, 'kneed a female boxer in the stomach with so much force that she had to immediately quit the match'[13]. Similarly, a boy has not just outjumped girls but set a new record[14]; and, therefore, there is a difference between girls and boys competing informally and a formal record being kept, which takes down a previous girl's record jump.

---

[12] Walt Heyer, April 1st 2015, "I Was a Transgender Woman": https://www.thepublicdiscourse.com/2015/04/14688/.

[13] Meder, October 23rd, 2024, "GERMANY: Transgender Martial Artist Who Kicked Female Opponent So Hard She Forfeited Match Aims To Compete As A Woman At The 2028 Olympics".

[14] Ryan Gaydos, February 27th, "Martina Navratilova takes shot at Gavin Newsom over California's trans-athlete policy": https://www.foxnews.com/sports/martina-navratilova-takes-shot-gavin-newsom-over-californias-trans-athlete-policy.

However, there is a possibility of a new "Bill" being passed in America which is designed to recognize biological sex and is otherwise called 'Protection of Women and Girls in Sports Acts of 2025'[15].

In contrast to recognizing Alsaleem's evidence, she was accused of "online harassment, abuse, and gender disinformation". In other words, another instance of name calling to discredit the speaker rather than to examine what Alsaleem has to say. What, then, is the vested interest that results in Alsaleem's document so quickly maligned and blighted? Have those who criticized it read it or just "reacted" to a script not their own? Similarly, a girl who objected to a boy on an all-girls basketball team, is being accused of bullying the boy[16]. In other words, a complete contradiction of common-sense justice.

As Alsaleem goes on to say, "Sex must be understood in its ordinary meaning to mean biological sex," Alsaleem said, quoting the landmark 1995 UN women's agreement at the Beijing conference. She went even further, suggesting that while the category of "sex" based on biology was established in international human rights law, the category of "gender" was not and that the two categories must not be confused.

"Nondiscrimination based on sex is recognized in all major international human rights agreements," she said whereas, "conflating sex and gender identity through the creation of a legal sex category (gender as

---

[15] Bill: 2025-01-03-Protection-of-Women-and-Girls-in-Sports-Act-Text.pdf. Under the Trump administration there are a number of developments which, collectively, are seeking to correct the inappropriate presence of men in women's sports and private spaces, and which are now making progress in the law.

[16] Warner Todd Hudson, February 28th, 2025, "Washington State Launches Bullying Investigation into Teen Girl Who Refused to Play Against Trans Opponent": https://www.breitbart.com/sports/2025/02/28/washington-state-launches-bullying-investigation-teen-girl-refused-play-against-trans-opponent/.

distinct from sex) has been confusing and problematic"[17]. In a recent judgment from 'A federal district court in Kentucky issued a decision … in *State of Tennessee v. Cardona* that blocks' Biden's government from trying to substitute 'gender identity' for 'sex'; thus ensuring the very point of 'Title IX', which was to protect women in sport and their spaces from men claiming to be women[18].

In the report itself, which is well worth reading, there is a tragic account of a kind of self-enclosed world of sport, with very little external regulation of justice to women and girls, which is a travesty in these modern times and cries out for attention and redress. In other words, if the UN takes itself seriously as a guarantor of human rights, this is a document to act on and to recover the truth expressed in its binding laws[19].

By contrast, Idaho has published legislation that takes out the confusion caused by using the term "gender identity" and restores the original meaning of male and female, not only banning men from women's spaces, but also preventing them from competing as "women" and taking the scholarships which were intended for women[20]. Similarly, another law

---

[17] By Stefano Gennarini, J.D. | October 10, 2024, "UN Official Defends Women's Sports Against Male Incursion": https://c-fam.org/friday_fax/un-official-defends-womens-sports-against-male-incursion/.

[18] Alliance Defending Freedom, January 10th, 2025, "Pro-family lawyer celebrates rejection of Biden's pro-LGBT Title IX rules: 'Colossal win'": https://www.lifesitenews.com/news/pro-family-lawyer-celebrates-rejection-of-bidens-pro-lgbt-title-ix-rules-colossal-win/.

[19] Reem Alsalem, in accordance with Assembly resolution 77/193, 27th August, 2024, "Violence against women and girls, its causes and consequences": https://documents.un.org/doc/undoc/gen/n24/249/94/pdf/n2424994.pdf; indeed, this is so clearly articulated it is a human rights document in its own right.

[20] Justine Brooke Murray | August 29, 2024, "Riley Gaines Celebrates Idaho As FIRST State to Block Men From Women's Spaces": https://www.mrctv.org/blog/justine-brooke-murray/riley-gaines-celebrates-idaho-first-state-block-men-womens-spaces.

mandates teachers 'to use pronouns that align with a student's biological sex, as listed on their birth certificate, rather than their "gender identity"' [21]. And, more generally, one wonders at the extent to which the law has been dominated by these kinds of disputes, necessary to restore justice – but unnecessary if biological sex had not been disputed.

The wider context of women in sport and the increasing recognition of design requirements that reflect women's needs

There are many commonsense reasons why women's sports need to be a protected category when it comes to men claiming to be women and thus they object to be left out of women's sports. In other words, the legal muscle that is used to bully women's sports into accepting men into women's competitions is clearly the injustice; not, by contrast, women seeking to keep women's sports for women. The fact that this is lost sight of because of gender ideology which says, in effect, I am whatever I call myself, means that justice is undone; and, if we read the evidence where is, literally, the equal footing between men and women? Where is the claim for evidence-based definitions of sporting justice?

Historically, 'Women were excluded from some sports until very recently: the FA banned women's football between 1921 and 1971. Women were only allowed to run in the Olympic marathon since 1984 and to participate in pole vault at the Olympics from 2000 and women were not allowed to compete in all sports on the Olympic programme until London 2012. Even now in 2023, 22% fewer girls than boys in England are playing

---

[21] Morgonn McMichael, 09/01/2024, "MORGONN MCMICHAEL: Texas school district mandates teachers use pronouns aligning with students' biological sex": https://humanevents.com/2024/09/01/morgonn-mcmichael-texas-school-district-mandates-teachers-use-pronouns-aligning-with-students-biological-sex.

team sport. That's 860,000 girls missing out, the equivalent to the capacity of every Premier League stadium'[22].

What is also very significant is that if sport can be a vehicle for women training to be leaders, especially in countries where their participation is undervalued[23], then, to change the focus to men competing in women's sports is to lose the personal and social impact of these initiatives. However, in another sense, all those women who are standing up for a woman's right to a woman's sport[24], are implicitly manifesting a willingness to take the lead in reasserting the reality of human rights and, simultaneously, demonstrating their political maturity[25]. The good, therefore, that they are doing goes beyond sport in that it is a part of recovering the real meaning of human rights based on a real grasp of human nature.

Moreover, this preoccupation with men in women's sports completely overlooks the question of why a man wants to play in a woman's team; and, therefore, the question of his general education about the needs and rights of women, which is separate to the right of women to their own sports. In one case, it seems, the timed performance of a man matched women's qualifying times but not that of the man's category; and,

---

[22] "Safe and Fair Sport Matters to Women and Girls on Every Level": https://womeninsport.org/safe-and-fair-sport-for-women-and-girls/.

[23] Cf. November 6th, 2024, "Faith and sports unite to empower women in Pakistan": https://www.faithonview.com/faith-and-sports-unite-to-empower-women-in-pakistan/.

[24] Cf. Valerie Richardson, October 15th, 2024, "Nevada governor backs volleyball players boycotting game over transgender rival": https://www.washingtontimes.com/news/2024/oct/15/joe-lombardo-backs-volleyball-players-boycotting-g/.

[25] Cf. Michael Reagan, November 8th, 2024, "Female Athletes Finally Stand Up to 'Men' Invaders": https://www.newsmax.com/reagan/hemales-sports/2024/10/29/id/1185829/.

therefore, he won in a woman's race but would not have qualified in a man's race[26].

Is it, as some say, a sign of 'prioritizing the feelings of trans-identifying males over the rights of female athletes'[27], in which case, what about women's feelings which reasonably express their right to separate, sex-specific events, when otherwise an injustice prevails? In another case, a woman volleyball player was hit in the head by a ball from a man on a woman's team and suffered a head injury and its consequences ever since. But, significantly, not only was there no apology but the attitude of the man showed a significant poverty in either appreciating what he had done or realizing, as a consequence, that he was in the wrong team for the sport[28]. Why were there no repercussions for him or those who were responsible for this unwarranted interference in a woman's match? What about those who determine the regulations for these sports; for, after all, was there not a reason why men and women's sports developed according to the requirements of each sex?[29]

Having said that, there are cases where justice is preserved in mixed sports between men and women, as in mixed doubles in tennis, horse racing, or any sport where that combination of non-contact and skill, makes

[26] Amy Hamm, December 29, 2024, "Trans-Identified Male Qualifies To Compete As "Female" In 2025 Boston Marathon, Sparking Outrage From Female Runners » :   https://reduxx.info/trans-identified-male-qualifies-to-compete-as-female-in-2025-boston-marathon-sparking-outrage-from-female-runners/.

[27] Calvin Freiburger, December 19th, 2024, "Republicans grill NCAA chief over men in women's sports, locker rooms": https://www.lifesitenews.com/news/republicans-grill-ncaa-chief-over-men-in-womens-sports-locker-rooms/.

[28] December 18th, 2024, "Volleyball Player Speaks Out After Life-Altering Injury by Trans Opponent": https://www.ndtv.com/world-news/volleyball-player-shares-story-in-new-docu-after-life-changing-injury-by-trans-opponent-7274620.

[29] Freiburger, December 19th, 2024, "Republicans grill NCAA chief over men in women's sports, locker rooms".

cooperation not just possible but equitable[30]. Having said that, the *British Lawn Tennis Association* has just banned men from entering women's categories, using scientific evidence of sex-based differences that persist even after lower 'testosterone levels or surgical procedures'[31] that mask being of the male-sex-at-conception; and, therefore, women's singles would be for women. In other words, justice needs a concrete expression.

In addition, the realization that the shape of men and women has a bearing on the design of seat-belts, police clothing and other items, means that it is increasingly noted that the default pattern of design was almost always for men; and, therefore, that it is realistic to reconsider designs which are both specific to women, such as women's protective clothing, or where there are two settings, one for women and one for men – perhaps especially with reference to women drivers and those with particular safety belt needs like pregnant women[32]. In other words, there is a growing sensitivity to sex-based differences which are critical for the everyday comfort and well-being of both women and men in the workplace.

These same sex-based differences feature in fairness in sport and, more widely, in the field of women's safety in situations in which women are vulnerable, as in shared locker rooms and other no longer protected spaces. In other words, while voyeurism, the look-with-lust, is objectionable generally, can this be excluded from those men who insist in being in

---

[30] Cf. Nadira Faber, July 31, 2012, "Should Men and Women be segregated in professional Sports?": https://blog.practicalethics.ox.ac.uk/2012/07/should-men-and-women-be-segregated-in-professional-sports/.

[31] Warner Todd Huston, 15 Dec 2024, "British Lawn Tennis Association Bans Transgender Players in Women's Event": https://www.breitbart.com/sports/2024/12/15/british-lawn-tennis-association-bans-transgender-players-in-womens-event/.

[32] Caroline Criado Perez, 23rd February, 2019, "The deadly truth about a world built for men – from stab vests to car crashes": https://www.theguardian.com/life-andstyle/2019/feb/23/truth-world-built-for-men-car-crashes.

women's protected spaces? Or is the "new" anthropology so naïve as to suggest there is no "alternative" motive for being in women's spaces other than the false claim to be a woman?

'When it comes to key factors that affect many different sports, men have:

- 10-12% faster times for most linear swimming and running events;
- 20% better results in jumping events;
- 35% greater weightlifting ability in weight-matched males and females;
- 50% greater weightlifting ability based on NHS average sizes for males and females'[33].

According to a football coach turned American Senator, if there are no restrictions on men competing in women's sports, then together with limited funding for women, 'there will be no women's sports left in five years'[34].

In general, then, there has been a remarkable blindness to the everyday effects of self-proclaiming sex-identities; and, if it were not for the misuse of the law, many of these would have died on the lips of those who suggested them. As regards our children growing up, do not many of them see that if an arbitrary claim can override reason and evidence, then what threshold is not beyond reach? In other words, if the evidence from physiological studies, characteristics of the effects of training on men and

---

[33] "Safe and Fair Sport Matters to Women and Girls on Every Level": https://womeninsport.org/safe-and-fair-sport-for-women-and-girls/.

[34] Elizabeth Troutman Mitchell | December 09, 2024, « Football Coach-Turned-Senator's Playbook for Saving Women's Sports": https://www.dailysignal.com/2024/12/09/alabama-senators-playbook-trump-admin-save-womens-sports/

women, and that engineers and clothes manufacturers are becoming increasingly sensitive to male and female differences, why are some clinicians, bureaucrats and sports officials unable to recognize irreversible and substantial differences in men and women?

In what follows, then, there is a reflection on the deepest roots of human identity, male and female; and, in view of this, the possibility that people will begin to reconsider the widespread fallacy of claiming that there is no difference between men and women.

Women in Sport

Dear Mary, you were a child once, maybe once running around and chasing other children and being chased, perhaps playing tag and running in and out of the washing lines or up and down the hills.

Did you race down, and tumble down, running and rolling down, or race back up, maybe not calling the loser a slug, but helping up who had fallen, heading back home for lunch, a clean-up and a rest too?

Dear Mary, you are renowned for appearing to the poor, not the fittest, fastest, or most agile of women, and yet there are those who love like you, your Son, who were full of the zipping zest for sport.

Did these zealous women, train harder, faster and higher, competing all the while to win medals of a glittering, temporary kind, and maybe they thought of St. Paul racing for an everlasting reward?

Dear Mary, you know how fashions have changed, once women were covered in cumbersome garments but now, the other extreme, pray for a step-back from barely enough to suitably modest clothing.

Did the media pick out the fastest, most graceful, delightful of faces, noting how the second helped the lead who collapsed to cross the line, leaving behind a ruthless win and winning in her humanity?
Dear Mary, women are not a race behind but leading the course,
some live the active life to the full, singing and dancing, tennis and horse riding, yielding only to death after entering religious life.

Did women believe the lie that there is no nobility and purpose in motherhood, so their hearts shrink while their influence seems to resound around the world, glamorizing singleness, only to regret all?

Dear Mary, did your family watch you play and then, calling you in, send you on an errand to the elderly, the housebound, those in need, and were you happy in these visits and on these missions to others?

Did you feel cheated of your childhood, visiting here and there, or are you shockingly happy to be sung through time, rejoicing in your Son's love, calling you out of total obscurity to light a way to Him?

Dear Mary, pray for the call to be like you, whether running on the field, jumping the bars of achievements, raising the level of love's loving the gift of womanhood, or just being you, loving to love all.

Did it matter that no one recorded your fastest run, your highest jump, your longest leap, as you outstripped us all in the race to pass through eternity's opening, as you ran home ahead of all mankind?

Dear Mary, turn our hearts and the hearts of all women, to the irreplaceable gift that each one is given, whether in the glory hall or the lowest place of all places where only the poorest are to be found.

Did you know we need you to help us, now more than ever, keeping us together in a mother's love between us, turning each from the other so that we are all turned together to hope in your only Son?

Chapter Four

Obstacles to Relationships and Marriage:
Looking for Answers

Advising about the use of dating apps, which seems to be on the increase as opposed to actually knowing someone from real sources, is like advising a person to do a reality check; but, in view of all we know in recent times, reality checks are in decline and may just be viewed in terms of being "out of date" on "how to date". But what confirmation is there that the person "pictured" and "described" is as he or she says is the case? In other words, what real-world evidence is there, in terms of who knows the person and is already a reliable witness to who the person is and the truth of what is said? What safeguards are there to deception? What evidence is there that this is not just another opportunity to opt out of what already exists and is difficult, 'as that is how marriage works'[1].

In a statement remarkable for its optimism unless, of course, this expresses the reality of true hope which is anchored in baptism and in heaven, itself, a novelist and social commentator says: 'When the tyrants and the propagandists and the experimenters have all gone, when the hatred and hopelessness has exhausted itself, the earth will grieve and be born again. The Church and family will remain. Then, all who have sown in struggle will reap a harvest of joy'[2].

'Would reviving marriage, 'revive families, thereby reviving the birth rate and ultimately reviving the country and maybe even the civilized

---

[1] Nancy Jo Sales, 18th November, 2023, "Relationships that begin online are less stable – I've seen it time and time again": https://www.theguardian.com/commentisfree/2023/nov/18/relationships-online-mates.

[2] Michael D. O'Brien, *The Family and the New Totalitarianism*, 2019, p. 24.

world'[3]? Now the call to revive marriage is indeed a good objective, especially as we have seen the trauma and fallout from divorce, gender distress and fatherlessness. Thus to rebuild marriages is also to restore hope to the children of once-divorced parents that, if they are called to marriage, reconciliation is possible in front of the cross, the unchosen but real obstacles to happiness in a marriage. Or maybe those entering marriage for the first time can see more clearly what marriage is, and that it draws on the reciprocal gift of husband and wife, open to the gift of life and supported in various ways by family, Church communities and, in some cases, society's deliberate help. But we have also entered times in which the call to conversion is raising, more and more, the need for prayer.

Indeed, with the incremental increase of a third world war, are we not ever more in need of prayer, the life of prayer, whether we are married, contemplating marriage or recovering from divorce? In other words, the foundations of a Christian life have not only to contend with the reality of people's lives in the midst of various kind of social disorder, but with the possibility that more than one vocation may be necessary for our times.

'Brad Wilcox from the University of Virginia, wrote an article in the New York Times, saying, "It turns out that the happiest of all wives in America are religious conservatives. Fully 73% of wives who hold conservative gender values and attend religious services regularly with their husbands have high-quality marriages."'

And, indeed, if there is widespread cultural agreement that men provide, procreate and protect[4], then clearly the abortion culture in which

---

[3] Chuck Chalberg, 9th of April, 2024, "Get Married! How American Families Can Save Civilization".

[4] Joy Lucius, October 6th, 2023, "Masculinity": https://www.afa.net/the-stand/family/2023/10/masculinity/.

men either silently or vociferously advocate for it, simultaneously destroys the groundwork of manhood.

'Cardinal Carlo Caffarra, … quoted Sister Lucia's words from … [her letter to the Pope]: "The final battle between the Lord and the kingdom of Satan will be about marriage and family . . . nevertheless, Our Lady has already crushed his head"'[5].

Why, we might ask, is the 'final battle … about marriage and family'? Is it because we are made in the image and likeness of God, that God Himself is, as it were, both intimately involved in each one of us coming to exist. As St. Paul says in the Acts of the Apostles, it is God 'who gives everything – including life and breath – to everyone' (Acts 17: 25). Therefore, the very identity of man and woman is a communication of the mystery of God; and, if that mystery is totally rejected, then that rejection shows itself in the vulnerability of marriage and family to destruction. Thus the conception of a human being expresses both the vulnerability of the human person to being extinguished and the action of God to being denied, overlooked or rejected. Consider that in America, for example, the promotion of abortion is higher than ever and the birth rate is lower than ever[6]: what message does this entail for marriage and family life?

---

[5] Mark Drogin, July 29th, 2021, "The Final Battle: Marriage and Family": https://www.hprweb.com/2021/07/the-final-battle-marriage-and-family/, quoting from a "Radio interview with Cardinal Caffarra following Mass at the tomb of Saint Padre Pio, February 16, 2008".

[6] Steven Ertelt, 25th April, 2024, "America's Fertility Rate Hits Record Low as Planned Parenthood Abortions Hit Record High": https://www.lifenews.com/2024/04/25/americas-fertility-rate-hits-record-low-as-planned-parenthood-abortions-hit-record-high/.

What is happening to people on-line and does it help boys and girls be ready,
   if they choose marriage, to court and marry?

We have already witnessed multiple social problems in the world in
which we live, some of them, like war, we have scarcely touched upon, even
if the event of war is a terrible and ongoing experience of everyday life becoming a desperate situation for so many people and the fear of the future
a source of anxiety for them and for us all. Rather, we have touched upon
the harmful, social media, somewhat extensively, as it is a groundbreaking
movement affecting so many of us, directly and indirectly; and, therefore,
let us examine a little more closely its impact on the possibility of marriage.
We know, from what many teenage girls, but also boys, are going through,
that many are confused or distressed about their identity; indeed, perhaps
not appreciating how deeply each one of us is male and female and, therefore, trying to migrate away from a given identity, thinking that it would
be better to be "other" than I am.

When I was a young man, my unhappiness was not connected to being
on social media but rather was deeply rooted in childhood humiliations
and a general state of being undeveloped, personally and socially. Indeed,
I neither had a computer nor a phone nor any of these items, even if they
existed somewhere they were not in my world. Nevertheless, I was deco-
rating a room in my parent's house and thinking, without thinking it
through, that it would be easier if I was a woman and did not have to worry
about what my talents were and what work or vocation I would do. As I
think back on those thoughts now, I see how unrealistic they were about
what a "woman" was and a kind a of hopelessness about my self-ignorance.
Moreover, there were other experiences I ran into, as it were, somewhat
unexpectedly. One was going out with a girl who said she was a lesbian
who lived with her mother and her estranged father was elsewhere; but, it
turned out, her lesbianism was relatively changeable in that she said it was

possible, she thought, to be open to marriage with a man if he was different to what she feared a man to be like. These and other experiences made me realize that our identities are impacted by our experiences but not totally governed by them; and, therefore, we need to reflect more deeply on what an identity is but, first, some further thoughts on what girls and boys are going through today

Now, however, we are amidst a different social situation: given the widespread use of social media, it is almost impossible to avoid some contact with it; and, therefore, the issue is about that contact being constructive and helpful. In general, parents, teachers, and friends are competitors for attention; and, therefore, it may be necessary to have some kind of tacit or explicit agreement about when phones can and cannot be used[7]. And, as has been said elsewhere, there is a growing need for face-to-face contact and good, general experience of life.

Clearly, with on-line users, there is a particular problem of who the "other" is, as the falsification of identity is very easy with the screen in between one person and another. Thus, I even warn my older children to find some other way of proving the identity of a person – certainly before actually meeting anyone. And, clearly, there are obvious reasons why meeting is better in a public place, with others who are known in the group. Moreover, there are work reasons why one person may be looking for others, but then there are obvious sources of verification, like a university or college address, published articles and biographies that either confirm or show up, by virtue of their scarcity, whether or not someone is worth contacting directly.

What we are dealing with here, then, is the question of how social media affects the development of girls and boys with respect to their ability to both to make and assess real relationships. One of the group effects is that young people were checking their phones in breaks, making less 'eye

---

[7] Heidt, *The Anxious Generation*, 2024, p. 293 etc.

contact' with each other, less laughing together and a lot less 'practice making conversation'[8]; and, as one of my sons who is not on a phone says, of school, he often feels left out owing to the eyes down and scrolling or texting activity.

Teen vulnerability seems particularly connected to 'how they look, especially as they begin to develop romantic interests'[9]. At the same time, if the world of adult men and women is compromised in so many ways, not least because of the money involved in on-line pornography, why is it surprising if this mentality begins in our youth? Clearly, this does not refer to those whose lives have been stolen so much as those who are taking advantage of "sin for profit"[10]. Indeed, as we see from more and more investigative journalism, the age in which children are mired in the muck is lower and lower:

'A new report by the Internet Watch Foundation (IWF), the first analysis of its kind, has revealed widespread online sexual abuse of three to six-year-old children while they are using household devices'[11].
The effect of social media on girls and women

'What do high heels, a pearl necklace, and a just-below-the-knee dress-wearing woman have in common with a tattooed, gun-slinging, boot-wearing and butt-kicking woman? You guessed it, absolutely nothing,

[8] Heidt, *The Anxious Generation*, 2024, p. 149.

[9] Heidt, *The Anxious Generation*, 2024, p. 154.

[10] ""Porn & OnlyFans Are Worse Than You Think!" - Brutal Advice For Men & Women | Jordan Peterson": https://www.youtube.com/watch?v=-LlhHIW3UUQ.

[11] Zoe Crowther, 23rd April, « "Devastating" Report Shows Thousands Of Children Under Six Being Sexually Abused Online": https://www.politicshome.com/news/article/devastating-report-shows-children-six-sexually-abused-online.

except for the fact that both images, though starkly different, have had a profound effect on women and womanhood in America and elsewhere. And let's not forget the images of braless-dancing and contorted twisting and twerking women dominating our music and entertainment industries today. They are also having an effect on women and womanhood.'

'When God transforms you, your life is no longer centered on you and "your truth"'[12].

If girls are concerned with a 'communion' that 'arises from striving to integrate the self in a larger social unit through caring for others'[13], then the use of social media to express that connection with a 'larger social unit' suggests that the young girl's acceptance or rejection by this "on-line" community has a profound bearing on her identity. In other words, being a part of a social group or not being a part of a social group seems to confer some kind of fundamental plank of the girl's identity. A part of being able to connect with others comes from being able to share emotions[14] and everyday experiences which, also, means that the girls are vulnerable to copying "mental illnesses" from others. From the point of view of the effect of social media, there are certain consequences that show, then, very quickly, that there is a kind of trapdoor through which, once a girl falls through, there are multiple problems. In 2019 it was beginning to be documented that there was a connection between 'the role of social media exposure and the possibility of social contagion in the onset of ROGD' [rapid onset

---

[12] Teresa Skepple, October 11th, 2024, "Unhinged No More: Understanding What It Means to Be a Transformed Woman of God": https://g3min.org/un-hinged-no-more-understanding-what-it-means-to-be-a-transformed-woman-of-god/.

[13] Heidt, *The Anxious Generation*, 2024, p. 152.

[14] Heidt, *The Anxious Generation*, 2024, pp. 161-165.

gender dysphoria][15]; and, moreover, 'when there are problems in parent-child relationships, teenagers are vulnerable' to all kinds of influence and 'some have speculated that "gender" is the new language of teenage rebellion'[16]. Furthermore, with the rise of social media access, there is the following escalation of identity crises, mostly among girls: 'For Americans 18-25, trans identity skyrocketed from just over half a percent of the population in 2014 to over 3% of the population in 2023'[17]. Now, in 2024, there is an immense social need to understand what is happening and to help any number of people with what they are going through[18] without exacerbating their problems with irreversible changes.

Using filters and tuning apps 'gave girls the ability to present themselves with perfect skin, fuller lips, bigger eyes, and a narrower waist … showcasing the most "perfect" parts of their lives' and, therefore, either comparing themselves favourably or unfavourably to others[19]. At the same time, owing to algorithms, if a teen looks up dieting, she will be inundated with thousands of videos to do with it[20]. In a rather striking interview, one of the "influencers" was living a lie in that she was underweight and suffering from the burden of excessive exercise and posting about herself when she was actually, regularly exhausted from her lifestyle. When, however, she wanted to have a child, she was advised to put on weight and

---

[15] *Gender Ideology and Pastoral Practice: A Handbook for Catholic Clergy, Counselors, and Ministerial Leaders*, 2024, pp. 40, 50-51 of Dowdell and Sodergreen, Chapter 3: "Becoming Who We Are".

[16] Dowdell and Sodergreen, Chapter 3: "Becoming Who We Are", p. 50.

[17] John Stonestreet, G. Shane Morris, Tuesday, October 29, 2024, "Yes, gender confusion is socially contagious": https://www.christianpost.com/voices/yes-gender-confusion-is-socially-contagious.html.

[18] "700% spike in LGBTQ+ helpline calls after Trump victory": https://www.faithonview.com/700-spike-in-lgbtq-helpline-calls-after-trump-victory/.

[19] Heidt, *The Anxious Generation*, 2024, p. 154, pp. 153-155.

[20] Heidt, *The Anxious Generation*, 2024, p. 157.

broke the silence on how much harm she was doing to herself on minimal diets and excessive exercise[21]. So, if for her, what about her followers? And if, as in her case, she eagerly awaited the return of her period and the possibility of conceiving a child, clearly these trends definitely impact on marriage and family life.

There is also the problem of boys intimidating girls into putting nude pictures on-line which the boys then know how to exploit for profit[22]. Not to mention the problem of the fact that the 'apps make little or no effort to restrict interactions between adults and minors'[23].

Presumably in America, one in five 'high school girls experienced cyber-bullying each year'[24]. If this social group turns into a bullying group, then it can turn the teen to depression and even suicide: 'physical death offers the end of pain, whereas social death is a living hell'[25].

The social identity of a girl, then, seems to be a very fragile identity and, at the same time, one which seems to somehow be independent of the family; and, indeed, if these girls are preoccupied with anything it seems to be "popularity", "appearance" and whether or not they are "attracted" to a boy or "catching" one of the psychological illnesses or distresses that seem to be circulating on social media. In other words, the very vulnerability of girls to being destroyed by social comparisons, being exploited by boys or men, suggests that they are entering adulthood with, almost inevitably, an inability to be clear about their own value. Certainly, there seems to be any number of girls who have entered adulthood vulnerable to damage by boyfriends, drugs and drinking; and, consequently, divorce has multiplied

---

[21] Julia Llewellyn Smith, interviews Alice Living, "I was constantly preoccupied with food", pp. 16-17, 19 of *The Sunday Times Style*, 30th June, 2024.

[22] Heidt, *The Anxious Generation*, 2024, p. 167.

[23] Heidt, *The Anxious Generation*, 2024, p. 166.

[24] Heidt, *The Anxious Generation*, 2024, p. 159.

[25] Heidt, *The Anxious Generation*, 2024, p. 158.

and, even without divorce, a definite uncertainty about the value of marriage.

One major sources of this damage, beyond the internet and its damaging influences, is the rogue mentality on university campuses, fuelled by "after the pill mentality" presuming the availability of young women for drink and sex, to the point where counsellors are raising the alarm about the abuse of young ladies[26]. Then, as the women get older and marry it turns out that the man is stagnating in pornography[27] and the woman has lost her drive on the pill: 'One study suggested that for some women who take the pill their libido [a component of the sex drive] might never return to its pre-pill level, as the impact on women's testosterone levels is permanent'[28].

Recovering womanhood

By contrast, there is the testimony of a young woman, whom we have already heard, who said that "'If I had been banned from social media as a child, I would not have transitioned," Strongin says'[29]. What is more, as the research shows, women who use testosterone to change their bodily behaviour, are discovering more and more that there are unruly, disruptive and distressing effects on their bladder and other pelvic functions even

---

[26] Mary Eberstadt, *Adam and Eve after the Pill: Paradoxes of the Sexual Revolution*, San Francisco: Ignatius Press, 2012, p. 83, and pp. 78- 93.

[27] Eberstadt, *Adam and Eve after the Pill*, p. 37, 50-53, 56, 62.

[28] Holly Grigg-Spall, no friend to Catholicism, but who recognizes just what good medicine teaches about the dangers of hormonal birth control and, therefore, shares across this divide the natural truths of good fertility management: *Sweetening The Pill: Or How We Got Hooked On Hormonal Birth Control*, Zero Books: Winchester, UK, 2013. With respect to the flattening of the woman's libido, p. 50.

[29] "From girl to 'boy' to woman: a detransitioner's story", May 29th, 2024: An email excerpt from drmorse@ruthinstitute.org

in their 20s; and, what is more, they were never told about these side-effects and, presumably, that is because no one had reported them. In other words, the use of these hormones in a non-treatment context, shows that they are harmful to healthy bodies[30]. At the same time, there are others who are on this path of the truth about who they are and what life is about. One young woman has found peace in recognizing that 'when we love our lives as they are, not as we wish they were. The peace we find when, ultimately, we are rooted in Christ'; and, at the same time, drawing on a decade of the rosary, time with nature and doing something for others[31]. With respect to the cause of rejecting one's own sex, there is another testimony of a young girl, abused as a child, trying to get away from her identity in order to recover from what she experienced; however, although she needed more than being taken further away from who she was, 'Nancy sought therapy for gender confusion. Unfortunately, her therapist thought there would be nothing wrong with Nancy becoming a man.' But, gradually, she saw that she was wounded and began to seek healing[32].

---

[30] Mairead Elordi, May 28th, 2024, "Trans-Identifying Women On Testosterone Suffering Menopausal Symptoms In 20s, Study Shows: The researchers looked at 68 trans-identifying women": https://www.dailywire.com/news/trans-identifying-women-on-testosterone-suffering-menopausal-symptoms-in-20s-study-shows; cf. also, "Pelvic Floor Dysfunction in Transgender Men on Gender-affirming Hormone Therapy: A Descriptive Cross-sectional Study" by Lyvia Maria Bezerra da Silva[1], Silvana Neves Dias Freire[2], Eduarda Moretti[3], Leila Barbosa[4,5]:

Conclusions: Transgender men on hormone therapy have a high incidence of PFD (94.1%) and experience a greater occurrence of urinary symptoms (86.7%). © 2024. The International Urogynecological Association: https://pubmed.ncbi.nlm.nih.gov/38662108/.

[31] Magdalene, May 19th, 2024, "Just a girl who loves Jesus: 3 ways to find peace": https://justagirlwholovesjesus1.wordpress.com/2024/05/19/3-tips-to-find-peace/.

[32] Nancy Charles, "Redemption from Abuse": Dr. Jennifer Roback Morse, drmorse@ruthinstitute.org; https://www.youtube.com/watch?v=99S1_mv903I.

As regards time with nature, one of my brothers in Christ puts it very well when he says, like the desert fathers of old, when we are close to God we will be closer to His work of creation. Another young lady literally lost her life in giving her life to serve others. Helena was full of life and ended up being killed by a robber while volunteering to help children; but, in the summary of her life, it was clear she lived life to the full:

> Helena Kmieć's 'life was filled with dreams and goals. One of the ideals she pursued was readiness to help. She described herself as a person with itchy feet and was always happy to engage in various activities and fields. Apart from singing and music, she led an active life: hiked in the mountains, cycled, and recently tried her hand at climbing'[33].

The effect of social media on boys

According to one account, the most important factor in the 'Sexual Identity Confusion … in Young Men' 'appears to be excessive time spent online', feelings of being an inadequate man and finding it difficult to identify with other men, which can lead to real-time relationships being neglected, use of pornography and a whole host of losing track of a personal identity that is being formed, more and more, by remote and questionable relationships that are even called '(pseudo) belonging'[34]. The advice to any person helping is to recognize and 'pay attention to the woundedness in these young men's lives that is in need of healing'[35].

---

[33] Helena Kmieć: https://helenakmiec.pl/english/.
[34] Moncher, Chapter 3.2: "Sexual Identity Confusion in Young Adult Males", pp. 62-64, of *Gender Ideology and Pastoral Practice*, 2024.
[35] Moncher, "Sexual Identity Confusion in Young Adult Males" p. 68.

In general, from the point of view of the effect of social media, it seems that boys are more concerned with 'agency' than with communion; and, in general, doing something rather than talking. Agency is defined in the following way: it 'arises from striving to individuate [a term usually used to denote becoming more genuinely individual] and expand the self and involves qualities such as efficiency, competence, and assertiveness'[36]. As regards agency, it has certainly bedevilled me almost all my life that I cannot do things as well as other people; for example, earn even a reasonable amount of money, learn languages and teach very well. At the same time, having been through a period of self-employment as a practical artisan and workman, I have acquired various practical skills which have been useful in family life. As we have noticed, however, even when discussing the effect of the media on girls, boys are already instrumentalizing girls and persuading them into pornography. Thus, already, boys are losing the perception, if they ever had it, of a girl or a woman as a gift to be appreciated and not exploited. What hope, then, is there for marriage?

Some boys are on-line a lot, and it seems to be about video games and pornography, even from an early age and, although boys are increasingly depressed it is reported less than in girls; however, the actual suicide rate is 'much higher' for boys[37]. So, maybe boys, who perhaps do not register their emotions so readily, are more depressed than they realize and simply take their life "out of the blue". As one social psychologist says: 'My story is more speculative than the one I told about girls ... because we just don't know as much about what's happening to boys'[38]. This was certainly my experience as a child. I had no idea I was so depressed and simply, one day, started taking an overdose of paracetamol; but then, "seeing" the possibility of being judged by Christ and His apostles, I panicked and started

---

[36] Heidt, *The Anxious Generation*, 2024, p. 152.
[37] Heidt, *The Anxious Generation*, 2024, p. 1175, but also pp.173-175.
[38] Heidt, *The Anxious Generation*, 2024, p. 176.

drinking water. The "vision" of Christ and His apostles was just as unexpected as my attempted suicide; and, in a certain way, as totally surprising given that I did not even pray or think about God, although I discovered later that my parents prayed regularly. So perhaps there was a kind of benefit to us children – even if we neither understood where it came from or why or, in my case, I did not take up praying until many years later.

Returning to the question of the media's impact on boys, although some will make a living from good work, and others will get money from what is not good, 'boys have increasingly disconnected from the real world and invested their time and their talents in the virtual world instead'[39]. In America, if boys' achievements have been in decline for some time and we are witnessing 'floundering young men'[40], then what are they doing with their time? The rise of "safetyism" led to boys losing 'rough and tumble play', with a dramatic drop in small accidents[41] and, with the internet, led to the Japanese phenomenon of "stay-ins" starting in America, with a rise of depression, loneliness, anxiety, self-harm, suicide and a lack of 'meaning or direction in their lives'[42]. In other words, the boys have gone from risky if not violent outbursts as they approach young adulthood to suffering from the 'internalising disorders (such as "I feel I can't do anything right")'; and, although the rate is still higher in girls, still it has climbed higher than was characteristic for boys by 2017[43].

What is more, in a gun and drug sub-culture, there are a whole variety of real-world risks, some of which motivate a young man to come out of this situation and make an impact doing good, hopefully leading a way out for others too, although some succumb and die. What is wonderful is that

---

[39] Heidt, *The Anxious Generation*, 2024, p. 176.
[40] Heidt, *The Anxious Generation*, 2024, p. 178.
[41] Heidt, *The Anxious Generation*, 2024, p. 184.
[42] Heidt, *The Anxious Generation*, 2024, p. 178, p. 179, and pp. 186-187.
[43] Heidt, *The Anxious Generation*, 2024, p. 181.

the young man who has come out of this dangerous culture is providing a route, as it were, through which others can come to help or can come out of the situation as he is doing[44].

Overall, pornography is 'potentially making boys who are heavy users turn into men who are less able to find sex, love, intimacy, and marriage in the real world'[45]. The combination, then, of gaming, pornography, dropping out of real-world activities, is that young men are both inexperienced in an everyday way about life and, increasingly, are either unsuitable or unprepared or both when it comes to the possibility of marriage. But, ultimately, whatever "world we come out of, whether on-line, real-world dangerous, or serial-relationships and their sufferings, God accompanies us and makes it possible for us to emerge, like becoming a chrysalis, into the reality of change: a progressive change that begins and continues with the action of the word of God (cf. Ez. 37: 1-14). But, conversely, if a person immerses himself in an "outward" life and, as it takes its toll in having no one with whom to disclose what is really going on, there is a danger that the anaesthesia, whether drugs or drink or both, begins to do harm to the person's integrity, the wholeness of their life, with the result of suicide:

'In 2012, ... [Tim Bergling, otherwise known as DJ Avicii] embarked on a 26-day US tour, which triggered stomach pains from his drinking, leading to hospitalisation and opioid prescriptions for worsening pancreatitis, starting a cycle of health issues and addiction'[46].

---

[44] Text from AP News story, https://apnews.com/article/baltimore-youth-gun-violence-poverty-entrepreneurship-1cb941be0cd302df626f7ba38bb96df6, by Lea Skene: https://apimagesblog.com/blog/2024/5/12/they-shared-a-name-but-not-a-future-how-two-kids-fought-to-escape-poverty-in-baltimore.

[45] Heidt, *The Anxious Generation*, 2024, p. 189.

[46] Alex Taylor, 16th June, 2024, "Avicii's dad: 'I miss him every minute, but I get angry at him for leaving'": https://www.bbc.co.uk/news/articles/c722jj9ep2wo

More widely and, in a sense, in a more everyday way, teachers in the UK are finding that the level of sexual language, intimidation, and porn use, even condoned by some parents, is showing itself as more and more adolescents are perpetrating these things. As regards respectful conversations or exchanges between the sexes, it seems less and less likely as the "cross-fire" is very "charged".

'There are even male teachers at my school who feel threatened and intimidated by the behaviour of the boys; from pupils blowing kisses to teachers to overhearing them say how they'd like to rape other students. It happens in the classroom and in the playground. It happens to female members of staff, and students'[47].

In a more recent survey of schools in the UK, it seems that the figures of children excluded are of growing concern; and so, for example, there are 'Teachers struggling with disruptive and violent behaviour … [as recorded in] 787,000 suspensions issued in 2022-23'. Of that figure, some '3,500 were excluded for violent behaviour towards children or adults'. And, what is more, the number of exclusions is rising in primary schools,

---

[47] Eleanor Peake, July 11th, 2024, I'm a teacher I see groping and rape threats daily at my school": https://inews.co.uk/inews-lifestyle/teacher-groping-threats-daily-school-3121848?ico=most_popular; and cf. Anna Davis, May 20th, 2024, "Two thirds of teachers say pupils assaulted each other in school in last term": https://ca.news.yahoo.com/two-thirds-teachers-pupils-assaulted-104426617.html?guce_referrer=aHR0cHM6Ly90LmNvLw&guce_referrer_sig=AQAAAGhl0zEmAqVCof8-3DKy926P6M_ol_WQSgiQDj-vkVBDcBDeO8v1MZhZpxPR6utbgMSMpUqzQBdCILeO9EYu7-ps7f3P8QTWLDJKGiWW54h5ozMbnfeI5cHO9BXx-TBAmWggq2_TXRsH-nlTsrE0OhKuO9il8kfSNqEydx5RGUNQG&guccounter=2.

as 'the number of children excluded in primary schools rose from 760 to 1,200 in a year'[48].

Carlo Acutis (1991-2006)

Even in view, however, of the negative impact of social media on young people, there is a singular young man who is an example to all, but particularly to the younger generation; his name is Carlo Acutis (1991-2006) and his cause for canonization has just taken a step closer owing to another miracle being recognized as through his intercession. This young man, who died at 15 from an aggressive cancer, prayed the rosary daily, designed and built websites, helped feed the poor, those 'struggling with homework', played soccer, video games, watched Pokémon and lived a full life of which he said: "'I'm happy to die because I've lived my life without wasting even a minute of it doing things that wouldn't have pleased God," according to carloacutis.com'[49]. In a small way, being computer incompetent myself, I can say that asking his help when I could not find the file that recorded an extract from this book, proved very successful. I discovered that I had not even made a file and, suddenly, pressing the right buttons, I not only made the recording but found where it was saved! We must ask his help to make good use of the internet and to "delete" the multitude of rubbish, which is worse than that blocking our rivers and polluting them, because this rubbish pollutes the heart!

---

[48] Richard Adams, 18th July, 2024, Education Editor, "Sharp increase in pupils suspended or excluded from schools in England": https://www.theguardian.com/education/article/2024/jul/18/sharp-increase-in-pupils-suspended-or-excluded-from-schools-in-england.

[49] Carol Glatz, May 23rd, 2024, "Pope Francis recognizes miracle needed for the first 'millennial' saint: Blessed Carlos Acutis": https://www.americamagazine.org/faith/2024/05/23/blessed-carlo-acutis-miracle-sainthood-248006.

Masculinity in crisis

In Japan, around 30,000, although this number is uncertain, mainly men are recorded as dying in isolation and not being discovered, very often, until the corpse has begun to break down. By implication, it seems, women fare far better at keeping integrated in society than men do[50]. We have already noted the problem of "un-connectedness" with American servicemen and construction workers and so, by way of another American confirmation of this phenomenon, we read:

'53 percent of older adults visiting primary care facilities report feeling lonely. These feelings significantly impact their physical and mental health, reducing their overall quality of life'[51]. And then, what is more, '31% of [Catholic] men have no close friendships with other parish men'[52]. In other words, men seem to be particularly vulnerable to either poor or non-existent relationships.

Discussing this with one of my daughters, she was of the view that boys seemed to follow each other around, having perhaps a sport in common;

---

[50] Matthew Bremner, June 26th, 2015, "The Lonely End:
In aging Japan, thousands die alone and unnoticed every year. Toru Koremura is there to clean up what they leave behind": https://slate.com/news-and-politics/2015/06/kodokushi-in-aging-japan-thousands-die-alone-and-unnoticed-every-year-their-bodies-often-go-unnoticed-for-weeks.html. Indeed, it is good to read the article, "The Lonely End", because it is also about a young, successful man coming out of business, having recognized that he neglected his grandmother, and going into the care of the dead.

[51] Contribution from Matt Higgins, March 20th, 2024, "Loneliness Worse For Health Than Obesity, Alcoholism, Even Smoking 15 Cigarettes Daily?": https://studyfinds.org/older-people-lonely/.

[52] "The State of Catholic Men": https://novamedia.us/wp-content/uploads/2024/03/State-of-Catholic-Men.pdf.

or, when there was nothing to play, doing what I did as a boy and ending up being a part, not exactly of a gang, but a stupidity group who did pranks and bullied others. As I got older, however, I do remember boys forming music groups around Led Zepplin and whatever else was going on; however, not being in touch with any kind of culture, I became increasingly isolated and played cards, losing my bus money and generally beginning to drop out of the social world that I was never integrated in in the first place.

Whereas girls, even if they can have their bully groups, seemed to form more socially positive groups, more interest based, even if they could have their drawbacks in terms of whether or not one person has fallen out with another and who will group around who.

Masculinity: toxic or not?

In general, social studies confirm men's domination of women: 'The issue of gender differences in the society is that of gender in-equality in which men usually dominate women'; however, even if the Church is imperfect and always in need of purification, there is a distinction between what is of God and endures and what needs to change. Therefore, while I agree that love equals equality[53], but not being identical, the priesthood is of Christ and not of a man's domination, except in so far as the priest is imperfect and in need of conversion. In other words, as with the work of popes, it is a part of the ministry of bishops and priests to develop the Church's understanding of male and female complementarity, as both a gift of God and a gift to be better understood.

Alternatively, there is an unscrupulous "soft, toxic masculinity" which is about exploiting vulnerable women by 'love-bombing': by overwhelm-

---

[53] Cf. Nantes Jr., F. (2021), « Masculine Domination », *Academia Letters*, Article 2065: https://doi.org/10.20935/AL2065.

ing a woman with attention that then becomes toxic through the undermining of the woman's confidence leading to her becoming a victim of this
punishing attention. While some form of 'love bombing' may be genuine,
in that expresses a tremendous gratitude in finding a person to love[54], there
needs to be discernment about whether this is genuine or the man is humiliating the woman and, on occasion, exploiting her vulnerability for
money. This, of course, raises the double question: Why is the woman so
vulnerable, aside from obvious reasons like a divorcee or wounded from a
previous failure in relationship? Why is the man exploitative, "playing" the
part of "love"? In other words, in both cases there is a clear want of either
discernment, as my father would say, what does the person do, not just
what do they say. But beyond evidence, we need recourse to a discernment
which goes beyond appearances and entails asking the question: Am I
called by God to marry this person? Seeking the will of God goes deeper
than adding up whatever he or she says and does and will either engage or
disengage the other person, the process of discernment becoming itself,
almost, a test of whether or not the relationship is authentic, sincere and
intending to be about marriage and not just about "getting together" or
"what can be got out of this relationship for either person".

Another factor involves the misuse of Christianity. 'In a *Christianity
Today* article, Brad Wilcox summarized his findings: "The most violent
husbands in America are nominal evangelical Protestants who attend
church infrequently or not at all."'

'It seems that nominal men hang around the fringes of the Christian
world just enough to hear the language of headship and submission but
not enough to learn the biblical meaning of those terms. They interpret

---

[54] Barbara Field, May 2nd, 2024, "The Dangers of Love Bombing":
https://www.verywellmind.com/what-is-love-bombing-5223611.

the words through a grid of male superiority and entitlement that they have absorbed from the secular world'[55].

With respect to another report, 'disengaged men are spending a great deal of time in front of screens that promote disembodied expressive individualism. This includes an average of 5.5 hours of movies and TV per day, not to mention the rise of exceedingly popular online pornography. Some estimate that Gen Z boys are being exposed to porn at the average age of nine. Studies indicate that pornography rewires the brain, causing boys and men to desire more and more novel content rather than a relationship with a real woman. Male employment is often tied to family structure, and marriage rates for low-income men have declined, demonstrating the unique causes and reinforcing mechanisms of the boy crisis.

But, in addition, if fashion and the media are taking up pain for pleasure, then the question arises is this advertising by shocking the public as well as downgrading both the man and the woman: 'Vogue magazine ran a seven-photo fashion spread [in 1975] featuring a man in a bathrobe battering a screaming model in a lovely pink jumpsuit'[56].

The devastating impact of the opioid epidemic is another factor. Some estimate that it could account for 43 percent of the decline in male labor force participation from 1999 to 2015. During that time, the number of overdoses quadrupled, and men made up almost 70 percent of

---

[55] Joy Lucius, October 6th, 2023, "Masculinity": https://www.afa.net/the-stand/family/2023/10/masculinity/.

[56] Eberstadt, *Adam and Eve After the Pill: Revisited*, pp. 166-167.

such deaths. The incarceration rate has also risen, and years behind bars reduce the likelihood of finding employment'[57].

More widely, in some cultures, however, the "toxic masculinity" seems to be more endemic and even encouraged by the more widespread "machismo" mentality: where masculine power is exaggerated, authoritarian and often violent, while also entailing 'a denigration of characteristics associated with the feminine'[58]. Or there is the brutal, male gang membership. All of which men are of the domineering kind (cf. Gn. 3: 16), irrespective of culture. Indeed, if the man who 'will dominate' is unleashed, as it were, by the fall, the loss of God's gift of completing grace, then this kind of man is both very prevalent and, at the same time, clearly in need of the antidote of the action of God to remedy it.

Why the decline in real fatherhood – Is it a decline in real-time in family life and in real friendships generally?[59]

In '1990, almost 70% of men had five or more close friends. By 2021, just 40% reported having that many. And the number who said they had *no* close friends quintupled. Women haven't fared well, either, though their friend groups haven't shrunk as rapidly'[60].

---

[57] Brenda Hafera, 2nd April, 2024, "The Tailspin of American Boys and Men": https://www.heritage.org/civil-society/commentary/the-tailspin-american-boys-and-men.

[58] "machismo: exaggerated masculinity": https://www.britannica.com/topic/machismo.

[59] Although the following article is about the decline, principally, of friendships between men, perhaps this decline of men-capable-of-relationships is about their availability for real-time relationships generally. Emily Katz, May 17th, 2023, "Three lessons from Aristotle on friendship": https://theconversation.com/three-lessons-from-aristotle-on-friendship-200520.

[60] Shane Morris, 24th of October, 2024, "Why nobody has friends anymore".

In general, between divorce, absent fathers, fathers or men who are not there to be positively imitated, it is necessary that in order 'To match our current moment, solutions to the boy crisis must encourage good, dialogical relationships rather than personal license'[61]. By contrast, then, there is the hope that men will not repeat the sins of their fathers and, if they do, that the word of conversion will bring an irrevocable change, albeit it may be gradual and over many years. So, while the past does not define us, it does need to be identified for the real effect it has upon us. What is more, then, the vocation to be a husband and father does need to go deeper, to see that the husband and father is not an "ad extra" but an expression of the gift of God[62]. More widely, one father asks, "Where *are* all the dads?" who can help a child to see that it is a help to a confused child to say that 'Good fathers know better than to encourage a permanent solution to a temporary problem'[63]. Indeed, there is a Canadian movement, including fathers, that is protesting against the usurpation of parental responsibilities: "pro-family Canadians are fighting to declare three things: that we are "one nation, one flag," that "Canada's parents will parent Canada's kids," and that "we won't allow our kids to be politicized"[64].

---

[61] Brenda Hafera, March 19th, 2024, "Men Without Meaning: The Harmful Effects of Expressive Individualism": https://www.heritage.org/progressivism/report/men-without-meaning-the-harmful-effects-expressive-individualism.

[62] Maureen Mackey, June 9th, 2024, "Why American fathers need to reject '3 damaging lies' in today's culture, says pastor: Dads have key roles to play in kids' well-being and 3 lies perpetuated by society should be rejected": https://www.foxnews.com/lifestyle/american-fathers-need-reject-3-damaging-lies-culture-pastor.

[63] Fritz Steiger, December 12, 2024, "In The Fight Against Transgender Experiments On Kids, Where Are All The Dads?": https://thefederalist.com/2024/12/12/in-the-fight-against-transgender-experiments-on-kids-where-are-all-the-dads/

[64] Clare Marie Merkowsky, August 22nd, 2024, "Canada's Million Person March against LGBT indoctrination has 'quadrupled' its support since last year":

Going back to fathers, specifically: Are the absent fathers absent because this society has alienated fathers from their children? Have fathers no capacity to think? Have fathers exempted themselves, as with abortion, from personal responsibility for their children? We do, however, as that father realized, need to go deeper, both in terms of seeing our own reality and drawing on the help of the word of God; for, as the word says, we need the Spirit of God '*to reconcile fathers to their children* and the disobedient to the good sense of the upright' (cf. Lk 1: 17). At the same time, do we not need a return to a 'maternal feminism' that looks to trust a man to become a husband and a father?[65]

In my own experience, a period of commuting gave me ample opportunity to pray about my own rejection of my father and attendant unwillingness to help in the house, to the point that he asked me to leave; and, when I became a father, and as our family grew, it was essential that I was reconciled to my history as the son who is not a son to his father cannot be a father to his own children (cf. Proverbs 10: 1; 15: 20)[66]. In other words, scrutinizing the Scriptures about fatherhood, reflecting on my own experience and asking God to both clarify my own history and to reconcile me to it are all essential parts of being able to be that "good parent" that we want to be.

How many men will not realize, until they die alone or are full of regrets, that they missed an opportunity to be the father of their child who, however, exists, whether aborted or abandoned later, and they will be accountable for that non-relationship, which is like the fruitless fig tree

https://www.lifesitenews.com/news/canadas-million-person-march-against-lgbt-indoctrination-has-quadrupled-its-support-since-last-year/.

[65] Erica Komisar, October 15th, 2024, "We Need a New Feminism That Embraces Motherhood as Meaningful Work": https://ifstudies.org/blog/we-need-new-feminism-that-embraces-motherhood-as-meaningful-work.

[66] Cf. Etheredge, *Lord: Do You Mean Me? A father-catechist!*: https://enroute-booksandmedia.com/doyoumeanme/.

which Christ admonished and it withered (cf. Mk. 11: 12-25)[67]; and, in a sense, that withering of the tree is a parable of what happens to our lives if we reject being connected with others, either through fatherhood, motherhood, family, friendship or service. But the fruit cannot be renewed without replanting, as it were, from the beginning and beginning again with love, mutual help and, if quarrelling, reconciling before sunset, and the mystery of marriage which then calls forth the following:

'Let us not forget, also, that for spouses it is essential to be open to the gift of life, to the gift of children, that are the most beautiful fruit of love, the greatest blessing from God, a source of joy and hope for every home and all of society. Have children! Yesterday, I received a great consolation. It was the day of the Gendarmerie Corps, and a gendarme came with his eight children! It was beautiful to see him. Please, be open to life, to what God may send you.

Dear brothers and sisters, love is demanding, yes, but it is beautiful, and the more we allow ourselves to be involved by it, the more we discover true happiness in it. And now, let each one of us ask themselves: How is my love? Is it faithful? Is it generous? Is it creative? How are our families? Are they open to life, to the gift of children?

May the Virgin Mary help Christian spouses. Let us turn to her in spiritual union with the faithful gathered at the Shrine of Pompeii for the traditional Supplication to Our Lady of the Holy Rosary'[68].

---

[67] Cf. Fr. Gordon J. MacRae, June 12th, 2024, "The Twilight of Fatherhood: Cry, the Beloved Country": https://beyondthesestonewalls.com/posts/the-twilight-of-fatherhood-cry-the-beloved-country.

[68] Pope Francis, "Angelus", 6th of October, 2024: https://www.vatican.va/content/francesco/en/angelus/2024/documents/20241006-angelus.html.

As one author puts it, 'The connection between contraception and the breakdown of marriage is well understood … the rise of birth control weakened the responsibility of men to their unmarried partner's pregnancy, increasing the incidence of both abortion and single motherhood'[69]. Again, however, we are not just seeing a change in values which puts mobility above stability or being child-free above welcoming children, the freedom of a lifestyle above the time and personal relationship between spouses and their children – so much as what helps us to accept, understand and enter into the mystery of suffering which relationships, inevitably, bring into our lives. But is not this a problem only for those who suffer from "affluenza"?[70] In other words, maybe what we are seeing is the implication that if a life is lived without close relationships, without the "suffering with" in family life, then there is not the depth of human experience that allows the word of the Gospel to root: that God loves us and comes close so that we can come close to Him and find meaning, consolation and help in daily life. But, if we are so inured owing to our wealth and wellbeing, then what opening is there, as it were, for God – especially if there are no children to strive to love throughout all their growing up and beyond.

But, as is obvious from the question of "toxic masculinity", whether "soft" or "hard", there is so much more to discovering the intentions of the human heart than just meeting another person; indeed, perhaps the scale of divorce demonstrates, in a way, the profound superficiality of our attraction to one another and, therefore, our vulnerability to seeking pleasure and not relationship. More widely, what kind of implications are there to this rejection-of-relationship? What about grandparents? What about

---

[69] Patrick T. Brown, June 5th, 2024, "The Cultural Roots of Our Demographic Ennui": https://www.thepublicdiscourse.com/2024/06/95062/.

[70] Cf. Brown, June 5th, 2024, "The Cultural Roots of Our Demographic Ennui".

aunts and uncles? What about the extended family? What about the child that died?[71] Given that 50% of somewhat older people who attend out-patients, indicate that they are lonely, the advantages of lasting marriage and family life are even being advocated in the press: 'The number of adults who have never been married or in a civil partnership has almost doubled in the past 30 years, and they now account for nearly 40 per cent of the population'. And, therefore, to imagine what life would be like if we had not married, 'is not just melancholy but meaningless: we would be different people, and the life would have happened to somebody else'[72].

Meaning includes and transcends what expresses it

When we examine the words of Scripture, that God made man male and female, we do not just examine the two words, "male", and, "female", we examine, as far as we can, what contributes to the meaning of these words[73]. Thus, examining the Hebrew text, we see that the language of masculine and feminine, while not extensively present in the lead up to the declaration that *man is made in the image of God, male and female he made them*, yet there are significant stepping stones from the opening words of Genesis to the creation of man, male and female. Thus God, *Elohim*, is a unique word, a masculine plural, meaning "two of", which takes a singular

---

[71] Cf. Bonnie Finnerty, June 11th, 2024, "We Need More Men Who Step Up and be Fathers Instead of Pushing Abortion": https://www.lifenews.com/2024/06/11/we-need-more-men-who-step-up-and-be-fathers-instead-of-pushing-abortion/.

[72] Stephen Bleach, "Couple up, kids – you'll be grateful when you're old and grey", *The Sunday Times*, June 30th, 2024, p. 25.

[73] "The Interpretation of the Bible in the Church": Presented by the Pontifical Biblical Commission to Pope John Paul II on April 23, 1993 (as published in *Origins*, January 6, 1994): https://catholic-resources.org/ChurchDocs/PBC_Interp-FullText.htm.

verb, bara, to create; and, therefore, opens up the fascinating possibility of referring to both "The Father" and "The Son". Then the word for the Holy Spirit, *Ruach*, is also connected to *Elohim*; but, together, the effect of their meaning is that *Ruach Elohim* expresses a feminine subject of the verb, *meraheffet*, referring to the presence of the Holy Spirit as a "feminine" presence over the original waters. When it comes, then, to a creation which is described as 'seed bearing' and, therefore, fertile, the sex of plants is understood. Again, more explicitly, the words for 'image' and 'likeness', are masculine and feminine, echoing the expressions of the 'heavens' and the 'earth', which are also masculine and feminine. In other words, and drawing on the whole understanding of man and woman being fertile and capable of procreation, the original text of Gensis is more than amply expressive of the deliberate intention that man is 'male and female'[74]. In other words, while words are a semi-physical event, whether spoken or written, their meaning is both communicated through and clarified by the context of being spoken or written. And, therefore, even if a point of view is very simply expressed, namely that Genesis refers to man, male and female, it does not follow that this is mistaken[75]; for, in its original and enduring meaning, it is what the writer's words refer to, namely, man and woman, which are confirmed by both Christ and our everyday experience. As the Lord Jesus said: 'the Creator from the beginning made them male and female' (Matthew 19: 4).

---

[74] Etheredge, *Scripture: A Unique Word*: "Chapter Eight: Creation: The Archetypal Action of God": https://www.cambridgescholars.com/resources/pdfs/978-1-4438-6044-4-sample.pdf; but, in the course of this book, there are many related investigations.

[75] Cf. Jack Jenkins, January 14th, 2025, "Speaker Johnson cites Genesis after House passes bill banning trans people from women's sports": https://religionnews.com/2025/01/14/speaker-johnson-cites-genesis-after-house-passes-bill-banning-trans-people-from-womens-sports/.

On the other hand, some argue that there is a division between the very events of life described as physically real *and* their significance; indeed, this philosophy is conveys what can be called a "denial of relationship": that one dimension of reality is unconnected to another. To admit meaning then is, in a sense, to admit that it is an expression of being-in-relationship: that our nature speaks, as it were, a voice that reveals us to ourselves. Thus what is revealed about ourselves is then there to be communicated to others. If, to the contrary, all interiority is denied or called "physical effects of neurones", a half-truth, concealing the whole truth that we are a psycho-somatic unity of body and soul, then we have swallowed, perhaps unwittingly, a distinction that destroys the unity of human being and experience. Take the following example of this: 'in all experiences that can make ... [a person] happier or better only the physical facts are 'real' while the spiritual elements are 'subjective'"[76]. After all, tp be 'subjective' has a meaning of "to speak from experience to experience"[77]. At the same time, however, if we recall that each of us is a bodily expression of a human soul[78], however difficult it is to understand the intimate unity of the person, we can see that even what is called the activity of our nervous system is the bodily expression of our human life and activities. Perhaps, considering these expressions, it is helpful to remember that the human person exists from the first instant of conception[79].

---

[76] C. S. Lewis, *The Screwtape Letters*, London, pp. 119-120.

[77] Cf. *Lived Experience and the Search for Truth: Revisiting Catholic Sexual Morality*, edited by Deborah Savage and Robert Fastiggi, Chapter 1: Deborah Savage: "When the Starting Place is Lived Experience: The Pastoral and Therapeutic Implications of Pope St. John Paul II's Account of the Person", pp. 17-55, and p. 30-31.

[78] Cf. St. John Paul II's, *Familiaris Consortio*, 11, and *Veritatis Splendor*, 48-50.

[79] Etheredge, Conception: An Icon of the Beginning: https://www.amazon.co.uk/Conception-Icon-Beginning-Francis-Etheredge/dp/1950108244. Reviewed by Bishop John Keenan of Paisley, Scotland.

What kind of being are we? Being-in-relationship

The more I read, therefore, and the more I reflect on this generation's search for an identity, the more I realise that growing up is like looking for keys that will unlock the question of who I am and what is the purpose of my life.

'And while each human person is an image-bearer of God [image-bearing is intrinsic], the Genesis creation account makes clear that image-bearing is not merely an individual responsibility or reality. Humanity as a community bears the image of God; there are aspects of image-bearing that can only be accomplished in community. A human being cannot "be fruitful and increase in number" alone. No single person can "fill the earth and subdue it." While each individual human being is created in the image of God and has the corresponding dignity and responsibility, there are broader dimensions of image-bearing that refer to communal realities.'

'The family is where the human person is first and most formatively socialized and acculturated into relations with other human beings.'

From the perspective of divine providence, each person is blessed—and in some cases burdened—with a particular background, set of talents and dispositions, resources and relationships, that God uses to further his purposes in the world.'

'An authentic anthropology does justice to the complexity of the human person in all dimensions—bodily and spiritually, individually and communally, earthly and heavenly'[80].

Even before I began the study of theology, I came from a psychological perspective that there were processes that enable or obstruct human development, like the recognition of suffering facilitates its integration whereas denying it, even unconsciously, acts like a dam on the development of consciousness and human identity. Thus, given the social prevalence of psychological sufferings, whether or not they involve sin as well, there had to be some beginning to human imperfection. In other words, the very presence of suffering in the lives of so many individuals and their families indicates a kind of global origin that is historical and antecedent to the development of society. There are instances of parental "blind-spots" which damage their children unintentionally. Thus the parent who did not believe his son had copied a picture so well led to the son rejecting his own gift. Therefore the son did not draw for maybe thirty years or so until his wife encouraged him to take advantage of Covid restrictions on what he normally did and go to art college. So there is no pretence that all is well in the sense that we are born perfect or born into perfect families.

However, the more clearly we examine the culture in which we live, the more obvious it becomes that questions about identity are like surf boards, riding whatever turning tide there is; and, therefore, gender crises are fuelled by social media and have escalated, along with the media, from a few in 1989 to thousands in 2024. But gender crises are symptomatic of the deeper, unidentified questions of who am I, what is my life about, what purpose does it have? These questions, however, take time, reading, discussion, silence and prayer, guidance and friendship. The "hell of noise",

---

[80] Jordan J. Ballor, June 6th, 2024, "Mere Humanity: An Ecumenical Anthropology for Human Flourishing": https://www.thepublicdiscourse.com/2024/06/95092/.

according to Cardinal Sarah, 'makes it nearly impossible to encounter God and suggests that many of our societal and personal issues stem from this disconnection'[81]. Instead, young people are very often offered attention seeking devices called i-phones, that are designed to sap the strength of your attention like a virus undermines your health. Therefore, instead of engaging, consistently, in the search for answers, there is the constant ebb and flow of information and various kinds of images.

What we have, then, in the place of a developing, philosophical, psychological and even theological engagement with the questions of life, is a kind of technological biologism: that the body answers the questions of life. That if a person is distressed, for example, by their gender, then they are in the wrong body. That if a person is unhappy, it is not because of failed relationships, isolation, confusion about careers, problems in the family – it is because of a chemical deficiency in the brain. If a person is troubled about when to give themselves away, but not in marriage, the answer is contraception. Never mind the mentality of a person making themselves available to others or the health consequences of taking unnecessary chemicals that impact upon a person's health. And then, if the girl or woman becomes pregnant, she aborts the child, as if the agony and distress afterwards are some kind of grief over a body-part, or a socially induced guilt – and not an actual registering of what was unclearly known, namely, that a baby died and there is a mother and a father of a child now "not there".

So what are the real keys to the real lock and what is opened by them? The real lock, as it were, is the question of identity: Who am I? What is the purpose of my life? Who can I make friends with? What makes a good friendship? These are the real and enduring questions which, although often engaged with indirectly, need to be discovered and addressed directly.

---

[81] Jen Arnold, September 22nd, 2024, "The Power of Silence According to Cardinal Sarah": https://catholicheartablaze.com/the-power-of-silence/.

What, then, are the keys that open upon the vista of human development? Not soul denying, psychologically quashing denials of subjectivity, but great and challenging demands on evidence, on reason, on asking for adequate answers that lead to more questions and build a real understanding of "Who I am" and "What life is about". In other words, we need to invite people to question, to think, to engage in critical dialogue with what is on offer as a so-called answer to human identity.

Let the question of what the body is surface beyond it being a biological process with no purposes beyond avoiding pain and seeking pleasure. In other words, let us ask the question of how it is even possible to ask a question? Why, if we are simply "flesh", as it were, are we even capable of asking a question? Thus, we begin, little by little, to appreciate that even if we are a bunch of wires, what we communicate comes from elsewhere than the wires themselves. If a man phones his wife, the phone does not make the content; rather, the phone transmits the message and, between them, they discuss what to do. Thus, thinking through the conception of human being, we begin to discover the edge of the deep philosophical answers of the past that still open us to the questions in the present: that the body communicates the soul: that there is an origin of communication in me, who I am, that seeks to communicate with another "I".

What is more, those who are conceived without knowing either who their "parent" or "parents" were, or who discover later in life that they are not related to those who have brought them up, go through a questioning of their identity which reveals how unregulated the transmission of life is in the laboratory and how fundamental are these questions of identity:

'It is not known how many donor-conceived individuals there are in the U.S because neither the U.S. federal government nor any states require tracking of this type of data'.

Our 'respondents reported significant disruptions in their personal identity, frequently thought about their own identity as a donor-conceived individual, and wondered about the identity of their biological parent. Additionally approximately half of our sample sought psychological help as a result of their discovery'[82].

In a word, the questions of identity are essential to growing up and that includes having parents, grandparents and the extended family; however, I am sure many people are nevertheless grateful to those who cared for them, even if they are not their natural parents or family. But, whether the dearth of knowledge is owing to artificial fertilization, absent parents or children rejecting their parents, this could well impact the capacity of these children to recognize who they are and be able to facilitate the identity of their own children.

---

[82] Rennie Burke, Yvette Ollada Lavery, Gali Katznelson, Joshua North, J. Wesley Boyd April 1, 2021, "How Do Individuals Who Were Conceived Through the Use of Donor Technologies Feel About the Nature of their Conception?": https://bioethics.hms.harvard.edu/journal/donor-technology.

Prose and a Prayer for Broiling Men:
"Kitchen Stinking"

Over forty, perhaps forty-five years ago, I was standing in a monastery, washing up, while wondering what my vocation was, whether I was called to the priesthood, the religious life or what, when it seemed as if there was a word: "that my vocation would involve the kitchen sink!" It was to be another twenty or more years before I married at forty and, increasingly, find that my vocation does indeed "involve washing up!"

"Engrossed in themselves" (Ps. 17: 10) and "When I awake I shall be filled with a vison of you" (Ps. 17: 15).

These two verses seem to encapsulate the difference that Jesus Christ can make in a person's life; and, indeed, apart from the words to follow below, about human imperfection and its tendency to self-destruction, a particular event summed up this difference for me. I was lying in hospital, unable to get off the bed owing to an acute case of a blocked urinary passage, due to a grossly enlarged prostate, and the drain was anchored to the bed and I did not have the energy to complain to busy emergency staff. My wife, a true helpmate, brought me the prayer of the Church, known as *The Office*; and, almost immediately, I began praying the different prayers of the day or night. By contrast to my willingness to collapse into a pit of self-pity, I noticed that I suddenly and energetically became interested in all and sundry who passed my bed, inquiring about their nationality, what brought them into nursing and hospital work. In other words, this prayer, literally took me from the temptation to become engrossed in my own predicament to welcoming the presence of others in my life.

This piece comes, then, from a long way off and is a kind of amalgam of grumbles and imperfections from numerous moments, but it captures some of the souring that is possible, both because of disappointment's

clutches or owing to the many ways that doing what we dislike doing is a
kind of dangerous bending of an already, almost sprung trap: a trap of falling into the pit of depicting ourselves as superman or supermen and discovering, in the reality of daily, repeated chores and difficulties, including
the aging process, that we are not the lovers of serving the family that we
thought we were!

Thus, like the person who finally admits his health is failing and falls on
the bed to discover he has pneumonia, pleurisy and clots on his legs and
lungs, as I once did, we have to discover that the wine has run out; indeed,
like the *Marriage Feast of Cana*, we may have been fortunate to discover
that the wine ran out on the wedding night and, ever after, we sought the
new wine that Christ gave at the behest of His mother (cf. Jn. 2: 1-12).
Therefore right from the beginning and from the very mystery of the sacrament of marriage itself, comes the reality of help: that just as God acts in
the sacrament of marriage itself, bringing about what man cannot sunder
(cf. Mt. 19: 6) so God continues to give the new wine of forgiveness, reconciliation, dialogue, when speaking and being civil is more than difficult
and needs an honest prayer of help.

So, even if marriage preparation involved a chaste courtship, common
prayer, recourse to the sacraments, advice and the helps of the Christian
life, reading the *Book of Tobit* together and taking the advice of Tobias and
Sarah praying together, there still comes the limits of human effort, goodwill, endurance and necessity of calling out to the Lord who created the
mystery of marriage and all it entails.

Let us, therefore, be willing to see that there are times when all seems lost,
when energy disappears, when problems of health, unemployment, studying, the multiplication of what makes life impossible, such as impending
homelessness, serious illnesses and dead ends all assail us – that yet there
is one who is there abiding and is abidingly helpful and, too, His community, the Church.

Kitchen Stinking

Dog walking again; washing up again; picking up towels, again;
Overtime again; up late again; dirty floors, again; no helping,
Again; re-cycling again; lost your glasses, phone and keys, again;
And, like polluted rain indoors, when it rains it spoils, acidifying
Again; and, like a drain, draws off what goodness was before it's
Long since gone, leaving the dregs of goodwill going rancid.

Swirly thinking, unlike drinking, more like swilling,
How many times am I doing what others have left undone,
Doing as I do the undoing of willing and working up a
Froth of feeling, resentment, begrudging – pillaging peace.

Un-shedded unwillingness, steeped in its ill-inward drilling,
Down downing, shrugging, still turning through botched cleaning,
Bunged up pipes, not swirling, only seeping and stinking, as
Suppression sticks with what I'm doing and others have not done.

But unable to be admitted, the barb bites, down below, sightless
And unwilling to share, staring rudely, imagining crudely, unsatisfyingly
ugly, not people but positions best undescribed, unholy longings amidst
the pots and pans and pained helping.

Hope was hope once but was hijacked into plotting unwelcome
Walks and talks, tackling dating as if dirty beaches, mud and filth,
Fill the horizon, dressed in photo-shopped stills showing nothing
But smiles, smart clothes, white teeth and clean, but empty hands.

Try as I might to fight, blighted sight, bloated with undisclosed Secrets, secretes its own glue, going down out of view down, down, And down again, sticky, sticking, sickly coagulation of inabilities, to Stop, to start again, to stay away from sinking into chained clutches.

With what joy I would leap up if but the spark of life ignites

The burning free, of rooted roots plunged in putrid flesh –

But can a damp, flickering flame destroy the rot to be rid of?

Or must I hope in conscience's dim grasp of a Great Other?

Chapter Five

Preliminaries: Turning Points

We do not begin from nothing, in the sense that God has brought us to exist with a desire for relationship: a relationship to our parents and family and a relationship to God. It may seem surprising, but when I was working on a farm as an adolescent, I can remember the noise of the tractor hiding the praise of God that I was singing; they were simple songs, simply the basic prayers that I knew, like the "Our Father" and "Glory be". Nobody prompted me to sing; but, in full view of the beauty of nature on a summer's day, I spontaneously sang. So, even if I did not understand going to Church or even want to be there, I responded to creation as having a Creator. Similarly, in terms of reasoning, the questions which arose, arose out of my history, why did I not know what I wanted to do with my life. Why did I fail every subject at school except religious studies? Why was I so obsessed with my own body's pleasure? In other words, I was full of questions and looking for answers; but, in view of my tired and scattered attention, I was like a man in a desert tying to remember under which sand-hill I had left myself. Thus, scattering sand, I wandered all over the place without finding a home, as it were, to my thoughts and experiences.

Making a history of our own investigations

Thinking back to different times in my life, I can remember the agonies I went through trying to understand the nature of mental illness, especially during my time as a trainee psychiatric nurse when, in retrospect, I can see more clearly now that there were two strands of thought. On the one hand, there was the chemical imbalance type of theory with its corresponding physical treatments like drugs, electro-convulsive therapy and,

occasionally, operations. And, on the other hand, there was the more subtle, painstaking, psychological investigations of a person's history, family
life, specific events and traumas and, in general, this was less taken up and
more marginalized as being too time consuming or uncertain. In other
words, there was already a medical model of mental illness firmly established even if, in terms of the literature, there was still work being done on
the basis of grappling with the relationship between an individual and his
or her family and social dynamics. Even now, as we have seen in the course
of these investigations into the use of puberty blockers and surgery, there
is an incredible emphasis on the physicality of the body being an answer
to problems of identity.

What began, then, as a kind of semi-academic question, involving the
pursuit of my own identity, went on to become an absorbing quest for the
foundations of human identity. I remember sitting in the canteen of a university one day and thinking about Christ as the fullness of human identity
without really knowing how or why; but, in some dim way, thinking that
it was true that we grow to the fullness of Christ or, at least, we are called
to do so. Indeed, it is as if that fullness of Christ, while an individual calling,
is also what the community is called to too: so that the gifts of God

> 'knit God's holy people together for the work of service to build up the
> body of Christ, until we all reach unity in faith and knowledge of the
> Son of God and form the perfect Man fully mature with the fullness of
> Christ himself' (Eph. 4: 12-13).

But this path to theology and philosophy was very roundabout and uncertain and went through many phases; and, in the end, only came together as I began the deliberate study of philosophy years later. But this
was not the disembodied, abstract philosophies of the mind, as if we can
"jump in" and make sense of what different people argue to be like a "ghost

in the machine" or others deny that it exists at all and claim that we are merely thinking machines, whatever that means, or some kind of advanced process that lives off, as it were, brain processes, like foam is generated by the sea. Rather, over many years of reading a wide range of books and, as it happens, the writing of popes, I began to synthesise the main ingredients of what made sense of being a human being: that I was a meaning seeker and that relationships were essential to self-discovery and to our very being as we are 'beings-in-relationship': both because relationships brings us into existence and relationship is the vehicle of self-discovery and purpose.

So, one way or another, each of us needs to chart, to visit our response to life-questions and to begin to build an understanding of reality. While it is not always easy to put together the different accounts of what constitutes human being, it is nevertheless worth it; and, here and there, we encounter really good summaries of that combination of the truth which is both universal and particular: both an integrated account of what makes each one of us both human and a personal human being. Thus a good philosophy takes account of the identity of man, male and female, as a whole, and, at the same time, recognizes that each person's subjective experience, which can yet be 'objectified'[1] and shown to be the evidence that we have in common between us. Thus, earlier in this book, I discussed my own experience of "passing through" the question of whether it would be "easier" to be a woman than a man; but, in passing through this experience, it was with a view to the inherent goal, if allowed to prevail, of discovering the fulfilment of my identity which takes up and takes account of being a man in search of himself. Therefore, objectifying this content of

---

[1] *Lived Experience and the Search for Truth: Revisiting Catholic Sexual Morality*, edited by Deborah Savage and Robert Fastiggi, Chapter 1: Deborah Savage: "When the Starting Place is Lived Experience: The Pastoral and Therapeutic Implications of Pope St. John Paul II's Account of the Person", pp. 17-55, and p. 30-31.

consciousness, discussing it, and realizing that others are going through these same questions, brings to light this capacity of human beings to "witness" to what is going on interiorly; and, as such, witnesses to what can be shared and understood by others as well as helping us to understand what another is going through.

Masculinity: Healed and connected

As Wendell Berry, an academic turned farmer, an essayist and a poet, says, living this reality in his own life: 'The word husbandry is the name of a connection. In its original sense, it is the name of the work of a domestic man, a man who has accepted a bondage to the household'[2].

Etymologically, 'husbandry' means a husband, householder, and farmer: 'c. 1300, "management of a household;" late 14c. as "farm management;" from husband (n.) in a now-obsolete sense of "peasant farmer" (early 13c.) + -ery'[3].

In a wonderful response to the many needs of those suffering the effects of 'floodwaters near Houston', an article celebrates the simplicity of men, many of whom are volunteers, risking their lives to help[4].

From a Christian account of the relationship of a man and a woman, 'domination' is not a true, natural state, of the relationship between them.

---

[2] John Cuddeback quotes Wendell Berry: John Cuddeback, June 19th, 2024, "'Husbandry' and Rethinking a Man's Bond with his Wife": https://life-craft.org/husbandry-and-rethinking-a-mans-bond-with-his-wife/.

[3] "husbandry": https://www.etymonline.com/word/husbandry.

[4] Mark Tapson, September 1st, 2017, "Houston Rescuers Prove the Lie of 'Toxic Masculinity'": https://www.nationalreview.com/2017/09/hurricane-harvey-toxic-masculinity-was-disproved-heroism/.

Rather, the domination by the man of the woman is both a consequence of the fall into the disobedience of God, which is sin, and, therefore, male domination is itself a fruit of that sin: 'Your yearning will be for your husband, and he will dominate you' (Gn. 3: 16). To which, among others, St. John Paul II replies, by returning us to the original gift of being male or female, which 'includes right from the beginning the nuptial attribute, that is, the capacity of expressing love, that love in which the person becomes a gift and - by means of this gift - fulfills the meaning of his being and existence'. Therefore, man and woman were originally, equally, each a gift for the other. So, speaking of the 'redemption of the body'[5], we are called back to the original, reciprocal gift of self, whole and entire, each for the other, through the great reciprocal gift of Christ for the Church and the Church for Christ (Eph. 5: 21-33).

At the same time, there are those social situations which facilitate the flourishing of equality in the home. In America at any rate, there has been a shift from a homegrown business in which the husband and wife worked together, with the father being present and introducing the children to the skills of his trade and, presumably, the wife and mother doing the same. But, with the advent of work outside of the home, it seems that the man has adopted a free-from-responsibility for the moral life of the home mentality, while the latter has fallen upon the wife and mother. In other words, there is the advent of the label of "toxic masculinity". It seems that men had become 'de-moralized' when, in origin, the word 'virtue comes from the Latin root vir, which means man, and the term originally had connotations of manly strength and honor[6].

---

[5] GENERAL AUDIENCE: Wednesday 16 January 1980: https://www.vatican.va/content/john-paul-ii/en/audiences/1980/documents/hf_jp-ii_aud_19800116.html/.

[6] Nancy Pearcey, from the May/June, 2023, edition of the Touchstone, "Common Good Men: The Lost Authority of Godly Men": https://www.touchstonemag.com/archives/article.php.

Now, however, there seems to be more of a recognition of the value of "husbandry": of being a husband and father who is connected to his family and to the land; and, indeed, whose vocation it precisely is to keep "things" together.

'A true husband tries to keep tied together many things that need to be kept together. Husbandry is a wonderfully vast enterprise that takes care of people, and so takes care of many 'things' in human life. A husband in the fullest sense is a man who has fallen in love with a woman, and then discovers that his love for her calls him to that vast enterprise, an enterprise calling for amazing, concrete applications. Imagine a world in which the concrete arts of life are driven by married love! It is always a matter of love, and love brings things together. A married man discovers that *his first* love does not narrow his life. Rather, by a deep magic the maturation of that love expands his heart, his vision, and the work of his hands to encompass more than he could have imagined.

In short, the seeming 'ambiguity' of the word husband points to a great truth: the arts of taking care of material things (in which the land has a unique but certainly not exclusive place) are closely tied to marriage. Somehow a man's being a husband to his wife—which again is the foundational commitment—calls him to a broader and deeply embodied husbandry. We can rediscover and rethink this husbandry and how to enact it today–first of all for the sake of our marriages. And then for most everything else too'[7].

And again, "Today, local economies are being destroyed by the 'pluralistic,' displaced, global economy, which has no respect for what works

---

[7] John Cuddeback, June 19th, 2024, "'Husbandry' and Rethinking a Man's Bond with his Wife".

in a locality. The global economy is built on the principle that one place can be exploited, even destroyed, for the sake of another place"[8].

By contrast, and by way of taking a slightly different positive development, for a variety of reasons, a number of people are rediscovering the "multigenerational home", in which grandparents and grandchildren interact with the middle generation of the parents; and, while this is not always without difficulties, it is at the very least a rediscovery of the social development which comes through this reality[9]. In a certain sense, we can say, the *Neocatechumenal Way*, in bringing generations together, is also contributing to the relationship enrichment which the reality of human nature needs to thrive.

Although these articles and references do not mention the "The Catholic Land Movement"[10], with the Catholic author, G. K. Chesterton (1874-1936) and Fr. Vincent McNabb (1868-1943), what is going on in America now is very reminiscent of what was being promoted in England and, in a way, is still very alive in those, wittingly or unwittingly, who cultivate the garden and the environment, although not in order to eradicate human beings but in order to cultivate a good relationship between human beings and indeed God the Creator.

Thus Fr. Vincent McNabb, a priest who took up the encouragement of Pope Leo XIII (1810-1903) to resisting public ownership of what deprives the working man of his opportunity to better himself, namely, an

---

[8] "Wendell Berry": https://www.poetryfoundation.org/poets/wendell-berry.

[9] Frank DeVito, July 10th, 2024, "Multigenerational Living: A Step Back to Healthy Communal Life": https://www.thepublicdiscourse.com/2024/07/95327/.

[10] "THE CATHOLIC LAND MOVEMENT": G. K. Chesterton, Fr. Vincent McNabb and Commander Herbert Shove: https://www.ecatholic2000.com/cts/untitled-495.shtml.

entitlement to his own income and property[11]. Thus *The Catholic Land Movement* sought to encourage a return to the land, to ownership and to the forming of a parish community, with a priest, and with a variety of workers who make possible the family, sufficiency, and purity of heart, adequate reasons for wholesome work, with a view to a dignified living and a good relationship to the family, its local situation and to God[12]. In other words, it is not just the vacancy of the countryside, as many left if for the cities and factory work, but also for the fact that profit and squalor, sexual temptations and inadequate opportunities to be together, are what encourages people to seek out a good way of life and not just an absence from the city-sins. My own mother-in-law's father was a part of that movement even if, being unable to sustain a living for a family, he eventually went on to sell milking equipment.

In a word, is the disruption or disorder between men and their wives and families a sign of their "disconnected" relationship to God? If, in other words, I have no relationship to God, and I am "unconnected to Him, am I also likely to be unconnected to my wife, children, family, fellow man and society? As Dr. Anthony Williams says who, in his retirement is exploring a new pilgrim path, that just as the Fathers of the Church and of monastic life came close to God and close to nature, so good environmentalism needs to recover its religious roots.

Even in a small way, and as we are too poor to own property and land, it is possible to make use of a garden and grow, as I do, various vegetables; and, therefore, there is an opportunity to be a living witness to the wonders and glories of creation even if what we grow comes mainly out of plastic

---

[11] Pope Leo XIII, wrote *Rerum Novarum*, Of New Things, published in 1891, on "Capital and Labor", article 5 etc.: https://www.vatican.va/content/leo-xiii/en/encyclicals/documents/hf_l-xiii_enc_15051891_rerum-novarum.html.

[12] "THE CATHOLIC LAND MOVEMENT": G. K. Chesterton, Fr. Vincent McNabb and Commander Herbert Shove: https://www.ecatholic2000.com/cts/untitled-495.shtml.

boxes. Thus, as I do my daily round, it is possible to talk to *Christ the Gardener*, and to Mary Magdalen, who first called Him this when, from one word, she then went on to recognize Him and to announce *the Good News of His Resurrection* to his disciples[13].

How many people must have welcomed Mother Teresa into heaven! As one writer has put it: 'Just as the beginning of life is a collaborative, relational act, death too ought to be communal'[14].

Divorce and annulment

If a couple come to marriage with a pre-nuptial agreement, determining who will receive what share of the property if the marriage does not work, then there is already a built-in failure of the possibility of marriage. For if marriage is life-long, until husband or wife dies, then it is clear that a pre-nuptial agreement introduces a provisionality into the relationship and, therefore, it is already not a marriage. In other words, we can live together as long as we are healthy, wealthy, and conflict free or whatever drives the provisionality; and, therefore, the couple has not entered into what marriage is. According to what is known, nothing was mentioned about this provisionality and the significance of suffering in marriage, except in so far as a 'lack of commitment' was referred to; rather, what was mentioned, were the symptoms. Thus marriage breakdown, if they were marriages in the first place, was attributed to one or more of the following: proximity to people who were already divorced, which suggests that being around people who had no experience of "going through" difficulties indicates that help was not forthcoming. Similarly, if one of the two was on

---

[13] Etheredge, The Unlikely Gardener: https://enroutebooksandmedia.com/anunlikelygardener/.

[14] Elizabeth Regnerus, June 10th, 2024, "Dying Alone": https://www.thepublicdiscourse.com/2024/06/95111/?utm_source.

his or her second "marriage", then again a "dead end" of inexperience in passing through or enduring suffering is indicated; even, for example, in thinking through what behaviour may be causing a problem in the marriage and being willing to acknowledge that there is the help of the word of God and the sacraments of the Catholic Church, as well as the wisdom of others to turn to and to benefit from.

'[L]acking commitment' was more commonly identified as a cause than even adultery, which leads into what constitutes this lack; is it an unwillingness to recognize a fault, such as bringing a mobile phone to the dinner table, or being unwilling to share the feelings around what is going on. Conflicts over money may be about "what is mine is not yours", whereas marriage entails a spirit of generosity, whereby it may be that a spouse scarcely "sees" any of his or her income because it is spent on the family. Other reasons given were abuse, alcohol or substance abuse, or the couple were married too young[15]. More and more, however, 'widespread sexual consumerism' leads to a consequence that 'would have been unthinkable until the last couple of decades: pornography is now a major contributor cited in divorces'[16]. Clearly, however, not all these reasons are of equal value and indeed, in some cases, like domestic violence, there is a need to protect the vulnerable spouse and to identify the "triggers" in the offending spouse. But, whatever the obvious cause of divorce, there still remains the discovery of what causes the cause, as it were, such that 'lacking commitment' may mean, as it did in my case, that a fear of an inescapable suffering was what prevented me from marrying for many years; but, in my case, it was only dimly perceived as the relationships were very often "on" and "off" and often entailed conflicts of conscience about how promiscuous we

---

[15] Kristy Bieber, J.D. , May 30th, 2024, "Revealing Divorce Statistics In 2024": https://www.forbes.com/advisor/legal/divorce/divorce-statistics/.

[16] Eberstadt, *Adam and Eve After the Pill: Revisited*, p. 86.

were. Indeed, conflicts of conscience for some, it seemed, did not exist at all, as if all that mattered was what was agreed.

Given the prevalence of divorce, however, this mentality can seep into a Christian understanding of marriage. And so, again, what is "given" turns out to be a conditional reality and not a permanent one. In other words, I will stay married if my spouse does not grow old, lose his or her vigour, have any imperfections or sin – as if Christ did not say, either 'cut off from me you can do nothing' (Jn 15: 5) or 'what God has joined together let not man divide' (Mt 19: 6).

Although, then, there is the question of why divorces occur, and even Christian counsellors can argue that God permits divorce[17], in reality, a valid Catholic marriage excludes divorce even in the case of adultery. Or rather, it is not so much whether there is adultery in the marriage as whether or not the marriage is validly celebrated by the man and woman and an action of God which cannot be rescinded (cf. Mt. 19: 6). In the case of an annulment, then, there is an investigation by the Church to see if there was a significant impediment to the celebration of the sacrament of marriage at the time it was celebrated; and, therefore, in the sense that there was a defect of some kind, marriage itself was never celebrated and God did not act to bring it about. Such a defect of intention would, for example, be an unwillingness to have children which, for some reason, was not evident before the marriage itself; and, for example, it was expressed to a friend but not to the prospective spouse so that he or she did not know that this mentality existed.

However, the pain and hurt may be no less or no different to what is recognized as a whole gamut of reactions, not least of which are the different ways that revenge can show itself[18]. It may, too, be unrealistic to

---

[17] "Sexual Betrayal/Cheating": https://www.healingsexualhurt.com/when_your_partner_cheats.

[18] "Sexual Betrayal/Cheating": as above.

emphasize, too much, the dependence of the healing of the marriage on how the "guilty" partner addresses what they have done. In other words, in the complexity of human marriage, people can turn to another for a variety of reasons, not least of which is the unbearable cross of another person's complaining, dissatisfaction with life, a revenge response for a previous spousal betrayal or any number of other factors; and, therefore, it is necessary to explore the whole reality of the marriage and not just the sin of adultery.

According to those who have investigated types of communication in relationships, albeit in a very secular way, disregarding what constitutes the central bond of being male and female, they nevertheless share what wisdom they have: 'Time and time again we hear of couples divorcing because of their problems, and then remarrying only to find they have similar or new problems in the new relationship'[19]. In other words, there are good reasons for investigating, either with each other or others, the nature of how couples communicate and what the obstacles really are to good communication. Indeed, the sin of adultery may disclose that there are either hidden sins or, at the very least, unaddressed problems. And, therefore, while not burdening the "innocent" person with responsibility for the wrong done to them, it may be necessary to be more open about the reality of the lived marriage resulting in one of the two turning away, however briefly, to another.

Population fears: Who benefits?

Thus one crisis tends to run into and combine with another, with abortion, the selling of body parts, euthanasia, contraception and the decision

---

[19] Cf. .John Gottman and Julie Schwartz with Doug Abrams and Rachel Carlton Abrams, Penguin Random House, UK, 2019, *Eight Dates: To keep your relationship happy, thriving and lasting*, p. 72.

to have no children, together with a strand of Muslim thought which says that, in time, the world will be Moslem as the West is destroying itself. Therefore, why should Muslims help defend human life when, by not doing so, the "West" plays into the hands of a country becoming Muslim by default – simply because the "West" are not having children whereas Muslims are. At the same time there are Muslims who have spoken with Pope Francis and who have otherwise argued that life begins from conception. In the words of Pope Francis, collaboratively expressed with the Grand Imam Ahmad Al-Tayyeb, "'In the name of innocent human life that God has forbidden to kill, affirming that whoever kills a person is like one who kills the whole of humanity, and that whoever saves a person is like one who saves the whole of humanity …'[20]. On the one hand, then, there are those who instrumentalize human life and destroy it with a view to bringing down the population and reducing the "carbon footprint" which, in this case, is the real footprint of human beings; and, on the other hand,

---

[20] Pope Francis, *Fratelli Tutti*: http://www.vatican.va/content/francesco/en/encyclicals/documents/papa-francesco_20201003_enciclica-fratelli-tutti.html#_ftnref262. In *Conception: An Icon of the Beginning*, there is a Muslim scholar who holds the view of human life from conception, p. 575: 'Germany, however, has gone before the world and enacted the following, 1991 legislation: "Act for the Protection of Embryos" (The Embryo Protection Act). This "word" of law, as it were, has become a world-wide teacher and a noted Muslim bioethicist commented, approvingly, on the German law: Hassan Hathut (1924-2009) 'referred to Germany, which banned all use of human embryos in biomedical research. As for the surplus of fertilized ova in the IVF processes, the law even banned initiating such a surplus …. Hathut concluded that this law goes in line with Islamic ethics (Hathut 1994, 175)' (citation on the Muslim scholar from: "'Islam, Paternity, and the Beginning of Life": "The Beginning of Human Life: Islamic Bioethical Perspectives" with Mohammed Ghaly, (*Zygon: Journal of Religion and Science*, vol. 47, No. 1, (March 2012), pp. 175-213: https://core.ac.uk/download/pdf/43497555.pdf, p. 207.' This whole passage and footnote is taken from Etheredge, *Unfolding a Post-Roe World*, p. 117.

there are those that see this as opportunity to bring down the human race or to bring in a different culture.

The irony of promoting contraception and abortion is that millions, if not billions, are spent on destroying human populations and polluting the environment in the name of some kind of environmentalism: an ideologically driven response to the needs of the environment rather than one which recognizes human rights and the help that people actually need to come out of the cities or poverty. In other words these advocates of environmentalism make money destroying human life and polluting the environment while claiming to do what is beneficial to both human beings and the environment. By contrast *Natural Family Planning* costs the training of a human being, invariably a woman, and the advocacy of good health and family practices and harms no one and nothing except the unscrupulous money makers. As we saw earlier, at the beginning of this book, pharmaceutical companies that have moved to manufacturing products that people, very often women, will take for many years is far more profitable than simply addressing, more immediately, the need to be treated and the treatment completed.

It maybe that the Catholic school and university system has even encouraged, not just a contraceptive mentality, but a mentality that takes us away from contemplating the Creator's contribution to the divine-human conception of a child. When our children were younger, there was a document which led their religious education and which promoted the understanding that a family meant two children, one of each sex; and, whether or not it explained how this was possible, it certainly distressed our eldest boy who came home wondering how it is that we have children over and above that number two: that we have eight. But, importantly, his question was: "How can we afford to have so many children?" And we explained that God exists and shows Himself in His Providence: that God acts in the circumstances of everyday life. So, many people make gifts to us of clothes that their own children have grown out of, owing to having three girls and five boys, clothes can be handed or swapped about and so we experience that God helps us.

And, therefore, children are not just conceived but prayed into existence, after the example of Sarah and Tobias who, on their wedding night, got up and prayed, Tobias saying to Sarah: 'Get up, my sister! You and I must pray and petition our Lord to win his grace and his protection' (Tobit, 8: 4). So, having been instructed to read the *Book of Tobit* during our marriage preparation, we have prayed every time we have come together as husband and wife, beginning with our wedding night; and, in addition, we have discussed all the factors that affect being open to life (cf. *Humanae Vitae*) and, in addition, hoped in the help of God whenever we came together.

Disquiet, discernment and decision

A girl who has now de-transitioned, as it is euphemistically called, from the process of altering her appearance to resemble a boy, who has now lost her breasts, and has realized how women around her were so negative about being a woman and thus, indirectly, helped to sell her the ideological position of being able to change her sex, says: 'As a budding adolescent, she was uncomfortable with her body, questioned her identity and place in the world, and wasn't yet considering her future as a mother'[21]. In other words, time and time again, the question of gender disquiet is more about the real question of identity and its psychological influences than the medicalization of the issue and its plethora of

---

[21] Madison Ayers, June 15th, 2024, "Is it true that puberty blockers "pause" puberty? Hint: The answer isn't what we've been told": https://naturalwomanhood.org/puberty-blockers-pause-puberty/.

unnecessary concrete proposals as regards the appearance of being male or female.

More widely there does seem to be a tendency to manufacture clothing styles that are not so much genderless as play down the feminine, expressing what one female writer said: 'I've realised this knee-jerk reaction to skirts and dresses is because they subject me to the male gaze – and I'm just not comfortable with that anymore'[22]. Would be fair to say that the woman is conscious of a predatory male gaze or just that she is not about being noticed for "just" being a woman? Either way her reaction may be about how men help or hinder a woman's expression of herself.

On the one hand, then, there are many philosophical positions, as it were, which, whether held explicitly or implicitly, whether by word or deed or word and deed, which indicate "where we are coming from"; however, none of this is adequate in its own right as, more often than not, each of us is on a path of discovering who we are and what we are like: a process of discovery which often entails many "repeats" because we never learnt from the lesson – we never listened to the voice of conscience.

On the other hand, then, what is necessary is that education of conscience: that listening to the objective evaluation of what we are doing which is not pretence but which proceeds from the voice which "knows" us from the depths of our heart and which, if we but reflect on what we discover, we would know ourselves too, in the depth of our human reality. Experience, while necessary, is insufficient, we also need that ability to listen to the 'still voice" within (cf. 1 Kings 19: 1-18): which enters us into a

---

[22] Lauren Bulla, 30th November, 2024, « Why I've stopped wearing women's clothes – and you should try it, too": https://www.independent.co.uk/voices/women-clothes-gender-men-male-gaze-b2654740.html.

dialogue with God: the voice that speaks the truth-in-love not to accuse but to enlighten, not to burden or blame but to free and to be a foundation in our lives.

On one occasion, then, while a young and inexperienced young man, I had met an equally young but experienced woman while travelling and, in a certain sense, it was obvious that there was an invitation to intimacy that somehow showed through our meeting very quickly. She saw, very clearly, how young and inexperienced I was and suggested that I go for a walk before taking this invitation further. As I walked around, relatively briefly, owing to the eagerness of the opportunity to engage with her, there was a very clear voice which said "no" to this opportunity; and, by contrast, my whole being seemed taken up with the romanticism of love only to discover, afterwards, that I was discarded as a "used being". And, while the romanticism persisted in my heart for no short-time afterwards, the ever-closed door and the presence of another man showed me very clearly that I was an "experience".

Thus, as I say, I was ill-prepared to listen and questioned, as it were, the truth or even the reality of what I heard the "no" to mean. In other words there was a voice of conscience that was totally unexpected and that I was totally unprepared to listen to, which brings home to me the absolute necessity of a formation which addresses the power to listen and indeed, in a way, enables it.

Thus one of the distinguishing features of the *Neocatechumenal Way* is precisely that: a training to listen; and, therefore, a listening that leads to obedience, which is listening in action. On the whole, then, while we traverse relationships as if we are in possession of ourselves, the disappointment and failure, in the event or events of life, shows us very clearly that we are more driven than driving, more desiring than loving, more falling than finding a real beginning.

So, in a somewhat unexpected way, I am thinking that discovering whether or not a person has an active conscience is probably more fundamental than I have thought, thinking about what leads to discernment in friendship, whether romantic or not. Indeed, thinking about it now, one of the ways to answer the question as to whether or not a person has an active conscience is what "going out" entails. No thanks to me but to the grace of God, the gift of 'chastity' made possible a chaste courtship and both I and my fiancé saw this as a definite act of God in favour of the possibility of us being called to marriage. In this instance, chastity meant not touching, caressing or kissing with a view to arousing each other; and, indeed, in view of our histories, accepting that no touching was, as I say, a gift of God.

Sexual ethics: Promoting the body's expression of the soul

Given that there are many problems in society, why focus on sexual ethics? To begin with, a culture that promotes the death of the ill or the unborn, through contraceptive chemicals which pollute the body and the planet, a body image that is fluid and can change from male to female or female to male, is already a culture that is teaching our contempories an understanding of what it is to be human: that our humanity is plastic, fluid, and capable of absorbing long term medications that are not, in fact, necessary for health and indeed, on the contrary, have many anti-life effects. In other words there is a widespread mentality which agrees that it is possible to treat the human being as an experimental subject, no matter the age, provided that boys and girls can be persuaded to take any number of medicalizing initiatives; and, for want of a better expression, medicalizing initiatives are drugs or surgery which are not a treatment of a disorder and, just as contraceptives are unnecessary, as contraceptives, so this leads to unnecessary surgery.

In other words, through the mentality of using a person for pleasure, pleasure is separated from the person and becomes an end in itself; and, therefore, if pleasure is separated from being a person, then what has become of being a person: a person has become an object of use. Never mind those who want to dignify animals with the title of person, presuming it will help human beings to care for them more, people have become less than animals in that people are not dignified with the integrity of being a whole: a psychosomatic whole of a body that expresses a soul and a soul that is expressed in the body (cf. *Familiaris Consortio*, 11).

Thus, as we live 'in a culture which promotes premarital sex and is intent on imposing acceptance of homosexual relations, as well as gender ideology. [And that] Most adults will enter into marriage or other conjugal relationships. [Therefore] Sexual morality "is of the utmost importance for the personal lives of Christians and for the social life of our times" (*Vatican Declaration on Certain Questions Concerning Sexual Ethics*, at 2)'[23].

It is not so much that the Church is addressing sexual ethics, particularly with respect to marriage, as if there is nothing else to address; indeed, it is rather that our society so generalizes everybody, that nobody exists as a personal subject. There are the unborn that can be aborted; and there are those who will want it, do it, and justify it. There are those who want to kill the ill, whether young or old, and there are those who will do it. There are those who are devastating human fertility and, irrespective of its consequences, devastating the fertility of the seas too, just because they want to devastate human fertility "for the sake of the planet": as if there is no such

---

[23] Richard P. Maggi Esq. December 24th, 2021, "The Church's Teaching on Marriage, Part One": https://www.hprweb.com/2021/12/the-churchs-teaching-on-marriage-part-one/.

thing as moral action – rather, only that which achieves their end. There are those who can be sterilized without knowing, deprived of passports and sent to war or imprisoned for being a particular race.

In other words, we live in a world where human beings are a subject, whether we like it or not; but, more and more, they are treated as less than a subject. What kind of society have we become? So, even if our laws identify, up to point, our common humanity, we live in a society in which, increasingly, there are exploiters and the exploited. Clearly, the exploiters seem to have lost an ability to identify the humanity of the exploited; and the exploited are exploited because the exploiters possess power, if not impunity before the law. So, naturally, the question arises, what has happened to our capacity to identity with each other: to recognize that my suffering unites me to yours; that your life is as precious as mine; that we have a common humanity that transcends our differences.

Revisiting the foundations of human identity and relevant disciplines

In view of all the controversy surrounding the use of physical treatments of what often are minors, political stability is clearly a key concern; and, where there are changes in government, it is especially important that policies are not ideologically driven but reflect the real evidence that is arising concerning the harm of certain treatments. And, therefore, it is crucial for ministers to be open to the evidence that is arising and to be able to see the good that can be continued because of it[24].

Finding a much-needed foundation for practice and policy, the revised *Constitution of the National Health Service* (NHS) will now say that "We

---

[24] July 15th, 2024, Ben Quinn and Peter Walker, "Wes Streeting expected to tell parliament why he backs puberty blockers ban": https://www.theguardian.com/politics/article/2024/jul/15/wes-streeting-defends-puberty-blocker-ban-decision-after-labour-criticism.

are defining sex as biological sex." And that patients will have a right to be on a ward of their own biological sex and to be seen by a member of staff who is also of the same biological sex[25]. On the other hand, if "men" are to be asked if they are pregnant[26], either the use of language is off the wall or there is a legitimate risk, owing to how women can identify as male, that in fact a real woman is pregnant even if she is claiming to be a man. In other words, while so much uncertainty surrounds who claims to be what, caution is necessary for the sake of the wellbeing of the woman her unborn child.

Therefore, presumably, the NHS ruling that men are biological men and women are biological women will allow parents, teachers and professional staff generally, to use biological sex as the normal foundation of addressing pupils and clients. Perhaps there will be clarity, too, for those who need help to understand themselves and for those who, for one reason or another, are in danger of accessing drugs which may well not be for them[27]. In some cases, then, this leaves people very distressed by the medical interventions that were supposed to allay distress, raising the profile of procedures which were rashly adopted and which, in retrospect, have raised more problems than they have solved; and, what is more, the presenting psychiatric issues may well have resolved over time anyway but which, if they have not, are now compounded with the aftermath of the effects of

---

[25] Kurt Zindulka, 30th April, 2024, "Win For Reality: UK's National Health Service Constitution to Declare 'Sex is Biological'": https://www.breitbart.com/politics/2024/04/30/win-for-reality-uks-national-health-service-constitution-to-declare-sex-is-biological/.

[26] Thomas Kingsley, Tuesday 29 March 2022, "Hospital is asking men if they're pregnant before taking scans 'as it's the least intrusive way to be safe'": https://www.independent.co.uk/news/uk/home-news/hospital-nhs-men-pregnant-walton-trust-b2046241.html.

[27] James Melley and Judith Burns, 02/05/2024, "Unregulated online clinic gave teen dangerous hormone dose": https://www.bbc.co.uk/news/uk-68944273.

what are being recognized, increasingly, as radically invasive treatments. But this is not a license for abuse of those who present as confused or unsure of their identity; and, therefore, it is not a matter of pointed remarks or undue emphases, so much as giving a ground plan to everyday communication.

But the debate seems far from over in terms of what is going on in our health service, especially in view of so many resignations from it:

'According to the Times, hundreds of members, including NHS leaders and former presidents of royal medical colleges, have expressed 'dismay' at union leaders for opposing the review's recommendations on gender identity services for children. They allege the union is being controlled by a 'vocal minority'[28].

One possible consequence of this departure of those with a reasoned objection to the refusal of the British Medical Association's rejection of the Cass Recommendations, is that the BMA becomes more radicalized to the detriment of the care provided to those seeking help from it. This, then, does not augur well for an NHS service that is set to open six new Gender Clinics by 2026: 'the NHS appears fully set to promote gender ideologies even more among children and young people'[29]. It is not enough to give "lip-service" to recognizing the need for far more time-consuming psychological assessment and counselling for those who ask for help. One of the basic problems is that the need for psychological assessment of those who present to these gender services is assessed on the premise that a person

[28] Makeda, 29th August, 2024, "Doctors quit BMA over Cass rejection": https://www.christianvoice.org.uk/index.php/doctors-quit-bma-over-cass-rejection/

[29] Makeda, August 15th, 2024, "Son of Tavistock: NHS to open six new children's gender clinics by 2026": https://www.christianvoice.org.uk/index.php/nhs-open-new-gender-clinics/.

experiences distress because of being rejected as trying to change sex, rather than trying to change sex being indicative of interior, psychological problems. Thus, a review of Australian gender services says:

> 'that elevated rates of depression, anxiety, self-harm, and suicide in gender-diverse children and adolescents are primarily due to experiences of stigma, discrimination, social exclusion, bullying, and/or barriers to gender-affirming care'[30].

On the one hand, then, it is perfectly legitimate to acknowledge that 'stigma' and other negative reactions are upsetting; however, on the other hand, it is another matter entirely to consider this sufficiently explanatory for the origin of the gender dysphoria and its history in the individual and their social situation. Clearly, a psychological explanation that "blames" others for gender dysphoria entails an acceptance of psychological explanations as valid but, for some reason, psychological explanations are often not regarded as sufficiently helpful for explaining the very existence of gender dysphoria. Why is this? One possibility is that there are other forces at work than just an open, discursive investigation of what is happening, namely, 'This suggests, as recently argued in a paper in this journal, that political pressure to increase access to rights may have overcome the usual medical safeguards designed to maintain patient safety'[31]. But now we have to ask: What is the supposed right invoked here: for the claim that there is a right to mutilate ourselves is contrary to the basic principle of all rights: do good and avoid harm.

---

[30]   Alison Clayton https://orcid.org/0000-0002-3634-234X alclayton@student.unimelb.edu.au, Andrew   James Amos https://orcid.org/0000-0002-9145-0212, and Patrick Clarke+1https://doi.org/10.1177/1039856224127633: "Implications of the Cass Review for health policy governing gender medicine for Australian minors" (or https://journals.sagepub.com/doi/10.1177/10398562241276335).

[31] https://journals.sagepub.com/doi/10.1177/10398562241276335.

Deeper than grave but external changes

Clearly, then, from the point of view of a person's readiness for marriage, for some people there may now be insuperable obstacles to this possibility. If, for whatever reason, you are considering suicide, consult the available helplines, beginning with those people whose judgement you trust[32]. But, even if there are dramatic disappointments as a person discovers that they have been betrayed into irrevocably destructive decisions, the Lord is merciful and answers with mercy, revealing the help that can show a person that happiness does come from love, but first of all it comes from the love God has for us! Even a young girl who was talked into transitioning and had her breasts removed, has now reversed the decision, married, and has a child.

'The desire to be a mother came to Daisy Strong after she had undergone a double mastectomy and started taking wrong sex hormones. The desire must have been shocking, because she had told herself that she would never get pregnant; she was going to be a man. And as everyone knows, men can't get pregnant. But if the desire to have children ever did come, she figured she could just use surrogacy. The desire to mother, moved her to reconsider her persona as a man, and move towards transitioning. While she and her husband were looking at surrogacy she realized that she had a body that could get pregnant, if what she had done didn't prevent her from becoming pregnant'[33].

Similarly, a homosexual man discovered that his activity did not define him and that God can act to change what we cannot and to heal the

---

[32] Speaking of Suicide: Resources: https://speakingofsuicide.com/resources/.

[33] Doing a 180 after Transitioning. Daisy Strongin on the Dr. J Show ep 237, May 24th, 2024: https://ruthinstitute.org/dr-j-show/doing-a-180-after-transitiond/

very real hurt that our behaviour can conceal; and so, for example, having lived this way for five years, and that 'trying to make a same-sex relationship is a living hell', admitting that 'Sin is fun', he realized he was 'so broken'. Reading the word of God started to heal him and 'counseling ... helped him realize that an absent father relationship is what caused him to sexualize male relationships when he reached puberty'[34]. Even if, then, after 15 years of marriage and the birth of his own children, life is a battle, he can see that God is with him, and his wife and family. As he goes on to say:

"Moms and Dads, don't give up on your kids. I don't know the time frame when God will answer your prayers, but I can encourage you that He is faithful"[35].

What this woman and man discovered is that being male or female is not skin deep and superficial, it is a reality that is deeply embodied in the very fact of human existence as, from conception, the very first instant of coming to exist as a whole being is the very first instant of the bodily embodiment of the soul. In other words, although to us, using words like body and soul, it seems as if there are two ingredients to being human; the language of body and soul is a way, as it were, of referring to what is innermost to human identity and what is the outward expression of it. Thus the body is the outward expression of the soul; and, therefore, the whole human person, a "being-in-relationship", is either male or female from

---

[34] Text excerpts from an email, drmorse@ruthinstitute.org drmorse@ruthinstitute.org], whereas the whole interview is to be found here: "Trading a Nightmare for Joy": https://theruthinstitute.locals.com/post/5750894/leaving-a-nightmare-gay-life-for-joy-in-family-jim-domen-on-the-dr-j-show-ep-240. Another reported on an 'early father wound' and, again, found healing: https://ruthinstitute.org/dr-j-show/integrating-self-and-leaving-a-double-life/.

[35] Excerpt the from testimony as above by the Ruth Institute.

conception. In reality, however, in that it is God who created the transmission of human life, drawing on the gifts of husband and wife, so it is God who, granting the gift of life to the child, at the very first instant of human conception, completes the personal gift of a personal God with the personal conception of each human person, at the first instant of their child coming to exist, one, whole and entire, whether boy or girl[36]. Thus being a human parent is an outward sign of the inward "parenthood" of God; and, therefore, "parenthood" is a whole gift of mother, father, and God: the outward gift a sign of the inward gift of God.

Being a father, however, is different from being a mother in that he contributes to the existence of a child by his self-gift, which transmits life, and therefore, is an outward sign of God's bringing to exist the human person, one in body and soul[37]; and, similarly, being a mother entails contributing to the existence of the child through giving both what will come to constitute the bodily expression of the child, the egg, and her welcoming the indwelling person who will, one day, be born from her and, therefore

---

[36] Cf. Etheredge, *Conception: An Icon of the Beginning*: https://enroutebooksandmedia.com/conception/; and, while Chapter 5 deals specifically with the embryological evidence, the whole book is dedicated to understanding the first instant of human conception: the conception of the whole person: the whole being-in-relationship of being a boy or a girl.

[37] I therefore think that the way Perry Cahall has put the relationship of the father to the child is undeveloped, even in his analogy between human and divine fatherhood; he says: 'A man can be a biological father, but he is a true father only when he chooses to enter into loving relationship with his offspring.', p. 181 of pp. 175-187, Chapter 10: "Why Did God Become Incarnate as a Man", in *Gender Ideology and Pastoral Practice*, 2024. So, while I do not disagree with Cahall's general thesis of father and mother expressing the mystery of God in a complementary way, it seems to me that 'biological fatherhood' is being expressed as if it does not express "psychological fatherhood", which reaches from the core of the man just as contributing to the conception of his child reaches from the depths of his being a husband. If, therefore, a man rejects fulfilling his relationship of fatherhood he disfigures his being, already, a father.

expresses the more intimate nature of the relational presence of God in whom 'we live, and move, and have our being' (Acts 17: 28). We are being-in-relationship, ultimately, because God is the "Being-in-Relationship"[38].

The forgetting of elemental truths

To pass over the development of embryology, the stimulation of philosophical questions of human identity, the contribution of psychology, and the insights of Scripture and theology, not to mention that 'theology and sociology cannot be pulled apart', as the one witnesses to the presence or the absence of the other[39], is like expecting a shrivelled and uprooted plant to blossom. But, more gravely, it is to put in front of already inexperienced, very often philosophically uncritical, untrained, and vulnerable parents and children, in a law-war environment, what is really ideologically driven advice which, in the end, neither serves the people it is meant to help or the scientific discipline of the adviser.

Mary Eberstadt 'points to alarming trends such as the rise in loneliness, psychiatric issues among children, and the increasing unhappiness of women since the sexual revolution. These issues, Mary notes, are intricately linked to the erosion of family structures and the diminishing regard for marriage. "Many people don't understand anymore why

---

[38] Cf. Etheredge, *Human Nature: Moral Norm*, "Part III: Drawing on the Doctrine of the Blessed Trinity". But this logic can also be seen in other accounts of reality: cf. Vern Poythress, November 23rd, 2024, "Trinitarian Metaphysics: The Difference the Trinity Makes in Evaluating Platonic and Aristotelian Ontologies—And Other Philosophical Proposals Too": https://frame-poythress.org/trinitarian-metaphysics-the-difference-the-trinity-makes-in-evaluating-platonic-and-aristotelian-ontologies-and-other-philosophical-proposals-too/.

[39] Society is "forgetting elemental human truths" - Mary Eberstadt interview with Tony Rucinski: https://www.youtube.com/watch?v=XgtBSbk_fWU.

people lived in families to begin with", she observes, adding that society is experiencing "a forgetting of elemental human truths" about family life'[40].

To put the matter in another way, if a many tentacled beast grows by virtue of the pruning of human vice, sin and ignorance being abandoned, then there is a social witness to the breakdown of family relationships which testifies, by contrast, to the presence of what had helped families exist and flourish, however imperfectly, namely, the appeal to God called prayer: the family that prays together stays together. Conversely, the family that does not pray, is a prey to what preys upon each and every one in it. One of the clearest, sociological signs of the breakdown of the family is the disappearance of religion which, in its roots, come from a root word meaning "to bind". And, therefore, while some societies employ force to maintain what is imposed upon its population, force, in the end, becomes counterproductive and incites rebellion. By contrast, then, seeking stability is another way of seeking God, as the great founder of the Benedictine order recognised, St. Benedict, that stability is a sign of the presence of a relationship to God as expressed in a relationship to a specific community. Thus there is a kind of parallel, possibly, between the decline of Benedictine spirituality and the decline of marriage: each entailing a relationship to a specific community or person, being life-long, and founded on a relationship to God.

What does Christian marriage express distinctly?

We have already encountered a false masculine Christianity which "uses" Christianity to justify abusive and domineering behaviour and,

---

[40] Quotes from the interview put together by "The Coalition for Marriage", by email: Coalition for Marriage admin@c4m.org.uk.

indeed, both historically and in recent times, popes have criticized mascu-line indifference to the woman with whom he has slept, the very existence of their children, the care of their children or the patriarchal abuse of power to impose a marriage on his daughters. There is, moreover, a con-trast between an 'exterior' and an 'interior' type of Christianity. An exte-rior kind of Christianity expresses an interiority that is about religion be-ing self-serving; and, therefore, a boyfriend who is willing to go to Church to please, superficially, his girlfriend, discovers that this is an inadequate reason to go and, therefore, stops going. A Christianity that expresses an interiority, a relationship to Christ and to his wife, is a Christianity that is rooted in faith and practice and is, therefore, more of a reliable indicator of a real relationship to Him. Given, then, that there is a genuine type of Christianity, where does it lead?

> Considering marriage a sacred union motivates new parents to find constructive solutions to conflicts, as the loss or deterioration of their bond would have negative spiritual and psycho-logical consequences for themselves and their child. Spiritual intimacy is related to investing in a relationship. It refers to the relationship behaviour when spouses are able to talk to each other about sensitive issues, they share their re-ligious experiences, their doubts, and the depths and heights of their quest for God[41].

There is the view that one man can have many wives, on the analogy of the bull and a herd of cows. However, the dignity and equality of human beings, male and female, does not admit of this comparison. The woman,

---

[41] P. 266 of CS. LAKATOS & T. MARTOS, "THE ROLE OF RELIGIOSITY IN INTIMATE RELATIONSHIPS": https://www.academia.edu/61338854/The_Role_of_Religiosity_in_Intimate_Relationships?email_work_card=thumb-nail

no less than the man, the man, no less than the woman, are equal and complementary; and, therefore, there is no other guarantee of this than that
marriage expresses this 'uni-duality'[42]. For while 'man is a "body" belongs
to the structure of the personal subject' both man and woman are equally
human, 'based on masculinity and femininity, … on two different "incar-
nations," that is, on two ways of "being a body" of the same human being
created "in the image of God" (*Gn* 1:27)'[43]. Not only, then, does the human
body express the soul (cf. *Familiaris Consortio*, 11); but marriage expresses
and confirms the goodness of the bodily expression of the soul-in-express-
ing love. In other words, marriage springs from, expresses, and celebrates
the difference between husband and wife; and, at the same time, communicates that equality does not mean being identical but being loved in our
human differences.

Marriage, then, of one man and one woman, begins to assume a social
significance which, on the one hand, makes 'Christian families … the principal agents of the family apostolate':

'Pope Francis has recognized that the Gospel of the family must be pro-
claimed. "Christian families, by the grace of the sacrament of matri-
mony, are the principal agents of the family apostolate, above all
through 'their joy-filled witness as domestic churches'" (*Amoris Laetitia*, at 200)'[44].

---

[42] Pope St. John Paul II, Letter to Women, 8: https://www.vatican.va/con-
tent/john-paul-ii/en/letters/1995/documents/hf_jp-ii_let_29061995_
women.html.

[43] Pope St. John Paul II, Wednesday, 7th November, 1979: https://www.vati-
can.va/content/john-paul-ii/en/audiences/1979/documents/hf_jp-ii_aud_
19791107.html.

[44] Richard P. Maggi Esq. December 24th, 2021, "The Church's Teaching on
Marriage, Part One": https://www.hprweb.com/2021/12/the-churchs-teaching-
on-marriage-part-one/.

But, on the other hand, the human integrity of being a man and a woman, equal in reality and in marriage, assumes an immense significance when it comes to communicating the value of the individual person: the real person who exists. Extreme individualism, then, is about a kind of divorce between our common humanity and the existence of each, actual and specific person, pursuing choices to the exclusion of a common understanding of being a human person; and, let us recall, that the term person has a real and historical origin with communicating the mystery of God as three persons in one God. In other words, the very term, "person", is richly theological and interpersonal; and, therefore, it can be expressed in the following way: that a person is a "being-in-relationship". Thus there is almost a point at which the denial of our relationship to others distorts the reality of being human, wherein "relationship" is integral to our humanity.

But, by contrast, the reality of one man one woman in marriage brings to the fore the real individuality and equality of the human person, one before the other; and, indeed, marriage begins to assume the social significance of safeguarding the perception of the wholesome nature of human personhood: of its real and common individuality that is also integrated into the communion of marriage and the society of family life. As one of my eldest sons said recently, he is often asked what is it like to be one of eight children; and, he replies, it is great on holiday! Note that holidays often involve the numerous cousins and aunts and uncles too! Thus a marriage open to life is also a witness to the good for children of siblings; and, indeed, for the good of society as our children welcome our guests too and share a little bit of their life and activities with those who eat at our table.

Again, however, marriage becomes a witness, increasingly as divorce and other crises rise and arise, of the presence of God in our human, everyday lives. Thus, the same God who called me out of serial relationships and sin into the possibility and event of marriage, calls me into an understanding of marriage as an ongoing relationship to God. Thus, while Christ said 'cut off from me you can do nothing' in terms of discipleship with Him, yet it also applies more widely in that whatever our Christian vocation, He calls us to be with Him and to draw upon His presence with and among us (Jn 15: 5). More explicitly, then, in terms of marriage, Christ speaks of marriage as an act of God, founding married life on a divine act which is, in its nature, irrevocably "for us": 'what God has joined together let not man divide' (Mt 19: 6). Furthermore, in the wonderful mystery of the marriage feast of Cana, not only Christ, His mother Mary, and His disciples are present, but Mary, in asking for the help this newlywed couple need to celebrate their marriage, is a sign that the presence of Christ and His Church is for the good of marriage (cf. John 2: 1-12).

All of which builds beautifully on the whole understanding of the Old and New Covenants as an understanding of the "marriage" between God and man within which, as it were, the sacrament of marriage between a man and a woman is both a fruit and a witness (cf. Eph 5: 21-33). And, lest this seem to be an impersonal account, it is deeply personal as the life of Christ is both understood as the life of a 'bridegroom' (Jn 3: 29) and, as Tobias and Sarah did, it involves the call for the husband and wife to pray together in the intimacy of marriage (cf. Tobit, 8: 4-8[45]).

In many and varied concrete ways, our married life was prepared through the help of Fr. Anthony Trafford, advising us to read the Book of Tobit, which we did, and we took from it the practice and now the habit of praying together, as Tobias and Sarah did, both generally and when we come together as husband and wife. Fr. Anthony also advised me to get a job, which I did, within the day, working as a laundry labourer on £3.50p an hour. Our parents and Christian community helped us with the

---

[45] Note that the numberings of the verses can vary but what is referred to here is the whole prayer, with both an introduction and a conclusion that says: 'And together they said, 'Amen. Amen,' and lay down for the night.'

celebration of marriage, seeing to the practicalities, so my fiancé and I enjoyed a simple, chaste courtship, of walking and talking. He was also a great help with my general recovery from sin and, when he left to go abroad as a missionary priest, I was almost bereft; but, as if by an inner voice and conviction, I knew that Christ was with me!

Prose and Prayer to Protect the Environment:

"Incorporation"

In what seems an extraordinary turnabout in the United Nations, there is the 'now paradoxical statement by the … [UN highlighting the value of people with disabilities and rejecting discrimination against them [which] is in open contradiction with the policies that this organization has promoted in all areas since the 1970s'[46]

Pope Francis' address to helping those with disabilities or, as he says, with 'different abilities because everyone has abilities', wherein he says: 'Ladies and Gentlemen, I view your work as a sign of hope for a world that all too often disregards people with disabilities or unfortunately rejects them before they are born, "returning them to the sender" after seeing a scan. I urge you to persevere in your efforts, inspired by faith and the conviction that each person is a precious gift to society'[47].

Let us think, therefore, of 'incorporation' as to 'unite in one body'[48]. In other words, the growth of the body of Christ, as it were, which is the Church, is an organic growth whereby anyone, anywhere, at any time, can be united in 'one body'. On the one hand, it seems so simple, that the whole

---

[46] Julio Tudela, October 2nd, 2024, "A surprising UN report now denounces discriminatory abortion practices in people with disabilities": https://bioethics-observatory.org/2024/10/a-surprising-un-report-now-denounces-discrimina-tory-abortion-practices-in-people-with-disabilities/47124/.

[47] Pope Francis, 17th October, 2024, "*ADDRESS OF HIS HOLINESS POPE FRANCIS TO THE DELEGATION OF MINISTERS PARTICIPATING IN THE G7 ON INCLUSION AND DISABILITY*": https://www.vatican.va/content/fran-cesco/en/speeches/2024/october/documents/20241017-g7-inclusione.html.

[48] "Incorporation (n)": https://www.etymonline.com/word/incorporation.

human race could be variously related to the one body of Christ; but, on the other hand, without His grace there would not even exist a Church, never mind one that is capable of unifying the whole human race. We might ask, though, how is this possible? Clearly, the main reason is that the founder of this Church, Jesus Christ, has taken into Himself all that is good, holy and true, and incorporated it into Himself, His family, and His mission. Thus, given that He was conceived, albeit mysteriously, the Son of God took to Himself all that is human in terms of developing embryonic human life, the absorption of minerals and vitamins and all that pertains to the wholesome food of His mother Mary. In other words, directly and indirectly, both through food and water and all He ate and did as He grew up. He interacted with His environment as well as, literally, absorbing it into His own bodily substance.

In addition, all the family and social relationships that arose out of the Jewish tradition of family life, pilgrimages, places of worship and ritual meals, like the Passover, indeed entering into the biblical culture that He inherited, He also made it His own. This unique relationship, of the true man and the true God, taking to Himself all this is good of the divine act of creation, is uniquely creative in recreating it in terms of the mystery of the Church and her mission which, in a sense, goes on reproducing His mystery throughout time, always taking what is good in creation, human work and bread and wine, and all else that is incorporated into the sacraments, and transforming them in that "prefiguring way" of what may well be involved in the transfiguration of creation at His Second Coming!

However, if we consider the good of the human environment overspilling, amply, to the benefit of creation as a whole, how much better it would be if all the unnecessary pharmaceutical products that interfere with the cycle of fertility and infertility, pregnancy, and body changes, was not washed down the toilet and into the waters of the world! Not to mention all the fashion clothes dumping and other dumps, like phones, bicycles, redundant windmill parts and all the other so difficult to reuse products of cheap or massed production, amassing in brooding mounds that await a long-coming response.

Incorporation

Dear Lord, you grew from the gift of your nourishing mother, Mary,
Who had drunk from the water and eaten from the food of the land:

What splashes of light, dazzled, broke and burst from the jars, as they
Filled to the brim, were scooped off to drink and poured off to wash.
What sounds of work, whether choosing and carrying the wood of a
Carpenter, toiling in the heat and sheltering in the shade of the foliage.
What contrasts in the flowers, colored shadows, coolness in the night,
Nurturing listening, listening again, and again talking with the *Father.*

Oh Creator-God, how amazing are the atomic particles which glue As
water whooshing, swirling and umbrelling into flowing shapes
Challenging us to think liquid, droplets, vapour and solid as the Rise
and fall of heat transports a "sticky" flow from state to state.

Dear Lord, you were baptised by the Baptist, in the Jordon waters off
mountains, passed by the land, into the liturgy of entering the Church:

What numberless times you healed broken hearts and bodies in Israel So
tendrils of praise reached, like in a lightning storm, to your Father.
What skies shone in the firmament, showing through from the Beginning,
the out of reach splendor of coloring swathes of heaven.
What time you gave to giving us a whole life, unhampered in the Giving,
taking into life all who came and did come and are coming.

Oh Creator-God, how human you have made us, making us to be Among each other, like the community that you are, giving each One of us a unique identity, conceived-in-relationship, raised in relationship, ready to meet you and us in this "place of meeting".

Dear Lord, you were born into a family, extended over time by the welcome of others, whether their parents died or were too ill to care.

What gathering of others and being gathered, whether walking and Working with Joseph, helping to bear the load of low-income living.
What is left of your garments, woven from plant threads, fibre science Passed from generation to generation, woven well into a single whole.
What everyday delights in the spaces between home and being away, In the fruit of the land, in the Synagogue and in the singing of psalms.

Oh Creator-God, how many gifts you poured into men and Women, from the use of human hands to shape and write, sing, invent, to philosophise, to understand, like good doctors, how to work with the grain of growth and to give a word from you to help.

Dear Lord, you took to yourself the goodness of creation and there, beheld, that wheat and grapes, worked by human hands, are changed:

What hours of work, from preparing the ground to planting, to Carefully picking off the slugs and bugs and giving them another diet.
What suffering as a blight takes hold and defeats the ingenuity of man, Who bleeds from his heart as the earth's yield diminishes and drops.
What hope arises with the help of God to persevere and plant again, Joined in so many ways to the help of others, sending grain-as-gifts.

Oh Creator-God, how intricately woven are the tiny organs, Encased within seeds, embryonic unfolding of plants, shooting Down and rising up, twirling around sticks, flowering orangy-red, Hosting insects, losing colour and growing beans and flowering.

Dear Lord, how we wrought a thorny crown out of what had grown, nails and hammer out of the ore of the earth and a cross from a tree.

What mangling of the human body we have practiced, especially Upon the innocent, the vulnerable, the undefended, in denial of death.
What freezing, experimentation, plans of torment we have explored In the flesh of the living, imagining we will not answer to our Maker.
What hidden wounds we have inflicted on ourselves at each turn of The pain that wells up, when we are addressed by our very actions.

Oh Creator-God, how beautiful is the recreation of the lost, the Poor and poor of heart, the broken and abandoned, the renewal of Planet home, the replanting, recycling, revisiting the places of Hatred with songs of reconciliation and understanding of wounds.

Dear Lord of the Resurrection, let us rise with you in time, hoping to begin the transfiguring ascent, taking what love everlastingly does!

Reflecting on the Discoveries

Coming to a book like this is like studying a mist and the shapes, as it were, that emerge and fade until, at a certain point, the landscape begins to clear and a certain clarity emerges. What, then, has become clear?

In a word, young people are particularly at risk of being caught up in a net of ideological strategies that aim to cripple the law, binding it to non-binding bureaucratic agreements, dividing families, schools, workplaces and society, enslaving people to the fear of being "called out" or "cancelled" for telling the truth about the human person: that man is male and female.

The only antidote is to express the truth of the human person with love, helping a person where they can be helped and praying for them whether they can be helped or not.

Initially, the end of this book was called "The Last Word"; but, as there is a sense that a last word is a contradiction in that there is always the possibility of, literally, another word, it makes more sense to reflect on one of the book's titles, which includes taking a "SnapShot". In other words, without any claim to being definitive, rather admitting that there may be many strands to our society, both global and local, that may have been left out, it is a matter of seeing what emerges from these pages.

On the one hand, then, this book has ranged over any number of crises and characteristics of our times, of which there are many and many more; and, as such, it is like zig-zagging through a culture, taking a sample here and a sample from there and looking at the various areas even if, like histology[1], we are not exactly examining living cells. But, like histology, cells can be kept alive and so taking slices through a social culture is not exactly about leaving it behind, as it is a part of what makes the whole; but, nevertheless, the contents of this book have a certain datedness as a cultural "snapshot" and, if I were to look back in a few years' time a lot of the articles would be written in 2024. So what is the value of something almost ephemeral, snapping shots that could be deemed idiosyncratic or too randomized to make a pattern? As with any gathering of impressions, information and insights, there is always going to be a selection process taking account of what is directly or indirectly relevant to the subject. So, as the book has developed, the chapters have rapidly outstripped the intention of being a prelude to chapters on marriage and other vocations which, now, will have to wait for another book. Thus, reflecting back on the book itself, it has come to be very focused on young people seeking an identity and getting caught up, as it were, in inadequate attempts to answer the question: "Who Am I?"

On the other hand, just as on a beach there is plenty of sand and, after a while of scrabbling it away, some stone shapes start to appear in different places; indeed, to begin with, it seems like they might be isolated rocks, however large or well buried and, gradually, the more sand is taken away the clearer it becomes that the various bits sticking up are connected and, the deeper the digging goes, the clearer it becomes that there is an underlying unity to it all. Nevertheless, there are other things in the sand which, like plastic bottles, cans, pieces of electronic equipment, all of which is, in a sense, useable or re-usable except, that is, for what is truly waste and belongs in the bin, the dump or the ground. Thus there will always be a work of discrimination and discernment, of deciding what is a part of the underlying rock and what is mistakenly mixed up with it, even if it is like a big boulder which happens to be in and around the same place but is not

---

[1] "histology, physiology": https://www.britannica.com/science/histology.

a part of the underlying rock formation. So it is with what we have found to be running through our culture; that is, a whole lot of disparate ideas that start to shape up into different places, as it were, in the intellectual landscape and, while there can be a forced coming together of a tin can and a flower, many things need to be separated and distinguished if we are to know where they belong and what we are to do with them.

Thus it is the same with ideas. There is a reality which, integrated as one, underlies the everyday nature of human life and, indeed, is constantly expressed in the course of it; but then there are those disparate ideas which, like wearing pieces of equipment and being confused about whether it is a natural part of us or not, we can eventually see that they are not, as such, a part of us. People, in other words, so used to the technological era, very often react very anxiously and alarmingly to the loss of their phone – even if it simply misplaced!

An emerging history of pharmacological companies profiting from exploitative practices and, over the years, the combination of "immunity from prosecution" and the "criminalizing" of legitimate opposition to contested practices

To be too general is to be as unjust as the unjust practices under discussion; and, therefore, to anchor the discussion a bit more practically, there were three classic cases of researchers exploiting patients which led to tragic outcomes – all of which unfolded after the tragedies of Nazi experiments and the ethical codes which emerged after the Second World War. One was Pincus' exploitation of patients in a hospital and on Peruvian women, testing unwitting subjects with vast amounts of hormones, which even arch feminists have been willing to recognize and to object to[2].

---

[2] Shulamith Firestone was obviously disturbed by this history (cf. my discussion in *Mary and Bioethics:* https://enroutebooksandmedia.com/maryand-

But there were two more cases. One of deliberately infecting children in order to study its effects on them and, secondly, of preventing patients with syphilis from receiving the modern treatment of antibiotics, both tragic scandals that helped, hopefully to move ethical safeguards to the fore – beyond the reach of unscrupulous researchers[3].

What we have, then, are pseudo medical practices, not for the good of the patient, but for the "research" kudos and income generated. Moreover, we have pharmaceutical companies which exploit the feedback from women as regards harmful effect of hormonal contraceptives, repackage them and remarket them as "new and improved"[4]. Similarly, with abortion itself, with its tragic outcome for the baby and mother, now moving into the field of unsupervised selling of abortion pills. What about the freezing of human embryos? How does it happen that unregulated companies can manufacture human beings, experiment on them, discard them, freeze them and all with legal impunity – how is this possible in a so-called ethically conscious age? At the same time as we have a law which outlaws giving help to women who think abortion is an answer to their problems, in America it has transpired that pro-life organizations have been targeted as "terrorist" and, so far, with impunity[5], while having peaceful protesters go to jail and others, protesting other causes violently, going free.

---

bioethics/; and Holly Grigg-Spall who began to object to this indeterminate flattening of mood and all the other ongoing objections to hormonal contraceptives (cf. my discussion with her in Etheredge, *Human Nature: Moral Norm*, 2023: https://enroutebooksandmedia.com/humannature/.

[3] Etheredge, *The Human Person: A Bioethical Word*, "Foreword" by Dr. Mary Anne Urlakis, pp. 11-16 etc. https://enroutebooksandmedia.com/bioethical-word/.

[4] Cf. Holly Grigg-Spall, *Sweetening The Pill: Or How We Got Hooked On Hormonal Birth Control*, Zero Books: Winchester, UK, 2013.

[5] Jake Smith, 25th, September, "Government Watchdog Urges Investigation of Army After Training That Called Pro-Life Americans Terrorists":

Moreover, living in a culture which both proclaims anything is possible and, at the same time, supposes there are no significant realities, such that a person can say they are any or no sex, can behave as if there is no sexed-reality to human life, can empty marriage of meaning by defining it according to what a person wants it to be rather than what it is – is it therefore any surprise that we have entered a period where the claim that reality is knowable, entailing an investigation into what it really is, people are now inventing what they want it to be and turning that "invention" into an icon of what it now is[6]. If a so-called scientist, wanting to exploit the possibilities of artificial conception of human beings, ingenuously argues that he cannot see that there is a beginning to human conception – then how is that he goes on to manufacture children precisely by "utilizing" the moment of human conception – is it surprising that these contradictions are overlooked because there is a claim that good has been done? What about all the discarded human embryonic children, the buying and selling of "reproductive" services, as if the human being is now a bottomless source of income? While it is true that a child is a child, however conceived, it is also true that this involves questions of identity, when it is discovered, beginning with the following: "'they said they felt "like lab experiments", "uncomfortable" and "different"'[7]. Which is extraordinary for how close to the truth this is; for the people who invented IVF, or fertilization in a dish,

---

https://www.lifenews.com/2024/09/25/government-watchdog-urges-investigation-of-army-after-training-that-called-pro-life-americans-terrorists/.

[6] Johnathon Van Maren, January 2nd, 2025, "Transgenderism has taken over the UK's iconic Trafalgar Square": https://www.lifesitenews.com/blogs/transgenderism-has-taken-over-the-uks-iconic-trafalgar-square/.

[7] Deborah Linton, November 27th, 2024, "I told my children they were born by IVF. I never expected they'd react like this": https://inews.co.uk/inews-lifestyle/told-children-born-ivf-never-expected-reaction-3401362

destroyed many human embryos in the process, and this procedure still does – but what is more IVF does not cure infertility it supplants it[8].

Now, then, we have moved into the area of mutilating children as if there are no legal consequences for those who do this only, rather, legal consequences for those who object. How is this possible that those who advocate and actually administer life-changing hormonal drugs, which are also used long term, and carry out mutilating surgeries are not prosecuted in the courts? In the words of one very clear advocate of evidence and rational argument:

'By their nature, these procedures involving the "sterilization and mutilation of children" are "involuntary" because minors lack the capacity to consent to such "trans-butchery" and therefore such an intervention equates to "a crime against humanity in accordance with UN definitions"[9].

And if those who object are "criminalized", so that they can lose custody of their children, the legal right to practice as professionals or even face imprisonment on "fictional" charges of discrimination, then clearly there are public problems in the systems of society. Similarly, those who object to abortion are criminalized if they pray or offer help outside of an abortuary. How have we got to the situation whereby legitimate and well-formed arguments, helpfulness and objections are facing an increasingly weaponized legal system? Where is the principle of an objective judiciary

---

[8] Cf. Etheredge, "On Regulating IVF": https://www.pdcnet.org/pdc/bvdb.nsf/purchase_mobile.

[9] Patrick Delaney, 25th of September 2024, "Jordan Peterson condemns 'trans-butchery of minor children' as 'a crime against humanity'": https://www.lifesitenews.com/news/jordan-peterson-says-trans-butchery-of-minor-children-is-a-crime-against-humanity/.

or legislative system that is fair to all? Where are the principles of natural justice, do good and avoid harm, and the use of scientific data with regard to basic questions of when a human child is conceived and what harms arise out of the use of hormonal drugs and unnecessary surgeries? How is it not relevant evidence about the beginning of human life that a child survives an abortion, or is transferred from being a frozen embryo and grows up to be a fully grown and mature adult? How is it not relevant evidence that children, getting older, regret the surgeries that have mutilated them and will not go back to those who promoted these practices? How is it not relevant that body-altering surgeries require interminable follow ups because of the disruption to bodily processes?

So how has it happened that we live in a society in which many people, otherwise well-trained, are unable to critically assess what is going on? In other words, if those who have weaponized the law have done so because they cannot defend their positions with argument and evidence, then is it any surprise that some people, of whatever discipline, do not know what anything is, and simply advance their own fiction and fuel the confusion in which our young people grow up? Thus we come to the point where laws, pitiably, have to be investigated as to whether they use the language of biological men or biological women, when man and woman are an integral, psychosomatic whole which does not change – but a court has to decide on the definition of a woman in the case of a particular law[10]: a definition that has existed from time immemorial and is only called into question precisely because the law has been weaponized. Discrimination, then, is different from protecting the legitimate interests and welfare of women who want, naturally, their public space; and, therefore, to invoke

---

[10] Maya Oppenheim, "How a battle over defining a woman ended up in the UK's highest court": https://www.msn.com/en-gb/news/uknews/how-a-battle-over-defining-a-woman-ended-up-in-the-uk-s-highest-court/ar-AA1uOjG7.

discrimination when a woman's right to a woman's space is being protected[11], is to make discrimination manipulation and to set about losing its
legitimate meaning. For, in the case of those who make claims about their
identity not rooted in their conception, other provision can be made until
the "pre-occupation" is discovered to be false and passes.

Connectedness? Both wholeness and in-relationship to others

Our first question is about "connectedness". That what often seems unconnected is connected. On the one hand, and this will be discussed more
fully later, there are bodily expressions of emotion; and, therefore, if I am
excited my heart rate increases, along with other physiological signs. The
excitement, however, is not fully defined by physiological changes and
could be due to a variety of situations. Therefore I am excited because I am
waiting for my exam results, a birthday present or a concert I am looking
forward to going to. Thus, the psychological interiority is profoundly relevant to determining what the physiological excitement is about; and, in
effect, we cannot know what the excitement entails if we are not the person
who is experiencing it and, therefore, giving an account of its interiority.
Although, having said that, there can be interior states where we repress
an emotional reaction to a pain, as I did as a child, and it profoundly frac-
tures the unity of personhood; however, rediscovering the experiences and
their emotions restored the integrity or wholeness of my physiological and
psychological being.

Therefore there is a whole, as it were, which is that we express ourselves
both interiorly and exteriorly and that both are necessary if we are to understand and to communicate with another or others. By implication,

---

[11]   "New   House   rules   target   Transgender   bathroom   access":
https://www.faithonview.com/new-house-rules-target-transgender-bathroom-
access/.

then, there is a relationship entailed in our reactions to what happens. I denied the pain of humiliating punishments in order to deprive others, or so I thought, of the satisfaction of seeing me cry; in reality, I was the one who suffered more from this act of pride, that I would not cry in front of others, than ever it would have humiliated me to have shed some tears in response to my suffering. Now, I cry readily, showing and sharing my reactions to what happens in the course of my relationship to myself or to others. Thus I can be moved to tears because of a word of God illuminating my life or touching a wound and I can share it with others so that they can see and hear what word touched what wound in a helpful way.

Relationality

To quote a voice about the disappearance of culture, which argues that in place of the dialogical progress of identity there is a box-ticking exercise: '*Complex, evolved, layered social identities are being replaced by a series of boxes, with freedom consisting of the right to choose your box at any one time (think about the way that sexual identity is coded into an endlessly multiplying series of letters)*'[12].

In other words, seeking an identity is not just adopting a letter, or calling myself anorexic[13], as it were, after our name, it is about exploring more fully who we are and all the entanglements, influences and education of our nature that that entails; indeed, it is about establishing a dialogue that develops us through real contacts with others in that

---

[12] John Fea, 26th of September, "Culture is being hollowed out by technology, data, globalisation, bureaucracy, and consumerist individualism": https://currentpub.com/2024/09/26/culture-is-being-hollowed-out-by-technology-data-globalisation-bureaucracy-and-consumerist-individualism/.

[13] This example was used by Dr. Helen Watt in an in-person conversation when she worked at the Linacre Centre, Oxford.

'Increased left- and right-wing references to 'identity' fail to confront this deeper crisis of culture and community. Our only option, Roy argues, is to restore social bonds at the grassroots or citizenship level'[14].

Clearly, however, to be able to communicate with the difficulties our children experience growing up, there has to be an attitude that is at least able to listen and, perhaps, to explore the identity problems without sounding off because of prejudice. But, nevertheless, the dialogue has to go further than just agreeing with ideas, even if it is out of love[15], for love also seeks to love the truth that sets us free (cf. Jn. 8: 31-32).

Alternatively, do we let our children go on and identify as "wolves"?[16]

So we come to a different but complementary type of connectedness which, really, shows that our reactions, emotions, are relational: they are about our being-in-relationship. Indeed, what arises from considering many facets of life is that we thrive, as human beings, if we are connected to others, whether that connection is familial, friendly or through a work or recreational culture. However, I remember when I was sixteen, living in a bedsit in London and working in an office, that the brief bit of office table-tennis at the end of the day was both good in itself and, at the same time, exacerbated my loneliness as and when I went back to the house

---

[14] More on the review of "The Crisis of Culture: Identity Politics and the Empire of Norms": https://www.hurstpublishers.com/book/the-crisis-of-culture/.

[15] Cf. Heather Hollingsworth, April 11th, 2024, "As his trans daughter struggles, a father pushes past his prejudice. 'It was like a wake-up'": https://apnews.com/article/trans-teen-bathroom-school-education-f40d2799609d6f95565e7bf90daf18de.

[16] Dr Tony Rucinski, « From boys and girls to wolves and furries – the results of redefinition": https://mailchi.mp/c4m/from-boys-and-girls-to-wolves-and-furries-the-results-of-redefinition?e=32b284b5cf.

where I lived and cooked alone. Note, by contrast to Japanese women who tend to be socially connected in numerous ways to others, that there are a growing number of Japanese men who die alone; indeed, Pope Francis speaks of women being 'better than men in terms of their insight and their ability to build communities"[17]. In an interesting variation of how the women cope with loneliness, according to a recent report, Japanese women are stealing to enter prison where there is company, free health-care, meals, work and warmth; indeed, some with nurse training, are even helping the increasingly elderly population with personal care[18]. In an-other and rather more attractive symbol of our times an American lone woman was invited out by her friend to dine for free, at Christmas, in a local restaurant, and so touched the staff with her thank you letter the owner is trying to trace her[19]. Recognizing, however, our human reality, does depend on some kind of awakening; and, in the case of one single woman's experience of Covid, it was the realization of the human help of a hug, a companion to watch television with and, therefore, a discovery of the human value of neighbours[20].

---

[17] Pope Francis remarking on the genius of women generally, Deborah Castellano Lubov, 20th June, 2024, "Pope to university students: 'Stay true to your convictions and faith'": https://www.vaticannews.va/en/pope/news/2024-06/pope-francis-students-in-building-bridges-across-asia-pacific.html.

[18] Jessie Yeung, Hanako Montgomery and Junko Ogura, CNN, Saturday, January 18th, 2025, "Japan's elderly are lonely and struggling. Some women choose to go to jail instead": https://edition.cnn.com/2025/01/18/asia/japan-elderly-largest-womens-prison-intl-hnk-dst/index.html.

[19] Rachel Paula Abrahamson, January 8th, 2025, "Elderly woman who dined at restaurant on Christmas leaves staff moving letter": https://www.today.com/food/people/woman-leaves-restaurant-letter-christmas-rcna186671.

[20] Marianne Power, November 7th, 2024, "At 47, I'm single and lonely – but stop telling me marriage is the answer": https://inews.co.uk/inews-lifestyle/single-lonely-47-marriage-not-answer-3366678.

Japanese men, by contrast, once they have retired – relinquishing their almost life-long relationship to the companionship of a company and passing, rapidly, into a state of isolation and depression, often end up dying alone and their death being so overlooked that their bodies may have even begun to decompose. What is more, as it was reported earlier, many young people are becoming "stay-ins", in which case their relationship to others is bordering on the virtual, as staying in a room does not encourage the everyday activities of eating, walking, gardening or doing anything together with another or others. Even those in a company, like builders or soldiers, if they are away long enough or out of contact long enough with their families, because of working away from home, are beginning to take their own lives. Even, then, if the culture is unfriendly, drug and violence driven, it nevertheless exerts an influence on us, as human begins, because we are social beings or beings who absolutely need relationships to function. Therefore, to be able to break free of addictive relationships, as it were, there are multiple factors involved which, in essence, entail forming relationships based on genuinely good interests – but that depends on coming to ourselves and developing those interests that can then be expressed and shared. Forty or fifty years ago, for example, I would never have dreamt that I could get excited about the size of a tomato grown in our garden or growing garlics from seeds or, more generally, seeing plants thrive and bear vegetable fruit. And, because of this, I can take my mother-in-law, a keen gardener, or anyone who will listen and talk about what is going on in the vegetable garden. Thus there is a wholeness to both the unfolding of a person's life and the possibility of the flourishing of personal relationships.

So when we come to recognizing the needs of young people, as I recall my own efforts to guide me, I note that for a long time my interests were very limited, as was my travelling, while working did mean that I travelled some of the time but, generally, I was often too tired to study, learn a language or run or do any sport. However, I did notice that working along-side others did provide me with many occasions for a discussion; and, therefore, it is important to remember how crucial having a variety of conversation partners is to both giving an account of ourselves and to developing a "world-view".

If I recall correctly, there was a sense of discovery when it came to discovering, suddenly, that a subject roused my interest and it would lead to a lot of questions, even to the point of annoying the person I was speaking to. Thus the subject of atomic structures sprung from nowhere, as it was not as if I was a mathematician or a physicist but there was a certain fascination with questions which, very quickly, connected with what is the nature of reality. So, for example, this question recurred with one of my own sons who wanted to argue that physics could account for the whole of reality; however, when asked how it could account for thought, he did not seem clear that it could account for the transmission of thought, either in the nervous system or on a phone line, but not for the origin of the thought itself.

Thought, as an expression of reason, I was to find out many years later, derives from a word which means to think through what is in the hands. In other words, there is a direct relationship between thought and activity; and, if young people are more preoccupied with the virtual world, and not necessarily critically, then this inhibits the development of thought from activities and experience. Obviously, however, people can talk about their use of phones but, in general, it seems like a "too" personal subject to be objective about although some young people have abandoned their "i-phones" for a more varied experience of life and even a "block phone". Clearly, however, a technologically orientated society is always advancing the use of the phone; however, the power to use the phone but not be used by it requires divine assistance! So many of us just end up endlessly scrolling, precisely because the phone is designed to be an attention hoover –

consuming for profit because of the sale of data, all our conscious hours or, certainly, as much as is possible, given that people still need to sleep. Indeed, is it likely that the books and articles that question the unlimited use of phones are going to "turn up" on the algorithm which feeds us endless "snap-snacks"?

Evidence and thoughts

What is a good starting point? So many people grow vegetables, flowers, whether as farmers but far more as ordinary gardeners, day in day out, watching a runner bean seed turn into a runner bean, watching a bee fertilize a flower and the resultant start of another bean, which swells and grows, seed after seed producing fruit after fruit. Runner bean seeds do not produce eggs, eggs do not produce runner bean seeds. In other words, there is a widespread and indeed universal nature to all that exists; and, if it is studied, it shows consistency, development and change, while remaining what it is: a bean plant; a chicken; or a human being. So, while there are many women gardeners, what about the men: the workmen who lay bricks, move snow, strive to making a living to give to their children and who, as one author says, '

My father — a bricklayer with eight kids — saw the world as a place of mystery and beauty, but that things could go so consistently, abysmally, wrong gnawed at him'[21]. How many ordinary dads does this include?! With whatever imperfections, so many of us go out into the garden and say: 'Look at that tomato; it is the biggest I have ever grown! And, what is more, if you had told me as a child that I would rave about vegetables, I would have said or thought you were mad! But now look at me!'

---

[21] 'Heather King, February 16th, 2024, "What is a man? Remembering my father": https://angelusnews.com/voices/what-is-a-man-king/

So, as we seen, there has been a trend away from outdoor activities, from seeing the landscape and understanding its reality, as well as just playing in it; and, owing to the change, many young people went "virtual". However, while prudence is necessary, there is no reason to reject the value of the outdoors for so many good experiences; and, therefore, note what Mariana Brussoni, play researcher, says, "Keep them as safe as necessary, not as safe as possible" (footnote 27)[22]. But, on the other hand, 'Safetyism is an experience blocker'[23] and imagining that we can go through life saying 'I should not have to experience negative emotions because of what someone else said or did. I have a right not to be "triggered"'[24]. On one side of my family, my grandparents never discussed death, as it was always assumed that my grandmother, being older, would die first; however, my recently retired grandfather went out one morning for a newspaper and died from a heart attack. My grandmother's world was shaken to the core. Never examining anything that is difficult, or challenging, leaves people profoundly unprepared for life; and, therefore, with sensitivity and understanding, questions need to be addressed that lead people into life and prepare them for it – rather than an avoidance, like living in-doors unnecessarily, that weakens our resistance to the point of catching every bug and infection going. In other words, society "numbs itself" into being unable to reflect, to argue, and to experience the real world; but, at the same time, this is not a license to insult, denigrate, or detract – but an exhortation to discuss, to explore, to experience reality in a multi-faceted way and to share and to dialogue about our findings.

Perhaps part of the problem is the virtual world: that so many people are detached from the actual world and do not think through what they

---

[22] Haidt, *The Anxious Generation*, 2024, Chapters 2- 3, p. 81. on what children need to do in childhood, discover and defence mode and the need for risky play.

[23] Haidt, *The Anxious Generation*, 2024, Chapters 2- 3, p. 97.

[24] Haidt, *The Anxious Generation*, 2024, Chapters 2- 3, p. 89.

see, do, bring about, or observe. But, at the same time many people are probably afraid of the law being used against them or their families, destroying livelihoods, relationships, and reputations. Furthermore, there are widespread "ideas" which have gained such currency that to go against them is to be branded an "extremist" or some other tag which does not engage with the points that are raised so much as simply side-steps them with a charge, as it were, of some imagined offence. Why, for example, is an organization that promotes contraception and abortion allowed to be exempt from national laws, as if the Gates Foundation is "above the law" and therefore exempt from any evaluation of its activities? As the Kenyan lawyer says: "'It is unfathomable that a private entity with no known national mandate would be granted consular status in Kenya, enabling it to operate with immunity under the Privileges and Immunities Act," said LSK Chief Executive Officer Florence Muturi'[25]. And so we live in a world where money is power and power, purportedly, is above the law. But why? When civilization depends not only on the rule of law on the rule of just laws.

In reality, however, some changes are radical but consistent, such as the chrysalis, from which emerges the butterfly. Similarly, the single-celled embryonic human being, encased in the embryonic wall, just as soon as the sperm makes contact with the egg, and then undergoes the most extraordinary but regular changes from a single-celled being to the manifestation of a person: one in physiological and psychological being. As argued before, then, as the inward capabilities of the human being develop, so the presence of co-developing psychological processes shows itself. Clearly, however, there are thresholds: so the ability to move goes beyond the

---

[25] Calvin Freiburger, November 27th, 2024, "Kenyan court temporarily blocks special immunity for pro-abortion Gates Foundation": LifeSite. https://www.lifesitenews.com/news/kenyan-court-temporarily-blocks-special-immunity-for-pro-abortion-gates-foundation/

natural movement of growth itself but is, in a way, a co-expression of it. Thus, it is possible for the mother to notice activity and rest, restlessness and reactions to stimuli such as sound and, increasingly, to the mother's voice and the presence of others. Furthermore, as focusing, facial recognition, smiling, and all the myriad and subtle responses that arise, show more and more the presence of a "relationship" between the baby and his or her mother and those, also, who are around, notably the father and other children, whether siblings or not.

This, too, is the common experience of men and women down the ages and, besides, if the child does not show these signs then either there is a recognition of a "late developer" or there is some obstacle to development beginning to show itself. But, in either case, this is the ongoing manifestation of the person conceived: the male-person or the female-person: the boy or the girl. While there are interactions and engagements with stimuli, interests, those around, there is that emerging vocalization of what is interior, from wailing as an expression of an urgent, sudden, and overwhelming sense of being hungry to, as the child gets older, laying the table before being asked as another form of saying, "I want to have dinner!" This externalization of what is internal, will go on and multiply in terms of all that is to be expressed and explored as the child recognizes being tired, hungry, helpful, and content. This externalization of what is interior includes speaking about the activities that he or she wants to do and indeed to be interested in. Furthermore, this revealing of a person's interior life includes what a person is distressed and unhappy about. Gradually, what are revealed are the reactions which contribute to our relationships and which enable us to be open, thus facilitating the process by which a person finds his or her talents and vocation. As insight matures, so we are able to share the difficulties that are being encountered in the course in the course of our lives.

The contribution of challenges: an incision

'Should this [bureaucratic] plan be adopted [of labelling pro-life groups 'anti-rights'], it clearly shows that the UN bureaucracy is choosing sides in a highly contested debate and willingly embracing the "anti-rights" rhetoric that will be used to shut down debate and exclude critical voices'[26]. Even a mixed group of feminist organizations are being called 'anti-rights' because they are 'critical of gender ideology', 'point out the harms that women suffer when women's-only spaces admit men', culminating in the following statement: '"UN Women should support the work of women for women's rights, not tell women that they need to place their concerns secondary to a newly declared group whose main aim is to claim women's rights for men," they write'[27].

Owing to a new intolerance, people who object to abortion and are called anti-rights, when to kill an unborn child is not a right, are slandered and accused of 'saying that they "hate" certain people when in fact they do not'[28].Indeed, the rhetoric betrays those who use it because the defenders of life, of all life, are those who love the living and want to help them! In general, there is an anti-life weaponizing of UN documents which, when frustrated, results in various kind of name calling, particularly when it comes to rejecting "reproductive rights" which, as officials are afraid to say what they are, has become a "code-word" for

---

[26] Rebecca Oas, September 30th, 2024, "Anti-Rights: The New Censorship Weapon of the Left": https://c-fam.org/definitions/anti-rights-the-new-censorship-weapon-of-the-left/.

[27] Rebecca Oas, Ph.D. | August 22, 2024, "Feminists Groups Criticize UN on Gender Ideology and Surrogacy": C-Fam. https://c-fam.org/friday_fax/feminists-groups-criticize-un-on-gender-ideology-and-surrogacy/

[28] Eberstadt, *Adam and Eve after the Pill: Revisited*, 2023, p. 48.

promoting abortion and other anti-life practices[29]. What is missing from these discussion is how to found a true human right on human nature and, therefore, to show its universality[30].

In other words, calling "anti-rights" groups those that oppose 'gender ideology, a framing of women's rights based on the right of a woman to access abortion, and opposition to ideologically extreme sex education for children' is a bureaucratic form of bullying with the intent of silencing debate on what, actually and profoundly, affects people in their daily lives[31]. Similarly, an attempt to redefine 'femicide', are legitimate if it is an attempt to include crimes against women; however, to "blame" prolife countries for driving women to unsafe abortionists, who are not prosecuted, is a roundabout way to foster an anti-life agenda[32]. What is more, this strategy of blaming prolife groups, falsely, for crimes against women, actually detracts and diverts energy and resources from studying why, genuinely, there are crimes against women. Note, for example, the rise of knife crime where women are attached because of a kind of anti-woman mentality which arises out of some

---

[29] Stefano Gennarini, J.D. | November 21, 2024, "Brave African Delegates Fight Abortion in Landmark UN Family Resolution": https://c-fam.org/friday_fax/brave-african-delegates-fight-abortion-in-landmark-un-family-resolution/

[30] Cf. Etheredge, *Human Nature: Moral Norm*: https://enroutebooksandmedia.com/humannature/.

[31] Cf. Stefano Gennarini, November 7th, 2024, "Biden Admin Praised UN Report Calling for Election Observers on LGBT Issues": https://c-fam.org/friday_fax/biden-admin-praised-un-report-calling-for-election-observers-on-lgbt-issues/.

[32] Rebecca Oas, Ph.D. | December 26, 2024, "UN Office Proposes Labeling Abortion-Related Deaths as Femicides": UN Office Proposes Labeling Abortion-Related Deaths as Femicides - C-Fam. https://c-fam.org/friday_fax/un-office-proposes-labeling-abortion-related-deaths-as-femicides/

internet sites that claim that seems to incite young men to 'harm [women] in order to reset a female-dominated world that works against you?'[33] Furthermore, a small group of bureaucrats are claiming legitimacy for hijacking feminism to not only promote abortion but to call for governments to enforce drastic restrictions on who can opt out conscientiously from carrying out an abortion[34].

Clearly, disregarding the rights of the unborn child, leads to disregarding a just recognition of who is at fault if a woman, regrettably, dies as a result of an abortion. The *United Nations*, then, is ceasing to be a forum for the good of all and is adopting language and practices that exclude those that disagree with abortion and question what words mean when they are used to slide in an agenda not properly voted upon[35]. In addition, this shows how ineffective are the arguments in defence of abortion if this international organization is now being used to outlaw debate[36]. What is more, when some social platforms restore the legitimacy of on-line debate, allowing discussion of contentious topics like 'gender', almost right away there is a claim that what the UN

[33] Jack Thorne, 18th March, 2025, "'The younger me would have sat up and nodded': Adolescence writer Jack Thorne on the insidious appeal of incel culture": https://www.theguardian.com/tv-and-radio/2025/mar/18/adolescence-writer-jack-thorne-incel-culture-netflix

[34] Stefano Gennarini, J.D. | January 16, 2025, "UN Group Says Government Must Force Medical Personnel to Provide Abortions": UN Group Says Government Must Force Medical Personnel to Provide Abortions - C-Fam. https://c-fam.org/friday_fax/un-group-says-government-must-force-medical-personnel-to-provide-abortions/

[35] Cf. Stefano Gennarini, November 15th, 2024, "Argentina Stands Alone at the UN/Hungary Stands with the Left": Argentina Stands Alone at the UN/Hungary Stands with the Left - C-Fam. https://c-fam.org/friday_fax/ argentina-stands-alone-at-the-un-hungary-stands-with-the-left/

[36] Rebecca Oas, September 30th, 2024, "Anti-Rights: The New Censorship Weapon of the Left": https://c-fam.org/definitions/anti-rights-the-new-censorship-weapon-of-the-left/.

was doing was not censorship[37] when, alarmingly, almost everything that comes from the UN bureaucrats is about suppressing the anti-abortion voice.

Thus, it is emerging more and more clearly from a variety of UN processes that, no matter the subject of debate, there are those who are constantly trying to advance an anti-life agenda. A recent example of this was an attempt to use language that would slip a pro-abortion, "gender" agenda into an agreement on measures to protect the world from Climate change in which "gender"[38] is not defined according to the binding Helsinki agreement in 1995: man means a biological man and woman means a biological woman. Furthermore, there are moves to alter the definition of these binding agreements so that 'misgendering' and refusing to provide abortion become 'crimes against humanity'[39] – completely contradicting the meaning of human rights as advancing the principle 'do good and avoid harm'. In other words, the United Nations, founded in 1945[40], needs reform: it needs to recall its founding principles and where it is now in relation to them. Moreover, as we are coming up to the 30th anniversary of the 'Beijing conference' this is a vital and opportune moment to affirm the

---

[37] Iulia-Elena Cazan | January 16, 2025, « UN Rights Chief Criticizes Facebook's Rollback on Censorship": UN Rights Chief Criticizes Facebook's Rollback on Censorship - C-Fam. https://c-fam.org/friday_fax/un-rights-chief-criticizes-facebooks-rollback-on-censorship/

[38] Iulia-Elena Cazan | November 28, 2024, « Gender Rejected at UN Climate Conference": Gender Rejected at UN Climate Conference - C-Fam. https://c-fam.org/friday_fax/gender-rejected-at-un-climate-conference/

[39] Stefano Gennarini, J.D. | October 17, 2024, «Do Pro-Lifers Commit Crimes Against Humanity?": https://c-fam.org/friday_fax/do-pro-lifers-commit-crimes-against-humanity/.

[40] "History of the United Nations": https://www.un.org/en/about-us/history-of-the-un.

truth, the good, and the beauty of being man, male and female[41]. Similarly, the preparatory report produced by the Secretary General of the UN reads like a radical reinterpretation of the outcome of the Beijing Conference on Women; and, therefore, reflects on advancing what was not agreed at that conference, namely abortion and other anti-life policies[42]. What is clear, however, is that a reform of the United Nations could draw on the *Universal Declaration of Human Rights* (UDHR) promulgated in 1948, followed by two Covenants: 'the 1966 Covenant on Civil and Political Rights and the 1966 Covenant on Economic, Social and Cultural Rights, which have become known collectively as the International Bill of Rights'[43]. This is because the UDHR has been incorporated into so many legal frameworks that it constitutes a foundational expression of human rights[44] to which appeal can therefore be made.

The President of Argentina, Javier Milei, cites 'the U.S. Declaration of Independence in defense of the fundamental rights to life, liberty, and property, and describes the United Nations Agenda 2030 as "a socialist project to establish a world government that feigns solutions to

---

[41] Stefano Gennarini, February 27th, 2025, « UN Commission Will Test Trump's Resolve on Gender Ideology": https://c-fam.org/friday_fax/un-commission-will-test-trumps-resolve-on-gender-ideology/.

[42] Rebecca Oas, February 27th, 2025, « Report Reveals Vast Divide on Gender Between UN Agencies, Member States": https://c-fam.org/friday_fax/report-reveals-vast-divide-on-gender-between-un-agencies-member-states/.

[43] Jane Adolphe, "The Holy See and UDHR: Towards a Legal Anthropology of Human Rights and the Family",

Ave Maria Law Review (2006): C:\Users\Francis\Downloads\HSand UDHR_ stamped.pdf., p. 351.

[44] Jane Adolphe, "The Holy See and UDHR: Towards a Legal Anthropology of Human Rights and the Family".

modern problems by way of attempts against the sovereignty of na-
tion-states."[45]

Milie goes on to say that the 'foreign policy "doctrine of the new Argentina" will hearken back to the founding principles of the United
Nations and hold the international organizations accountable to the
essential standard of "cooperation between nations, united in defense
of liberty."[46]

However, the reform of UN would be no easy task as a number of the
bureaucrats are accusing pro-lifers of an ant-rights agenda; however,
the bureaucrats are anti-defence of human life and, therefore, are anti-
rights group themselves.[47]

In addition, part of the reform could be the introduction, in the *European Parliament*, of global anti-Christian monitoring, alongside the existing anti-Islamic and anti-Semitic monitors[48]. Note, too, a call for reform
in Pope Francis' address to the Diplomatic Corps, early in 2025, of the
many institutions founded around 80 years ago:

---

[45] Jane Adolphe, "The Holy See and UDHR: Towards a Legal Anthropology
of Human Rights and the Family".

[46] Stefano Gennarini, 27th March, 2025, "Argentina's Milei Fights Alongside
Trump Against Gender and DEI": https://c-fam.org/friday_fax/argentinas-milei-
fights-alongside-trump-against-gender-and-dei/.

[47] Rebecca Oas, 27th March, 2025, "The "anti-rights" campaign at the UN
Heats   Up": https://c-fam.org/friday_fax/the-anti-rights-campaign-at-the-un-
heats-up/.

[48] Guillaume de Thieulloy: https://mailchi.mp/lesalonbeige.fr/lunion-eu-
ropenne-face-la-perscution-des-chrtiens?e=f99fc8fc7b. The original French text
translated by Google translate.

'Many of them are in need of reform, bearing in mind that any such reform needs to be based on the principles of subsidiarity and solidarity, and respect for the equal sovereignty of states. Regrettably, the risk exists of a "monadology" and of a fragmentation into *like-minded clubs* that only let in those who think in the same way'[49].

Similarly in Australia, "Christian pro-life advocate and law professor, Dr Joanna Howe has won the anti-bullying case she brought against her employers at the University of Adelaide after it attempted to halt her pro-life research efforts'[50]. Medical language, in some cases, is being turned into propaganda as, at a conference, speakers said: "When they used the word "woman," they explained it was only to mirror the older, less politically correct research they referenced' – as if woman is not a universal term, along with man, identifying the sexes as a reality and not as a fictional version of it.

What happened to the declarations on human rights from the post Second World War period, notably those which prioritized vulnerable groups for particular protection when it came to the risk of harm? As defined, 'Vulnerable groups may include individuals who cannot give fully informed consent or those individuals who may be at elevated risk of unplanned side effects. Examples of vulnerable participants include pregnant women, children younger than the age of consent, terminally ill

---

[49] Pope Francis, 9th January, 2025, "*ADDRESS OF HIS HOLINESS POPE FRANCIS TO MEMBERS OF THE DIPLOMATIC CORPS ACCREDITED TO THE HOLY SEE*": https://www.vatican.va/content/francesco/en/speeches/2025/january/documents/20250109-corpo-diplomatico.html.

[50] *Madalaine Elhabbal* | Aug 14, 2024 | *Adelaide, Australia*, "Christian Professor Wins Case Against University That Tried to Stop Her Pro-Life Research": https://www.lifenews.com/2024/08/14/christian-professor-wins-case-against-university-that-tried-to-stop-her-pro-life-research/.

individuals, institutionalized individuals, and those with mental or emotional disabilities'[51].

How many of these groups are properly safeguarded in the current climate of abortion procedures, experiments on human embryonic life, euthanasia and children subject to puberty blockers and mutilating surgeries? For if pro-abortionists and those who experiment on human embryos very often claim that there is real medical uncertainty surrounding when a human life begins, then clearly this is a reason to consider abortion and embryo experimentation as research and to stop it in order to prevent harm to the subjects. Similarly, if there are other treatments for those seeking death because of how to help people suffering mental or physical illness, then again euthanasia, which trials drugs for killing people, is an experimental practice as well as being totally against life and harmful. Finally, taking advantage of young people's confusion about their identity and fast-tracking puberty blockers and mutilating surgeries when there are other treatments available – how are these practical procedures, adopted without proper evidence, not experimental?

In this account of the dynamics at work in society, more generally, with individuals, pressure groups and campaigners exploiting the law to the end of silencing objections or debate around single subject programmes which, according to them are claimed as rights, there is a looming sense of mental crippling: that the painstaking collection of evidence, ideas, their evaluation, the citing of alternative points of view and the giving of answers to these objections, all of which are classical academic tasks, from ancient times, are leading to an impoverished grasp of reality and an incapacity to

---

[51] Jennifer M. Barrow; Grace D. Brannan; Paras B. Khandhar, September 18th, 2022, "Research Ethics": https://www.ncbi.nlm.nih.gov/books/NBK459281/; and cf. Dr. Mary Anne Urlakis' "Foreword", pp. 1-21 of *The Human Person: A Bioethical Word*.

think critically, except where criticism is simply about rejecting the "other" point of view[52].

I think, then, that what is so unexpected but which has emerged from the research in this book is that there is a dearth of critical debate where real objections, like puberty-blockers jeopardizing a person's health, are not side-stepped but are answered head on: if these are already found facts, what is holding up the medical profession from taking this "evidence-based-medicine" for what it is and arresting the carnage wrought in young people's health? Clearly, as has been noted throughout this book, there is a mentality abroad which wants to silence opposing views in order to drive both the protection of protagonists of health-harming effects on children and, at the same time, to "imprison" their opponents. In other words, we live in a culture that substitutes 'conformism' for dialogue[53]; and, in the process, strips the intellectual development of those who resort to silencing rather than showing the weakness of their political opponents.

How, then, if the world at large cannot cope with engaging deeply with the crises in our society, calling out and debating the pros and cons of controversial decisions and their consequences, then what possibility is there of our young people being formed critically as opposed to just reiterating inaccurate and implacable one-line answers about which they have scarcely thought. In a very straight answer to how we got here, it seems that feminism has been side-lined by the view that there is no male or female. But feminism, and the legitimate rights of women, have not been

---

[52] Cf. Genevieve Gluck, September 20, 2024, "FRANCE: Trans Activists Set Off Explosion in Attempt to Sabotage Conference Critical of Gender Ideology": https://reduxx.info/france-trans-activists-set-fire-to-venue-in-attempt-to-sabotage-conference-critical-of-gender-ideology/.

[53] September 26th, 2024, "Lucinda Creighton challenges 'cancel culture' in address at pro-life dinner": https://prolifecampaign.ie/lucinda-creighton-challenges-cancel-culture-in-address-at-pro-life-dinner/.

side-lined, but powerfully supplanted[54]. What is more, the law is being used to oppose opposition to the equation that gender identity equals a person's sex[55] – as if any gender identity claim determines a person's sex rather than a person's sex informs a person's identity.

But, as Pope Francis has recently said, if the power of pornography is beyond the power of human beings to resist[56], then it follows that its eradication is not simply a rational but also a spiritual battle. Therefore, if there is a corporate unwillingness to undertake the changes necessary, it is because there is an attachment to the wealth that it generates or the vice that it is. And, as in so many of these scenarios, which surround and entrap our young people, the Gospel adage that we cannot serve two masters, both God and wealth (cf. Mt. 6: 24), is proving to be more and more an account of the spiritual reality of our times but, in the words of Christ, if we are caught in the trap of wrongdoing, let us beg to be delivered from it (cf. Mt. 18: 9).

In the end, reason and faith

Althusius, *Politica*: 'There is no civil law, nor can there be any, in which something of natural and divine immutable equity has not been mixed. If it departs entirely from the judgment of natural and divine law (*jus naturale et divinum*), it is not to be called law (*lex*). It is entirely unworthy of this name, and can obligate no one against natural and divine equity'[57].

---

[54] Anderson, *When Harry Became Sally*, p.206-211.

[55] Anderson, *When Harry Became Sally*, pp. 192-196.

[56] Pope Francis: "General Audience, 25.09.2024": https://press.vatican.va/content/salastampa/en/bollettino/pubblico/2024/09/25/240925b.html.

[57] Cited by Nicholas K. Meriweather, June 22nd, 2024, "Natural Law: An Introduction, Part 5": https://worldviewbulletin.substack.com/p/natural-law-an-introduction-part-f60.

Taking the advice of a modern proponent of the natural and divine law, Pope Francis says: "'What characterizes women, that which is truly feminine, is not stipulated by consensus or ideologies, just as dignity itself is ensured not by laws written on paper, but by an original law written on our hearts," he said'[58].

In a new development, there is a growing opposition, across both professional bodies and individuals, opposing the unverified assertions that have led to the use of puberty blockers and mutilating surgeries advanced as "so-called treatments". The umbrella organization is called: "Doctors Protecting Children Declaration", with signatories across 60 countries[59].

To make this more concrete, when a father asked his daughter why she wanted to be a man, the daughter was eleven and had been interviewed twice by a gender clinic and programmed for puberty blockers, she answered in a way that made her gender confusion understandable. The daughter said:

it was because she didn't like the way women were treated and feared being sexually assaulted.' Following this admission and a thorough going conversation with her dad about what puberty blockers are, why they were invented and what the risks are, the daughter reverted to being happily who she was: a girl[60].

---

[58] Elise Ann Allen, 28th September, 2024, "Pope's rhetoric on women in Belgium stirs protest": https://cruxnow.com/vatican/2024/09/pope-says-men-and-women-not-rivals-wants-discussion-free-of-ideology.

[59] "Doctors Protecting Children Declaration": https://doctorsprotectingchildren.org/.

[60] David Southwell for Daily Mail Australia, https://archive.md/o/T3nG9/ https://www.dailymail.co.uk/profile-314/david-southwell.html, 31st December,

Thus, reason and evidence prevailed in a very simple and well-informed discussion about why the man's daughter wanted to be different and how, listening to her in a totally different way to the gender clinicians, helped her recover her original identity as a girl.

In brief, the foundational principle of the natural law, do good and avoid harm, has been cited; and, at the same time, this natural law principle is self-evident, for it is implicitly expressed in every true and upright act. At the same time, while the perfection of human action is constantly challenged by human imperfection and sin, the more we depart from the good of the person the more we endanger the common good. What would happen if the so-called mandate to insist on puberty blockers and mutilating surgery were to be extended to society as a whole – society as a whole would cease to exist, both because of the totalitarianism of the dictate and the practical infertilization of everyone. Similarly, the law of non-contradiction[61] entails that we examine the contradiction between the harm caused by puberty blockers and mutilating surgery and the claim that this does not harm the subject. Alternatively, if we do not examine this contradiction then we have abandoned the basic rule of reason and evidence; indeed, the possibility that many people have abandoned the use of reason is summed up in the following way: we live in a time of 'a "signature irrationalism", a demand that we cancel Aristotle and believe "A and not-A at

---

2024, "When Brad's 11-year-old daughter said she was a boy, he made a decision that could have cost him everything. Now, a crucial question we must all ask: have our doctors been making a terrible mistake with our children?": https://archive.md/T3nG9.

[61] 'Message of the Holy Father on the occasion of the Workshop "Aquinas' Social Ontology and Natural Law in Perspective"', 07.03.2024: https://press.vatican.va/content/salastampa/en/bollettino/pubblico/2024/03/07/240307h.html.

once"[62]. In other words, we are asked to believe that a man or a woman is not a man or a woman. Or we recognise the relationship between identity and evidence and say, albeit in Pope Francis' inimitable words: 'In this regard, the pope in an off-the-cuff remark condemned sex-change and transgenderism, saying, "It's ugly when a woman wants to be a man, no, she's a woman!"'

And, if we have abandoned the basic rule of reason then we are proceeding on the basis of unsubstantiated claims which run contrary to the reality of the good of human life and, in so doing, we inflict harm not just on specific people but on the social good to which all particular goods are ordered: the common good which governs our relationships to one another and which becomes disordered to the extent that it is contradicted by particular laws – bearing in mind that the law has a teaching function and influences many aspects of society.

Having given many reasons, and cited much evidence, for the ongoing and unfolding nature of human development, integrally physical and psychological, it is clear that we are addressing many weaknesses in our educational practice, that even professionals cannot engage in respectful debate without turning to the law to legislate or bureaucracies to insinuate a consensus on anti-life practices when there is none, instead of answering with reason and evidence as to why a certain practice does good and avoids harm. In other words, if professionals cannot debate the pros and cons of a particular type of treatment, then how does this augur for young people who come into contact with a gender service that cannot acknowledge a diversity of opinion and evidence which is tending, realistically, to increasingly discredit the use of puberty blockers and mutilating surgeries? In other words, why are so-called professionals, who claim to be driving evidence-based treatments, so incapable of assessing the evidence? In other

---

[62] Eberstadt, *Adam and Eve after the Pill: Revisited*, 2023, p. 12, from the "Foreword" by Cardinal George Pell.

words, it is not a matter of dialogue but of a power struggle that simply defines those that are against puberty blockers and mutilating operations as 'practicing "hate," and cannot be reasoned with or in any way tolerated, only conquered'[63]. Thus, the very people who are incapable of assessing evidence and argument mount a campaign against those who can instead of answering the legitimate objections to the harm these non-treatments are causing to a widespread group of people.

How profoundly significant is it that young people, in the very throes of self-understanding and developing their outlook, are meeting people who cannot dialogue: who cannot engage in the reality-based discussion of what it means to be growing up, going through puberty, under the influence of social media influencers, whether peer groups or others, never mind the concrete realities of long-term, life-changing drugs and mutilating surgeries! In one particular state, for example, the counsellor can agree and fast-forward a self-identifying claim that "I am in the wrong body"; but, according to the law, that same counsellor cannot explore the other possibilities, particularly the influence of trauma and social influence. Thus, one counsellor says: 'According to the state, children and teens are more than mature enough to decide for themselves whether they want to identify as male or female; they're just not mature enough to rethink that decision'[64]. In other words, this is not counselling this is selling a solution.

More widely, then, not only is there a profound disregard of human development that passes through childhood and adolescence to adulthood, exploring ideas and images in the course of it but, too, there is a profound inability to argue, objectively, that the "temporary identity" that

---

[63] Rod Dreher, Live Not By Lies: A Manual for Christian Dissidents, Sentinel: An Imprint of Penguin Random House, LLC, 2022, p. 61.

[64] Kaley Chiles, Dec 11, 2024, "GUEST COLUMN: Colorado thinks kids can make gender decisions — but not rethink them": https://gazette.com/opinion/guest-column-colorado-thinks-kids-can-make-gender-decisions-but-not-rethink-them/article_9d315660-b650-11ef-b527-3f208eb77a86.html.

occurs in the course of growing up, like a claim about "being in the wrong body", is more than the temporary claim that it is. For "being in the wrong body" is not a life-goal which originates with the person but an "adopted" goal which, according to the statistical rise of cases, originates more with social media and trauma than his or her real nature.

Seeking the help that is beyond us

In a recent article on UK 21 to 34 year-olds, there is a jump from 5% spending it alone in 1955 to 11% spending it alone in 2024[65].

Thus 'The newest disease of civilization across the infertile and greying West is the thoroughly documented "epidemic" of loneliness'[66]. Vulnerability to social media targeting is very real[67], especially if 'An adolescent who is lonely, friendless, mentally ill or who doesn't fit in … is an easy target for online seduction of all sorts'[68].

And, indeed, while it would be good to identify the varieties of loneliness, a common experience of families and parents, when it comes to a

---

[65] **Sammy Gecsoyler**, 24th December, 2024, "Major increase in young people spending Christmas Day alone in UK": https://www.theguardian.com/lifeandstyle/2024/dec/24/sharp-rise-young-people-spending-christmas-day-alone-uk-study-finds.

[66] Eberstadt, *Adam and Eve after the Pill: Revisited*, 2023, p. 168, plus her own work called *Primal Screams: How the Sexual Revolution Created Identity Politics*, 2018.

[67] Cf. Hasson, Chapter 22: "Targeting Children, Dividing Families", p. 369 of pp. 357-371 of *Gender Ideology and Pastoral Practice*, 2024.

[68] Hasson, Chapter 22: "Targeting Children, Dividing Families", p. 368 of pp. 357-371 of *Gender Ideology and Pastoral Practice*, 2024.

child declaring gender confusion, is 'Isolation: "I feel so alone. There is no one I can talk to about this"'[69].

But, let us remember that what develops in us, does not necessarily develop in isolation of our personal and family history, which brings with it its own need for awareness, sensitivity and healing. Where this applies, 'Families find it helpful when clergy and pastoral leaders either know the family or take the time to learn about the family and the transgender-identifying child'[70] avoiding, where possible, labels and self-identifications[71].

We need to be aware, too, that 'loneliness' is a dead end and frustrates our vocation to be-in-relationship; and, therefore, there needs to be various kinds of welcome in the parish, for both families and, particularly, by 'creating a culture for youth that can fill their need for community and communion'[72].

But seeking the help we need takes discernment[73]: recognizing that a person 'can be sincerely welcomed by the Church without affirming the

---

[69] Hasson, Chapter 19: Gender Ideology's Harmful Effects on Families", p. 321 of pp. 315-331 of *Gender Ideology and Pastoral Practice*, 2024.

[70] Hasson, Chapter 19: Gender Ideology's Harmful Effects on Families", p. 316 of pp. 315-331 of *Gender Ideology and Pastoral Practice*, 2024.

[71] Hasson, Chapter 19: Gender Ideology's Harmful Effects on Families", p. 318 of pp. 315-331 of *Gender Ideology and Pastoral Practice*, 2024.

[72] Hasson, Chapter 22: "Targeting Children, Dividing Families", pp. 370-371 of pp. 357-371 of *Gender Ideology and Pastoral Practice*, 2024.

[73] A note of caution that while good and true and wise counsel can be found in many places, nevertheless discernment is necessary as to how wholesome it is; for example, some "Christian" resources are 'not grounded in a theology or anthropology compatible with Catholic teaching' and end up being, therefore, contradictory as to what they offer and claim is good for the person who needs help.

ideological roots supporting their position'[74]; indeed, little by little, introducing them to the truth that sets them free (cf. Jn. 8: 32). And that help can be comprehensive, covering many aspects: prayer; study; spiritual reading; conscience; reflection; friends; pastors; the sacraments[75]; participation; and spiritual direction[76]. At the same time, it is important that a school or university culture takes full advantage of a good anthropology; and, if it is Catholic, of an anthropology that sets out, builds, and explains the mysterious identity of man and woman made in the image of God[77].

However, in view of the very mixed culture in which we live, it is possible that there needs to be a discernment, too, about whether or not there is a diabolical influence in a person's life; but, this is not to be entered upon carelessly and entails a whole caution, proceeding carefully through a range of assessments. Thus a suitably trained exorcist, having also benefited from an apprenticeship with one with experience, and who is fully committed to his prayer life, 'using gentle methods of

---

p. 278 of pp. 271-279 of Selner-Wright, Chapter 16: "Responding to Non-Catholic Christian Approaches" in *Gender Ideology and Pastoral Practice*, 2024.

[74] Billy, Chapter 13: "Spiritual Discernment", p. 229 of pp. 229-242 of *Gender Ideology and Pastoral Practice*, 2024.

[75] With respect to the sacraments of the Church, the founding sacrament is Baptism; and, therefore, as this normally founds the identity of the child, it is advisable, if not already practiced, to add son or daughter to the register. This is not only a record of fact but, upon it, rests the notation that may illuminate whether or not a person is free to marry, enter the religious life or become a priest; 'And so, as asserted, we can see that the baptismal record is a master record for a Catholic.', p. 265 of pp. 257-270 of Chapter 15: "Canonical Issues" of *Gender Ideology and Pastoral Practice*, 2024.

[76] Billy, Chapter 13: "Spiritual Discernment", pp. 236-239 of pp. 229-242, of *Gender Ideology and Pastoral Practice*, 2024.

[77] Cf. Farnan, Chapter 23: "Male and Female He Created Them", pp. 373-389 of *Gender Ideology and Pastoral Practice*, 2024.

diagnosis it should be possible to distinguish mental distress from diabolical obsession/vexation/possession'[78].

And so the Lord says come to me all who need help: "Those who are
well have no need of a physician, but those who are sick; I came not to call
the righteous, but sinners" (Mark 2: 17). Thus, do we know our need of
help or are we so immersed in a virtual environment that all possible, particularly negative feedback, is either explained away, neutralized or blamed
on the 'other'?

It may take time, however, and setbacks, to discover the path to repentance and reconciliation with God, with our history and with each other;
indeed, I was once helpfully refused absolution by a priest as it was not
clear to him that I rejected marrying in a registry office instead of in the
Church. This was a helpful refusal of absolution as it made me think more
clearly about what and why I was willing to do what I wanted; and, basically, it came down to me wanting to "get" what I wanted which was not,
in reality, a good disposition to either marry or receive absolution. And,
similarly, in the case of anyone coming to the confessional, it is both matter
of being well disposed, willing to listen and, if necessary, being helped to
understand both the natural law and the teachings of the Church[79]. But,
what I would recommend from years of experience, is the value of preparing to receive confession, or the sacrament of reconciliation as it is called,
by meditating on the word of God and even listening to an exhortation,
based on the word of God, to help prepare for the sacrament[80].

---

[78] Tiso, Chapter 18: "Pastoral Care for the Spiritually Afflicted", p. 308 of pp.
297-313 of *Gender Ideology and Pastoral Practice*, 2024.

[79] Cf. Fastiggi, Chapter 12: "Moral Principles and Subjective Culpability", pp.
209-225 of *Gender Ideology and Pastoral Practice*, 2024.

[80] I note here that this is the common practice of the liturgical celebration of
the sacrament of Reconciliation in the *Neocatechumenal Way*.

The social woes which afflict so many of us in so many societies are related to our relationships with each other, whether in the family, because of divorce, aborting siblings[81], and fatherlessness, as well as the tragic disappointment of abuse. These and other raging conflicts are a call to a relationship with God[82]; for, given the nature of these breakdowns, we need a relationship to God to reestablish our relationships with one another.

'14 psychiatrists … asked the [Dutch] prosecution office to investigate the death by euthanasia of a 17-year-old, 'questioning the right of a minor to opt for euthanasia and whether it is right to assume that mental suffering cannot be cured'[83].

On the other hand, it is also clear that there are forces at work in our own lives whereby it is possible to be ensnared by mental anguish, enslaved by a technological device, never mind in terms of certain contents and practices, such that we are also in front of a spiritual landscape in which, in reality, the spirit of man has disappeared. He is either a machine, a form of materialism, or a kind of processor of data, and often not even regarded as a psychological subject. Thus we need conversion. And conversion is not to be confused with anything coerced; and, it is interesting to note, that while 'conversion therapy' has been outlawed by transgender ideologues, they use the word 'transition' in such a way as they are converting young people to transgenderism.

---

[81] Eberstadt, *Adam and Eve after the Pill: Revisited*, 2023, p. 119.

[82] Cf. Eberstadt, *Adam and Eve after the Pill: Revisited*, 2023, p. 116.

[83] Alex Schadenberg, October 2nd, 2024, "Netherlands euthanasia death of 17-year-old criticised": https://alexschadenberg.blogspot.com/2024/10/netherlands-euthanasia-death-of-17-year.html.

'The false accusation is sometimes made that to question gender affir-mation is to support some form of 'conversion therapy.' This seems meant to discourage those who question or challenge certain proce-dures from speaking out, in clinics, schools, doctors' offices, universi-ties, etc. Yet hardly anyone uses that term. Rather, it is interesting that those who support early transition are themselves involved in an at-tempt to 'convert,' except the word 'transition' is used'[84]. In other words, a good possibility, like offering a person help to resolve their questions of identity, is made illegal, while funnelling young people, without a differentiating diagnosis, is not.

Religious conversion, however, is a free recognition that we need the help of God because we can see we are stuck and unable to move away from what entraps us. What is more, conversion is a gift of God which proceeds from His love[85]: conversion is an act whereby God "crosses" the divide between His own "otherness" and our sinfulness; and, in so doing, effects a change totally beyond us but which is, at the same time, fruitful in a change of life. My own experience at 40, confirms this, the which I have written about elsewhere in this and other books.

---

[84] Dr. Moira McQueen and Bambi, in the January 15th, 2025, edition of "CCBI News: Gender Affirmation – Changing Approaches": Canadian Catholic Bioeth-ics Institute – Affiliated with the University of St. Michael's College in the Univer-sity of Toronto. **https://www.ccbi-utoronto.ca/**

[85] Cf. Michael Haynes, January 14th, 2025, "Pope Francis says God loves ho-mosexuals 'as they are' in new memoir": https://www.lifesitenews.com/news/pope-francis-god-loves-homosexuals-as-they-are-in-new-memoir/ - LifeSite; and, as regards the blessings of people, Pope Francis is clear that he is not advo-cating the blessing of unions that do not accord with the truth of love expressed in the Catholic Church's teaching on marriage. See my discussion of this in *The Word in Your Heart: Mary, Youth, and Mental Health*: https://enroute-booksandmedia.com/wordinyourheart/

Indeed, while there may be goodwill and objective merit in clearing un-
helpful materials from schools, it takes the graced truth to enlighten our
hearts and bring about the abstinence[86] so necessary to people who, it
seems, are spreading fire rather than being able to keep it in the grate and
warm the home with it. We need Judith who, with the help of God, overcame the overwhelming army of Nebuchadnezzar, and freed the land from
the imposition of a false god (cf. *The Book of Judith*).

As discussed at the beginning of the book, there are innumerable sufferings that afflict us, our families and society, many of which arise because
we cannot understand suffering: that with the passing of Christianity from
many people's lives there has passed, too, a sense of the purpose, value and
meaning of suffering with it. Therefore, while the statistics speak for themselves in terms of the numbers of people in prison, albeit mainly men, the
number of pregnant women and young people who are accessing mental
health services, raises urgent questions about the many people's lives that
have become unintelligible to them or, conversely, were never intelligible
to begin with. As problems surfaced, so the question of what a person's life
is about and what meaning it has, suggests that people need help to get to
the point of some self-understanding. However, if along with the breakdown of family, there is a breakdown of faith, there is also a breakdown in
the processes of communication which enable young people to form a stable identity and developing world view.

Wider considerations concerning spiritual help

While, then, what Pope Francis says was particularly applicable to
priests, it raises the question more widely, namely, that many people may

---

[86] Cf. Rebecca Crosby and Noel Sims, 25th of September, 2024, "Florida bans
instruction on contraception and consent in sex ed classes": https://popu-
lar.info/p/florida-bans-instruction-on-contraception.

need help to have insight into their lives. This is not to suggest that all these kinds of sufferings are to do with sin, but it is to suggest that we need to know ourselves, to cite an old adage.

What Pope Francis said, then, to priests, applies more widely to all of us, that we tend to be entrapped in our own bubble of preoccupation and need help to evaluate it from the heart; and, therefore, to discuss the piercing pain of discovering that we are sinners in need of help – but he does not stop there!

'The origin of the term [*compunction*] has to do with *piercing*. Compunction is "a piercing of the heart" that is painful and evokes tears of repentance'.

'Compunction is the remedy for this, since it brings us back to the truth about ourselves, so that the depths of our being *sinners* can reveal the infinitely greater reality of our being *pardoned* by grace – the joy of being pardoned. It is not surprising, then, that Isaac of Nineveh could say: "The one who forgets the greatness of his sins forgets the greatness of God's mercy in his regard"'.

'Those who are willing to be "unmasked" and let God's gaze pierce their heart receive the gift of those tears, the holiest waters after those of baptism'[87].

And, if we avail ourselves of the help of the word of God and His sacrament of reconciliation, of forgiveness, let us hear the words of Pope Francis to priests:

---

[87] "Chrism Mass in the Vatican Basilica, 28.03.2024": https://press.vatican.va/content/salastampa/en/bollettino/pubblico/2024/03/28/240328a.html.

'Dear friends, the task entrusted to you in the confessional is beautiful and crucial, because it enables you to help so many brothers and sisters to experience the sweetness of God's love. I encourage you, therefore, to live every confession as a unique and unrepeatable moment of grace, and to give the forgiveness of the Lord generously, with affability, fatherliness and, I dare say, even with maternal tenderness'[88].

At the same time as we discover our weakness, its history, its depth and dimensions, let us pray with St. Paul who 'glories in his weaknesses and trusts in the grace of the Lord (cf. *2 Cor* 12:8-10) [which] is a gift that we must ask for in prayer, for ourselves and for others'[89].

And, therefore, as we discover our vulnerability and weakness, let it help us to identify how to help others; and, instead of the exploitation of the vulnerable, let there be a community outreach, as it were, of the vulnerable to the vulnerable: 'Human trafficking is a "systemic" evil, and therefore we can and must eliminate it through a systematic, multilevel approach. Trafficking is fuelled by wars and conflicts, thrives on the effects of climate change and socio-economic disparities, and takes advantage of the vulnerability of those forced to migrate, as well as the conditions of inequality in which they find themselves, especially women and girls'[90].

---

[88] Pope Francis: "Audience with participants in the Course on the 34th Internal Forum organized by the Apostolic Penitentiary, 08.03.2024": https://press.vatican.va/content/salastampa/en/bollettino/pubblico/2024/03/08/240308a.html.

[89] *"Message of His Holiness Pope Francis to the Participants in the Third Latin American Conference "Vulnerability and Abuse."* [Panama, 12-14 March 2024]: https://www.vatican.va/content/francesco/en/messages/pont-messages/2024/documents/20240301-messaggio-congresso-latinoamericano.html.

[90] May 23rd, 2024, "Pope Francis Reveals the Key to Eliminate the "systemic" Evil of Human Trafficking": https://www.catholicnewsworld.com/2024/05/pope-francis-reveals-key-to-eliminate.html

Pope Francis, speaking of how Christ is vulnerable with the vulnerable, says: 'Think of the Magdalene: tormented by seven demons, she became the first witness of the Risen Jesus. In short, vulnerable people, encountered and welcomed with Christ's grace and with His style, can be a presence of the Gospel in the community of believers and in society'[91].

At the same time, the Church is made up of sinners and is constantly in need of purification: 'the Church, however, clasping sinners to her bosom, at once holy and always in need of purification, follows constantly the path of penance and renewal'[92]. And, therefore, as Pope Francis says to the young, approaching God with the sins of the Church, 'like beggars', which harm both her mission and those who are sinned against, '"How could we be credible in mission," he asked, "if we do not acknowledge our mistakes and stoop to heal the wounds we have caused by our sins?"'[93].

'To these … representatives of the young, Pope Francis then consigned a copy of the Gospel, entrusting to them and their contemporaries the mandate to proclaim the Good News to future generations, in the hopes of "a better mission, ever more faithful to the logic of the Kingdom of God"'[94].

---

[91] Pope Francis: "Audience with participants in the Conference "Vulnerability and community, between welcome and inclusion", 01.03.2024": https://press.vatican.va/content/salastampa/en/bollettino/pubblico/2024/03/01/240301b.html.

[92] *Catechism of the Catholic Church*, 827, drawing on *Lumen Gentium*, 8, the document of the Second Vatican Council on the Church.

[93] Christopher Wells, October 1st, 2024, "Pope Francis at Vigil: We are here as beggars of God's mercy": https://www.vaticannews.va/en/pope/news/2024-10/pope-francis-at-vigil-we-are-here-as-beggars-of-god-s-mercy.html.

[94] Wells, October 1st, 2024, "Pope Francis at Vigil: We are here as beggars of God's mercy".

Talking to a group of students from different parts of the world, and taking account of this book, which is almost an account of what happens if people are isolated from others, Pope Francis speaks of the need to recognize our vulnerability and to seek help:

'The Holy Father spoke to the first group about feeling a sense of belonging to society, and how our 'belonging' heightens our security in ourselves and our own human dignity.

All these factors, he noted, "save us from vulnerability, because today youth are very vulnerable. We must always defend this sense of belonging in order to ward off vulnerability".

"Look at where you are most vulnerable, and ask someone to help you," he said'[95].

And so we need hope, which is the theme of both an interview with a Phoenix Bishop John Dolan who has lost three members of his family to suicide[96] and the words of Pope Francis for the coming World Meeting of Youth:

'embraced by God and born again in him, you too can become open arms to embrace your many friends and peers who need to feel, through your welcome, the love of God the Father. May each of you

[95] Deborah Castellano Lubov, June 20th, 2024, "Pope to university students: 'Stay true to your convictions and faith'": https://www.vaticannews.va/en/pope/news/2024-06-pope-francis-students-in-building-bridges-across-asia-pacific.html.

[96] Catherine Hadro, September 30th, 2024, "Bishop Who Lost 3 Siblings to Suicide: 'Get Help, and Don't Give Up Hope'": https://www.ncregister.com/interview/bishop-john-dolan-on-losing-3-siblings-to-suicide.

give even just "a smile, a warm gesture of friendship, a kind look, a ready ear, a good deed, in the knowledge that, in the Spirit of Jesus, these can become, for those who receive them, rich seeds of hope" (ibid., 18), and thus become *tireless* missionaries of joy'[97].

What emerges, then, specifically for the Church, is that her guardianship of the truth, both natural and supernatural, is ever a service for the times in which we live![98]

---

[97] Pope Francis: "Message of the Holy Father Francis for the 39th World Youth Day 2024, 17.09.2024": https://press.vatican.va/content/salas-tampa/en/bollettino/pubblico/2024/09/17/240917d.html.

[98] Cf. Farnan, pp. 195-203, of Chapter 11: "Catholic Teaching on Gender Ideology", pp. 189-208 of *Gender Ideology and Pastoral Practice*, 2024.

And Thus to End

'And as we reflect, we can see that there is an even greater reality that enlightens us and transcends us: *the truth*. What is truth? Pilate asked this question. Without truth, our life loses its meaning. Studying makes sense only when it seeks the truth with a critical mind. Finding truth requires critical thinking. This is the way for moving forward. Do not forget that studying makes sense when it seeks the truth. When seeking it we understand that we are made in order to find it. Truth is meant to be found, for it is inviting, accessible and generous'[1].

And 'Formation in the truth on the unchanging teachings of the Church concerning human nature is essential for anyone who *serves the suffering*'[2]. Indeed, we notice more and more that the less people are formed, holistically in the truth, ranging from the natural to the supernatural nature of it, the more vulnerable people are to being "ideologically hijacked"; and, therefore, as so many others have said, we need to revisit all the ways that formation can come to the fore, in our homes, parish communities, universities and, by implication, in the wider culture in which we live[3].

---

[1] Pope Francis, Address to Students at the *Aula Magna of the Université Catholique de Louvain, Saturday, 28 September 2024*: https://www.vatican.va/content/francesco/en/speeches/2024/september/documents/20240928-belgio-studenti-universitari.html.

[2] Italics added to a quotation from p. 289 of pp. 283-296 of Chapter 17: "Pastoral Care for Regretters and Detransitioners" in *Gender Ideology and Pastoral Practice*, 2024.

[3] Cf. Rod Dreher, *The Benedict Option*, New York: Sentinel, Penguin Random House, 2017.

An end, like a beginning, is a bit like dipping into a stream and, although a scoop or two will come out in cupped hands, so some will fall back into the water as well as the water rushes all the while and by and by goes on its way, bearing the possibility of a trace that it was once interrupted but is ever flowing on and through and away.

Sometimes an end is in view, involving drawing together some of the different strands that run through a work; but, in this case, the end came about because of a poem written by the poet James Sale which I discovered, like a twitching stick sensing water, and so I decided to run with what I found and find what I can from taking a little time to react to it.

So there are all kinds of links, not least of which is that of gathering little lights together, like a light here and a light there, an insight here and an insight there, a truth here and a truth there and, as they come together, so the light grows, each lighting the other and all becoming one light, lighting and growing brighter because of it.

What we have, then, is that truth is not ours, it is not a personal possession or invention but it takes wit and work to gather it from all kinds of sources, whether they be experiential accounts of what has happened in people's lives or a statistic. Even as a statistic on the number of young people who have become Japanese "stay-ins" is about actual lives, indeed 700, 000 actual lives, along with families and those they know; indeed, in a more recent article, the number of people affected by loneliness in Japanese society has risen to 1. 5 million 'living as recluses'. What is more, where there is an actual account of what precipitates becoming a "stay in", one has the impression that it can be about "losing face" because of a disappointment, such as not getting into college and, when this is aggravated by negative comments, a person seems to be unable to face his own family[4]. Thus the

---

[4] Nicola Smith, 31st July, 2024, "How Japan is tackling 'hikikomori' – a syndrome that created a generation of recluses": https://www.telegraph.co.uk/global-

reality of human nature "speaks", as it were, about the need for humility: of not being discouraged by disappointments or hurts but discovering that they make us humbler and more human. And so, along with every other kind of principle, practice, good or harmful, altogether amounting to a blazing bonfire of fact and truth gathering which, one hopes, lights for all and sundry just as the warning fires of old were set upon a mountain top to alert a kingdom of an invasion: an invasion, in this case, of losing the reality of our lives when there is no word to enlighten us.

May our young people, then, becoming light gatherers, collecting from wherever it can be found and, as with a real bonfire, seeing that like burns with like and truth and truth ignite, in the hope that God, "The Father of All Lights" is able to come to our aid and not just our aid but to the aid of this generation and inspire more truth telling and hope begetting and worldview forming that takes people into life, able to circumvent the traps of falsehood and to thrive as light upon light leads to love: a love which is essentially communion with God and each other, dispelling the cruelty of isolation, loneliness, false groups and leading to the beacon-like saving fellowship of the Church which, potentially, can guide the pilgrim home.

Whoever we are, then, at whatever stage of life, but particularly as we emerge from childhood, we are called and invited, by the very impulse of our nature and appetite for 'we are made in order to find' the truth and the Truth is there to be sought and to be found, just as those who knock, who seek, who love, will find that the truth that opens on reality and, ultimately, through the gift of the Holy Spirit, is the Truth that is Jesus Christ (Jn. 14: 6) – is the Truth who is, all the while, seeking us!

Thus, in a word, implicit to the specific injustice to some of our young people growing up is, perhaps, the injustice of depriving them, and their parents and advisers, of an education: of an education about themselves,

health/climate-and-people/japan-recluse-generation-hikikomori-shut-in-syndrome/.

their changes, their inner impulse to make sense of themselves and the world and society's social responsibility in assisting them to do this! Together, then, with this weakening if not disabling of peoples' capacity to think critically, is the cumulative effect of laws and pressure groups tending to dominate and to give us a "group think" which is neither good for us nor the generations to come! I hope, therefore, that the many good resources upon which I have drawn may yet contribute to many works which can still promote the good, the true and beautiful gifts of God.

What follows is a "Spiritual Autobiography" of James Sale, 'a poet of the Lord' and his piece "The Father of All Lights", followed by my reasons for choosing it as an "End Piece" for this book.

The Spiritual Autobiography of James Sale, a 'Poet of the Lord'

To talk of one's spiritual autobiography as a Christian is difficult, except as it appertains to revealing the mercy and the glory of God Almighty who, one comes to understand, has made everything, sustains everything, and – quite incredibly – seems to take an inordinate interest in humanity generally, and specifically in me (for the purpose of this writing). I cannot – as Job noted – even swallow my own spittle without His presence being felt.

My family were atheists, even deep atheists, and my father told me that he would give God a piece of his mind if there were such a thing as the afterlife. I was the only person with him when he actually died in 1996; it took about thirty minutes, and what I witnessed was some conversation he was having with some invisible entity as he mumbled repeatedly some self-justifications; it was terrifying to behold – for, truly, it is a terrifying thing to fall into the hands of the living God.

For many years I was an atheist, right up to my twenties. I always argued against religion and against God, though I was aware that something in me prompted me to do so because something else in me knew that these arguments were both false and self-serving; for what we really want is to have no moral constraints on our own behaviour. Through and through, I sinned then, and have sinned ever since, though the presence of the Holy Spirit since my conversion has acted as my Comforter and guide to better ways.

The key intellectual event that enabled me to become a low-church evangelical in my mid-twenties was my being led by the Spirit to repeatedly examine the evidence for the Resurrection of Jesus Christ. And the more one examined it, the surer it seemed to be. Like CS Lewis, I became a reluctant convert. But after 5 years I left the Evangelical denomination; I had moved, my life was messy, and evangelicalism seemed too rigid an interpretation of Christianity – wholly biblically based, but ignoring tradition, and also the inner witness.

During several years, I continued to believe, but drifted, not attending any church. Then a Catholic friend of mine got me to attend two spiritual retreats on the Isle of Wight (Verbum Dei). I thought of becoming a Catholic but in attending a local Catholic church three or four times, and seeing the priest, I was massively disappointed. On the rebound from this, I went to the opposite theological extreme and became a Quaker for 15 years!

In 2011 I nearly died of a malignant cancer and was in hospital for 3 months and on Nil-by-Mouth for 29 days during which time I lost nearly 5 stone in weight. And also, during this period, I had an out-of-body experience – the greatest experience of my life – in which I cried out to the

Lord and He saved me. I did not want to 'come back' but he sent me anyway.

Eventually, as well, I came to see – especially after a trip to Ravenna in Italy where I saw the glorious cathedrals and mosaics through which the faithful had glorified God through the centuries – that Quakerism whilst containing many 'good' people, was itself becoming increasing Pelagian in its belief: the glory of God had been exchanged for education, progress and human 'good works'. The shift from orthodoxy to orthopraxy meant that you could hardly distinguish it from devout humanism.

Through the Spirit, my wife – inspired – said to me: 'James, stop agonising about where next. Just go to the local church next door.' So, I did. That was 7 or so years ago. It was an Anglo-Catholic Church, devoted to St Francis, and I became a member. My wife too, who'd not attended church before. We found a spiritual home, and found that high church is what we like and want. And we like it because the glory and mercy of God are always being praised there and we celebrate the Mass of our Lord.

Recently I was described by an American literary critic on the pages of NY's The Society of Classical Poets, as 'a poet of the Lord'. The word 'a' indicates I am not the only one, but I am one – one of His poets: it was to this end that the Lord God called me from my mother's womb – to fall short of praising His glory adequately, but to attempt to do so anyway. Like David, to see the beauty of the Lord is my deepest desire.

The Father of All Lights

*"Every good thing given and every perfect gift is
from above, coming down from the Father of
lights, with whom there is no variation or
shifting shadow"* —*James 1:17*

How much more to please him, then,
__The Father of all lights,
We should—if so then might we shine,
__Attain to brilliance.
And what a shining that would be—
__Accepting discipline,
Which now of course lash-heavy seems,
__But shall be kissing-soft.
From his vantage, advantage point
__He sees and we do not
But the Father declares his love
__And shining we too see
That everything's invisible
__Except the trash that's here—
Fit fuel for a fire He will light
__And yes, one day, appear[5].

---

[5] Used with permission by the author of "The Father of All Lights", James
Sale, by email, 5/10/2024; and cf. James Sale: https://englishcantos.home.blog/.

And My Response

"A-Lighting Together"

Another's scented words that I have read, brushing off on
Me as I read, and then reread, realising that there was a
Light to which, like a moth, I turned and turned towards
Again and again, to seek more clearly the scent of a certain Meaning,
overspilling between the beginning and the end.

Indeed, a bit like brushing against tomato plant leaves and
Discovering, slowly, the lingering scent and going back,
Almost for more, but more deliberately than before,
Searching amidst the leaves and fronds for both the
Big enough fruit and that free perfume presently given.

So, after turning and returning, again and again, it seems
As if this poet had undergone a wine-press making process
Distilling, a kind of boiling off that does not so much leave
An essence as, in this case, more than the bones of the lived
Christian life – even that life which took flesh according to God's Word
to the prophet and prefigured the One who was to come.

Thus this almost scarce but well-defined run of words is certainly a Gift;
and, in this case, the poem has certainly excelled in a kind of Cascading
descent from "The Father of All Lights" to that promised Presence, 'And
yes, [He will,] one day, appear' in a terrible glory.

Think too of that 'Fit fuel for a fire He will light' as already lit alight And
that, therefore, there is One Love expressed in a three-fold fire:

The first loving fire is Love's eternally enabling the lover to live;

The second loving fire being that Love which spans the broiling, Burning off whatever 'trash' impedes and obstructs the flow of Love's loving to return, like the rising of the plumed heat to the sun;

And the third loving fire, and the most appalling of all, the ever- Pained possibility of Love's love being lavished upon one who is Eternally unable to ignite and remains ever unable to arise alight.

And so with such heart-thought-through words as these, passing
More by inspiration than mining with effort the possibilities of
Meanings that abound, loose and looking for capture, amongst the Sayings of the day and the daylight hours of working for words,

I come to say "let us go forward into that dim light, lighting that it
Be brighter be, as we each bring together a little light to be a little
Brighter be so, betwixt you and I and a middle Thee, may our light Be
brighter be, bringing about a brightening meant for others to see.

May the Lord, His Holy Mother Mary, her spouse St. Joseph and all The saints and angels intercede for us and for the times we live in!

Postscript: On the heart's desire (Psalm 20: 4)

But just as the truth is a person, the person of Jesus Christ, so we are called to encounter the truth in the *healing heart of Christ*. And, even if we are among the hard hearted, those who are unable to listen or who reject the evidence of the harm that flows from our unthought through ways, we are still called to the heart of Christ to encounter the love that loves to love and overflowers for us and for others.

On the other hand, while politicians come and go and, for a time, their policies endeavour to establish what is good, what emerges is that if a society has no principled understanding of human nature, what good that can and will be done will pass too! In other words, we need to recognize that if the good is to prevail, we need to build on sound ground: on true principles that endure the test of time: do good and avoid harm. But, recognizing our human weakness, we need the help of what is beyond us for our principled work to prevail after us. If the Catholic Church teaches *The Truth* then 'all other truths incline toward this truth as iron shavings incline to a magnet'[6].

And if, speaking of the heart of Christ, may God 'grant … your heart's desire' (Psalm 20: 4), then the Lord, whose whole love is lived
for our salvation, has expressed in every possible way that He comes to save us, where saving us is to meet us in love's redeeming love. In other words, all the words of truth come together in the sacraments, particularly the Sacraments of Baptism, Reconciliation and the Eucharist, where we meet the heart of the redeeming Christ. And if, speaking of the depths of our own 'heart's desire', we discover that amidst all that is unworthy of this love, is the very desire that the Lord has planted to meet Him in the mystery of His divine-human presence of the Eucharist. Then let us hasten and help each other, like the disciples on the road to Emmaus, to meet Him in the blessed breaking of the bread (Luke 24: 30).

---

[6] Slightly adapted quotation from George Weigel, *The Truth of Catholicism: Ten Controversies Explored*, Leominster: Gracewing, 2001, p. 6.

An Appendix

The Brief Development of a Dialogue
with a Catholic Psychiatrist

Posing the Question

Clearly the principle of totality permits removal of non-damaged organs if there is a proportionate greater good of the person eg orchidectomy (to stop testosterone release) post prostatectomy for CA prostate. Or prophylactic mastectomy in those with high familial risk of cancer etc.

Do you think that some may in good conscience believe that Transition Related Medical Interventions for those with profound gender dysphoria and high suicidal risk is a proportionate mutilation to serve the good of preserving life?

Some preliminary points

'Psychologists used to call inappropriate feelings of discomfort with one's own sex "dysphoria," at term indicating a pathological mismatch between what one is and what one feels'[1]. And, moreover, there are some people who identify as blind but have normally functioning eyes, or identify as 'paralysed and ask to have their spinal cords severed'. These are considered a 'serious disorder, called body identity dysphoria'. In other words,

---

[1] *Lived Experience and the Search for Truth: Revisiting Catholic Sexual Morality*, 2024, J. Budziszewski, Chapter 9: "Transexualism as Transhumanism", p. 224.

considering oneself to be in the 'wrong body' and mutilating it 'is not therapeutic, because it destroys the order of the body'[2].

To return, then, to the case of the aforementioned three examples, the first two involve actual cancer and the question of how to treat it; and, as such, is a careful question of medical experience and skill. However, as a medical procedure, there will be factors to do with the age of the patient, whether or not they hope to have children and the discovery of what else may be relevant. After all, if an initial treatment does not succeed, then presumably a more decisive surgery is a backstop position.

As regards the third case, prophylactic mastectomy in those with high familial risk of cancer, there is not an actual cancer so much as a 'high familial risk of cancer'. It is not clear, therefore, that this is a sufficient reason for removing one or both breasts, especially as breast tissue can remain even after this surgery. In the case of a young woman and the possibility of marriage and motherhood, there is even more reason to be less convinced of "circumstantial" factors, even that of a family history of breast cancer, for even considering the removal of breasts. Again, as it was said before, the complete removal of breast tissue does not appear to be possible; and, in reality, what is being removed is not actually cancerous breast tissue – but healthy breast tissue.

In sum, there is a need for differential diagnoses; and, even if a particular person suffers from multiple conditions, the necessity of distinguishing between them.

---

[2] *Lived Experience and the Search for Truth: Revisiting Catholic Sexual Morality*, 2024, J. Budziszewski, Chapter 9: "Transexualism as Transhumanism", p. 225.

More Specifically in the case of Gender Dysphoria

Comparing, then, these procedures, with **profound gender dysphoria**, has this drawback: a physical remedy is being considered for a physical condition (except, possibly, in the previous scenario, where breast removal may be more about alleviating anxiety than actually being a preventative treatment), whereas the accumulating evidence is that gender dysphoria is a psychological condition. And, as we have seen in the course of this book, there is very often a contributing factor of sexual abuse in the genesis of the psychological condition. Otherwise, in addition, there is also the possibility of a "media contagion" whereby whatever the personal and familial reasons for this, there is an "in-group" to which admittance is by identification with the group, in this case, gender dysphoria.

The principle of moral action is do good and avoid harm. How are irreversible infertility, bone density damage, irreversible surgery, constant recourse to expensive drugs and multiple operations as a further consequence of initial, invasive puberty blockers and surgeries, not a case of obvious harm? Moreover, good cannot be done by doing harm. Surgery itself, when justified, is a proportionate incision to remove or repair an actual tumour or rupture, which is not in itself a psychological condition, although it may well have psychological effects. In the case of the use of catheters for draining the bladder, especially when it is "in situ" for some time, there is clearly an impact on the possibility or even the desirability of a married couple coming together.

In the case of **profound gender dysphoria**, however, more than a majority of cases resolve in favour of the child's sex at conception. However, there is a necessity for a variety of clear distinctions. The person who is convinced of their gender dysphoria, for whatever reason, is one case, and needs appropriate help. There are, though, other possibilities. A person is exploiting gender dysphoria for their own reasons, particularly that of destabilizing the stability of the family. Or, alternatively, there is a goal of obtaining a win or a medal when, competing with his own sex, it would not be possible. And, although difficult to determine, a person is exploiting the question of his identity for the sake of invading the privacy of women.

Secondly, suicide ideation seems to increase, following mutilating surgery, not decrease. In other words, the very effect of the surgery, profoundly disfiguring a child or young adult, is clearly a traumatic event in its own right. What is more, when a child or young person regrets this procedure, confirming the transitory nature of the condition, they do not want to revisit the very gender counsellors who advocated this one help fits all.

Thirdly, there seems to be rigid program of gender clinics offering, only, pronoun and dress change, puberty blockers and surgery. However, both the Cass Report and many other authorities around the world, recognize that young people present with multiple psychological problems - but they are assessed as if there is only one presenting condition, namely gender dysphoria.

Fourthly, there is a phenomenal relationship between the rise of social media, around 2010-2015, the coming of the pandemic and children being on-screen in a radically new immersion of influencers. Thus the rate of Gender Clinic admissions or referrals went from a handful in the early days of the 1980s, to thousands upon thousands in more recent times. The change from outdoor to indoor play and the rise of unsupervised internet access and the spiked rising of gender dysphoria, are not mere coincidences because the young, philosophically vulnerable age-group is particularly influenced by others.

Fifthly, and this receives almost no attention in the press, there is an overwhelming number of young people turning to suicide, in the UK it is the highest killer between 10–19-year-olds and the greatest killer in men under 50. What is more, in the UK 420,000 families and young people were referred for psychiatric help in one month, in 2022. In the USA, a third of all teenagers between 10-17 are referred for mental health issues. In other words, there is a widespread context of psychological malaise in which **profound gender dysphoria** is appearing. In a word, young people do not have the maturity to understand what they are going through and are therefore particularly vulnerable to ideological pressures, whether parental, peer or others.

Sixthly, the **gender dysphoria** related operations are hugely expensive and a source of income that is attracting surgeons irrespective of the morality or justification of the procedures. At the same time, there is the question of funding: How did a fringe discussion become mainstream?

Seven, there is an immense propaganda campaign, including lawfare, also emanating from the United Nations bureaucracy which constantly wants to advance anti-population measures - all of which rolls into being a program of pro-abortion, contraception, and mutilating operations (cf. Cfam, Stefano Genarini etc). Thus, in the coming 30th anniversary of Beijing's Conference on Women, there has to be a very careful examination of terminology, as it is clear that a commonly understood word can by hijacked to introduce an alien concept to what otherwise was a well understood term.

More widely, the manipulation of language is very serious and has been pursued in the contraception debate, calling the unnecessary medicalization of a woman's body, 'reproductive rights'. In the abortion debate, 'Not

Your Body, Not Your Life, Not Your Choice'[3], is a slogan used to defend abortion; but, clearly, it could be the words of the child in the womb to those who would end his or her life: "Not Your Body; Not Your Life; Not Your Choice". And as regards the IVF scenario, it was never a remedy for infertility, in that the original woman who had a problem suffered from blocked fallopian tubes[4]; and, therefore, it was a pretext for "experimenting" with human conception and implantation. Thus, in conclusion, the abandonment of what words mean, to what they correspond in reality, has brought us now to "transgenderism" and the claim that it is possibility of a person being in the 'wrong body'. Where will the abandonment of truth take us next?

Thus, the answer is very simple, to return to the truth that conception means a beginning and that that beginning, if uninterrupted, manifests the human person conceived at the first instant of fertilization. And that, in principle, human beings are called to do good and to avoid harm, not forgetting that it is not just the goal of human action that needs to be good, but that the act which accomplishes the goal has to be good too! And, finally, that truth, ultimately, is the ground of our being human, the diet of human relationships, and the name of Christ who loves us beyond measure: "I am the Way, the Truth, and the Life" (John 14: 6).

In the end, then, we need both faith and reason, one complementing and not excluding the other and, as we enter Lent, the whole help of the Christian life in that God, who sees our need in every aspect of our lives and that

---

[3] Greg Barradale, 3 Mar 2025, "Revealed: How 'sinister' lack of access to surgical abortions puts lives at risk": https://www.bigissue.com/life/health/surgical-abortions-care-scotland-england-women-health/.

[4] Francis Etheredge, "On Regulating IVF": https://www.pdcnet.org/em/content/em_2016_0041_0007_0001_0002.

of society, comes to help us. And, while inevitably we focus on a pressing need, we do not forget the myriad needs of others; and, therefore, we do what we can, where we can, for whom we can, in the hope of the help of God and the whole Church in the crises of our times[5].

At the same time, as we have seen throughout this book, governments, scientists, and journalists, have a contribution to make for the good; and, in some cases, have either continued to do so or have, once again, turned towards the common good and are promoting the welfare of their people. But, clearly, as we have seen, the freedom to speak the truth is necessary to the good of society; and, conversely, the unnecessary obstruction of it impoverishes the good of all.

But let us recall where we began, that with Pope Francis we distinguish the ideology, "transgenderism", from the needs of individual people who are suffering, in whatever way, from gender dysphoria. Similarly, we distinguish the need for scientific clarity when, according to the evidence that is already available, puberty blockers and surgery, that attempts to change the natural sex of a person, renders them infertile, and suffering from multiple, harmful consequences of what has been done to them. Thus 'This approach is not an 'anti-trans' objection, but a scientific argument concerning lack of evidence on which to base treatment that could endanger a young person's health and fertility'[6]. Moreover, then, the possibility of continuing tests on young people, using puberty blockers, risks both denying the evidence already collected and continuing to damage young people

---

[5] Pope Francis, "Let us Journey Together in Hope": Message of the Holy Father Francis for Lent 2025, 25.02.2025": https://press.vatican.va/content/salastampa/en/bollettino/pubblico/2025/02/25/250225b.html.

[6] Dr. Moira McQueen and Bambi, in the January 15th, 2025, edition of "CCBI News: Gender Affirmation – Changing Approaches": https://www.ccbi-utoronto.ca/.

under a "research protocol" which is already redundant. On the one hand, it is necessary to argue against the false claims of transgender ideology; and, on the other hand, it is necessary to help those who suffer from the harm it causes, or who are otherwise misguided by the anti-population mentality that it expresses. Thus, in the end, observing and communicating the good of woman, can only but be beneficial to particular women. And, ultimately, the clearer we are about the identity of woman, the clearer it will be to differentiate the reasons why some men claim to be women. Ultimately, then, improving our understanding of both what it is to be a man and a woman is both good for society as a whole and the individual man or woman.

Finally, the quest for an identity is very often an ongoing task, even when we have identified what is foundational. On the one hand, in my formative years, I very often threw away, as it were, the cumulative insights into who I was and whether or not God existed. This was owing to an inveterate, almost compulsive questioning of everything, whether it was an answer to a question or even why I went on questioning even the answers I obtained. And, indeed, some people's search for who they are seems to go through many changes making it difficult to give superficial answers to a person's identity[7]. Nevertheless, in my own experience, and that of innumerable others, there are answers which constitute a framework for life, beginning with accepting what I am conceived to be, a boy or a girl, and a man or a woman. Furthermore, that whatever difficulties and sufferings I encounter in the unfolding of that identity, all the relationships that that entails, my gifts and talents, that God loves me and that His love is ever fruitful for my

---

[7] Cf. Dennis Uhlman, March 17th, 2025, "What Does *A Complete Unknown* Teach Us About Finding Our Identity?": https://christandpopculture.com/what-does-a-complete-unknown-teach-us-about-finding-our-identity/.

life, whether I remain single, marry, become a priest, a religious sister or a brother.

May God bless whoever reads or benefits from this book.

www.ingramcontent.com/pod-product-compliance
Lightning Source LLC
Chambersburg PA
CBHW050642270326
41927CB00012B/2843